Software Engineering of
Fault Tolerant
Systems

SERIES ON SOFTWARE ENGINEERING AND KNOWLEDGE ENGINEERING*

Editor-in-Chief: **S K CHANG** (*University of Pittsburgh, USA*)

Published

Vol. 6 Object-Oriented Software: Design and Maintenance
edited by Luiz F. Capretz and Miriam A. M. Capretz (Univ. Aizu, Japan)

Vol. 7 Software Visualisation
edited by P. Eades (Univ. Newcastle) *and K. Zhang* (Macquarie Univ.)

Vol. 8 Image Databases and Multi-Media Search
edited by Arnold W. M. Smeulders (Univ. Amsterdam) *and Ramesh Jain* (Univ. California)

Vol. 9 Advances in Distributed Multimedia Systems
edited by S. K. Chang, T. F. Znati (Univ. Pittsburgh) *and S. T. Vuong* (Univ. British Columbia)

Vol. 10 Hybrid Parallel Execution Model for Logic-Based Specification Languages
Jeffrey J.-P. Tsai and Bing Li (Univ. Illinois at Chicago)

Vol. 11 Graph Drawing and Applications for Software and Knowledge Engineers
Kozo Sugiyama (Japan Adv. Inst. Science and Technology)

Vol. 12 Lecture Notes on Empirical Software Engineering
edited by N. Juristo and A. M. Moreno (Universidad Politécrica de Madrid, Spain)

Vol. 13 Data Structures and Algorithms
edited by S. K. Chang (Univ. Pittsburgh, USA)

Vol. 14 Acquisition of Software Engineering Knowledge
SWEEP: An Automatic Programming System Based on Genetic Programming and Cultural Algorithms
edited by George S. Cowan and Robert G. Reynolds (Wayne State Univ.)

Vol. 15 Image: E-Learning, Understanding, Information Retrieval and Medical
Proceedings of the First International Workshop
edited by S. Vitulano (Università di Cagliari, Italy)

Vol. 16 Machine Learning Applications in Software Engineering
edited by Du Zhang (California State Univ.,) *and Jeffrey J. P. Tsai* (Univ. Illinois at Chicago)

Vol. 17 Multimedia Databases and Image Communication
Proceedings of the Workshop on MDIC 2004
edited by A. F. Abate, M. Nappi and M. Sebillo (Università di Salerno)

Vol. 18 New Trends in Software Process Modelling
edited by Silvia T. Acuña (Universidad Autónoma de Madrid, Spain) *and María I. Sánchez-Segura* (Universidad Carlos III de Madrid, Spain)

Vol. 19 Software Engineering of Fault Tolerant Systems
edited by P. Pelliccione, H. Muccini (Univ. of L'Aquila, Italy), *N. Guelfi* (Univ. Luxembourg, Luxembourg) *and A. Romanovsky* (Univ. of Newcastle upon Tyne, UK)

*For the complete list of titles in this series, please go to

http://www.worldscibooks.com/series/ssekes_series

Series on Software Engineering and Knowledge Engineering Vol. 19

editors

P. Pelliccione
University of L'Aquila, Italy

H. Muccini
University of L'Aquila, Italy

N. Guelfi
University of Luxembourg, Luxembourg

A. Romanovsky
University of Newcastle upon Tyne, UK

Software Engineering of Fault Tolerant Systems

World Scientific

NEW JERSEY • LONDON • SINGAPORE • BEIJING • SHANGHAI • HONG KONG • TAIPEI • CHENNAI

Published by

World Scientific Publishing Co. Pte. Ltd.
5 Toh Tuck Link, Singapore 596224
USA office: 27 Warren Street, Suite 401-402, Hackensack, NJ 07601
UK office: 57 Shelton Street, Covent Garden, London WC2H 9HE

British Library Cataloguing-in-Publication Data
A catalogue record for this book is available from the British Library.

Series on Software Engineering and Knowledge Engineering — Vol. 19
SOFTWARE ENGINEERING OF FAULT TOLERANT SYSTEMS

ISBN-13 978-981-270-503-7
ISBN-10 981-270-503-1

Printed in Singapore by World Scientific Printers (S) Pte Ltd

PREFACE

This book is a collection of peer-reviewed research papers focusing on various aspects of software engineering and fault tolerance. The growing importance of this area is recognised by many researchers and practitioners, and is due to an urgent need to support building fault tolerant systems in a disciplined and rigorous fashion, ensuring proper integration of fault tolerance concerns from the earliest steps of system development. The challenge here arises from the fact that this area sits on the borderline between several well-established research domains, such as *software engineering, dependability* and *formal methods.* The book is intended as a major step toward a future time when these communities will have established long-term close cooperation. It is clearly only a beginning of and an indication of the huge potentials in the fruitful cooperation between them.

In addition to the nine high-quality technical papers selected through a thorough peer-revision process, we decided to include an introductory chapter to give our personal view of the area and explain the motivation which has driven the book. Its preparation started after a successful workshop on the same subject organised in Luxembourg in June 2006. This 1.5 day workshop consisted of 6 selected technical talks, 2 invited talks and a tool demonstration followed by two discussion sessions, and attracted more than 25 participants from all over the world. After the workshop we invited all workshop contributors and a number of external researchers with a strong background in related topics to submit their papers. Nine papers were finally selected for inclusion.

We are grateful to the authors for their thorough work and to the reviewers for their help in selecting the papers and improving their quality. We would like to acknowledge the contribution of several projects which supported our work on this book: EC FP6 IST RODIN, CORRECT (funded by the Luxembourg Ministry of Higher Education and Research) and EC FP6 IST PLASTIC.

Patrizio Pelliccione, *University of L'Aquila, Italy*
Henry Muccini, *University of L'Aquila, Italy*
Nicolas Guelfi, *University of Luxembourg, Luxembourg*
Alexander Romanovsky, *Newcastle University, UK*

February 10, 2007

Workshop on Engineering of Fault-Tolerant Systems (EFTS 2006)

12–14 June 2006, Luxembourg

International Advisory Committee

Bondavalli Andrea	Univ. Florence, Italy
Castor Filho Fernando	State University of Campinas, Brazil
Coleman Joey	Univ. Newcastle upon Tyne, UK
Cortellessa Vittorio	Univ. L'Aquila, Italy
Crnkovic Ivica	Mälardalen University, Sweden
De Lemos Rogério	Univ. Kent, Canterbury, UK
Di Nitto Elisabetta	Politecnico di Milano, Italy
Ebnenasir Ali	Michigan Technological University, USA
Garcia Alessandro	Computing Department, Lancaster University, UK
Gnesi Stefania	CNR, Italy
Göschka Karl M.	Vienna University of Technology, Austria
Grassi Vincenzo	Univ. Roma Tor Vergata, Italy
Guelfi Nicolas	Univ. Luxembourg, Luxembourg
Jimenez-Peris Ricardo	Univ. Politecnica de Madrid, Spain
Kharchenko Vyacheslav	National Aerospace University, Ukraine
Kienzle Jörg	McGill University, Montreal, Canada
Majzik Istvan	BME, Budapest, Hungary
Mirandola Raffaela	Politecnico di Milano, Italy
Muccini Henry	Univ. L'Aquila, Italy
Pelliccione Patrizio	Univ. L'Aquila, Italy
Romanovsky Alexander	Univ. Newcastle upon Tyne, UK
Ruiz Juan Carlos	Technical University of Valencia, Spain
Schoitsch Erwin	ARC Seibersdorf Research (AARIT), Austria
Zorzo Avelino	Ponthifical Catholic University of RS, Brazil

CONTENTS

INTRODUCTION

PATRIZIO PELLICCIONE and HENRY MUCCINI

Dipartimento di Informatica, University of L'Aquila
Via Vetoio, 1, 67100 L'Aquila, ITALY
E-mail: {pellicci, muccini}@di.univaq.it

NICOLAS GUELFI

Laboratory for Advanced Software Systems, University of Luxembourg
6, rue Richard Coudenhove-Kalergi, LUXEMBOURG
E-mail: nicolas.guelfi@uni.lu

ALEXANDER ROMANOVSKY

School of Computing Science, Newcastle University
Newcastle upon Tyne, NE1 7RU, UK
E-mail: alexander.romanovsky@newcastle.ac.uk

1. Motivations for the Book

Building trustworthy systems is one of the main challenges Faced by software developers, who have been concerned with dependability-related issues since the first day system was built and deployed. Obviously, there have been plenty of changes since then, including the nature of faults and failures, the complexity of systems, the services they deliver and the way society uses them. But the need to deal with various threats (such as failed components, deteriorating environments, component mismatches, human mistakes, intrusions and software bugs) is still in the core of software and system research and development. As computers are now spreading into various new domains (including the critical ones) and the complexity of modern systems is growing, achieving dependability remains central for system developers and users.

Accepting that errors always happen in spite of all the efforts to eliminate faults that might cause them is in the core of dependability. To this end various fault tolerance mechanisms have been investigated by researchers and used in industry. Unfortunately, more often than not these solutions exclusively focus on the implementation (e.g. they are provided as middleware/OS services or libraries), ignoring other development phases, most importantly the earlier ones. This creates a dangerous gap between the requirement to build dependable (and fault tolerant) systems and the fact that it is not dealt with until the implementation step step.[1] One consequence of this is that there is a growing number of situations reported in which fault tolerance means undermine the overall system dependability as they are not used properly.

We believe that fault tolerance needs to be explicitly included into traditional software engineering theories and practices, and should become an integral part of all steps of software development. As current software engineering practices tend to capture only normal behaviour, assuming that all faults can be removed during development, new software engineering methods and tools need to be developed to support explicit handling of abnormal situations. Moreover, every phase in the software development process needs to be enriched with phase-specific fault tolerance means. Generally speaking, integrating fault tolerance into software engineering requires:

- integrating fault tolerance means into system models starting from the early development phases (i.e. requirement and architecture);
- making fault tolerance-related decisions at each phase by explicit modelling of faults, fault tolerance means and dedicated redundant resources (with a specific focus on fault tolerant software architectures);
- ensuring correct transformations of models used at various development phases with a specific focus on transformation of fault tolerance means;
- supporting verification and validation of fault tolerance means;
- developing dedicated tools for fault tolerance modelling;
- providing domain-specific application-level fault tolerance mechanisms and abstractions.

This book consists of an introduction and 9 chapters, each of which describes a novel approach to integrating fault tolerance into the software development process. It covers a wide range of topics, including fault tolerance during the different phases of software development, software engineering techniques for verification and validation of fault tolerance means, and languages for supporting fault tolerance specification and implementation.

Accordingly, the book comprises the following three parts:

- Part A: *Fault tolerance engineering: from requirements to code*
- Part B: *Verification and validation of fault tolerant systems*
- Part C: *Languages and Tools for engineering fault tolerant systems*

The next section of this chapter briefly introduces the main dependability and fault tolerance concepts. Section 3 defines the software engineering realm, while sections 4, 5 and 6 introduce the three areas corresponding to the parts above and briefly outline the current state or research. The last section summarises the content of the book.

2. Dependability and Fault Tolerance

Dependability is usually defined as system ability to deliver service that can be justifiably trusted.[2] Ensuring the required dependability level for complex computer-based systems is a challenge faced by many researchers and developers working in various relevant domains. The problems here have multiple origins, including the high cost of making system dependable, the growing complexity of modern applications, their pervasiveness and openness, proliferation of computer-based systems into new emerging domains, a greater extent to which society relies on these systems. Apart from that it can be difficult to assess the impact which various dependability means have on the resulting system dependability, as well as to define realistic and practical assumptions under which these means are to be applied, set dependability requirements and trace them through all development phases, etc.

Dependability is an integrated concept encompassing a variety of attributes, including availability, reliability, safety, integrity, and maintainability. Generally, there are four means to be employed to attain dependability:[2] fault prevention, fault tolerance, fault removal, and fault forecasting. Clearly, in practice one needs to apply a combination of all these to ensure the required dependability. It is important to understand that all these activities are built around the concept of faults: where possible, faults are prevented or eliminated by using appropriate development and verification techniques, while the remaining ones are tolerated at runtime to avoid system failures and estimated to help predict their consequences.

This chapter adheres to the use of the dependability terminology Introduced in ,[2] which specifies the following causal chain of dependability threats. A system failure to deliver its service is said to be caused by an erroneous system state, which, in its turn, is caused by a triggered fault.

That means that faults can be silent for some time and that their triggering does not necessarily cause immediate failure. Errors are typically latent and the aim of fault tolerance is to detect and deal with them and their causes before they make systems fail.

This book focuses on *fault tolerance means that are used to avoid system failures in the presence of faults.* The essence of fault tolerance[3] is in detecting errors and carrying the subsequent system recovery. Generally speaking, during system recovery one needs to perform two steps: error handling and fault handling.

Error handling can be conducted in one of the following three ways: backward error recovery (sometimes called rollback), forward error recovery (sometimes called rollforward) or compensation. Backward error recovery returns the system into a previous state (assumed to be correct). The techniques which are typically used to achieve this are checkpoints, recovery points, recovery blocks, conversations, file backup, application restart, system reboot, transaction abort, etc. Forward error recovery moves the system into a new correct state. Recovery of this type is normally carried out by employing exception handling techniques (found, for example, in many programming languages, such as Ada, Java, C++, etc.). Note that backward error recovery is usually interpreted as a particular case of forward error recovery. There has been a considerable amount of research on defining exception handling mechanisms suitable for different domains, development and modelling paradigms, types of faults, execution environments, etc. (see, for example, a recent book[4]). It is worth noting here that, on the whole, the rollforward means are more general and run-time efficient than the rollback ones as they take advantage of their precise knowledge of the erroneous state and move the system into a correct state by using application-specific handlers. To perform compensation, one needs to ensure that the system contains enough redundancy to mask errors without interrupting the delivery of its service.

Various replication and software diversity techniques fall into this category as they mask erroneous results without having to move the system into a state which is assumed to be correct. A wide range of software diversity mechanisms, including recovery blocks, conversations and N-version programming, has been developed and widely used in industry.

Fault handling activity is very different in nature from error handling as it is intended to rid the system of faults to avoid new errors the former might cause in a later execution. It starts with fault diagnosis, followed by the isolation of the faulty component and system reconfiguration. After that the system or its part needs to be re-initialized to continue to provide its service. Fault handling is usually much more expensive than error handling and is more difficult to apply as it typically requires some part of the system to be inactive to conduct reconfiguration.

Fault tolerance never comes free as it always requires additional (redundant) resources which are employed in runtime to perform detection and recovery. Specific fault tolerance mechanisms require various types of redundancy such as spare time, additional memory or disk space, extra exchange channels, additional code or messages, etc. Typically, each scheme uses a combination of redundant resources, for example, a simple retry always uses time redundancy, but may need extra disk space and code to save the checkpoints if we need to restore the system state before retrying.

The choice of the specific error detection, error handling and fault handling techniques to be used for a particular system is defined by the underlying fault assumptions. For example, replication techniques are normally used to tolerate hardware faults, whereas software diversity is employed to deal with software design bugs.

Let us now briefly discuss the main challenges in developing fault tolerant systems.[5] First of all, fault tolerance means are difficult to develop or use as they increase system complexity by adding a new dimension to the reasoning about system behaviour. Their application requires a deep understanding of the intricate links between normal and abnormal behaviour and states of systems and components, as well as the state and behaviour during recovery. Secondly, fault tolerance (e.g. software diversity, rollback, exception handling) is costly as it always uses redundancy. Thirdly, system designers are typically reluctant to think about faults at the early phases of development. This results in decisions ignoring fault tolerance being made at these stages, which may make it more difficult or expensive to introduce fault tolerance at the later ones. More often than not, the developers fail to apply even the basic principles of software fault tolerance. For example, there is no focus on (i) a clear definition of the fault assumptions as the central step in designing any fault tolerant system, (ii) developing means for early error detection, (iii) application of recursive system structuring for error confinement, (iv) minimising and ensuring error confinement and error recovery areas, and (v) extending component specifications with a concise or complete definition of failure modes. We can refer here to a recent paper[6] reporting a high number of mistakes made in handing exceptions in the C programs or to the Interim Report on Causes of the August 14th 2003 Blackout in the US and Canada,[7] which clearly shows that the problem was mostly caused by badly designed fault tolerance: poor diagnostics of faults, longer-than-estimated time for component recovery, failure to involve all necessary components in recovery, inconsistent system state after recovery, failures of alarm systems, etc. It is worth recalling here as well that the failure of the Ariane 5 launcher was caused by improper handling of an exception.[8]

Given all of the above, it is no wonder that a substantial part of system failures are caused by deficiencies in fault tolerance means.[1] We believe that a closer synergy between software engineering phases, methods and tools and fault tolerance will help to alleviate the current situation.

3. Defining Software Engineering

Software engineering (SE) is quite a new field of Computer Science, recognized in the 1968 NATO conference in Garmisch (Germany) as an emergent discipline. Today, many different definitions of software engineering have been proposed, aiming to describe its main characteristics:

- "Application of *systematic, disciplined, quantifiable approach* to the *development, operation, and maintenance* of software";[9]
- "Software engineers should adopt a *systematic and organised approach* to their work and use appropriate tools and techniques depending on the problem to be solved, the development constraints and the resources available";[10]
- "Software Engineering is the field of computer science that deals with the building of software systems that are *so large or so complex* that they are built by a team or teams of engineers";[11]
- "Software engineering is the branch of systems engineering concerned with the development of *large and complex software intensive systems*". ... "It is also concerned with the *processes, methods and tools* for the development of software intensive systems in an *economic and timely manner*"[12] .

Most of these well known definitions point out different characteristics or perspectives to be considered when looking at software engineering as a research area. Several examples of the systems developed in the last forty years will help us to identify the key points common to most of the definitions of SE and to illustrate why and when the software engineering discipline is needed. Ariane 5, the Therac-25 radiation therapy machine, Denver Airport and others big software failures,[13] as well as the example of excellent work by on-board shuttle group[14] will be used for this purpose.

3.1. *If Software Fails, This May Cost Millions of Dollars and Harm People*

As already pointed in Section 1, software is pervasive (it is everywhere around us, even if we do not see it), it controls many devices used everyday, and more and more critical systems (i.e., those systems whose malfunctioning can injure people or cause great material losses).

Ariane 5, Therac-25 radiation-treatment machine and Denver Airport are some examples of critical systems which, due to software systems malfunctioning, ended up being big catastrophic failures[a]. The Ariane 5 shuttle, launched on June 4th 1996, broke down and exploded forty seconds after initiation of the flight sequence, due to a software problem. People were killed. The Therac-25 radiation-treatment machine for cancer therapy harmed and even killed several patients by administering a radiation overdose. The Denver Airport software, responsible for controlling 35 kilometers of rails and 4000 tele-wagons never worked properly and after 10 years of recurring failures it was recently dismissed;[15] millions of dollars were wasted. In all three cases, the main causes of failure were undisciplined management of requirements, imprecise and ambiguous communication, unstable architectures, high complexities, inconsistency of requirements with design and implementation, low automation, and insufficient verification and validation.

3.2. *How to Make Good Software*

While the previous examples described what might happen when software engineering techniques are not employed, the on-board shuttle group example of excellence (taken from the 1996 white-paper written by Fishman[14]) shows results that can be achieved when best software engineering practices are applied in practice. It describes how the software operating a 120-ton space shuttle is conceived: such a software system is composed of around 500,000 lines of code, it controls 4 billion dollars' worth of equipment, and decides the lives of a half-dozen astronauts. What makes this software and their creators so extraordinary is that it never crashes and is bug free (according to[14]). The last three versions of the program (each one of 420,000 lines of code) had just one fault each. The last 11 versions of this software system had a total of 17 faults. Commercial programs of equivalent complexity would have 5,000 faults. How did the developers achieve such high

[a]These and many other examples of catastrophic failures are described in paper [13] .

software quality?

It was simply the result of applying most of the SE best practices:

- *SE allows for a disciplined, systematic, and quantifiable development:* The on-board shuttle group is the antithesis of the up-all-night, pizza-and-roller-hockey software coders who have captured the public imagination. To be this good, the on-board shuttle group's work is very had to be a focused, disciplined, and methodically managed creative enterprise;
- *SE does not only concern programming:* Another important factor discussed in Fishman's report[14] is that about one-third of the process of writing software happens before anyone writes a line of code. Every critical requirement is documented. Nothing in the specification is changed without the rest of the team's agreement. No coder changes a single line of code without carefully outlining the change;
- *SE takes into consideration maintenance and evolution:* As explicitly stated in,[9] maintenance and evolution are important factors when engineering software systems. They allow system evolution, while limiting newly introduced faults;
- *SE is for mid-to large systems:* Applying SE practices is quite expensive and requires effort. While non-critical, small systems may require just a few SE principles, applying the best SE practices for the development of critical, large software systems is mandatory;
- *Development cost and time are key issues:* The main success of this example is not the software but the software process the team uses. Recently, much effort has been spent on identifying new software processes (like the Unified Software Process[16]), and software maturity frameworks which allow the improvement of the software development process (like the Capability Maturity Model – CMM[17] or the Personal Software Process – PSP[18]). Nowadays software processes explicitly take into consideration tasks such as managing groups, setting deadlines, checking the system cost to stay on budget, to deliver software of the required quality.

4. Fault Tolerance Engineering: from Requirements to Code

In the past, fault tolerance (and specifically, exception handling) used to be commonly delayed until late in the design and implementation phases of the software life-cycle. More recently, however, the need for explicit use of exception handling mechanisms during the entire life cycle has been advocated by some researchers as one of the main approaches to ensuring the overall system dependability[19,20] .

It has been recognised, in particular, that different classes of faults, errors and failures can be identified during different phases of software development. A number of studies have been conducted so far to investigate where and how fault tolerance can be integrated in the software life-cycle.

In the remaining part of Section 4 we will show how fault tolerance has been recently addressed in the different phases of the software process: requirements, high-level (architectural) design, and low-level design.

4.1. *Requirements Engineering and Fault Tolerance*

Requirements Engineering is concerned with identifying the purpose of a software system, and the contexts in which it will be used. Various theories and methodologies for finding out, modelling, analysing, modifying, enhancing and checking software system requirements[21] have been proposed.

Requirements being the first artefacts produced during the software process, it is important to document expected faults and ways to tolerate them. Some approaches have been proposed for this purpose, the best known analysed in[20,22,23] and subsequent work.

In[22,24,24] the authors describe a process for systematically investigating exceptional situations at the requirements level and provide an extension to standard UML use case diagrams in order to specify exceptional behaviour. In[20] it is described how exceptional behaviours can be specified at the requirements level, and how those requirements can drive component-based specification and design according to the Catalysis process. In[23] an approach to analysing the safety and reliability of requirements based on use cases is proposed: normal use cases are extended with exceptional use cases according to,[22] then use cases are annotated with their probability of success and subsequently translated into Dependability Assessment Charts, eventually used for dependability analysis.

4.2. *Software Architecture and Fault Tolerance*

Software Architecture (SA) has been largely accepted as a way to achieve a better software quality while reducing the time and cost of production. In particular, a software architecture specification[25] represents the first complete system description in the development life-cycle. It provides both a high-level behavioural abstraction of components and their interactions (connectors) and a description of the static structure of the system.

Typical SA specifications model only the *normal* behaviour of the system, while ignoring *abnormal* ones. This means that faults may cause the system to fail in unexpected ways. In the context of critical systems with fault tolerance requirements it becomes necessary to introduce fault tolerance information at the software architecture level. In fact, error recovery effectiveness is dramatically reduced when fault tolerance is commissioned late in the software life-cycle[19] .

Many approaches have been proposed to modelling and analysing fault tolerant software architectures. While a comprehensive survey of this topic is given in,[26] this introductory chapter simply identifies the main topics covered by the existing approaches, while providing some references to the existing work.

- Fault Tolerant SA specification: as discussed in many papers (e.g.,[27–29]) a software architecture can be specified using box-and-line notations, formal architecture description languages (ADLs) or UML-based notations. As far as the specification of fault tolerant software architectures is concerned, both formal and UML-based notations have been used. The approaches proposed in[30–32] are examples of formal specifications of Fault Tolerant SA: traditional architecture description languages are usually extended in order to explicitly specify error and fault handling. The approaches in, e.g.,[20,33,34] use UML-based notations for modelling Fault Tolerant SA: new UML profiles are created in order to be able to specify fault tolerance concepts;
- Fault Tolerant SA analysis: analysis techniques (such as deadlock detection, testing, checking, simulation, performance) allow software engineers to assess a software architecture and to evaluate its quality with respect to expected requirements. Some approaches have been proposed for analysing Fault Tolerant SA: most of them check the conformance of the architectural model to fault tolerance requirements or constraints (as in[35,36]). A testing technique for Fault Tolerant SA is presented in;[34]
- Fault Tolerance SA styles: according to,[37] an architectural style is "*a set of design rules that identify the kinds of components and connectors that may be used to compose a system or subsystem, together with local or global constraints on the way the composition is done*". Many architectural styles have been proposed for Fault

Tolerant SA: the idealized fault tolerant style (in[34]), the iC2C style (which integrates the C2 architectural style with the idealized fault tolerant component style[30]), the idealized fault tolerant component/connector style;[38]

- Fault Tolerance SA middleware support: when coding software architecture via component-based systems, middleware technology can be used to implement connectors, coordination policies and many other features. In paper [39] a CORBA implementation of an architectural exception handling is proposed. In[40] the authors outline an approach to exception handling in component composition at the architectural level with the support of middleware. Many projects have been conducted to provide fault tolerance to CORBA applications, like AQuA, Eternal, IRL, and OGS (see[41]). More Discussion of fault tolerance middleware follows in Section 6 .

4.3. *Low-level Design and Fault Tolerance*

The low-level design phase (hereafter simply called "design") takes information collected during the requirement and architecting phases as its input and produces a design artefact to be used by developers for guiding and documenting software coding. When dealing with fault tolerant systems, the design phase needs to benefit from some clear and domain-specific tools and methodologies to drive the implementation of a particular fault tolerance technique.

In papers[42,43] two approaches are presented to progressing from architectural design to low-level design using fault tolerance design patterns. In[33] an MDA approach is introduced: given a specification of a Coordinated Atomic Action [44] it enables the automatic production of Java code. This approach has been subsequently refined in other papers, and recently presented in[45] . In[20] an approach to fault tolerance specification and analysis during the entire development process is proposed. It considers both normal and exceptional requirements to be defined, shows how to use them for driving the system specification and design phase, and how to implement the resulting system using a Java-based framework. The proposed software process is based on the Catalysis. In[34] a similar strategy is adopted based on the UML Components Process.

5. Verification and Validation of Fault Tolerant Systems

Fault tolerance techniques alone are not sufficient for achieving high dependability, since unexpected faults cannot always be avoided or tolerated.[46] In addition it is important to note that fault tolerant systems inevitably contain faults. Verification and validation (V&V) techniques have proved to be successful means for ensuring that expected properties and requirements are satisfied in system models and implementation.[34] This is why V&V techniques are typically used for removing faults from the system. This section will discuss the use of V&V techniques for fault tolerance.

Different classes of faults, errors, and failures must be identified and dealt with at every phase of software development, depending on the abstraction level used in modelling the software system under development. Thus, each abstraction level requires specific design models, implementation schemes, verification techniques, and verification environments.

Verification and validation techniques aim to ensure the correctness of a software system or at least to reduce the number or severity of faults both during the development and after the deployment of a system. There are two different classes of verification methods: exhaustive methods, which conduct an exhaustive exploration of all possible behaviours, and non-exhaustive methods, which explore only some of the possible behaviours. The exhaustive class there are model checking, theorem provers, term rewriting systems, proof checker systems, and constraint solvers. The non-exhaustive class comprises testing and simulation, the well-established techniques which can nevertheless easily miss significant errors when verifying complex systems. Several approaches have been proposed in literature in the recent years, aiming to apply V&V techniques to fault-tolerant systems, which are surveyed in the following subsections. In particular, Section 5.1 reports the use of model checking techniques, Section 5.2 summarises experiences with theorem provers, Section 5.3 shows approaches that exploit constraint solvers for verification, and finally Section 5.4 describes how testing techniques can complement fault tolerance. Furthermore, with the introduction of UML[47] as the de-facto standard in modelling software systems and its widespread adoption in industrial contexts, many approaches have been proposed to using UML for modelling and evaluating dependable systems (e.g.,[48–51]); these are reported in Section 5.5.

5.1. *Model Checking*

Model checkers take as input a formal model of the system, typically described by means of state machines or transition systems, and verify it as to whether it satisfies temporal logic properties[52] .

Several approaches have been proposed in the recent years focusing on model checking of fault tolerant systems, such as[53–55] .

The application of these approaches to real case studies indicates that model checking is a promising and successful verification technique. First of all, model checking techniques are supported by tools, which facilitates their application. Secondly, in case verification detects a violation of a desired property, a counter example showing how the system reaches the erroneous state in which the property is violated is produced.

To be used in fault tolerant systems, model checking approaches typically require specification of normal behaviours, failing behaviours, and fault recovering procedures. Thus, fault tolerant systems are subjected to the state explosion problem that also afflicts model checkers in verifying systems that do not consider exceptional behaviours.

One approach that can be used for avoiding the state explosion problem is the partial model checking technique introduced in[56] . This technique, which aims to gradually remove parts of the system, is successfully applied for security analysis, and an attempt to use it for fault tolerant systems is described in[57] .

5.2. *Theorem Provers*

Interactive theorem provers start with axioms and try to produce new inference steps using rules of inference. They require a human user to give hints to the system. Working on hard problems usually requires a skilled user. A logical characterisation of fault tolerance is given in[57] , while approaches that apply theorem prover techniques to fault tolerant systems are in[58–61] .

5.3. *Constraint Solvers*

Given a formula, expressed in a suitable logic, constraint solvers attempt to find a model that makes the formula true. Typically, this model is a match between variables and values. One of the most famous constraint solvers, based on the first-order logic, is Alloy Analyzer, the verification engine of Alloy.[62] In,[63] the authors propose an approach that exploits Alloy for modelling and formally verifying fault-tolerant distributed systems. More precisely, they focus on systems that use exception handling as a mechanism for fault tolerance and in particular they consider systems designed by using Coordinated Atomic Actions (CAA).[44] CAA is a fault-tolerance mechanism that uses concurrent exception handling and combines the features of two complementary concepts: the conversation and the transaction. Conversation[64] is a fault-tolerance technique for performing coordinated error recovery in a set of participants that are designed to interact with each other to provide a specific service (cooperative concurrency).

5.4. *Testing*

Testing refers to the dynamic verification of system behaviour based on the observation of a selected set of controlled executions, or test cases.[65] Testing is the main fault removal technique.

A real world project involving 34 independent programming teams for developing program versions of an industry-scale avionics application is presented in[66] . Detailed experimentations are reported which study the nature, source, type, delectability, and effect of faults uncovered in the programming versions. A new test generation technique is also presented, together with an evaluation of its effectiveness.

Another approach from[67] shows how fault tolerance and testing can be used to validate component-based systems. Fault tolerance requirements guide the construction of a fault-tolerant architecture, which is subsequently validated with respect to requirements and submitted to testing.

5.5. *UML-based approaches to modelling and validating dependable systems*

The approaches considered in this section share the idea of translating design models into reliability models.

A lot of solutions have been proposed in the context of the European ESPRIT project HIDE.[50] This project aims at creating an integrated environment for designing and verifying dependable systems modelled in UML. In[49] authors propose automatic transformations from UML specifications, augmented with additional required information (i.e., fault occurrence rate, percentage of permanent faults, etc...), to Petri Net Models.

A modular and hierarchical approach to architecting dependable software using UML is proposed in.[51] It relies on a refinement process allowing the critical parts of the model to be described when information becomes available in the subsequent design phases.

In[48] authors convert UML models to dynamic fault trees. In this study the translation algorithm uses the logical system structure available in the UML model, but it can also be applied to the non-UML models provided they have similar logical structures.

6. Languages and Frameworks

It is of great importance that engineers have, in their development tools, features available to them to help them deal with the increase in complexity due to the incorporation of fault-tolerance software techniques into software. Each development tool studied in this section helps to separate the code which implements a software system function (as described by its functional specification) from that which implements the service restoration (or simply "recovery"), when a deviation from the correct service was detected (by the implemented error detection technique, of course). The choice of recovery features depends on the classes of faults to be tolerated. For example, transient faults, which are the faults that eventually disappear without any apparent intervention, can be tolerated by error handling.

Each of the tools that are presented below allows engineers to achieve the separation described above, sometimes with several possibilities. Which solution path will depend on costs in terms of money, processing power (performance), and memory size as well as the consequences (whether measurable in terms of cost or not) brought about by the failure of the software system, which is the most important one to evaluate precisely in order to decide on the requirements to fault tolerance.

This section addresses three types of development environments: programming languages, fault-tolerance frameworks and advanced fault-tolerance frameworks. The choice from these three categories will depend on the complexity of the fault tolerance requirements.

6.1. *Programming Languages Perspectives*

Some programming languages incorporate fault tolerance techniques directly as part of their syntax or indirectly through features that allow engineers to implement them. One reason for having fault tolerance support at the programming language level is an increased performance due to the application-specific knowledge. Another is for programmers who need to use standard programming languages to be offered a capability to design and develop fault-tolerant applications more easily.

6.1.1. *Exception Handling*

As stated in the previous section, one of the features to be provided by a fault tolerance technique is to support the separation of fault tolerance instructions (for recovery objectives) from the rest of the software and to activate them automatically, when necessary. The obvious moment to activate the recovery behaviour is when it is impossible to finish the operation that the software is carrying out. An exception is defined precisely as an event signalling the impossibility of finishing an operation: the software is going to fail if no action is taken. In order to keep the software running and avoid a failure, fault tolerance instructions are applied. This is called *Exception handling* (EH), which is the most popular fault tolerance mechanisms used to implement modern software systems.

Nowadays, various exception handling models are part of practical programming languages like Ada, C++, Eiffel, Java, ML and Smalltalk. Almost all languages have similar basic types of exceptions and constructs to introduce new exception types and to handle exceptions (e.g. *try/throw/catch* in Java). Thus, exception handling is a good technique to implement fault-tolerant sequential programs.

In the context of distributed concurrent software (a network of computing nodes), the situation is different. Exception handling needs to be defined according to the semantics of concurrency and distribution. ERLANG[68] is a declarative language for programming concurrent and distributed software systems with EH features. This language has primitives which support the creation of processes (separated unit of computation), communication between processes over a network of nodes and the handling of errors when a failure causes a process to terminate abnormally. The *spawn* statement allows a process to create a new process on a remote node. Whenever a new process is created, the new process will belong to the same process group as the process that evaluated the *spawn* statement. Once a process terminates its execution (normally or abnormally), a special signal is sent to all processes which belong to the same group. The value of one of the parameters that compose the signal is used to detect if the process terminated abnormally. In order to avoid propagating an abnormal signal to the other processes of the group (i.e. to ensure failure containment), the default behaviour has to be changed. This is achieved by using the catch instruction, which defines the recovery context (scope) where the errors which occurred on the monitored expression will be dealt with.

6.1.2. *Atomic Actions*

Fault tolerance in distributed concurrent software systems can also be achieved using the general concept of atomic actions. A group of components (participants, threads, processes, objects, etc.) that cooperate to achieve a joint goal, without any information flow between the group and the rest of the system for the period necessary to achieve the goal, constitutes an atomic action. These components are designed to cooperate inside the action, so that they share work and exchange information in order to complete the action successfully. Atomicity guarantees that if the action is successfully executed, then its results and modifications of shared data become visible to other actions. But if an error is detected, all the components take part in a cooperative recovery in order to ensure that there are no changes in the shared data. These characteristics of the atomic actions allow the containment and recovery to be easily achieved since error detection, propagation and recovery all occur within a single atomic action. Therefore fault tolerance steps can be attached to each atomic action that forms part of the software, independently from each other. The first fault-tolerance atomic action scheme proposed was the conversation scheme[64] . It allows tolerating design faults by making use of software diversity and participant rollback. Other schemes including fault tolerance have been proposed and developed as part of programming languages since then. For example, Avalon[69] takes advantage of inheritance to implement atomic actions in distributed object-oriented applications. Avalon relies on the Camelot system[70] to handle operating-system level details. Much of the Avalon design was inspired by Argus[71] .

6.1.3. *Reflection and Aspect-Orientation*

Other software technology which is related to programming languages and has been considered for handling software faults is "reflection"[72] . Reflection is the ability of a computational system to observe its own execution and, as a result, make changes in it. Software based on reflective facilities is structured into different levels: the base level and one or more metalevels. Everything in the implementation and application (syntax, semantics, and run-time data structures) is "open" to the programmer for modification via metalevels[73] . Metalevels can be used to handle fault tolerance strategies. Therefore, this layered structure allows programmers to separate the recovery steps (part of the metalevels) from those necessary to achieve the functional goal (part of the base level). The fact that metalevels can observe the base level computation allows its execution to be halted when any deviation (according to the view adopted on what constitutes normal behaviour) is observed and the recovery to be started.

General approaches to implementing fault tolerance that can be chosen at the level of programming languages are as follows:

- extending the programming language with non-standard constructs and semantics;
- extending the implementation environment underlying the programming language to provide the functionality, but with an interface expressed using the existing language constructs and semantics;
- extending the language with specific abstractions, implemented with the existing language constructs and semantics (e.g. abstract data types intended to support software fault tolerance) perhaps expressed in well-recognised design patterns;
- or combinations of the above.

Aspect-orientation has been accepted as a powerful technique for modularizing crosscutting concerns during software development in so-called aspects. Similarly to reflection, aspect-oriented techniques provide means to extend a base program with an additional state, and describe additional behaviour that is to be triggered at well-defined points during the execution of the program. Experience has shown that aspect-oriented programming is successful in modularizing even very application-independent, general concerns such as distribution and concurrency, and examples of using aspect-orientation to achieve fault tolerance are given in[74–78] .

However, if an application needs to meet complex fault tolerance requirements, relying just on the programming language will be risky, and a framework will then need to be applied.

6.2. *Frameworks for Fault Tolerance*

According to[79] , *"a framework is a reusable design expressed as a set of abstract classes and the way their instances collaborate. It is a reusable design for all or part of a software system. By definition, a framework is an object-oriented design. It doesn't have to be implemented in an object-oriented language, though it usually is. Large-scale reuse of object-oriented libraries requires frameworks. The framework provides a context for the components in the library to be reused."*

CORBA (Common Object Request Broker Architecture), which was conceived to provide application Interoperability, is a good example of a framework,. Unfortunately, CORBA and other traditional frameworks often cannot meet high quality of service (QoS) requirements (including the fault-tolerance ones) for certain specialised applications. This is why these frameworks are often extended to include fault tolerance techniques in order to become predictable and reliable. This is what is done in the FT CORBA specification[80] , which defines an architecture, a set of services, and associated fault tolerance mechanisms that constitute a framework for resilient, highly-available, distributed software systems. Fault tolerance is achieved through features that allow designers to replicate objects in a transparent way. A set of several replicas for a specific object defines an object group. However, a client object is not aware that the server object is replicated (server object group). Therefore, the client object invokes methods on the server object group, and the members of the server object group execute the methods and return their responses to the client, just like a conventional object.

The same approach has also been pursued at higher levels of abstraction. The well-known coordination language Linda[81] , which has been extended to facilitate programming of fault-tolerant parallel applications, is a good example. FT-Linda[82] is an extension of the original Linda model, which defines new concepts, such as stable tuple spaces (stable TSs), failure tuple and new syntax, to achieve atomic execution of a series of TSs operations. A stable TS represents a tuple that survives a failure. This tuple stability is achieved by replicating the tuple on multiple hosts that together form the distributed environment where software is deployed. FT-Linda uses monitoring to detect failures. The main type of failure that is addressed by FT-Linda corresponds to the host failure, which means that the host has been silent for longer than a pre-defined interval. When a failure of this type is detected, the framework automatically notifies all processes by signalling a failure tuple in a stable TS available to them. Note that there must exist a specific process in the software responsible for detecting a failure tuple and starting the corresponding recovery process. Atomic execution is denoted by angle brackets and represents the all-or-none execution of the group of tuple space operations enclosed by them. There are also some language primitives that allow tuples to be moved or copied from one TS to another one.

Another extension of Linda, oriented towards mobile applications using the agent paradigm, is CAMA[83] . It brings fault tolerance to mobile agent applications by using a novel exception handling mechanism developed for this type of applications. This mechanism consists in attaching application-specified handlers to agents to achieve recovery. Therefore, to a set of primitives derived from Linda (e.g. create, delete, put, get, etc.), CAMA adds some primitives to catch and raise inter-agent exceptions (e.g. *raise*, *check*, *wait*).

Linda has strongly influenced the JavaSpaces[84] system design. They are similar in the sense that they store collections of information (resources) which can be later searched by value-based lookup in order to allow members of distributed software systems to exchange information. JavaSpaces is part of the Jini Network Technology[85] , which is an open architecture that enables developers to create network-centric service. Jini has a basic mechanism used for fault-tolerance resource control, which is referred to as Lease. This mechanism is used to define a holding interval of time on a resource by the party that requests access to such resource. It produces a notification event (error detection) when the lease expires, so that actions (recovery) on lease expiry can be taken by the requestor party.

While these framework extensions are good tools for implementing fault-tolerance, they are still "extensions" of the existing tools. The next section will present frameworks that have been designed with the central objective to support the design and implementation of fault tolerance.

6.3. *Advanced Frameworks for Fault Tolerance*

In general, frameworks were defined to allow designers/programmers to develop fault-tolerant software by implementing fault tolerance techniques share the following characteristics[86] :

- many details of their implementation are made transparent to the programmers;
- they provide well-defined interfaces for the definition and implementation of fault tolerance techniques;
- they are recursive in nature (each component can be seen as a system itself).

One of such frameworks is Arjuna[87] , programmed in C++ and Java. It allows the construction of reliable distributed applications in a relatively transparent manner. Reliability is achieved through the provision of traditional atomic transaction mechanisms implemented using only standard language features. It provides basic capabilities for the programmer to handle recovery, persistence and concurrency control, while at the same time achieving flexibility of the software by allowing those capabilities to be refined as required by the demands of the application.

Other similar work is OPTIMA[77] , which is an object-oriented framework (developed for Ada, Java and AspectJ) that provides the necessary runtime support for the "Open Multithreaded Transactions" (OMT) model. OMT is a transaction model that provides features for controlling and structuring not only accesses to objects, as usually happens in transaction systems, but also threads taking part in the same transaction in order to perform a joint activity. The framework provides features to fork and terminate threads inside a transaction, at the same time restricting their behaviours in order to guarantee the correctness of transaction nesting and isolation among transactions.

The DRIP framework[88] provides technological support for implementing DIP[89] models in Java. DIP combines Multiparty Interactions[90,91] and Exception Handling[92] in order to support design dependable interactions among several processes. As an extension to DRIP, the CAA-DRIP implementation framework[45] provides a way to execute Java programs designed using the COALA design language[93] that exploits the Coordinated Atomic actions (CA actions) concept[94] .

Other advanced frameworks for fault-tolerance are currently being designed. For example, the MetaSolve design framework, supporting dynamic selection and parallel composition of services, has been proposed for developing dependable systems[95] . This approach defines an architectural model which makes use of service-oriented architecture features to implement fault tolerance techniques based on meta-data. Furthermore, the software implemented using the MetaSolve approach will be able to adapt itself at run-time in order to provide dynamic fault-tolerance. Such ability to dynamically respond to potentially damaging changes by adapting itself in order to maintain an acceptable level of service is referred to as dynamic resilience. Within this approach, software architecture relies on dynamic information about software components in order to make dynamic reconfiguration decisions. Such metadata will then be used in accordance with some resilient policies which ensure that the desirable dependability requirements are met.

7. Contribution of this Book to the Topic

The contribution of this book to the area of Software Engineering of Fault Tolerant Systems consists of nine papers, briefly described below and categorised according to the three parts identified in section 1:

- Part A: *Fault tolerance engineering: from requirements to code*
  - *In "Exploiting Reflection to Enable Scalable and Performant Database Replication at the Middleware Level" Jorge Salas, Ricardo Jimenez-Peris, Marta Patino-Martinez and Bettina Kemme* introduce a design pattern for data base replication using reflection at the interface level. It permits a clear separation between the regular function and the replication logic. This design pattern allows good performance and scalability properties to be achieved.
  - *In "Adding Fault-Tolerance to State Machine-Based Designs", Sandeep S. Kulkarni, Anish Arora and Ali Ebnenasir* present a non-application specific approach to automatic re-engineering of code in order to make it fault-tolerant and safety. This generic approach uses model-based transformations of programs that must be atomic in terms of their access to variables.
  - *In "Replication in Service-Oriented Systems", Johannes Osrael, Lorenz Froihofer and Karl M. Goeschka* present state of the art replication protocols and replication in service-oriented architectures supported by middleware. They show how to enhance the existing solutions provided in the service-oriented computing with the designs for replication already developed for traditional systems.
- Part B: *Verification and validation of fault tolerant systems*
  - *In "Embedded Software Validation Using On-Chip Debugging Mechanisms", Juan Pardo, José Carlos Campelo, Juan Carlos Ruiz and Pedro Gil* explain how to use on-chip debugging in practice to perform fault-injection in a non-intrusive way. This portable approach offers a verification and validation means for checking and validating the robustness of COTS-based embedded systems.
  - *In "Error Detection in Control Flow of Event-Driven State Based Applications", Gergely Pinter and Istvan Majzik* introduce a formal approach using state-charts to detect two classes of faults: those which occurred during state-chart refinement (using temporal logic model-checking) and those which happened during implementation (using model-based testing).
  - *In "Fault-Tolerant Communication for Distributed Embedded*

Systems", Christian Kühnel and Maria Spichkova present a formal specification using the FOCUS formal framework of FlexRay and FTCom. This paper provides a precise semantics useful for analysing dependencies between FlexRay error rate and FTCom replication component configuration, and for verification of the existing implementations (using Isabelle/HOL).

- Part C: *Languages and Tools for engineering fault tolerant systems*

  - *In "A Model Driven Exception Management Framework", Susan Entwisle and Elizabeth Kendall* propose a model-driven engineering approach to the engineering of fault tolerant systems. An iterative development process using the UML 2 modelling language and model transformations is proposed. The engineering framework proposes generic transformations for exception handling strategies, thus raising exception handling to a higher level of abstraction than only implementation.
  - *In "Runtime Failure Detection and Adaptive Repair for Fault-Tolerant Component-Based Applications", Rong Su, Michel Chaudron and Johan Lukkien* formally present a fault management mechanism suitable for systems designed using a component model. Run-time failures are detected, and the repair strategy is selected using a rule-based approach. An adaptive technique is proposed to dynamically improve the selection of the repair strategy. A forthcoming development framework, Robocop, will provide an implementation of this mechanism.
  - *In "Extending the Applicability of the Neko Framework for the Qualitative and Quantitative Validation and Verification of Distributed Algorithms", Lorenzo Falai and Andrea Bondavalli* describe a development framework written in Java, allowing rapid prototyping of Java distributed algorithms. An import function allows for direct integration of C and C++ programs via glue-code. The framework offers some techniques for qualitative analysis that can be used specifically for the fault tolerance parts of the distributed program developed with its help.

Acknowledgments

The book editors wish to thank Andrea Bondavalli and Rogerio de Lemos for their helpful comments on this introductory chapter and Alfredo Capozucca and Joerg Kienzle for their comments and contribution to Section 6.

References

1. A. Romanovsky, A Looming Fault Tolerance Software Crisis?, in *2006 NATO Workshop on Building Robust Systems with Fallible Construction (also CS-TR-991 Newcastle University, UK)*, 2006.
2. A. Avizienis, J.-C. Laprie, B. Randell and C. E. Landwehr, Basic Concepts and Taxonomy of Dependable and Secure Computing, *IEEE Trans. Dependable and Sec. Comput.* **vol. 1, numb. 1**, 2004.
3. P. Lee and T. Anderson, *Fault Tolerance: Principles and Practice, Second Edition* (Prentice-Hall, 1990).
4. C. Dony, J. L. Knudsen, A. Romanovsky and A. Tripathi, *Advances in Exception Handling Techniques*, LNCS-4119 edn. (Springer-Verlag, 2006).
5. A. Romanovsky, Fault Tolerance through Exception Handling in Ambient and Pervasive Systems, in *SBES 2005 - 19th Brazilian Symposium on Software Engineering, Brazil*, October 6, 2005.
6. M. Bruntink, A. van Deursen and T. Tourwe, Discovering faults in idiom-based exception handling, in *ICSE 2006: Proceedings of the International Conference on Software Engineering*, (ACM Press, Shanghai, China, 2006).
7. The U.S. Secretary of Energy and the Minister of Natural Resources Canada, *Interim Report: Causes of the August 14th Blackout in the United States and Canada. Canada U.S. Power System Outage Task Force,* 2003.
8. J.-L. Lions, *Ariane 5 flight 501 failure. Technical report* (ESA/CNES, 1996).
9. Recommended Practice for Architectural Description of Software-Intensive Systems, in *The Institute of Electrical and Electronics Engineers (IEEE) Standards Board*, (IEEE-Std-1471-2000, September 2000)
10. I. Sommerville, *Software engineering (8th ed.)* (Addison-Wesley Longman Publishing Co., Inc., Boston, MA, USA, 2006).
11. C. Ghezzi, M. Jazayeri and D. Mandrioli, *Fundamentals of Software Engineering*, second edn. (Prentice Hall, September 2002).
12. W. Emmerich, *Engineering Distributed Objects* (John Wiley and Sons Ltd, 2000).
13. I. Peterson, *Fatal Defect: Chasing Killer Computer Bugs* (Vintage, 1996).
14. C. Fishman, They Write the Right Stuff (in the FastCompany magazine, Issue 06, Dec 1996/Jan 1997, Page 95).
15. D. Jackson, Dependable Software by Design *Scientific American* June 2006.
16. I. Jacobson, G. Booch and J. Rumbaugh, *The Unified Software Development Process* (Addison Wesley, Object Technology Series, 1999).
17. The capability maturity model. http://www.sei.cmu.edu/cmm/.
18. The personal software process. http://www.sei.cmu.edu/tsp/psp.html.

19. R. de Lemos and A. Romanovsky, Exception Handling in the Software Lifecycle *International Journal of Computer Systems Science and Engineering* **vol. 16, numb. 2** (CRL Publishing, March 2001).
20. C. M. F. Rubira, R. de Lemos, G. R. M. Ferreira and F. C. Filho, Exception handling in the development of dependable component-based systems *Softw. Pract. Exper.* **vol. 35, numb. 3** (John Wiley & Sons, Inc., New York, NY, USA, 2005).
21. B. Nuseibeh and S. Easterbrook, Requirements Engineering: A Roadmap, in *ACM ICSE 2000, The Future of Software Engineering*, ed. A. Finkelstein, year 2000.
22. A. Shui, S. Mustafiz, J. Kienzle and C. Dony, Exceptional Use Cases, in *MoDELS*, 2005.
23. S. Mustafiz, X. Sun, J. Kienzle and H. Vangheluwe, Model-driven assessment of use cases for dependable systems, in *MoDELS*, 2006.
24. A. Shui, S. Mustafiz and J. Kienzle, Exception-aware requirements elicitation with use cases *Advanced Topics in Exception Handling Techniques, Springer, Berlin* 2006.
25. D. E. Perry and A. L. Wolf, Foundations for the study of software architecture, in *SIGSOFT Software Engineering Notes*, Oct 1992.
26. H. Muccini and A. Romanovsky, Architecting Fault Tolerant Systems: a Comparison Framework *University of L'Aquila Technical Report* 2007.
27. N. Medvidovic and R. N. Taylor, A Classification and Comparison Framework for Software Architecture Description Languages *IEEE Transactions on Software Engineering* **vol. 26, numb. 1,** January 2000.
28. N. Medvidovic, D. S. Rosenblum, D. F. Redmiles and J. E. Robbins, Modeling Software Architectures in the Unified Modeling Language *ACM Transactions on Software Engineering and Methodology (TOSEM)* **vol. 11, numb. 1,** January 2002.
29. D. Garlan, Formal Modeling and Analysis of Software Architecture: Components, Connectors, and Events, in *Formal Methods for Software Architectures*, (Lecture Note in Computer Science, 2804, 2003).
30. F. C. Filho, P. A. de C. Guerra and C. M. Rubira, An Architectural-Level Exception-Handling System for Component-Based Applications, in *LADC03*, 2003.
31. F. C. Filho, P. H. S. Brito and C. M. F. Rubira, A framework for analyzing exception flow in software architectures, in *ICSE 2005 Workshop on Architecting Dependable Systems (WADS05)*, 2005.
32. C. Gacek and R. de Lemos, *Structure for Dependability: Computer-Based Systems from an Interdisciplinary Perspective* (Springer-Verlag, 2006), ch. Architectural Description of Dependable Software Systems, pp. 127–142.
33. N. Guelfi, R. Razavi, A. Romanovsky and S. Vandenbergh, DRIP Catalyst: An MDE/MDA Method for Fault-tolerant Distributed Software Families Development, in *OOPSLA and GPCE Workshop on Best Practices for Model Driven Software Development*, 2004.
34. P. H. da S. Brito, C. R. Rocha, F. C. Filho, E. Martins and C. M. F. Rubira, A method for modeling and testing exceptions in component-based software

development, in *LADC*, 2005.
35. F. C. Filho, P. H. Brito and C. M. Rubira, Modeling and Analysis of Architectural Exceptions, in *Workshop on Rigorous Engineering of Fault Tolerant Systems Event Information, in conjunction with Formal Methods 2005. 18-22 July 2005, University of Newcastle upon Tyne, UK*, 2005.
36. R. de Lemos, Idealised Fault Tolerant Architectural Element, in *DSN 2006 Workshop on Architecting Dependable Systems (WADS06)*, 2006.
37. M. Shaw and P. Clements, A Field Guide to Boxology: Preliminary Classification of Architectural Styles for Software Systems, in *COMPSAC97, 21st Int. Computer Software and Applications Conference*, 1997.
38. R. de Lemos, P. A. de C. Guerra and C. Rubira, A Fault-Tolerant Architectural Approach for Dependable Systems *IEEE Software, Special Issue on Software Architectures* March/April 2006.
39. V. Issarny and J. Banatre, Architecture-based Exception Handling, in *HICSS '01: Proceedings of the 34th Annual Hawaii International Conference on System Sciences (HICSS-34)-Volume 9*, (IEEE Computer Society, Washington, DC, USA, 2001).
40. Y. Feng, G. Huang, Y. Zhu and H. Mei, Exception Handling in Component Composition with the Support of Middleware, in *ACM Proc. Fifth International Workshop on Software Engineering and Middleware (SEM 2005)*, 2005.
41. A. Bondavalli, S. Chiaradonna, D. Cotroneo and L. Romano, Effective fault treatment for improving the dependability of COTS- and legacy-based applications *IEEE Transactions on Dependable and Secure Computing* **vol. 1, numb. 4**, 2004.
42. D. M. Beder, A. Romanovsky, B. Randell and C. M. Rubira, On Applying Coordinated Atomic Actions and Dependable Software Architectures in Developing Complex Systems, in *4th IEEE International Symposium on Object-Oriented Real-time Distributed Computing (ISORC'01)*, (Magdeburg, Germany, 2001).
43. A. F. Garcia and C. M. Rubira, *Advances in Exception Handling Techniques* (Springer-Verlag, LNCS-2022, April 2001), ch. An Architectural-based Reflective Approach to Incorporating Exception Handling into Dependable Software.
44. J. Xu, B. Randell, A. Romanovsky, C. M. F. Rubira, R. J. Stroud and Z. Wu, Fault tolerance in concurrent object-oriented software through coordinated error recovery, in *FTCS '95: Proceedings of the Twenty-Fifth International Symposium on Fault-Tolerant Computing*, (IEEE Computer Society, Washington, DC, USA, 1995).
45. A. Capozucca, N. Guelfi, P. Pelliccione, A. Romanovsky and A. Zorzo, CAA-DRIP: a framework for implementing Coordinated Atomic Actions, in *The 17th IEEE International Symposium on Software Reliability Engineering (ISSRE 2006)*, 7-10 November 2006 - Raleigh, North Carolina, USA.
46. P. Ammann, S. Jajodia and P. Liu, *A Fault Tolerance Approach to Survivability*, tech. rep., Center for Secure Information Systems, George Mason University (April 1999).

47. Object Management Group, OMG/Unified Modelling Language(UML) V2.0 (2004).
48. G. J. Pai and J. B. Dugan, Automatic Synthesis of Dynamic Fault Trees from UML System Models *13th International Symposium on Software Reliability Engineering (ISSRE'02)* (IEEE Computer Society, Los Alamitos, CA, USA, 2002).
49. A. Bondavalli, I. Majzik and I. Mura, Automatic dependability analysis for supporting design decisions in UML, in *Proc. of the Fourth IEEE International Symposium on High Assurance Systems Engineering*, eds. R. Paul and C. Meadows (IEEE, 1999).
50. A. Bondavalli, M. D. Cin, D. Latella, I. Majzik, A. Pataricza and G. Savoia, Dependability analysis in the early phases of UML-based system design. *Comput. Syst. Sci. Eng.* **vol. 16, numb. 5**, 2001.
51. I. Majzik, A. Pataricza and A. Bondavalli, Stochastic dependability analysis of system architecture based on uml models, in *Architecting Dependable Systems, LNCS 2677*, eds. R. De Lemos, C. Gacek and A. RomanovskyLecture Notes in Computer Science (Springer-Verlag, Berlin, Heidelberg, New York, 2003) pp. 219–244.
52. E. M. Clarke, O. Grumberg and D. A. Peled., *Model Checking* (The MIT Press, Massachusetts Institute of Technology, 2001).
53. C. Bernardeschi, A. Fantechi and S. Gnesi, Model checking fault tolerant systems *Software Testing Verification and Reliability* **vol. 12**, 2002.
54. T. Yokogawa, T. Tsuchiya and T. Kikuno, Automatic verification of fault tolerance using model checking, in *Proc. 2001 Pacific Rim International Symposium on Dependable Computing*, (IEEE Computer Society, Los Alamitos, CA, USA, 2001).
55. G. Bruns and I. Sutherland, Model checking and fault tolerance, in *AMAST '97: Proceedings of the 6th International Conference on Algebraic Methodology and Software Technology*, (Springer-Verlag, London, UK, 1997).
56. H. R. Andersen, Partial model checking, in *LICS '95: Proceedings of the 10th Annual IEEE Symposium on Logic in Computer Science*, (IEEE Computer Society, Washington, DC, USA, 1995).
57. S. Gnesi, G. Lenzini and F. Martinelli, Logical specification and analysis of fault tolerant systems through partial model checking, in *Proceedings of the International Workshop on Software Verification and Validation (SVV 2003), Mumbai, India*, eds. S. Etalle, S. Mukhopadhyay and A. Roychoudhury (Elsevier, Amsterdam, December 2003).
58. J. J. Kljaich, B. T. Smith and A. S. Wojcik, Formal verification of fault tolerance using theorem-proving techniques *IEEE Trans. Comput.* **vol. 38, numb. 3** (IEEE Computer Society, Washington, DC, USA, 1989).
59. L. Pike, J. Maddalon, P. Miner and A. Geser, Abstractions for fault-tolerant distributed system verification, in *Theorem Proving in Higher Order Logics (TPHOLs)*, eds. K. Slind, A. Bunker and G. Gopalakrishnan, Lecture Notes in Computer Science, Vol. 3223 (Springer, 2004).
60. B. Bonakdarpour and S. S. Kulkarni, Towards reusing formal proofs for verification of fault tolerance, in *AFM (Automated Formal Methods) August 21,*

2006, Seattle. USA,

61. S. Owre, J. Rushby, N. Shankar and F. von Henke, Formal verification for fault-tolerant architectures: Prolegomena to the design of pvs *IEEE Transactions on Software Engineering* **vol. 21, numb. 2** (IEEE Computer Society, Los Alamitos, CA, USA, 1995).
62. D. Jackson, Alloy: a lightweight object modelling notation *ACM Trans. Softw. Eng. Methodol.* **vol. 11, numb. 2** (ACM Press, New York, NY, USA, 2002).
63. F. C. Filho, A. Romanovsky and C. M. F. Rubira, Verification of coordinated exception handling, in *SAC '06: Proceedings of the 2006 ACM symposium on Applied computing*, (ACM Press, New York, NY, USA, 2006).
64. B. Randell, System Structure for Software Fault Tolerance *IEEE Transactions on Software Engineering. IEEE Press* **SE-1**, 1975.
65. A. Bertolino, Software testing research and practice, in *Abstract State Machines 2003. Advances in Theory and Practice: 10th International Workshop, ASM 2003, Taormina, Italy, March 3-7, 2003. Proceedings. Book Series Lecture Notes in Computer Science. Volume 2589/2003*, (Springer Berlin / Heidelberg, 2003).
66. M. R. Lyu, Z. Huang, S. K. S. Sze and X. Cai, An empirical study on testing and fault tolerance for software reliability engineering, in *ISSRE '03: Proceedings of the 14th International Symposium on Software Reliability Engineering*, (IEEE Computer Society, Washington, DC, USA, 2003).
67. A. Bucchiarone, H. Muccini and P. Pelliccione, Architecting fault-tolerant component-based systems: from requirements to testing, in *2nd VODCA Views On Designing Complex Architectures proceedings. To appear on ENTCS (Electronic Notes in Theoretical Computer Science)*, 2006.
68. J. Armstrong, R. Virding, C. Wikström and M. Williams, *Concurrent Programming in Erlang*, second edn. (Prentice-Hall, 1996).
69. D. Detlefs, M. Herlihy and J. Wing, Inheritance of synchronization and recovery properties in avalon/c++ *IEEE Computer* **vol. 21, numb. 12**, 1988.
70. A. Z. Spector, R. F. Pausch and G. Bruell, Camelot: A flexible distributed transaction processing system., in *COMPCON'88, Digest of Papers, Thirty-Third IEEE Computer Society International Conference, San Francisco, California, USA, February 29 - March 4, 1988*, (IEEE Computer Society, 1988).
71. B. Liskov, The argus language and system, in *Distributed Systems: Methods and Tools for Specification, An Advanced Course, April 3-12, 1984 and April 16-25, 1985 Munich*, (Springer-Verlag, London, UK, 1985).
72. B. Randell and J. Xu, Object-Oriented Software Fault Tolerance: Framework, Reuse and Design Diversity *Predictably Dependable Computing System (PDCS 2)* **First Year Report**, 1993.
73. P. Rogers, Software Fault Tolerance, Reflection and the Ada Programming Language, PhD thesis, Department of Computer Science, University of YorkOctober 2003.
74. J. Kienzle and R. Guerraoui, AOP - Does It Make Sense? The Case of Concurrency and Failures, in *16th (ECOOP'2002)*, ed. B. Magnusson, (2374) (Malaga, Spain, 2002).

75. S. Soares, E. Laureano and P. Borba, Implementing distribution and persistence aspects with AspectJ, in *Proceedings of the 17th ACM Conference on Object- Oriented Programming, Systems, Languages, and Applications*, (ACM Press, 2002).
76. A. Rashid and R. Chitchyan, Persistence as an aspect, in *Proceedings of the 2nd International Conference on Aspect-Oriented Software Development - AOSD'2003*, ed. M. Aksit (ACM Press, March 2003).
77. J. Kienzle, *Open Multithreaded Transactions - A Transaction Model for Concurrent Object-Oriented Programming* (Kluwer Academic Publishers, 2003).
78. J. Fabry and T. Cleenewerck, Aspect-oriented domain specific languages for advanced transaction management, in *International Conference on Enterprise Information Systems 2005 (ICEIS 2005) proceedings*, (Springer-Verlag, 2005).
79. R. Johnson, http://st-www.cs.uiuc.edu/users/johnson/frameworks.html (1997).
80. R. Martin and S. Totten, Introduction to Fault Tolerant CORBA (2003).
81. D. Gelernter, Generative communication in linda *ACM Trans. Program. Lang. Syst.* **7** (ACM Press, New York, NY, USA, 1985).
82. D. Bakken and R. Schlichting, Supporting fault-tolerant parallel programming in linda *IEEE Transactions on Parallel and Distributed Systems* **6**, 1995.
83. B. Arief, A. Iliasov and A. Romanovsky, On Using the CAMA Framework for Developing Open Mobile Fault Tolerant Agent Systems, in *SELMAS 2006 Workshop, as part of the 28th International Conference on Software Engineering*, (ACM Press, 2006).
84. Jini JavaSpaces, http://www.sun.com/software/jini/specs/jini1.2html/js-spec.html.
85. Jini, http://www.sun.com/software/jini/.
86. L. L. Pullum, *Software fault tolerance techniques and implementation* (Artech House, Inc., Norwood, MA, USA, 2001).
87. G. D. Parrington, S. K. Shrivastava, S. M. Wheater and M. C. Little, The Design and Implementation of Arjuna *Computing Systems* **vol. 8, numb. 2**, 1995.
88. A. F. Zorzo and R. J. Stroud, A distributed object-oriented framework for dependable multiparty interactions, in *OOPSLA '99*, (ACM Press, 1999).
89. A. Zorzo, Multiparty Interactions in Dependable Distributed Systems, PhD thesis, University of Newcastle upon Tyne, Newcastle upon Tyne, UK1999.
90. M. Evangelist, N. Francez and S. Katz, Multiparty interactions for interprocess communication and synchronization *IEEE Transactions on Software Engineering* **15**, 1989.
91. Y.-J. Joung and S. A. Smolka, A comprehensive study of the complexity of multiparty interaction *J. ACM* **43** (ACM Press, New York, NY, USA, 1996).
92. F. Cristian, Exception Handling *Dependability of Resilient Computers (ed. T.Anderson)* (Blackwell Scientific Publications, 1989).
93. J. Vachon, COALA : a design language for reliable distributed systems, PhD thesis, Swiss Federal Institute of Technology Lausanne (Thesis no 2302)2000.

94. B. Randell, A. Romanovsky, R. J. Stroud, J. Xu and A. F. Zorzo, *Coordinated Atomic Actions: from Concept to Implementation*, Tech. Rep. 595 (1997).
95. G. D. M. Serugendo, J. Fitzgerald, A. Romanovsky and N. Guelfi, Towards a Metadata-Based Architectural Model for Dynamically Resilient Systems, in *SAC'07, March 11-15, Seoul, Korea*, (ACM Press, 2007).

PART A

Fault Tolerance Engineering: From Requirements to Code

EXPLOITING REFLECTION TO ENABLE SCALABLE AND PERFORMANT DATABASE REPLICATION AT THE MIDDLEWARE LEVEL*†

J. SALAS, R. JIMÉNEZ-PERIS and M. PATIÑO-MARTÍNEZ

Facultad de Informática, Universidad Politécnica de Madrid
Madrid, Spain
E-mail: {jsalas, rjimenez, mpatino}@fi.upm.es

B. KEMME

School of Computer Science, McGill University
Montreal, Quebec, Canada
E-mail: kemme@cs.mcgill.ca

Database replication has gained a lot of attention in the last few years since databases are often the bottleneck of modern information systems. Database replication is often implemented at the middleware level. However, there is an important tradeoff in terms of scalability and performance if the database is dealt with as a black box. In this paper, we advocate for a gray box approach in which some minimal functionality of the database is exposed through a reflective interface enabling performant and scalable database replication at the middleware level. Reflection is the adequate paradigm to separate the regular functionality from the replication logic. However, traditional full-fledged reflection is too expensive. For this reason, the paper focuses on the exploration of some lightweight reflective interfaces that can combine the architectonic advantages of reflection with good performance and scalability. The paper also evaluates thoroughly the cost of the different proposed reflective mechanisms and its impact on the performance.

Keywords: Database Replication, Reflection, Middleware, Fault-Tolerance.

---

*This chapter is an extension of the paper "Lightweight Reflection for Middleware-based Database Replication" that was published at the 25th IEEE Symposium on Reliable Distributed Systems (SRDS'06).

†This work has been partially funded by the European EUREKA/ITEA S4ALL project, the Spanish Ministry of Education and Science (MEC) under grant #TIN2004-07474-C02-01, and the Madrid Regional Research Council (CAM) under grant #0505/TIC/000285 with support from FEDER and FSE.

1. Introduction

Database replication is a topic that has attracted a lot of research in the last years. There are two main reasons. Firstly, databases are frequently the bottleneck of more complex systems such as multi-tier architectures that need high throughput. Secondly, databases store critical information that has to be continuously available. With database replication, the database system can provide both scale-up and fault-tolerance. A critical issue of database replication is how to keep the copies consistent when updates occur. That is, whenever a transaction updates data records, these updates have to be performed at all replicas. Traditional approaches have studied how to implement replication within the database, what we term the *white box* approach.[1–4] However, the white box approach has a number of shortcomings. Firstly, it requires access to source code. This means that only the database vendor will be able to implement it. Secondly, it is typically tightly integrated with the implementation of the regular database functionality, in order to take advantage of the many optimizations performed within the database kernel. While this might lead to better performance, it results in the creation of inter-dependencies between the replication code and the other database modules, which is hard to maintain in a continuously evolving codebase.

Recent research proposals have looked at replication solutions outside the database,[5–14] typically as a middleware layer. However, nearly none of them is truly a *black-box* approach in which the database is used exclusively based on its user interface since this would lead to very simplistic and inefficient replication mechanisms. Instead, some solutions require specific information from the application. For instance, they parse incoming SQL statements in order to determine the tables accessed by an operation.[7] This allows performing simple concurrency control at the middleware layer. More stringent, some solutions require the first command within a transaction to indicate whether the transaction is read-only or an update transaction,[13] or to indicate the tables that are going to be accessed by the transaction.[8,9,15] Nevertheless, many do not require any additional functionality from the database system itself. However, this can lead to inefficiencies. For instance, it requires update operations or even entire update transactions to be executed at all replicas which results in limited scalability. We term this approach *symmetric processing.* An alternative is *asymmetric processing* of updates that consists in executing an update transaction at any of the replicas and then propagating and applying only the updated tuples at the remaining replicas. Reference 16 shows that the asymmetric approach results in a dramatic increase of scalability even for workloads with a large proportion of update transactions (80% and above). However, retrieving the writesets and applying them at remote sites is non-trivial and is most efficient if the database system provides some support. We believe that additional replication efficiency could be achieved if the database exposed even more functionality to the middleware layer.

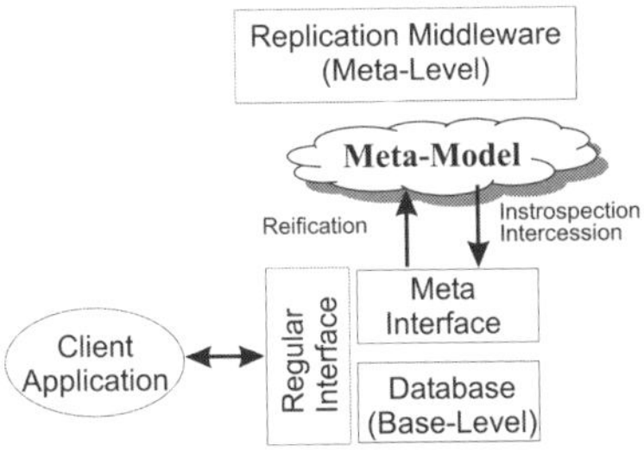

Fig. 1. A Reflective Database

Thus, in this paper we try to combine the advantages of white and black box approaches by resorting to computational reflection.[17] The essence of computational reflection lies in the capability of a system to reason about itself and its behavior, and act upon it. A reflective system is structured around a representation of itself or *meta-model*. This meta-model might provide different abstractions of the underlying system with different levels of detail. A reflective system is split into two level. The regular computation takes place at the *base-level* (the database in Fig. 1). The *meta-level* only sees the meta-model of the underlying base-level. The meta-model provides the meta-level with an abstraction of the computation of the base-level, based on which the meta-level provides extended functionality (the replication middleware in Fig. 1). *Reification* is the process by which changes in the base-level are reflected in the meta-model. *Introspection* is the mechanism that enables the meta-level to interrogate the base-level about its structure and/or behavior, and update the meta-model accordingly. *Intercession* is the mechanism through which the meta-level can change the state and/or behavior of the base-level.

We use reflection to expose some functionality of the database resulting in what we term a *gray box approach* to database replication (Fig. 1). Unlike previous reflective approaches for middleware,[18,19] our goal is not to propose a full-fledged meta-model of a database, since the inherent overheads are prohibitive and incompatible with the high performance requirements of databases. Our aim is to identify a set of composable, minimal and lightweight reflective interfaces that enable high performance replication at the middleware level. We start by a set of basic interfaces which are essential for the practicality of the approach. Functionality provided by such interfaces is already implicitly used by existing protocols. In this paper, we make their use more explicit. Then, we reason about more advanced functionality which we have identified of being beneficial for database replication. These advanced interfaces allow obtaining the combined benefits of black and white box approaches. On the one hand separation of concerns is achieved by having separate components for the regular database functionality and the replication code. On the other hand, sophisticated optimizations can be performed in our replication middleware.[12]

In the following, Section 2 presents two replication algorithms that will serve as examples to discuss our needs for reflection. Section 3 provides a series of interesting reflective interfaces. Section 4 presents the implementation and evaluation of some specific reflective interfaces. Section 5 presents related work and Section 6 concludes the paper.

2. Two Basic Database Replication Protocols

In this section we want to give an intuition of how a typical database replication protocol works. Database replication aims at providing one-copy correctness (1CC), that is, that the replicated database behaves as a non-replicated one. The traditional 1CC is one-copy-serializability (1CS) in which a replicated database behaves as a serializable non-replicated one. Other 1CC criteria have been defined recently such as one-copy-snapshot isolation,[14] in which a replicated database behaves as a centralized database with snapshot isolation. There are two families of replication protocols: pessimistic and optimistic. Pessimistic protocols are characterized because they prevent the violation of 1CC. That is, they only allow the execution of transactions when it is known that they will not violate 1CC. In contrast, optimistic protocols allow unconstrained execution of transactions and before they commit, they check whether they satisfy 1CC.

We look at two basic protocols, one being pessimistic, the other optimistic. Both protocols provide 1CS, and use group communication systems[20] that provide total order multicast (all messages are delivered to all replicas in the same order). For simplicity of description, we ignore reliability of message delivery in this paper.

The pessimistic replication protocol is a simplified version of the one proposed in Ref. 5. It performs symmetric processing of transactions and assumes single statement transactions or multiple statement transactions sent in a single request. A client sends its transaction requests to one of the replicas. The replica multicasts these requests in total order to all the replicas which process all received requests sequentially. Transaction execution can be summarized as follows:

I. Upon receiving a transaction request from the client: send the request to all replicas using total order multicast.
II. Upon delivering a transaction request: enqueue the request in a FIFO queue.
III. Once a request is the first in the queue: submit transaction for execution.
IV. Once a transaction finishes execution: remove it from queue. If local return response to client.

This basic protocol only needs minimal reflective support in order to forward transactions to all replicas. We discuss later how it can be enhanced to improve performance and functionality, and how these improvements require extensions to the reflective interface.

The optimistic protocol is more advanced. It is a simplified version of Ref. 21 and performs asymmetric processing of updates. For simplicity of description we assume that each request is one transaction (multiple request transactions could be handled in the same way). A client submits a request to one of the replicas where it is executed locally. If the transaction is read-only the reply is returned to the client immediately. Otherwise, a distributed validation is needed that checks whether 1-copy serializability has been preserved. If not, the validating transaction is aborted.

I. Upon receiving a transaction request from the client: execute it locally.
II. Upon completing the execution:
   1. If read-only: return response to client.
   2. If update transaction: extract the readset (RS) and writeset (WS) and multicast them in total order.
III. Upon delivering RS and WS of transaction tv: validate it with all transactions tc that committed after tv started.
   1. If $\exists tc : WS(tc) \cap RS(tv) \neq \emptyset$: if tv local, abort tv and return abort to client (tv should have read tc's update but might have read an earlier version), otherwise ignore tv.
   2. If $\forall tc : WS(tc) \cap RS(tv) = \emptyset$: if tv not local, apply the writeset of tv in form of a remote transaction and commit. If local, commit tv and return commit to user.

3. Reflective Interfaces for Database Replication

In this section we study which reflective interfaces can be exhibited by databases to enable the implementation of the protocols presented in the previous section at the middleware level. Additionally, we also discuss how these protocols can be enhanced and which extensions to the reflective interface these enhancements require.

3.1. *Reflective database connection*

Clients open a database (DB) connection by means of a DB connectivity component (e.g. JDBC) running at the client side, through which they submit transactions. The DB connectivity component forwards the connection request and the transactions to the DB server that processes them. The DB server then returns the corresponding replies that the connectivity component relays to the client. Finally, the client can close the connection. Since database functionality is split into a client and server part, we have a meta-model, and base- and meta-levels at both the client and server side. The client base-model is the client connectivity component. The database base-level is the connection handler. The well-known *request interception* reflective technique can be applied at the connectivity component and the connection handler to implement replication as a middleware layer. Request interception is used by nearly all replication approaches to allow the middleware layer control over the execution.

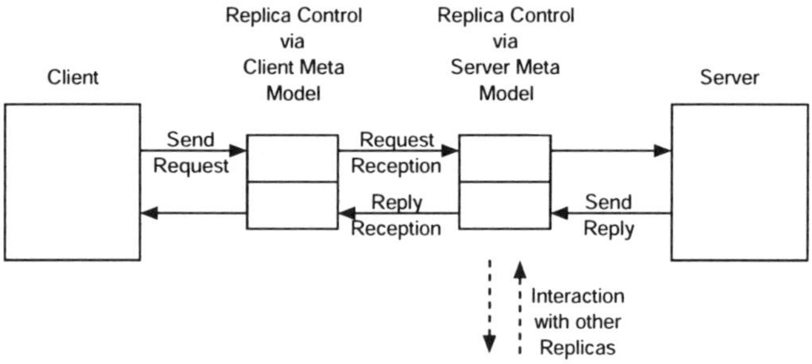

Fig. 2. Reflective Database Connection

3.1.1. *Basic algorithm*

Figure 2 shows how reflective support is required from the DB connectivity component and the connection handler to enable the pessimistic basic algorithm presented in the previous section. First, since the client is not aware of the replication, the connection request should be intercepted by the meta-level. This provides the first hook to insert the replication logic (*SendRequest*). The connection request will be reified and at the meta-level the connection will be established by first executing a replica discovery protocol (e.g. by means of IP-multicast as in Middle-R[14]) to discover the available replicas. Then, one is chosen and the connection is established with it. This result will be reified (*ReplyReception*) to the client meta-level so that it can keep track of the replica to which it is connected. The standard client transaction requests and the corresponding responses from the server can be intercepted in the same way. However, for the basic protocol no special actions are needed, and requests and responses are simply forwarded. In order to perform its tasks the client-meta level only needs a very simple meta-model representing the underlying DB connectivity component. It only needs to distinguish between connection related requests/responses and transaction related requests/responses.

Let us now examine what is required at the server side. At each replica, execution is split between meta-level (replication logic) and base-level (the original database). A request to the database server is reified (*RequestReception*) to the server meta-level. If it is a connection request the meta-level registers the client. That is, the connection is now actually established between the meta-level at the client and the metal-level at the database replica. Upon a transaction request, it needs to be multicast in total order to the meta-levels of all replicas. At each replica, upon receiving a transaction request the meta-level triggers transaction execution in a serial manner at the base-level as a form of intercession. When execution is completed at the server base-level the result is reified (*SendReply*) to the server meta-level which can perform additional replication logic. For instance, for the response to a transaction request, only the local replica has to return the result to the client. The meta-model used by the meta-level treats the database as a completely black box. However, as the client metal-level it must distinguish between connection and transaction requests.

When looking at the optimistic algorithm, a simple reflective mechanism at the database connection level is not enough. Hence, we defer the discussion of this protocol to the next sections.

3.1.2. *Fault-Tolerance*

A reflective database connection can furthermore enhance the pessimistic protocol (and in a similar way the optimistic protocol), by providing the right hooks to integrate fault-tolerance. A client should stay connected to the replicated system even if a replica fails. Ideally, the client itself is not even aware of any failures but experiences an uninterrupted service. Reflection at the connection level can achieve this.[14] As mentioned before, when a client wants to connect to the system, the client meta-level can detect existing replicas and connect to any of them. In a similar way, when the replica to which the client is connected to fails, the failure needs to be reified to the client meta-level. Then, the meta-level can automatically reconnect to a different replica without the client noticing. For that, the client meta-level has to do extra actions when intercepting transaction requests and their responses. A possible execution can be outlined as follows. When the meta-level receives a request it tags it with a unique identifier and caches it locally before forwarding the tagged request to the server. If the meta-level receives a failure exception or times out when waiting for a response, it can reconnect to another replica and resubmit the request with the same identifier. The server meta-level of each replica keeps track of the last request and its response for each client using the request identifier. Hence, when it intercepts a request, it first checks whether it is a resubmission. If yes, it returns immediately the result. Otherwise, it is multicast and executed at all replicas as described above. At-least-once execution is provided by letting the client meta-level resubmit outstanding requests. At-most-once is guaranteed by detecting duplicate submissions. The server meta-level has to remove the request identifier from the request before the request is forwarded to the base-level server in order to keep the regular interface unmodified.

3.2. *Reflective requests*

The basic pessimistic protocol executes both read-only and update transactions serially at all sites. In order to enable more efficient replication protocols, read-only transactions need to be executed at only one replica, and a minimum degree of concurrency should be allowed. In order for the replication middleware to achieve this, a more advanced meta-model is needed. This meta-interface will enable to perform introspection on the request and might also provide access to application-dependent knowledge on the transaction access pattern. Therefore, this meta-interface can offer information about transaction requests with different levels of detail. At level 1, it can classify the transaction as read-only or update. At level 2, it can provide information about the tables that are going to be accessed by the transaction and in which mode (read or update). At level 3, it can determine the conflict classes to be accessed by the transaction. Conflict classes is an application defined concurrency control in which data are grouped in sets called conflict classes and it is known a priori which conflict classes each transaction accesses.

Level 1 can be achieved, for instance, if the application uses the `SetConnectionToReadOnly` method offered by the JDBC drivers. For our simple pessimistic protocol, this allows read-only transactions to not be forwarded to all replicas but only to be executed at the base-level of the replica to which the request was submitted (as used in Ref.[5]). Distinguishing between read-only and update transactions is also needed by primary copy replication.[13] In this case, the replication protocol can redirect update transactions to the base-level of the primary server and read-only transactions to any other replica. Levels 2 and 3 are used to implement concurrency control at the middleware level. Level 2 can be easily achieved through a SQL parser run at the meta-level (either at client or server side) as has been done in Ref. 22. Level 3 requires a meta-interface so that application programmers can define conflict classes and attach to transactional requests the set of conflict classes they access. Level 3 can be exploited by conflict aware schedulers such as in Refs. 7–9,15,23. Middle-R[12] has an implementation of such interface. If levels 2 or 3 are available, then the basic pessimistic protocol can be extended. Instead of having one FIFO queue, there can be a queue per table or conflict class and requests are appended to the queues of tables/classes they access. Hence, transactions that do not conflict (i.e. are stored in different queues) can be submitted concurrently to the base-level.

3.3. *Reflective transactions*

Reflective connections and requests are not enough to execute the optimistic asymmetric protocol presented in Section 2. While the optimistic concurrency control could be achieved through reflective requests, the coarse conflict granularity achieved at this level (on a table or conflict-class basis) is likely to lead to many aborts. Thus, in order for optimistic concurrency control to be attractive, conflicts should be detected on the tuple level. Furthermore, we need to retrieve and apply writesets for asymmetric replication. Therefore, we need what we call reflective transactions.

3.3.1. *Writesets*

Since the optimistic protocol performs asymmetric replication, the meta-model of the server side needs the concept of a writeset. The meta-level needs to be able to obtain the writeset of a transaction from the base-level and apply a writeset at the base-level. The first requires reification, the second intercession. The writeset contains the updated/inserted/removed tuples identified through their primary keys. The meta-interface can provide access to writesets in three different forms. The first form provides the writeset as a black box. In this case, writesets can only be used to propagate changes to all replicas. The second form consists in a reflective writeset providing an introspection interface itself. This interface allows the analysis of the content of the writeset, for instance, to identify the primary keys of the updated tuples. This is needed for the optimistic protocol to detect conflicts. The third form offers a textual representation of the writeset. This could be a SQL update statement identifying the tuples to be updated by their primary keys. However, other textual representations are possible, for instance, XML. With this, replication could be performed across heterogeneous databases since one could retrieve a writeset from a PostgreSQL database and apply it to an Oracle instance. Heterogeneous replication is useful to tolerate bugs in databases as done in Ref. 24 or to have inexpensive backups as in Ref. 13.

The writeset meta-interface can be implemented efficiently. At the time updates are physically processed at the database, the updates can be recorded in a memory buffer. The meta-interface just provides access to this buffer. A binary meta-interface for PostgreSQL is used in Refs 22,23, an introspective writeset meta-interface exists for PostgreSQL 7.2,[14] and we have just completed a textual writeset based on SQL statements for MySQL. If the database itself does not provide writeset functionality, it can be implemented through different means such as triggers.[13]

3.3.2. *Readsets*

In order to perform the validation of our optimistic replication algorithm, we also need the readset information. In contrast to the writeset inteface, the readset meta-interface only needs to know the primary keys of the read tuples (and possibly some timestamp or version information), not the entire tuples. The implementation is also relatively simple. Whenever a physical read takes place, the primary key (and version number) is recorded in a buffer. However, the practicality of the approach might be limited. Writesets are usually small, while readsets can become very large, e.g., if complex join operations are used. Thus propagating readsets might be prohibitive. Also, performing validation on readsets can be very expensive. Therefore, although the readset can be supported at the meta-interface, so far, very few protocols use it.

3.4. *Reflective log*

The log of a database contains undo and redo records for updated tuples in order to guarantee transaction atomicity. A reflective log provides an introspection interface that enables the retrieval of the records written by a given transaction in order to generate its writeset. Although conceptually similar to the writeset approach presented above, there is a very important difference. With the previous meta-interface writesets are obtained before transaction completion, while a reflective log typically only provides writesets of already committed transactions. This difference prevents the use of the reflective log approach for eager replication which requires to multicast updates before transaction commit. In particular, if the writeset is needed for conflict detection before transaction commit the reflective log cannot be used. Furthermore, making the log reflective can have a negative effect on performance. Typically, the log file is stored on a separate disk for efficiency reasons. The append-only semantics of log writes leads to fast disk writes since the disk head is always on the right track. A reflective log, however, requires read access to the log leading to random disk access, and thus, will slow down both read and write access.

Reflective logs are already provided by some commercial databases such as Microsoft SQLServer, Oracle, and IBM DB2. This reflective interface is usually known as log sniffer/reader/miner. Log sniffers are usually used for lazy replication in which updates are propagated as separate transactions.

3.5. *Reflective concurrency control*

Reflective transactions described in section 3.3 allow the meta-level to implement its own concurrency control mechanism. However, the base-level has already a sophisticated fine-granularity concurrency control system in place, of which the meta-level might need to be aware of. As a first option, one could consider a full-fledged meta-model making the meta-level aware of all concurrency control actions at the base-level. For instance, for locking based concurrency control, every lock request and release would be reified to the meta-level giving it opportunity to keep track of actual conflicts.

This meta-model would be very powerful but also very expensive due to the large number of locks obtained by a transaction.

Therefore, it is necessary to resort to a slimmer meta-model. For this, one has to understand what is really needed by the middleware level. Assume our optimistic asymmetric protocol is implemented over a database system that uses locking. The replication protocol first executes a transaction at the local replica and then applies it at the other replicas. Two transactions that are executed locally at one replica are scheduled by the lock manager of the base-level. The meta-level then detects conflicts between transactions executed at different replicas optimistically when the writeset of one of the transaction arrives at the other replica. Typically, the transaction whose writeset arrives first may commit, the other has to abort. This means, a local transaction should abort when a conflicting writeset arrives. For this to happen, however, the meta-level (1) needs to know about the conflict even before the local transaction might retrieve its writeset and (2) be able to enforce an abort. Ref. 14 discusses how these things are difficult to achieve in a black box approach, slowing down the replication mechanism. Two simple meta-level interface functions could simplify the problem.

3.5.1. *Conflict reification/introspection*

A first interface could provide the meta-model information about blocked transactions. One possibility could be to reify the blocking of transactions (a callback mechanism) such that when a SQL request is made to the database and the transaction becomes blocked on a lock request, the base-level automatically informs the meta-level about this blocking and the transaction that caused the block (i.e., the one holding a conflicting lock). In the previous protocol, this enables the meta-level to detect whether a writeset is blocked on a local transaction. Alternatively to a reification mechanism, the meta-level might use introspection via a "get-blocked-transactions" method to retrieve information about all blocked transactions. This method can be easily implemented in PostreSQL 7.2 in which there is a virtual view table with the transactions blocked on a lock. By querying this view it becomes possible to find out which transactions are blocked.[25]

3.5.2. *Indirect abort*

The second interface enables the abort of a transaction at any time. Usually, a client cannot enforce the abort of a transaction during the execution of an operation. Instead, abort requests can typically only be submitted when the database expects input from the client, i.e., when it is currently not executing a request on behalf of the client. However, in the case described above, the replication protocol might need to abort a local transaction at any time. A meta-interface offering such indirect abort would provide a powerful intercession mechanism to the meta-level.

3.5.3. *Lock release intercession*

One can go even further. A transaction usually releases all locks at commit/abort time. Different lock implementations use different mechanisms to grant the released locks to waiting transactions. Lock requests could be waiting in a FIFO or other priority queue. Alternatively, they could be all woken up and given an equal chance to be the next to get the lock granted. However, the replication protocol might like to have its own preference of whom to give a lock, for instance, to guarantee the same locking order at all replicas. Hence, intercession mechanisms that give access to the priority queue or allow the meta-level to decide in which order waiting transactions are woken up can be useful.

3.5.4. *Priority transactions*

Another way to enforce an execution order on the base-level is by allowing transactions to have different priority levels. The simplest solution consists in providing a simple extension of the writeset interface that forces the database to apply the writeset in spite of existing conflicting locks. In case that a tuple contained in the writeset is blocked by a different transaction, the database aborts this transaction giving priority to the transaction installing the writeset. This could allow the replication middleware to enforce the same serialization order at all replicas. More advanced, transactions could be given different priority levels. Then the base-level database would abort a transaction if it has a lock that is needed by a transaction with a higher priority. In this case, local transactions could be given the lowest priority, and writesets a higher priority.

4. Evaluation

In this section we provide an extensive evaluation of the costs and benefits of reflective writeset functionality, since it has shown to have a tremendous effect on performance.[16] We consider a wide number of mechanisms to collect the writeset. Our first two implementations are true extensions of the database kernel, and they return the writeset either in binary or in SQL textual form. Furthermore, we have implemented a trigger based writeset retrieval, and a log based writeset retrieval, both of them return the writeset in SQL text format. The binary writeset retrieval has been implemented in PostgreSQL and was used by Middle-R.[12,23] The SQL text writeset retrieval is implemented in MySQL. The trigger and log based writeset mechanisms are implemented in a commercial database [a].

For applying writesets at remote replicas, we have two implementations. One uses the binary writeset provided by the binary writeset service, the other requires as input a writeset with SQL statements (as provided by all other generation techniques).

Since the different reflective approaches are implemented in different databases we show the results separately for each database. We compare the performance of a regular transaction execution without writeset retrieval with the performance of the same database with writeset retrieval enabled. This allows us to evaluate the overhead associated with the writeset retrieval mechanism. A similar setup is used for evaluating the costs of applying a writeset. In here, we compare the cost of executing an update transaction with the cost of just applying the writeset of the transaction. This enables us to measure what is gained by performing asymmetric processing of updates. We also evaluate the impact in performance of the level of reflection provided by requests. The cost of reflective concurrency control is also evaluated using the lock view facility provided by PostgreSQL. Finally, to show the effect of the different alternatives to generate and apply writesets we derive analytically the scalability for different workloads and number of replicas.

4.1. *Experiment setup*

The experiments have been made using the "Buy Confirm" transaction from the TPC-W benchmark. The database is compliant with TPC-W. The database size has been defined through the two standard parameters NUM_EBS and NUM_ITEMS with values of 50 and 10000, respectively. The resulting table sizes in number of tuples are summarized in Table 3.

The transaction "Buy Confirm" starts with a shopping cart that contains several items and formalizes the shopping order updating the stock of the bought items and registering the order and credit card details.

---

[a]The license does not allow to name the benchmarked database.

Table Name	Table size (in tuples)
CUSTOMER	144,000
ADDRESS	288,000
AUTHOR	2,500
ORDERS	129,600
COUNTRY	92
ITEM	10,000
SHOPPING_CART	TXN_PER_CLIENT * MAX_NUM_CLIENTS
SHOPPING_CART_LINE	TXN_PER_CLIENT * MAX_NUM_CLIENTS * NUM_ITEMS

Fig. 3. Size of the Tables in the Experiments

The load is injected through a variable number of clients from 1 to 10. Each client submits sequentially 600 transactions. Each transaction resulted in 4 updated tuples with a writeset size of 642 bytes.

4.2. *The cost of reflective writeset retrieval*

Let us first look at the results of the reflective mechanisms that are typically available when using a commercial database system at the base-level, namely log and trigger-based reflection. Figure 4 shows the throughput and execution times with an increasing load for transactions when no writeset is generated, and when writeset retrieval is enabled via logging or triggers. Without the overhead of generating writesets, the maximum achievable throughput is 45–50 transactions per second, and the response time is 35 ms at low loads and increases to 205 ms at high loads.

The writeset retrieval via log mining exhibits a very bad performance. The throughput drops to 3.5 transactions per second, i.e., a reduction of throughput compared to no writeset retrieval of over 90%. In fact, the system cannot cope with more than 5 clients submitting transactions. The response time is also very bad being between 300 and 1400 ms. The main reason for this behavior is that the additional log access creates a very high contention at the log disk converting it into a bottleneck.

When capturing the writeset via triggers the behavior is quite different. Although higher throughput can be achieved than with log mining, the maximum achievable throughput is only around half of the throughput that can be achieved when writeset retrieval is not activated. Response times, however, are only slightly affected by the triggers capturing the writeset.

Figure 5 shows the effects of generating SQL writesets in the MySQL kernel. The maximum achievable throughput in MySQL without generating writesets is over 330 transactions per second, while the peak with writeset retrieval enabled is 220 transactions, resulting in a throughput loss of 33%.

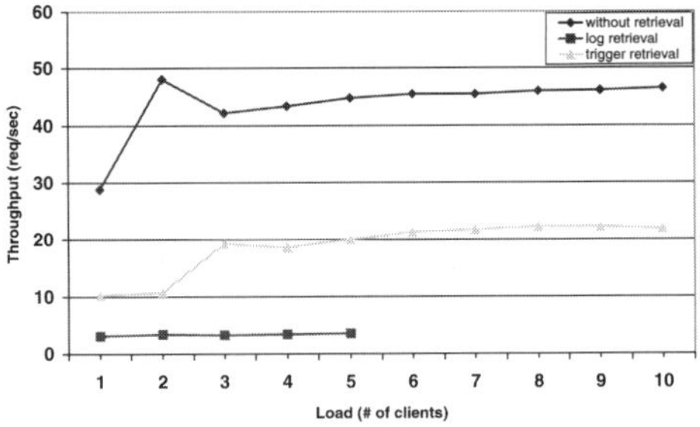

(a) Throughput

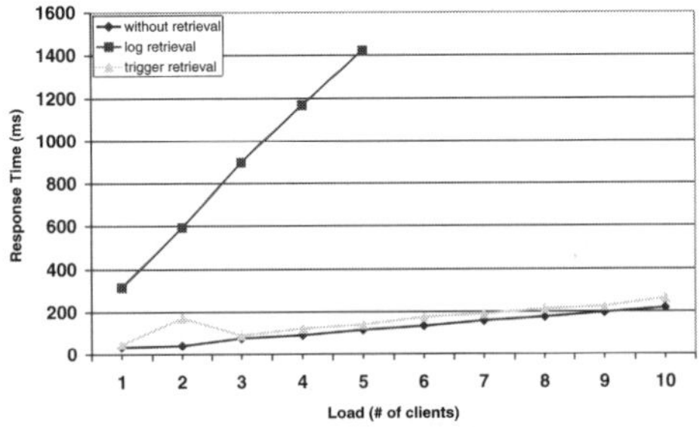

(b) Response time

Fig. 4. Log Mining and Trigger Writeset Retrieval for a Commercial DB

However, at a large number of clients, writeset retrieval leads to a faster degradation of the system and the achievable throughput drops faster than without writeset retrieval. The reason is that there is some non-neglible cost involved in retrieving the SQL writesets, and when the system is close to saturation this cost makes to degrade faster. The response time of MySQL without generation starts at around 8 ms and stabilizes at around 50 ms for high loads. Capturing the writeset only increases response times slightly up to 6 clients. However, close to the saturation point, it leads to an explosion of the response time.

Figure 6 shows the results for the binary writeset retrieval in PostgreSQL. The maximum achievable throughput of PostgreSQL without writeset retrieval is around 11 tps. When enabling the binary writeset retrieval, the throughput remained almost the same. With respect to response time PostgreSQL has a response time of 200 ms with up to two simultaneous clients, and it increases linearly with the number of clients up to 900 ms. Generating writesets does not lead to a visible increase of the re-

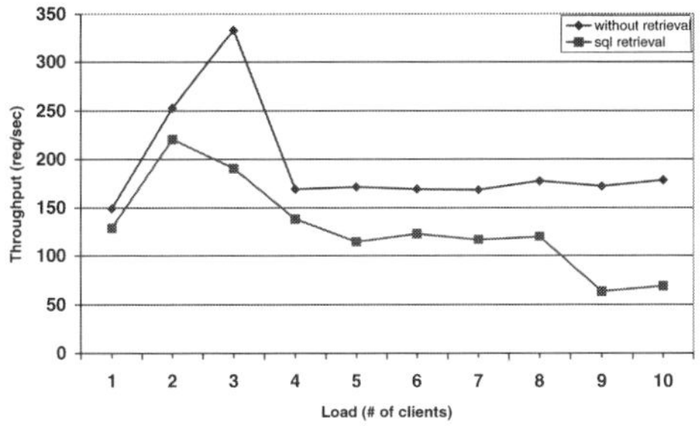

(a) Throughput

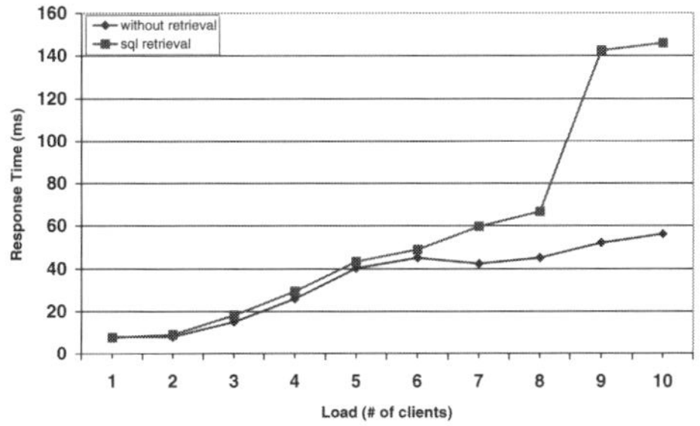

(b) Response time

Fig. 5. SQL Writeset Retrieval in MySQL

sponse time. This means that the binary writeset retrieval has negligible cost showing the best potential to attain high scalability. Although the version of PostgreSQL used in this experiment achieved generally a very low throughput for the injected workload, we do not expect the writeset retrieval to behave worse for lighter transactions with higher throughputs or more performant databases since it is a very local task which is not affected by more concurrency in the system.

In summary, trigger and log-based reflection turned out to be too heavy weight with an unacceptable cost in the case of log mining and a very high cost in the case of triggers. In contrast, the reflective services implemented in MySQL and PostgreSQL are very lightweight with affordable cost, the binary writeset retrieval exhibiting an extremely low overhead.

4.3. *The gain of reflective writeset application*

In here, we evaluate how much can be gained when applying writesets compared to executing the entire transaction. We evaluate two approaches,

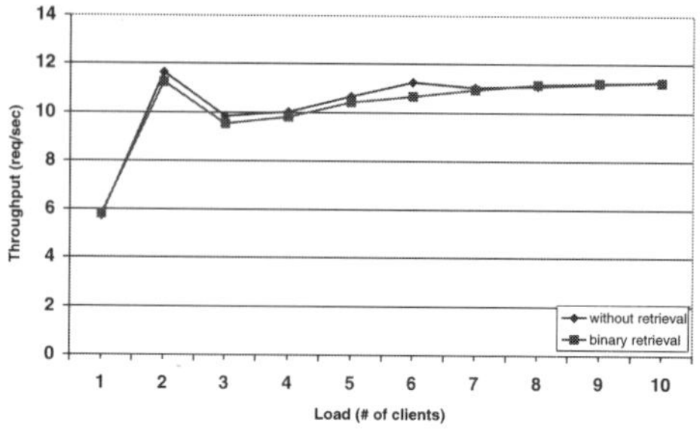

(a) Throughput

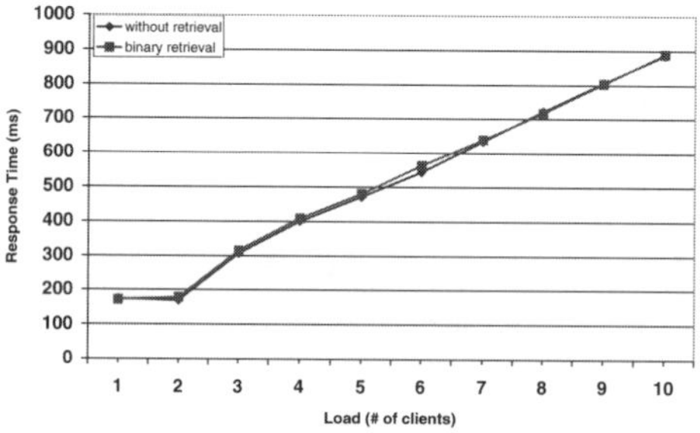

(b) Response time

Fig. 6. Binary Writeset Retrieval for PostgreSQL

namely applying binary writesets and SQL writesets. SQL writesets are obtained by most of the mechanisms evaluated in the previous section. Binary writesets are only generated by the binary writeset reflective service we implemented in PostgreSQL. We use PostgreSQL for this evaluation since it is the only one in which we have implemented both kinds of writeset application.

Figure 7 shows the throughput and the response time with increasing load when fully executing transactions in PostgreSQL, when applying the SQL writesets, and when applying the binary writesets. Applying writesets achieves higher throughputs than executing normal transactions. The application of SQL writesets reaches a peak of 345 transactions per seconds and the application of binary writesets a peak of 362 transactions per second. These peaks are reached when there are around 3 clients submitting writesets concurrently. When there are more clients, the achievable throughput lies between 170–100 transactions for SQL writesets, and between 210–115 transactions per second for binary writesets. This means that binary write-

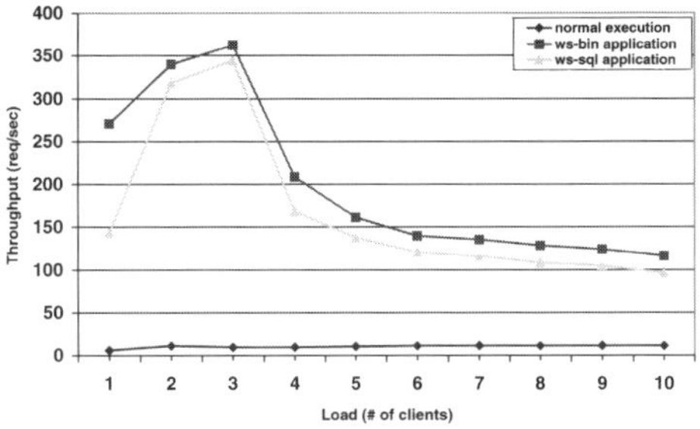

(a) Throughput

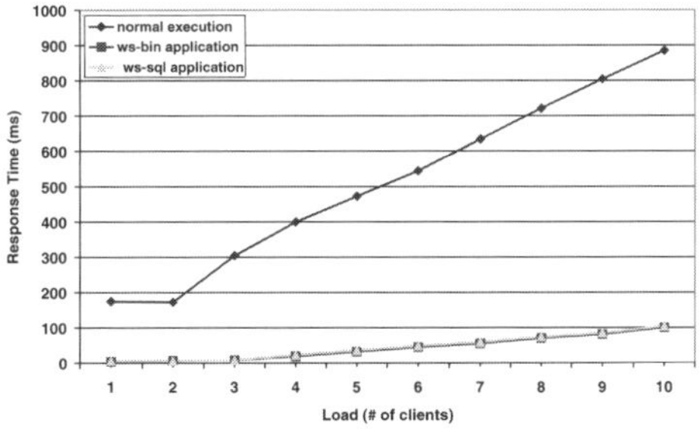

(b) Response time

Fig. 7. SQL and Binary Writeset Application for PostgreSQL

sets can obtain a throughput between 5–20% higher than SQL writesets. Furthermore, applying writesets can achieve throughputs that are 100–350 times higher than executing the update transactions.

With regard to response time, the situation is similar. The response time for full execution of update transactions in PostgreSQL is between 170 and 900 ms depending on the load while writeset application only requires between 7 and 100 ms.

4.4. *The impact of reflective requests*

Many replication protocols implemented at the middleware level have as main shortcoming that they restrict transaction concurrency, and therefore, potentially the scalability and performance of a replicated database. This section aims at quantifying the impact of transaction concurrency on database performance. We evaluate the different reflective request interfaces proposed in Section 3.2. More concretely, level 1 only distinguishes between read only and update transactions. Based on this, we implemented the basic pessimistic replication protocol where update transactions are submitted sequentially to the database. Level 2 provides information about the tables a transaction accesses. This allows us to submit update transactions that access different tables in parallel to the database. Finally, level 3 (conflict classes) allows more concurrency. In this case we use two different granularities 50 and 100 conflict classes. We implemented levels 2 and 3 and compare the results of the three levels with the unrestricted concurrent execution of transactions that provides the best possible performance.

The experiment is run over a non-replicated database of 10 tables. Each table contains three integers and a string. Each transaction reads a tuple and updates a tuple in a number of tables. The database management system used for the experiment was SQLServer. The conflict classes were materialized as horizontal partitions over sets of attributes for each table. That is, each table was partitioned in a set of conflict classes, depending on the value of one attribute. We have run the experiments with transactions accessing an increasing number of tables (1 and 4 tables, respectively). We show both throughput and response time as performance metrics.

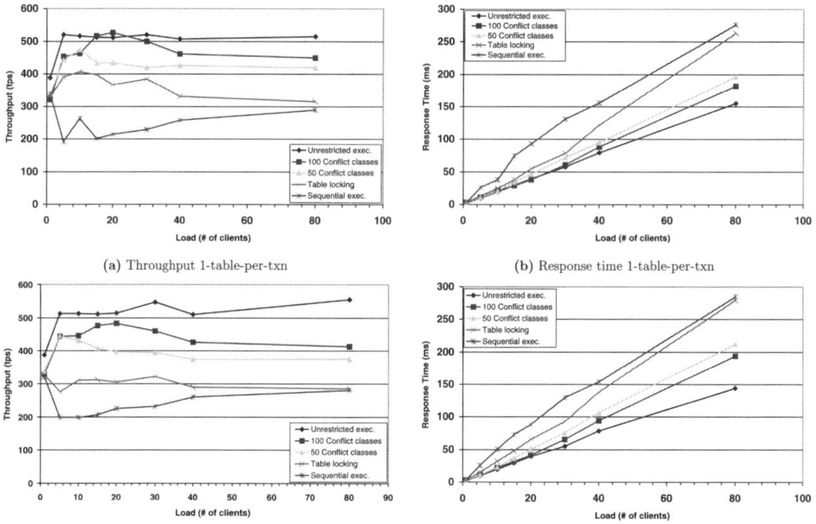

(a) Throughput 1-table-per-txn

(b) Response time 1-table-per-txn

(c) Throughput 4-tables-per-txn

(d) Response time 4-tables-per-txn

Fig. 8. Performance Analysis of Different Concurrency Granularities

Figure 8(a-b) shows the difference in performance of the different reflective approaches for transactions accessing a single table. The most noticeable fact is that sequential execution throughput shows a sharp degradation of over 60% with respect to unrestricted execution. For high loads, the throughput degradation is smaller, around 40–50%. The reason is that sequential execution represents a strict load control which can be beneficial under saturation. Table locking lies in between unrestricted execution and sequential execution. The throughput degradation is around 20% for low loads, reaching 50% with high loads. In the case of 50 conflict cases, the degradation is about 10% over the unrestricted execution. For 100 conflict classes, the performance is between 0 and 10% worse compared to the performance of an unrestricted execution.

In terms of response time (Fig. 8(b)), the performance degradation is quite different. Sequential execution has clearly a noticeably increased response time over unrestricted execution. For table level locking, the response time only increases with high loads. For the two conflict classes curves the response time is almost the same as unrestricted execution except for the highest load in which there is a small increase.

We can see in Fig. 8(c-d) the effects of increasing the conflict probability of transactions by accessing 4 tables per transaction. Table locking has now a much bigger degradation since conflicts are more likely and therefore, there is less concurrency. The performance in terms of throughput and response time is close to the one of sequential execution, since at most two transactions can execute in parallel (each accessing 4 different tables out of the 10 available). For conflict class execution, the throughput loss compared to unrestricted execution is more visible than when only one table is accessed, however the loss is small thanks to the finer granularity of conflict classes. In regard response time, the difference is only slightly higher than for execution on one table.

In summary, conflict classes provide a finer concurrency control than table level locking or simple sequential execution of update transactions. This high level of concurrency yields a throughput close to the one of unrestricted execution, which uses the underlying system's tuple level locking. Only for high conflict levels, accessing 4 tables out of 10, there is some small degradation for the conflict class approach, especially for 50 conflict classes and high loads. In terms of response time the increase is small and only becomes perceptible at high loads with a high conflict level (accessing 4 tables per transaction). Table locking shows serious performance degradation both in terms of throughput and response time with respect unrestricted execution. Finally, sequential execution shows the highest performance degradation. Therefore, the finer the concurrency control at the middleware level is, the better the throughput of a replicated database.

4.5. *The cost of reflective concurrency control*

In this section we evaluate an introspection interface for conflict detection. The goal of this interface is to detect the blocking of conflicting transactions by the replication middleware. For this purpose we will use the *pg_locks* view of PostgreSQL. This view provides information about the locks held by transactions. When the pg_locks view is accessed, the data structures of PostgreSQL's lock manager are momentarily locked, and a copy is made for the view to be displayed. This ensures that the view produces a consistent set of results, while not blocking the normal operations of the lock manager operations longer than necessary. The experiment aims at quantifying the impact on the performance of consulting this view. The impact on performance will depend on the frequency of the access to this view. The level of conflicts will increase the size of the view and will also have an impact on the performance. Therefore, we measure the impact on performance of these two parameters.

The experiment injects an increasing load with different levels of conflict and queries the lock view with different frequencies. The conflict level has been materialized in the experiment through a small table that acts as hot spot. All transactions access this table and modify a random tuple of it. The chosen hot spot sizes are 100 and 1000 tuples. The frequencies for consulting the lock view are 100, 500, and 1000 ms.

Figure 9(a-b) shows that for a large hotspot, 1000 tuples, the impact of consulting the lock view table is negligible. In this case, the probability of conflicts is low, even for high loads. With 80 concurrent clients, at most 80 random tuples from 1000 tuples are modified concurrently. When the hotspot becomes smaller, 100 tuples, there is a more noticeable degradation but still it only shows up when the database is already saturated (Fig. 9(c-d)). For frequencies of 500 and 1000 ms the loss of throughput is around 15%, whilst for a frequency of 100 ms the loss is over 20%. In terms of response time the behavior is highly correlated with the throughput observations.

In summary, it can be concluded that the locks view reflective mechanism is quite effective and shows a negligible performance degradation. Only for very small hot spots and saturating loads some performance degradation can be observed.

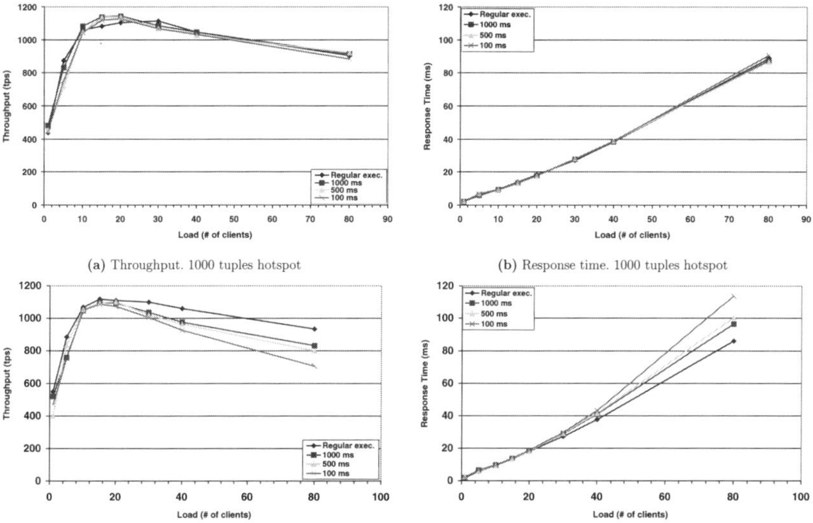

(a) Throughput. 1000 tuples hotspot

(b) Response time. 1000 tuples hotspot

(c) Throughput. 100 tuples hotspot

(d) Response time. 100 tuples hotspot

Fig. 9. Performance Analysis of Conflict Introspection

4.6. *Analytical scalability*

In the previous sections we have evaluated the cost of the different reflective mechanisms. In this section we evaluate the potential scalability by extending the analytical model presented in Ref. 16 to consider the cost of capturing the writesets, since in that analytical model that cost was considered negligible and only took into account the ratio between the application of the writesets and the full transaction execution.

Let L be the total processing capacity of the system, i.e., the maximum number of transactions per time unit that can be handled by the aggregation of all sites. Let $L_w = w \cdot L$ and $L_r = (1 - w) \cdot L$ be the load created by update and read transactions, being w the proportion of update transactions in the load. Let t be the processing capacity of a single site in terms of transactions per time unit. t and L exhibit the following relation:

$$t = P_w \cdot L_w + P_r \cdot L_r = L \cdot (w \cdot P_w + (1 - w) \cdot P_r)$$

Where P_r and P_w are the probabilities of executing a read and a write operation. The global scalability of a replicated system is given by the total processing capacity of the entire system (L) divided by the processing

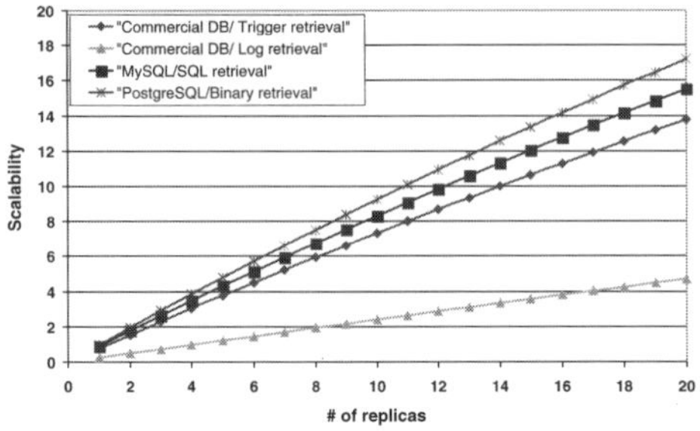

(a) w = 0.25

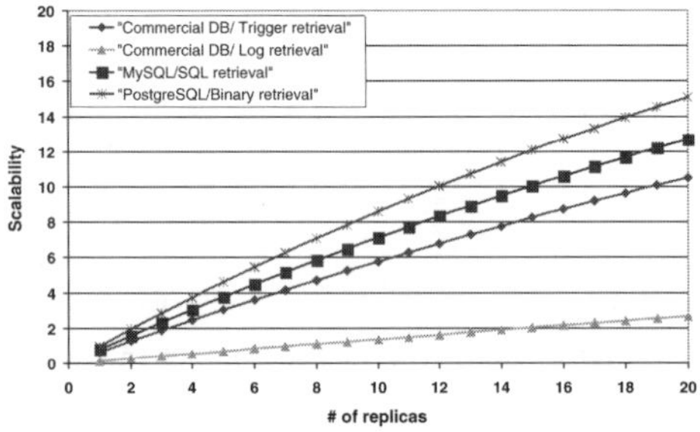

(b) w = 0.50

Fig. 10. Scalability for the Different Reflective Writeset Handling Mechanisms

capacity of one site (t):

$$so = \frac{L}{t} = \frac{1}{w \cdot P_w + (1 - w) \cdot P_r}$$

Taking into account that writes are processed asymmetrically the probability for a site to execute a write transaction can be split into: $P_w = P_w^L + P_w^R$, where P_w^L is the probability of being the site fully executing the write transaction (local site for the transaction) and P_w^R is the probability of applying the writeset of an update transaction (remote site for the transaction). Then, we need to distinguish the cost of fully executing an update transaction, which is considered to be 1, the cost of fully executing the transaction including capturing the writeset by means of a particular mechanism, which we denote as *writeset retrieval overhead* or *wro*, and the cost of applying the writeset, which we denote as *writeset application overhead* or *wao*. As seen before, for asymmetric systems, $wro \geq 1$ and $0 < wao \leq 1$. In contrast, $wro = wao = 1$ represents a symmetric system.

With this the scalability, *so* of a replicated system is:

$$so = \frac{L}{t} = \frac{1}{w \cdot wro \cdot P_w^L + w \cdot wao \cdot P_w^R + (1-w) \cdot P_r}$$

We can now feed the analytical model with different values of *wro* and *wao* extracted from the experimental evaluation performed in the previous sections. *wro* is obtained as the ratio between the maximum throughput with writeset retrieval enabled and the maximum throughput for regular transaction execution. Similarly, *wao* is computed as the ratio between the maximum throughputs of writeset application and regular transaction execution. The computation of these values is made for each implemented reflective writeset mechanism in the different DBs. The empirically obtained values of wao and wro are summarized in Fig. 11.

DB and Reflective Mechanism	wro	wao
PostgreSQL binary retrieval	1.037845	
PostgreSQL binary application		0.032181
PostgreSQL SQL application		0.033856
Commercial DB trigger retrieval	2.160964	
Commercial DB logreader retrieval	13.35062	
MySQL SQL retrieval	1.508986	

Fig. 11. Empirical values of writeset retrieval and application overheads

In Figure 10 we can find the scalability of the different approaches for a percentage of write operations of 25% and 50%. The graph shows in the y-axis the relative power of the replicated system compared to a non-replicated system, that is, how many times the throughput of a replicated system multiplies the throughput of a centralized non-replicated system. For instance, a value of 10 in the y-axis, means that the maximum throughput is 10 times the one of a single non-replicated site. The x-axis shows the number of replicas. Since all the graphs are relative, it does not matter that the curves might belong to different databases.

The first observation is that the higher the value of w (percentage of update transactions) the more noticeable the difference among the different approaches. This is intuitive since, the more updates, the more impact has how efficiently they are handled. When comparing all the approaches, it becomes clear that the log mining approach is not an alternative for database replication. Trigger-based writeset retrieval pays the cost of a heavy weight reflective mechanism. However, it has the advantage that it can be implemented as an application, and hence, does not require changes to the database kernel. Finally, the two reflective services implemented within the database kernel (binary and SQL writeset retrieval) have the best scalability. Their scalability is very competitive. In the case of SQL retrieval, the scalability is somewhat lower, since capturing the writeset requires some additional processing for generating the SQL statements. Secondly, there is also the slightly higher cost for applying the writeset that has also some impact on scalability.

If we compare the binary writeset service approach with the others, we can see that for 20 replicas, it provides 10–23% more scalability than the SQL writeset service approach. With respect to the trigger approach, it has 20–41% better scalability. It beats the log mining approach with an enhancement in scalability of 73–88%.

5. Related Work

Reflection has become a popular paradigm to introduce non-functional concerns with a clean architecture without tangling the code of the regular functionality. A number of approaches have been taken to introduce reflection in middleware systems such as OpenORB[19] and DynamicTAO[18] to disentangle the implementation of nonfunctional cross-cutting concerns from the implementation of the functional aspects. Some new middleware systems have been designed from the very beginning to provide reflective components that can be composed into new reflective components.[26]

Reflection to introduce transactional semantics has been explored by some researchers. Early approaches relied simply on inheritance (without reflection) to provide flexible transactional semantics.[27] Reference 28 extends a legacy TP-monitor with transactional reflective capabilities to implement advanced transaction models at the meta-level. Reflection[29] and aspects[30] have been exploited to introduce transactions in object oriented and component based systems.

Reference 31 is a seminal paper on dependability through reflection. The paper takes advantage of reflection in an actor-based language to implement dependable protocols. Reference 32 is also one of the early approaches to implement fault-tolerance exploiting reflection. This paper explores how to perform process replication in three different flavors, active, semiactive and passive, using linguistic reflection in object oriented languages, that is, by means of a meta-object protocol (MOP). The use of MOPs to implement fault-tolerant CORBA systems has been studied in Refs. 33,34. More recently, reflective design patterns have been studied for implementing fault tolerance.[35] It has also been studied how to integrate reflective systems, for instance, how to integrate a fault-tolerant middleware on top of an operating system.[36]

6. Conclusions

In this paper we have proposed a wide set of lightweight reflective mechanisms for databases that enable to perform replication at the middleware level. These mechanisms have explored all the main functionalities of the database, database connectivity, request handling, concurrency control and logging. Some of the reflective mechanisms are already widely used, others are quite novel and an efficient implementation would be very useful for middleware based replication. From there, a thorough comparison of different implementations of reflective mechanisms for writeset retrieval and application, requests, and concurrency control has been performed. The main conclusion has been that some reflective mechanisms are quite effective and have a negligible overhead enabling scalable and performant database replication.

References

1. Y. Breitbart and H. F. Korth, Replication and Consistency: Being Lazy Helps Sometimes, in *Proc. of ACM Symp. on Principles of Database Systems (PODS)*, pp. 173–184 (Tucson, Arizona, United States, 1997).
2. Y. Breitbart, R. Komondoor, R. Rastogi, S. Seshadri and A. Silberschatz, Update Propagation Protocols for Replicated Databates, in *Proc. of the ACM Int. Conf. on Management of Data (SIGMOD)*, pp. 97–108 (Philadelphia, Pennsylvania, United States, 1999).
3. B. Kemme and G. Alonso, Don't Be Lazy, Be Consistent: Postgres-R, A New Way to Implement Database Replication, in *Proc. of the Int. Conf. on Very Large Data Bases (VLDB)*, pp. 134–143 (Cairo, Egypt, 2000).
4. B. Kemme and G. Alonso, A New Approach to Developing and Implementing Eager Database Replication Protocols, *ACM Trans. on Database Systems (TODS)* **25**(3), pp. 333–379 (ACM Press, September 2000).
5. Y. Amir and C. Tutu, From Total Order to Database Replication, in *Proc. of the IEEE Int. Conf. on Distributed Computing Systems (ICDCS)*, pp. 494–503 (Vienna, Austria, 2002).
6. L. Rodrigues, H. Miranda, R. Almeida, J. Martins and P. Vicente, Strong Replication in the GlobData Middleware, in *Proc. of the Workshop on Dependable Middleware-Based Systems (Part of Dependable Systems and Networks Conference, DSN)*, pp. G96–G104 (Washington D.C., USA, 2002).
7. E. Cecchet, J. Marguerite and W. Zwaenepoel, C-JDBC: Flexible Database Clustering Middleware, in *Proc. of USENIX Annual Technical Conf., Freenix track*, pp. 9–18 (Boston, MA, USA, 2004).
8. C. Amza, A. L. Cox and W. Zwaenepoel, Distributed Versioning: Consistent Replication for Scaling Back-end Databases of Dynamic Content Web Sites, in *ACM/IFIP/Usenix Int. Middleware Conf.*, pp. 282–304 (Rio de Janeiro, Brazil, 2003).

9. C. Amza, A. L. Cox and W. Zwaenepoel, Conflict-Aware Scheduling for Dynamic Content Applications, in *Proc. of the USENIX Symp. on Internet Technologies and Systems (USITS)*, pp. 71–85 (Seattle, Washington, USA, 2003).
10. S. Gancarski, H. Naacke, E. Pacitti and P. Valduriez, Parallel Processing with Autonomous Databases in a Cluster System, in *Cooperative Information Systems (CoopIS)*, pp. 410–428 (Irvine, California, USA, 2002).
11. E. Pacitti, M. T. Özsu and C. Coulon, Preventive Multi-Master Replication in a Cluster of Autonomous Databases, in *Int. Conf. on Parallel and Distributed Computing (Euro-Par)*, pp. 318–327 (Klagenfurt, Austria, 2003).
12. M. Patiño-Martínez, R. Jiménez-Peris, B. Kemme and G. Alonso, MIDDLE-R: Consistent Database Replication at the Middleware Level, *ACM Trans. on Computer Systems (TOCS)* **23**(4), pp. 375–423 (ACM Press, Nov. 2005).
13. C. Plattner and G. Alonso, Ganymed: Scalable Replication for Transactional Web Applications, in *Proc. of the ACM/IFIP/USENIX Int. Conf. on Middleware*, pp. 155–174 (Toronto, Canada, 2004).
14. Y. Lin, B. Kemme, M. Patiño-Martínez and R. Jiménez-Peris, Middleware Based Data Replication Providing Snapshot Isolation, in *Proc. of the ACM Int. Conf. on Management of Data (SIGMOD)*, pp. 419–430 (Baltimore, Maryland, 2005).
15. M. Patiño-Martínez, R. Jiménez-Peris, B. Kemme and G. Alonso, Scalable Replication in Database Clusters, in *Proc. of the Int. Conf. on Distributed Computing (DISC)*, pp. 315–329 (Toledo, Spain, 2000).
16. R. Jiménez-Peris, M. Patiño-Martínez, G. Alonso and B. Kemme, Are Quorums an Alternative for Data Replication?, *ACM Trans. on Database Systems (TODS)* **28**(3), pp. 257–294 (ACM Press, September 2003).
17. P. Maes, Concepts and Experiments in Computational Reflection, in *Conf. Proc. on Object-oriented Programming Systems, Languages and Applications (OOPSLA)*, pp. 147–155 (Orlando, Florida, United States, 1987).
18. F. Kon, M. Román, P. Liu, J. Mao, T. Yamane, L. C. Magalhaes and R. H. Campbell, Monitoring, Security, and Dynamic Configuration with the DynamicTAO Reflective ORB, in *IFIP/ACM Int. Conf. on Distributed Systems Platforms (Middleware)*, pp. 121–143 (New York, NY, United States, 2000).
19. G. S. Blair, G. Coulson, A. Andersen, L. Blair, M. Clarke, F. Costa *et al.*, The Design and Implementation of Open ORB v2, *Special Issue of IEEE Distributed Systems Online on Reflective Middleware* **2**(6) (IEEE Distributed Systems Online, November 2001).
20. G. V. Chockler, I. Keidar and R. Vitenberg, Group Communication Specifications: a Comprehensive Study, *ACM Computing Surveys* **33**(4), pp. 427–469 (ACM Press, December 2001).
21. F. Pedone, R. Guerraoui and A. Schiper, The Database State Machine Approach, *Distributed and Parallel Databases* **14**(1), pp. 71–98 (Kluwer Academic Publishers, July 2003).
22. J. M. Milán, R. Jiménez-Peris, M. Patiño-Martínez and B. Kemme, Adaptive Middleware for Data Replication, in *Proc. of the ACM/IFIP/USENIX Int. Conf. on Middleware*, pp. 175–194 (Toronto, Canada, 2004).

23. R. Jiménez-Peris, M. Patiño-Martínez and G. Alonso, Non-Intrusive, Parallel Recovery of Replicated Data, in *Proc. of the IEEE Symp. on Reliable Distributed Systems (SRDS)*, pp. 150–159 (Osaka, Japan, 2002).
24. I. Gashi, P. Popov, V. Stankovic and L. Strigini, On Designing Dependable Services with Diverse Off-The-Shelf SQL Servers, in *Chapter of the book "Architecting Dependable Systems II", LNCS-3069*, pp. 196–220 (R. de Lemos, C. Gacek and A. Romanovsky (editors), Springer, 2004).
25. F. D. Muñoz-Escoí, J. Pla-Civera, M. I. Ruiz-Fuertes, L. Irún-Briz, H. Decker, J. E. Armendariz-Inigo and J. R. Gonzalez de Mendivil, Managing Transaction Conflicts in Middleware-based Database Replication Architectures, in *Proc. of the IEEE Symp. on Reliable Distributed Systems (SRDS)*, pp. 401–420 (Leeds, UK, 2006).
26. ObjectWeb, Fractal (http://fractal.objectweb.org).
27. S. K. Shrivastava, G. N. Dixon and G. D. Parrington, An Overview of the Arjuna Distributed Programming System, *IEEE Software* **8**(1), pp. 66–73 (IEEE Computer Society Press, January 1991).
28. R. S. Barga and C. Pu, A Reflective Framework for Implementing Extended Transactions, in *Advanced Transaction Models and Architectures*, pp. 63–90 (S. Jajodia and L. Kerschberg (editors), Kluwer Academic Publishers, 1997).
29. Z. Wu, Reflective Java and a Reflective Component-based Transaction Architecture, in *Proc. of the ACM Workshop on Reflective Programming in Java and C++ (OOPSLA)*, (Vancouver, BC, Canada, 1998).
30. J. Kienzle and S. Gélineau, AO Challenge - Implementing the ACID Properties for Transactional Objects, in *Proc. of the Int. Conf. on Aspect-oriented Software Development (AOSD)*, pp. 202–213 (Bonn, Germany, 2006).
31. G. Agha, S. Frølund, R. Panwar and D. Sturman, A Linguistic Framework for Dynamic Composition of Dependability Protocols, in *Proc. of the IFIP Conf. on Dependable Computing for Critical Applications (DCCA)*, pp. 197–207 (Palermo, Sicily, Italy, 1992).
32. J-C. Fabre, V. Nicomette and Z. Wu, Implementing Fault-Tolerant Applications Using Reflective Object-oriented Programming, in *Proc. of the Int. Symp. on Fault-Tolerant Computing (FTCS)*, pp. 489–498 (Pasadena, California, USA, 1995).
33. M-O. Killijian, J-C. Fabre, J. C. Ruiz-Garcia and S. Chiba, A Metaobject Protocol for Fault-Tolerant CORBA Applications, in *Proc. of the IEEE Symp. on Reliable Distributed Systems (SRDS)*, pp. 127–134 (West Lafayette, Indiana, USA, 1998).
34. J-C. Fabre and T. Pérennou, A Metaobject Architecture for Fault-Tolerant Distributed Systems: The FRIENDS Approach, *IEEE Trans. on Computers (TC)* **47**(1), pp. 78–95 (IEEE Computer Society, January 1998).
35. L.L. Ferreira and C.M.F. Rubira, Reflective Design Patterns to Implement Fault Tolerance, in *Proc. of the ACM Workshop on Reflective Programming in Java and C++ (OOPSLA)*, (Vancouver, BC, Canada, 1998).
36. F. Taiani, J-C. Fabre and M-O. Killijian, Towards Implementing Multi-Layer Reflection for Fault-Tolerance, in *Int. Conf. on Dependable Systems and Networks (DSN)*, pp. 435–444 (San Francisco, CA, USA, 2003).

ADDING FAULT-TOLERANCE TO STATE MACHINE-BASED DESIGNS

SANDEEP S. KULKARNI

Computer Science and Engineering Department
Michigan State University
East lansing MI 48824
E-mail: sandeep@cse.msu.edu

ANISH ARORA

Computer Science and Engineering Department
The Ohio State University
Columbus Ohio 43210 USA
E-mail: anish@cse.ohio-state.edu

ALI EBNENASIR

Department of Computer Science
Michigan Technological University
Houghton MI 49931 USA
E-mail: aebnenas@mtu.edu

Late detection of new types of faults often results in the evolution of fault-tolerance requirements while developers have already created design artifacts. Thus, the reuse of an existing design in the development of a fault-tolerant version thereof has the potential to reduce the overall development costs. Moreover, the automation of such a reuse yields a fault-tolerant design that is correct by construction, given that the existing design is correct. To facilitate such an automation, we present an approach, where we add three levels of fault-tolerance, namely *failsafe, nonmasking*, and *masking*, to functional designs represented as state machines. Intuitively, failsafe fault-tolerance requires that safety specification is met even in the presence of faults. In the presence of faults, nonmasking fault-tolerance guarantees recovery to states from where safety and liveness specifications are satisfied. Masking fault-tolerance stipulates that (i) recovery is provided to states from where safety and liveness specifications are met, and (ii) safety specification is satisfied during such a recovery. Specifically, we present sound and complete deterministic algorithms for automated addition of (failsafe/nonmasking/masking) fault-tolerance to the functional design of concurrent programs. These polynomial-time algorithms are especially useful in model-driven development of fault-tolerant systems, where models are automatically checked and modified. We also discuss (1) the effect of distribution and safety specification model on the complexity of adding fault-tolerance, and (2) the impact of the proposed algorithms on the addition of multitolerance.

Keywords: Software design, Addition of fault-tolerance, Model-driven development

1. Introduction

We focus our attention on the problem of *redesign for fault-tolerance* where new fault-tolerance requirements arise while developers have already created some design artifacts that meet functional properties. To address this problem, we propose an approach for automated addition of fault-tolerance concerns to an existing design represented as a state machine. Such an automated addition of fault-tolerance is especially useful as it has the potential to reuse the existing design of a program while generating a fault-tolerant version thereof. More importantly, if the existing design is correct with respect to its specification, then the automatically generated fault-tolerant design will also be correct by construction.

Existing automated techniques[1–7] for the synthesis of fault-tolerant designs mostly focus on generating a design from a satisfiability proof of its specification (i.e., specification-based approach). For example, Attie and Arora and Emerson[1] present a specification-based approach for synthesizing fault-tolerant programs from their temporal logic specification. In the synthesis of reactive programs,[2,7] the program/environment interaction model is based on two-player games where players take turn in making moves and one player can only affect the state of the other player through specific interface variables. Instead, in the context of adding fault-tolerance properties, faults may perturb the state of programs to any state.

We present efficient algorithms for adding fault-tolerance to a given fault-intolerant design of a concurrent program in such a way that the addition is done *solely* for the purpose of dealing with faults; i.e., we do not introduce new ways to satisfy the specification *in the absence of faults.* While our previous work[8–10] on *manual* design has shown that transforming a fault-intolerant design into a fault-tolerant design is possible and desirable, we expect that an *automated* algorithm will further help in adding fault-tolerance to existing designs. More specifically, such an automated algorithm will obviate the need for constructing the proof of correctness of the synthesized fault-tolerant design, which is often supported by theorem proving or model checking methods.[11] This advantage is especially useful when designing fault-tolerant concurrent (respectively, distributed) programs as it is well-understood that manually constructing proofs of correctness for such programs is hard. Next, we layout the context in which we model programs, specifications and levels of fault-tolerance.

The choice of computation model. If we consider a very general model of computation, e.g., processes that communicate via messages with unbounded message queues, then adding fault-tolerance becomes undecidable.[12] Hence, we need to consider simpler models of computation where the complexity of the addition problem is manageable. We consider a *high atomicity model* of computation, where a program can read and write all its variables in an atomic step. In other words, the high atomicity model allows the program to perform operations such as 'test-and-set' over program variables.

The choice of safety specification model. Intuitively, a safety specification stipulates that nothing bad ever happens in program computations. We model a safety specification as a set of *bad* transitions that must not occur in program computations. Our *bad transitions* (BT) model is a restricted version of Alpern and Schneider's[13] model of safety specifications, where one represents safety by a set of finite *sequences* of transitions that must not occur in program computations. We adopt the BT model for specifying the safety specification of programs since (i) the complexity of adding fault-tolerance will significantly increase to the class of NP-hard problems if one uses Alpern and Schneider's general model of safety specifications,[14] and (ii) the BT model is sufficiently expressive for specifying the safety of a wide range of practical problems as we have already synthesized several fault-tolerant designs for industrial applications (e.g., altitude switch controller, cruise control, and token ring[15]) using the BT model.

Levels of fault-tolerance. The level of fault-tolerance identifies the extent to which the original specification is satisfied when faults occur. Although one could consider arbitrary levels of fault-tolerance, experience shows that for most programs, the fault-tolerance level falls into one of the three levels, *failsafe, nonmasking* or *masking.* These levels are based on Alpern and Schneider's[13] definition where they show that a specification can be decomposed into a safety specification and a liveness specification. More specifically, these levels are based on whether the fault-tolerant program satisfies the safety specification, the liveness specification or both.

In the presence of faults, a failsafe fault-tolerant program only satisfies its safety specification. Failsafe fault-tolerance is often used in safety-critical systems. For nonmasking fault-tolerance, we observe that satisfying the liveness specification alone is not very useful as the liveness specification does not impose any restrictions on finite computations of a program. Hence, in the presence of faults, we allow safety to be violated, and when faults stop occurring, we require recovery to states from where both safety and liveness specifications are satisfied. Nonmasking fault-tolerance is often used in networking related applications (e.g., routing, spanning tree maintenance, etc.) where maintaining safety in the presence of faults is either too expensive or impossible. Finally, a masking fault-tolerant program guarantees to (i) recover to states from where both safety and liveness specifications are satisfied, and (ii) satisfy its safety specification during such a recovery. Masking fault-tolerance is the ideal level of fault-tolerance and it is used in database applications as well as in several problems (e.g., leader election, mutual exclusion, etc.) in distributed systems.

Contributions of the chapter. The main contributions of this chapter are as follows: We present sound and complete algorithms that solve the problem of adding failsafe/nonmasking/masking fault-tolerance to state machine-based designs of programs. The complexity of our approach is polynomial in the state space of the fault-intolerant design (see Sections 4, 5 and 6). Moreover, we discuss the role of our proposed algorithms in (i) adding fault-tolerance to the design of distributed programs, (ii) developing a software tool for adding fault-tolerance during model-driven development of software systems, and (iii) adding *multitolerance* to program designs, where a multitolerant program is subject to multiple types of faults and provides different levels of fault-tolerance corresponding to each fault-type.

Organization of this chapter. This chapter is organized as follows: We provide the definitions of a program design, specifications, faults, and fault-tolerance in Section 2. Using these definitions, we state the addition problem in Section 3. In Section 4, we show how to add failsafe fault-tolerance to fault-intolerant designs. In Section 5, we present an algorithm for adding nonmasking fault-tolerance to fault-intolerant designs. Subsequently, in Section 6, we solve the problem of adding masking fault-tolerance. We demonstrate our algorithms for adding fault-tolerance to the program of a parking lot gate controller. In Section 7, we discuss related work. In Section 8, we give an overview of the current results and open problems regarding automatic addition of fault-tolerance. Finally, we make concluding remarks in Section 9.

2. Preliminaries

In this section, for the sake of completeness, we recall the definitions of a program design, problem specifications, faults, and fault-tolerance. The design of a program is defined in terms of its state space and its transitions. Hereafter, we use the terms design and program interchangeably as we use finite state machines to represent the design of a program. The definition of specifications is adapted from Alpern and Schneider.[13] The definitions of faults and fault-tolerance are due to Arora and Gouda[16] and Arora and Kulkarni.[8]

2.1. *Program Design Model*

A program p (denoted $p = \langle S_p, \delta_p \rangle$) is specified by a finite state space, S_p, and a set of transitions, δ_p, where δ_p is a subset of $S_p \times S_p$. A state predicate of p is any subset of S_p. A state predicate S is closed in the program p iff (if and only if) the condition $(\forall s_0, s_1 :: (((s_0, s_1) \in \delta_p) \wedge (s_0 \in S)) \Rightarrow (s_1 \in S))$ holds. A sequence of states, $\sigma = \langle s_0, s_1, ... \rangle$ with $len(\sigma)$ states, is a computation of p iff the following two conditions are satisfied: (1) $\forall j : 0 < j < len(\sigma) : (s_{j-1}, s_j) \in \delta_p$, and (2) if σ is finite and terminates in state s_l then there does not exist state s such that $(s_l, s) \in \delta_p$. A sequence of states, $\langle s_0, s_1, ..., s_n \rangle$, is a computation prefix of p iff $\forall j : 0 < j \leq n : (s_{j-1}, s_j) \in \delta_p$, i.e., a computation prefix need not be maximal.

The projection of program p on state predicate S, denoted as $p|S$, is the program $\langle S_p, \{(s_0, s_1) : (s_0, s_1) \in \delta_p \ \wedge \ s_0, s_1 \in S\} \rangle$. In other words, $p|S$ consists of transitions of p that start in S and end in S.

Notation. When it is clear from the context, we use p and δ_p interchangeably. For example, a state predicate S is closed in p iff S is closed in δ_p. We also say that a state predicate S is true in a state s iff $s \in S$.

2.2. *Specifications and Correctness Criteria for Functional Designs*

A *specification* is a set of infinite sequences of states that is *suffix closed* and *fusion closed*. *Suffix closure* of the set means that if a state sequence $\sigma = \langle s_0, s_1, ... \rangle$ is in that set then so are all the suffixes of σ, where a suffix of σ is a sequence $\langle s_i, s_{i+1}, ... \rangle$ for some finite i such that $i \geq 0$. *Fusion closure* of the set means that if state sequences $\langle \alpha, x, \gamma \rangle$ and $\langle \beta, x, \delta \rangle$ are in that set then so are the state sequences $\langle \alpha, x, \delta \rangle$ and $\langle \beta, x, \gamma \rangle$, where α and β are finite prefixes of state sequences, γ and δ are suffixes of state sequences, and x is a program state. Intuitively, fusion closure of the specification means that a design that implements the specification must execute its next transition only based on its current state; i.e., the history of a computation does not affect the next move of the program.

Following Alpern and Schneider,[13] we rewrite the specification as the intersection of a *safety specification* and a *liveness specification*. For our addition algorithms, the safety specification is specified in terms of a set of bad transitions that must not occur in program computations. That is, for program p, its safety specification is a subset of $S_p \times S_p$. A computation violates the safety specification if it contains a bad transition. A computation satisfies the safety specification if it does not violate the safety specification. We represent the liveness specification by a set of infinite sequences of states. A computation satisfies the liveness specification if it contains a suffix that is in the liveness specification. We show that a fault-tolerant program satisfies the liveness specification in the absence of faults iff its fault-intolerant version satisfies the liveness specification.

Remark. Since the specification is suffix-closed and fusion-closed, it is possible to specify a safety specification as a set of bad transitions. This result was proved earlier in[10] (see Page 26, Lemma 3.6 of[10]). Moreover, we have illustrated[14] that if one adopts Alpern and Schneider's general model of safety specification instead of our restricted model (i.e., the *bad transitions* model) then the complexity of adding fault-tolerance will significantly increase. Hence, for efficient synthesis, based on which tool support[15] can be provided, we represent safety with a set of bad transitions that must not occur in program computations.

Given a program p, a state predicate S, and a specification *spec*, we say that p *refines spec* from S iff (1) S is closed in p, and (2) every computation of p that starts in a state where S is true satisfies (safety and liveness of) *spec*. If p refines *spec* from S and $S \neq \{\}$, we say that S is an *invariant* of p for *spec*.

For a finite sequence (of states) α, we say that α *maintains spec* iff there exists a sequence of states β such that $\alpha\beta \in$ *spec*. Likewise, we say that α *violates spec* iff it is not the case that α maintains *spec*. We say that p maintains *spec* from S iff S is closed in p and every computation prefix of p that starts in a state in S maintains *spec*.

Notation. Let *spec* be a specification. We use the term *safety of spec* to mean the smallest safety specification that includes *spec*. Also, whenever the specification is clear from the context, we will omit it; thus, S *is an invariant of* p abbreviates S *is an invariant of* p *for* spec.

2.3. *Faults*

We systematically represent the faults that perturb a program by a set of transitions in program state space. We emphasize that such representation is possible notwithstanding the type of the faults (be they stuck-at, crash, fail-stop, omission, timing or Byzantine), the nature of the faults (be they permanent, transient, or intermittent), or the ability of the program to observe the effects of the faults (be they detectable or undetectable). Formally, a class of *fault* f for program p is a subset of $S_p \times S_p$. We use $p \; [] \; f$ to denote the transitions obtained by taking the union of the transitions in p and the transitions in f. We say that a state predicate T is an f-span (read as *fault-span*) of p from S iff the following two conditions are satisfied: (1) $S \subseteq T$ and (2) T is closed in $p \, [] \, f$. Thus, at each state where an invariant S of p is true, an f-span T of p from S is also true. The closure of T in $p \, [] \, f$ means that if any transition in f (respectively, p) is executed in a state where T is true, then T is also true in the resulting state. It follows that for all computations of p that start at states where S is true, T is a boundary in the state space of p up to which (but not beyond which) the state of p may be perturbed by the occurrence of the transitions in f.

As we defined a computation of p, we say that a sequence of states, $\sigma = \langle s_0, s_1, ... \rangle$ with $len(\sigma)$ states, is a computation of p in the presence of f iff the following three conditions are satisfied: (1) $\forall j : 0 < j < len(\sigma) : (s_{j-1}, s_j) \in (\delta_p \cup f)$, (2) if σ is finite and terminates in state s_l then there does not exist state s such that $(s_l, s) \in \delta_p$, and (3) $\exists n : n \geq 0 : (\forall j : j > n : (s_{j-1}, s_j) \in \delta_p)$. The first requirement captures that in each step, either a program transition or a fault transition is executed. The second requirement captures that faults do not have to execute; i.e., if the program reaches a state where only a fault transition can be executed, it is not required that the fault transition be executed. It follows that fault transitions cannot be used to deal with deadlocked states. Finally, the third requirement captures that the number of fault occurrences in a computation is finite. This requirement is the same as that made in previous work[16–19] to ensure that eventually recovery can occur.

2.4. *Fault-Tolerance*

We now define what it means for a program to be fault-tolerant. We define three levels of fault-tolerance; *failsafe, nonmasking and masking*. Irrespective of the level of tolerance, in the absence of faults, a program should refine its specification from its invariant. The level of fault-tolerance characterizes the extent to which the program refines *spec* in the presence of faults. Intuitively, a failsafe fault-tolerant program ensures that in the presence of faults, the safety of *spec* is maintained. A nonmasking fault-tolerant program ensures that in the presence of faults, the program recovers to states from where *spec* is refined. A masking fault-tolerant program ensures that in the presence of faults both these properties are satisfied. Thus, we reiterate the definitions of these three levels of fault-tolerance (from[8,16]) as follows:

Program p is *failsafe f-tolerant* to *spec* from S iff the following two conditions hold: (1) p refines *spec* from S, and (2) there exists T such that (i) T is an f-span of p from S, and (ii) $p \, [] \, f$ maintains *spec* from T.

Program p is *nonmasking f-tolerant* to *spec* from S iff the following two conditions hold: (1) p refines *spec* from S, and (2) there exists T such that (i) T is an f-span of p from S, and (ii) every computation of p [] f that starts from a state in T has a state in S.

Program p is *masking f-tolerant* to *spec* from S iff the following two conditions hold: (1) p refines *spec* from S, and (2) there exists T such that (i) T is an f-span of p from S; (ii) p [] f maintains *spec* from T, and (iii) every computation of p [] f that starts from a state in T has a state in S .

Notation. Henceforth, whenever the program p is clear from the context, we will omit it; thus, "S is an invariant" abbreviates "S is an invariant of p" and "f is a fault" abbreviates "f is a fault for p". Also, whenever the specification *spec* and the invariant S are clear from the context, we omit them; thus, "f-tolerant" abbreviates "f-tolerant for *spec* from S", and so on.

3. Problem Statement

In this section, we formally specify the problem of adding fault-tolerance to a fault-intolerant program, say p, in order to generate a fault-tolerant program, say p'. Towards this end, we first identify constraints so that p' is obtained from p by adding *only* fault-tolerance. Then, we discuss the soundness and the completeness issues in the context of the addition problem.

As described in Section 2, a fault-intolerant program p is specified in terms of its state space S_p , its transitions, δ_p , and its invariant, S. The safety of specification *spec* provides a set of bad transitions that should not occur in program computations. The faults, f, are specified in terms of state transitions. Likewise, the fault-tolerant program p' is specified in terms of its state space S_p , its state transitions, say δ'_p , its invariant S' , its specification *spec*, and the level of fault-tolerance it provides.

Now, we consider what it means for a fault-tolerant program p' to be *derived* from p. As mentioned in the introduction, our derivation is based on the premise that p' is obtained by adding fault-tolerance alone to p, i.e., we should be able to prove that p' refines *spec* from S' in the absence of faults by simply using that 'p refines *spec* from S'. To precisely state this requirement, we consider the relation between (1) the invariants S and S', and (2) the transitions δ_p and δ'_p.

- If S' contains states that are not in S then, in the absence of faults, p' will include computations that start outside S. However, we cannot prove that such computations are in *spec* by just using the fact that p refines *spec* from S as we have no information about computations of p that originate outside S. Therefore, we require that $S' \subseteq S$ (equivalently, $S' \Rightarrow S$).

- Regarding the transitions of p and p', we focus only on the transitions of $p'|S'$ and $p|S'$. If $p'|S'$ contains a transition that is not in $p|S'$, p' can use this transition in order to refine *spec* in the absence of faults. Once again, we cannot prove that the resulting computation is in *spec* by just using the fact that p refines *spec* from S. Therefore, we require that $p'|S' \subseteq p|S'$.

Using the above two requirements, we define the addition problem as follows:

The Addition Problem
Given p, S, *spec* and f such that p refines *spec* from S,
Identify p' and S' such that:
$S' \subseteq S$,
$p'|S' \subseteq p|S'$, and
p' is $\mathcal{L}$ f-tolerant to *spec* from S', where
$\mathcal{L}$ is failsafe, nonmasking or masking. □

In order to define soundness and completeness in the context of the addition problem, we define the corresponding decision problem:

The Decision Problem
Given p, S, *spec* and f such that p refines *spec* from S,
Does there exist p' and S' such that:
$S' \subseteq S$,
$p'|S' \subseteq p|S'$, and
p' is $\mathcal{L}$ f-tolerant to *spec* from S'?
(where $\mathcal{L}$ is failsafe, nonmasking or masking) □

Notations. Given p, *spec*, S and f as input, we say that p' and S' solve the addition problem for this input iff p' and S' satisfy the three conditions of the addition problem. We say p' (respectively, S') solves the addition problem iff there exists S' (respectively, p') such that p' and S' solve the addition problem.

Soundness and completeness. An algorithm for the addition problem is *sound* iff for any given input, its output, namely p' and S', solves the addition problem. An algorithm for the addition problem is *complete* iff for any given input if the answer to the decision problem is affirmative then the algorithm always finds a program p' and a non-empty state predicate S'.

Note that our notion of completeness is *relative* to the input fault-intolerant program p and its invariant S. That is, a complete algorithm finds a fault-tolerant version of p iff a fault-tolerant program p' exists that solves the addition problem for p.

4. Adding Failsafe Fault-Tolerance

In this section, we present an algorithm for the addition of failsafe fault-tolerance. We also illustrate the soundness and completeness of our algorithm. As mentioned in Section 2, we represent a safety specification as a set of bad transitions that should not occur in program computations. Given a bad transition (s_0, s_1), we consider two cases: (1) (s_0, s_1) is not a transition of f, and (2) (s_0, s_1) is a transition of f.

For case (1), we claim that (s_0, s_1) can be removed while obtaining p'. To see this, consider two subcases: (a) state s_0 is reached in the computations of $p' \; [] \; f$, and (b) state s_0 is never reached in any computation of $p' \; [] \; f$. In the former subcase, the transition (s_0, s_1) must be removed as the safety of *spec* can be violated if $p' \; [] \; f$ ever reaches state s_0 and executes the transition (s_0, s_1). In the latter subcase, the transition (s_0, s_1) is irrelevant and, hence, can be removed.

For case (2), we cannot remove the transition (s_0, s_1) as it would mean removing a fault transition. Therefore, we must ensure that $p' \; [] \; f$ never reaches the state s_0. In other words, for all states s, the transition (s, s_0) must be removed in obtaining p'. Moreover, if any of these removed transitions, say (s_{-1}, s_0), is a fault transition then we must recursively remove all transitions of the form (s', s_{-1}) for each state s'.

Using the above two cases, our algorithm for obtaining a failsafe fault-tolerant program is as follows. First, it identifies states from where the execution of a sequence of fault transitions violates safety. This is done by a (smallest) fixpoint calculation where we begin with the empty set. Then, we add state s_0 to this set if there exists a fault transition (s_0, s_1) such that either (1) (s_0, s_1) violates safety, or (2) s_1 is added to this set earlier. Thus, the set of *marked states* (denoted *ms*) from where faults alone can violate safety is the smallest fixpoint of the following equation:

$$X = X \cup \{s_0 :: (\exists s_1 :: (s_0, s_1) \in f \; \wedge \; (s_1 \in X \vee (s_0, s_1) \text{ violates } spec))\}$$

Then, we compute the set of *marked transitions* (denoted *mt*) that must be removed from p. These transitions fall in two categories: (1) transitions that reach states in *ms*, and (2) transitions that violate the safety of *spec*.

If there exist states in the invariant such that execution of one or more fault transitions from those states violates the safety of *spec*, then we recalculate the invariant by removing those states. The recalculation of the invariant is a (largest) fixpoint calculation. As shown in Theorem 4.2, any invariant S' that solves the addition problem must be a subset of $S-ms$. The same theorem also shows that if p' solves the addition problem then $p'|S'$ must be a subset of $p-mt$. Moreover, we show that if p' and S' solve the addition problem then no state in S' can be a deadlock state. Hence, the invariant S' equals $RemoveDeadlocks(S-ms, p-mt)$, where $RemoveDeadlocks(S, p)$ is the (largest) fixpoint of the equation:

$$X = (X \cap S) - \{s_0 : (\forall s_1 : s_1 \in X : (s_0, s_1) \notin p)\}$$

Finally, we compute the transitions of the fault-tolerant program by removing transitions of $p-mt$ that start from a state in S' but reach a state outside S'. Thus, our algorithm is shown in Figure 1 (As mentioned in Section 2, we use a program and its transitions interchangeably.):

```
Add_failsafe(p, f : transitions, S : state predicate, spec : specification)
{
    ms := smallestfixpoint(X = X ∪ {s0 :: (∃s1 : (s0, s1) ∈ f ∧
                                  (s1 ∈ X ∨ (s0, s1) violates spec))})
    mt := {(s0, s1) : ((s1 ∈ ms) ∨ (s0, s1) violates spec) };
    S' := RemoveDeadlocks(S − ms, p−mt);
    if (S'={}) declare no failsafe f-tolerant program p' exists;
    else p' :=EnsureClosure(p−mt, S')
}

RemoveDeadlocks(S : state predicate, p : transitions)
// Returns the largest subset of S such that computations of p
// within that subset are infinite
  { return largestfixpoint(X = (X ∩ S) −
                                  {s0 : (∀s1 : s1 ∈ X : (s0, s1) ∉ p)}) }
EnsureClosure(p : transitions, S : set of states)
  { return p−{(s0, s1) : s0 ∈ S ∧ s1 ∉ S} }
```

Fig. 1. Addition of failsafe fault-tolerance.

Theorem 4.1 Algorithm *Add_failsafe* is sound. (See[20] for proof) □
Theorem 4.2 Algorithm *Add_failsafe* is complete. (See[20] for proof) □

The proofs of the above theorems show the maximality of the invariant and the transitions within them. Thus, we have

Corollary 4.3 The invariant output by *Add_failsafe* is the largest invariant that solves the addition problem. □

Corollary 4.4 Let the output of *Add_failsafe* be the fault-tolerant program p' and its invariant S'. If p'' and S' solve the addition problem then $p''|S' \subseteq p'|S'$. □

Theorem 4.5 Algorithm *Add_failsafe* is in P. (Proof in[20]) □

Remark. We do not explicitly identify the fault-span in *Add_failsafe*. If the fault-tolerant program output by *Add_failsafe* is p' and its invariant is S', we can compute the fault-span by identifying states reached in the computations of $p' \, [] \, f$ starting from a state in S'. However, this is not the weakest possible fault-span. The weakest possible fault-span is $true - ms$, i.e., it includes all states except those from where faults alone violate safety. Moreover, we can obtain maximal transitions within the fault-span if we add to p' all transitions that (1) begin in a state outside S' and (2) are not in mt. We leave it to the reader to check that the program obtained by adding these transitions solves the addition problem.

4.1. *Case Study: Parking Lot Problem*

In order to illustrate the algorithms presented in this chapter, we use the parking lot problem (see Figure 2). The parking lot contains three spots for cars (marked a, b and c). There are two gates to enter the parking lot. Immediately after each gate, there is a space where the customer can drop the car off (marked l and r). If the gate is open, the customer may leave the car in this spot. The car will then be moved to one of the spots (a, b or c). We assume that if the car is being moved from l or r to a, b or c, no car can enter during this move. At the exit, there is one door. A car parked in spots a, b or c can leave through this door. However, only one car can leave the parking lot at a time. All doors are one-way, i.e., cars in spots l and r cannot leave and a car cannot enter in spots a, b or c.

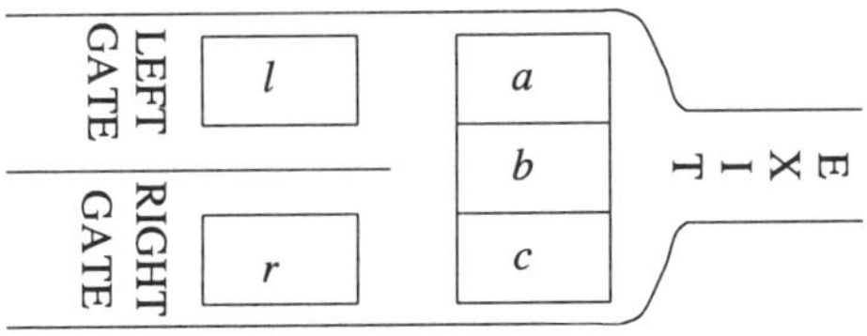

Fig. 2. Parking Lot Problem.

Thus, in the parking lot problem, there are three possible events: (1) a car could be dropped off at the left gate and (possibly) moved to spots a, b or c, (2) a car could be dropped off at the right gate and (possibly) moved to spots a, b or c, or (3) a car could exit. For simplicity, we assume that each event is atomic. Also, we assume that in each spot there can be at most one car. Now, we describe the state space of the fault-intolerant program, its invariant, its safety specification, and its transitions. The fault-intolerant program, invariant, specification and faults identified in this section are used as input to the addition problem. We use the same input for *Add_failsafe* (this section), *Add_nonmasking* (in Section 5.1), and *Add_masking* (in Section 6.1).

Variables and the state space of fault-intolerant program, IP. To model the parking lot, we maintain three variables; x, y and z. The variable x denotes the number of cars that can be let in through the left gate, y denotes the number of cars that can be let in through the right gate, and z denotes the number of cars in the lot. Hence, the left (respectively, right) gate is open when x (respectively, y) is positive. The domain of x and y is $\{0, 1, 2, 3\}$. The domain of z is $\{0, 1, 2, 3, 4, 5\}$. A state of IP is obtained by assigning each variable a value from its domain. The state space of IP, thus, contains 4x4x6 (=144) states.

Safety specification, $spec_{IP}$. The safety specification requires that any car in the parking lot should be able to leave. Clearly, a car in spots a, b or c can leave. However, if spots a, b and c are occupied and there is a car in spot l (respectively, r) then that car cannot leave. Hence, it is required that the value of z is at most three. Also, to model the assumption that only one event (entry/exit) can occur at a time, it is required that the value of x, y and z can change at most by 1. Thus, the safety specification rules out the following transitions:

$$\begin{aligned} spec_{IP} = \{(s_0, s_1) : & \ z(s_0)>3 \ \lor \ z(s_1)>3 \ \lor \\ & |x(s_1) - x(s_0)|>1 \ \lor \ |y(s_1) - y(s_0)|>1 \ \lor \ |z(s_1) - z(s_0)|>1\} \end{aligned}$$

Note that the above safety specification allows x, y and z to change simultaneously. To model the requirement that if a car enters the left gate then another car cannot enter the right gate at the same time, we could strengthen the above safety specification to include a predicate of the form: 'if the value of x is changed then the value of y cannot change.' However, we have chosen the above specification to simplify the presentation, especially while adding masking fault-tolerance.

Transitions δ_{IP}. For brevity, we write program transitions in terms of guarded commands.[21] A guarded command is of the form $g \longrightarrow st$, where

g is a state predicate and st is a statement that updates the variables in the program. The guarded command $g \longrightarrow st$ corresponds to the set of transitions $\{(s_0, s_1) : g$ is true in state s_0 and s_1 is obtained by *atomic* execution of st in state $s_0\}$. The fault-intolerant program IP contains four actions: The first two actions let a car enter, and the last two actions let a car exit. Upon exit, the value x (or y) is non-deterministically increased so that a new car can enter. For simplicity, we do not model the actions corresponding to the movement of the car inside the parking lot. Thus, the transitions of the fault-intolerant program, δ_{IP}, are captured by the following actions.

$$
\begin{array}{llcl}
IP1 :: & x>0 \ \wedge \ z<5 & \longrightarrow & x,z := x-1, z+1 \\
IP2 :: & y>0 \ \wedge \ z<5 & \longrightarrow & y,z := y-1, z+1 \\
IP3 :: & y<3 \ \wedge \ z>0 & \longrightarrow & y,z := y+1, z-1 \\
IP4 :: & x<3 \ \wedge \ z>0 & \longrightarrow & x,z := x+1, z-1
\end{array}
$$

Invariant, S_{IP}. We let the invariant of the fault-intolerant program, S_{IP}, be $x+y+z = 3$.

Once again, this is not the only possible invariant; $x+y+z \leq 3$ is another possibility. We have chosen S_{IP} as it describes several facets of the algorithm while keeping the presentation simple.

Faults. For our case study, we consider two faults. The first fault action, $F1$, allows a car to sneak in. We will use this fault to demonstrate an example where failsafe and masking fault-tolerance cannot be designed. The second fault action, $F2$, allows a car to sneak out. This fault action will be used to demonstrate an example where fault-tolerance can be added. Thus, the fault actions are as follows:

$$
\begin{array}{llcl}
F1 :: & z<5 & \longrightarrow & z := z+1 \\
F2 :: & z>0 & \longrightarrow & z := z-1
\end{array}
$$

Now, given the transitions δ_{IP}, faults $F1/F2$ and the specification $spec_{IP}$, we add fault-tolerance to program IP.

Adding failsafe fault-tolerance to $F1$. First, we compute the set ms, the set of states from where faults alone can violate safety. Towards this end, consider states s_1, s_2, s_3 and s_4 where the value of x and y is 0 and the value of z in state s_j is j, for $1 \leq j \leq 4$. Observe that (s_3, s_4) is a transition of fault $F1$ that violates safety. It follows that s_3 should be included in ms. Also, (s_2, s_3) is a transition of $F1$ that reaches s_3 and, hence, s_2 is included in ms. Continuing thus, state s_1 will also be included in ms. Following this discussion, it is easy to see that starting from an arbitrary state, fault $F1$ can cause the value of z to be greater than 3. Thus, ms includes all states. And, since ms contains all possible states, it follows that mt contains all possible transitions.

Now, the first argument to RemoveDeadlocks (see Figure 1), $S_{IP}-ms$, is the empty set. Hence, RemoveDeadlocks will return the empty set. Subsequently, *Add_failsafe* will declare that failsafe fault-tolerance cannot be added. (This is an expected result; if the fault can continue to increase the value of z, it will not be possible to guarantee that z will be at most 3.)

Adding failsafe fault-tolerance to $F2$. Once again, we compute ms for $F2$. Observe that if the value of z in a state is 3 or less, execution of $F2$ cannot violate safety. However, if the value of z in a state is 4 or 5, execution of $F2$ violates safety. Hence, ms equals the set $\{s_0 : z(s_0) > 3\}$. Thus, $S_{IP}-ms$ equals S_{IP}.

The set mt includes the set $spec_{IP}$ and the set of transitions that reach ms. It follows that mt equals $spec_{IP}$. Using the values of ms and mt, RemoveDeadlocks is called with parameters S_{IP} and $\delta_{IP}-mt$. We leave it to the reader to verify that RemoveDeadlocks returns the set S_{IP}.

The transitions of the failsafe fault-tolerant program are obtained by calling RemoveDeadlocks. RemoveDeadlocks removes transitions of IP that originate in S_{IP} but reach a state outside S_{IP}. Since S_{IP} is an invariant of IP, no such transitions exist. Thus, the transitions of the failsafe fault-tolerant program, δ_{FP} are as follows:

$$\delta_{FP} = \{(s_0, s_1) : (s_0, s_1) \in \delta_{IP} \ \wedge \ z(s_0) \leq 3 \ \wedge \ z(s_1) \leq 3\}$$

From the above discussion, the invariant of the failsafe fault-tolerant program is S_{IP} and its transitions are those transitions of IP where the value of z in the initial and final state is 3 or less. In the presence of faults, the failsafe fault-tolerant program may reach a state where $x+y+z$ is less than 3. In this case, the failsafe fault-tolerant program can deadlock if it reaches a state where x, y and z are 0.

Remark. Note that the execution of $F2$ from states in S_{IP} did not violate the safety specification. Hence, the invariant of the fault-tolerant program remained unchanged. If we had considered the fault where z could be increased only if the initial value of z was 3 then in that case the invariant of the fault-tolerant program would have been $S_{IP} \wedge (z < 3)$.

5. Adding Nonmasking Fault-Tolerance

In order to design a nonmasking f-tolerant program p', we ensure that if p is perturbed by faults f then it eventually recovers to a state in S. To obtain the nonmasking f-tolerant program, for each state s_0, $s_0 \notin S$, we add a transition (s_0, s_1) such that $s_1 \in S$. We present our algorithm for adding nonmasking f-tolerant to programs in Figure 3:

```
Add_nonmasking(p, f : transitions,
        S : state predicate, spec : specification)
{
    S' := S;
    p' := (p|S) ∪ {(s0, s1) : s0∉S ∧ s1∈S}
}
```

Fig. 3. Addition of nonmasking fault-tolerance.

Comment on the Add_nonmasking algorithm. Adding nonmasking fault-tolerance has important applications in the design of resilient network protocols and reactive programs where a program provides recovery in the presence of failures. In the high atomicity model, the addition of such recovery to an existing program is straightforward since processes can read/write all program variables in an atomic step. Hence, we only need to add single-step recovery transitions from states outside the invariant to the invariant. However, we have shown[22,23] that adding nonmasking fault-tolerance to distributed programs is non-trivial and the *Add_nonmasking* algorithm provides an upper bound for checking the feasibility of adding recovery to distributed program.

Theorem 5.1 Algorithm *Add_nonmasking* is sound and complete.

Proof. By construction, p' and S' satisfy the conditions of the addition problem. Thus, the algorithm is sound. Also, the algorithm always finds a solution to the addition problem. □

Corollary 5.2 The invariant output by *Add_nonmasking* is the largest invariant that solves the addition problem. □

Corollary 5.3 Let the output of *Add_nonmasking* be the fault-tolerant program p' and its invariant S'. If p'' and S' solve the addition problem then $p''|S' \subseteq p'|S'$. □

Theorem 5.4 Algorithm *Add_nonmasking* is in P. (The proof is trivial, hence omitted.) □

Note. The results of this section also hold for Alpern-Schneider's general model of safety specifications (for high atomicity programs) as the invariant is not modified and preserving safety is not required while adding recovery. However, the complexity of adding nonmasking fault-tolerance to distributed programs in Alpern-Schneider's model is still unknown.

5.1. *Parking Lot Problem: Adding Nonmasking Fault-Tolerance*

We consider the problem of adding nonmasking fault-tolerance to $F1$ and $F2$ identified in Section 4.1. Applying *Add_nonmasking* to program IP with invariant S_{IP}, the invariant and the transitions of the nonmasking fault-tolerant program, say OP are as follows:

$$S_{OP} = S_{IP}$$
$$\delta_{OP} = \{(s_0, s_1) : (s_0 \in S_{IP} \ \wedge \ (s_0, s_1) \in \delta_{IP}) \ \ \vee \ \ (s_0 \notin S_{IP} \ \wedge \ s_1 \in S_{IP})\}$$

Thus, in states in S_{IP}, the nonmasking program has the same transitions as IP. From states outside S_{IP}, OP simply recovers to any state where S_{IP} is true. Note that some of these recovery transitions violate safety; for example, a transition that changes the value of x (respectively, y or z) by more than one is included in these transitions. In the derivation of a masking fault-tolerant version of IP, we need to ensure that such transitions are not executed. In other words, it is necessary that the recovery to the invariant should occur without these transitions.

6. Adding Masking Fault-Tolerance

In order to design a masking f-tolerant program p', we proceed to identify the weakest invariant S' (which is stronger than S) and the weakest fault-span T'. As argued in Theorem 4.2, our first estimate of S' is S_1 where S_1 = RemoveDeadlocks($S - ms, p - mt$). Likewise, we estimate T' to be T_1 where $T_1 = true - ms$, i.e., T_1 includes all states except those in ms.

The calculation of the invariant and the fault-span for the masking fault-tolerant program is also a (largest) fixpoint calculation. However, due to the nesting involved in this fixpoint calculation, for simplicity, we present it operationally as a loop (Lines 5-13 in Figure 4) where we strengthen S_1 and T_1 while ensuring that if some S' solves the addition problem then $S' \subseteq S_1$. This loop contains three key steps (Lines 7, 8 and 9). Line 7 is a simple statement that computes the transitions, p_1, that may be used if S_1 is the invariant and T_1 is the fault-span. Lines 8 and 9 are fixpoint calculations for the fault-span and the invariant respectively. The value of p_1 is used to compute these fixpoints. These steps are as follows:

(1) To compute the set of transitions, say p_1, that can be included in the masking fault-tolerant program, first, we include transitions that start from a state in S_1; i.e., $p|S_1$. Then, we consider transitions that start from a state in T_1–S_1. By the closure of the fault-span, these transitions

include those that reach a state in T_1. Finally, we remove the transitions mt from this set (Line 7).

(2) We recompute the fault-span on Line 8 in Figure 4 using a (largest) fixpoint calculation. For this fixpoint calculation, we first remove states in T_1 from where it is not possible to reach a state in S_1 using the transitions of the program identified in Step 7; i.e., p_1. Now, if there are states, say s_0 and s_1, such that s_0 is in the fault-span, s_1 is outside the fault-span and (s_0, s_1) is a fault transition then s_0 must be removed from the fault-span. Thus, we strengthen T_1 to ConstructFaultSpan($T_1 - \{s : S_1$ is not reachable from s in p_1 $\}$, f), where ConstructFaultSpan(T, f) is the (largest) fixpoint of the following equation:

$$X = (X \cap T) - \{s_0 :: (\exists s_1 :: (s_0, s_1) \in f \;\wedge\; s_1 \notin X)\}$$

(3) Since S_1 must be a subset of T_1, we recalculate (line 9 in Figure 4) the invariant using RemoveDeadlocks($S_1 \wedge T_1, p_1$) where RemoveDeadlocks itself is a (largest) fixpoint calculation.

We continue the loop on Lines 5-13 until we achieve the largest fixpoint for S_1. After the largest fixpoint is found, we compute the program transitions by assigning ranks to all states in T_1 and removing cycles outside S_1. We present our algorithm for adding masking fault-tolerance in Figure 4.

Theorem 6.1 Algorithm *Add_masking* is sound. (See[20] for proof) □

Theorem 6.2 Algorithm *Add_masking* is complete. (See[20] for proof) □

The proofs of the above theorems also show the maximality of the invariant and the transitions within it. Thus, we have

Corollary 6.3 The invariant output by *Add_masking* is the largest invariant that solves the addition problem. □

Corollary 6.4 Let the output of *Add_masking* be the fault-tolerant program p' and its invariant S'. If p'' and S' solve the addition problem then $p''|S' \subseteq p'|S'$. □

Theorem 6.5 Algorithm *Add_masking* is in P.

Proof. Note that the repeat-until loop can be executed only for a polynomial number of times as in each iteration either size of S_1 or size of T_1 decreases. As in the proof of Theorem 4.5, each statement in *Add_masking* is in P. Thus, the algorithm *Add_masking* is in P. □

Modification for stepwise synthesis. As discussed earlier, the invariant and the fault-span computed by an algorithm that solves the addition problem should be maximal if the output of the addition algorithm is to be used as an input when fault-tolerance is added in a stepwise fashion. Corollaries 6.3 and 6.4 show the maximality of the invariant and the tran-

Add_masking(p, f : transitions, S : state predicate, *spec* : specification)
{
$ms := smallestfixpoint(X = X \cup \{s_0 :: (\exists s_1 : (s_0, s_1) \in f \wedge$
$(s_1 \in X \vee (s_0, s_1)$ violates $spec))\})$ (1)
$mt := \{(s_0, s_1) : ((s_1 \in ms) \vee (s_0, s_1)$ violates $spec)\};$ (2)
$S_1 :=$ RemoveDeadlocks$(S - ms, p - mt);$ (3)
$T_1 := true - ms;$ (4)

repeat (5)
$T_2, S_2 := T_1, S_1;$ (6)
$p_1 := p|S_1 \cup \{(s_0, s_1) : s_0 \notin S_1 \wedge s_0 \in T_1 \wedge s_1 \in T_1\} - mt;$ (7)
$T_1 :=$ ConstructFaultSpan$(T_1 -$
$\{s : S_1$ is not reachable from s in $p_1\}, f);$ (8)
$S_1 :=$ RemoveDeadlocks$(S_1 \wedge T_1, p_1);$ (9)
if $(S_1 = \{\} \vee T_1 = \{\})$ (10)
`declare no masking` f`-tolerant program` p' `exists;` (11)
exit (12)
until $(T_1 = T_2 \wedge S_1 = S_2);$ (13)

For each state $s : s \in T_1$: (14)
$Rank(s)$ = length of the shortest computation prefix of p_1 (15)
that starts from s and ends in a state in S_1;
$p' := \{(s_0, s_1) : ((s_0, s_1) \in p_1) \wedge (s_0 \in S_1 \vee Rank(s_0) > Rank(s_1))\};$ (16)
$S' := S_1;$ (17)
$T' := T_1$ (18)
}

ConstructFaultSpan(T : state predicate, f : transitions)
// Returns the largest subset of T that is closed in f.
{
return $largestfixpoint(X = (X \cap T) - \{s_0 : (\exists s_1 : (s_0, s_1) \in f \wedge s_1 \notin X)\})$
}

Fig. 4. Addition of masking fault-tolerance.

sitions inside it. Regarding the fault-span, these conditions are satisfied by the value of T_1 and p_1 at the end of *Add_masking*. However, to ensure that the fault-tolerant program does not remain in $T_1 - S_1$ forever, we removed certain transitions from p_1. This removal may be premature if the output of *Add_masking* is to be used as an input to add fault-tolerance to another fault. We have addressed[24] this problem by developing sound and complete algorithms for stepwise addition of fault-tolerance.

6.1. *Parking Lot Problem: Adding Masking Fault-Tolerance*

In this section, we demonstrate the addition of masking fault-tolerance in the context of the parking lot example.

Adding masking fault-tolerance to $F1$. As in the case of failsafe fault-tolerance, we begin with computation of ms, mt and the first guess at the invariant of the fault-tolerant program. As discussed in Section 4.1, the invariant S_1 computed on Line 3 is the empty set and, hence, *Add_masking* will declare that masking fault-tolerance cannot be added. Once again this is expected; if a fault could increase the value of z arbitrarily, we cannot ensure that z is bounded by 3.

Adding masking fault-tolerance to $F2$. As in the case of failsafe fault-tolerance, the invariant S_1 on Line 3 will be equal to S_{IP}. Also, since ms equals the set $(z>3)$, the value of T_1 on Line 4 is $z\leq 3$.

Now, we consider the first iteration of the loop on Lines 5-13. On Line 7, we compute p_1 as follows. First, we include a transition that originates in S_{IP} (i.e., where the value of $x+y+z$ equals 3) iff it is in δ_{IP}. Then, we add a transition that originates in $T_1 - S_{IP}$ (i.e., where the value z is less than 3 but the sum of x, y and z is not 3) iff it reaches a state in T_1. Then, we remove the transitions in mt (i.e., transitions where the value of x (or y or z) changes by more than 1 and transitions where the value of z is more than three).

Now, observe that from each state in T_1, it is possible to reach a state in S_{IP} by using the transitions in p_1. (From any state in T_1, we can systematically increase or decrease x, y and z by 1 so that $x+y+z$ equals 3.) Hence, the value of T_2 is the same as T_1. Subsequently, on Line 9, S_1 is also the same as S_2. Thus, the loop on Line 13 terminates.

After the loop terminates, we consider the transitions in p_1 and decide the rank of each state in T_1. Consider the state where $x=0, y=0$, and $z=0$. From this state, in one transition, we can reach a state where $x=1, y=1$ and $z=1$, and the resulting state is in S_1. Hence, the rank of the state where $x=0, y=0$ and $z=0$ is 1. Likewise, the rank of the states where the sum of x, y and z is in the set $\{0,1,2,4,5\}$ is 1.

For states where $x+y+z$ equals 6, if all three variables are non-zero, in one transition a state in S_1 is reached (by decreasing each x, y and z). Hence, the rank of these states is 1. Now, consider a state, say s, where the value of one variable, say x, is 0. If $x+y+z$ equals 6 then the values of y and z must be 3. From s, it is not possible to reach S_1 by using one transition. However, by using two transitions, it is possible to reach a state in S_1. Hence, the rank of a state, where $x+y+z$ equals 6 and the value of

x (respectively, y or z) is 0, is 2.

Finally, the rank of the states where $x+y+z$ equals 7, 8 or 9, is 2.

Now, to obtain the transitions of the masking fault-tolerant program (Line 16), we use the transitions of p_1 where the rank decreases by 1. Thus, the transitions of the masking fault-tolerant program, p' are as shown in Figure 5.

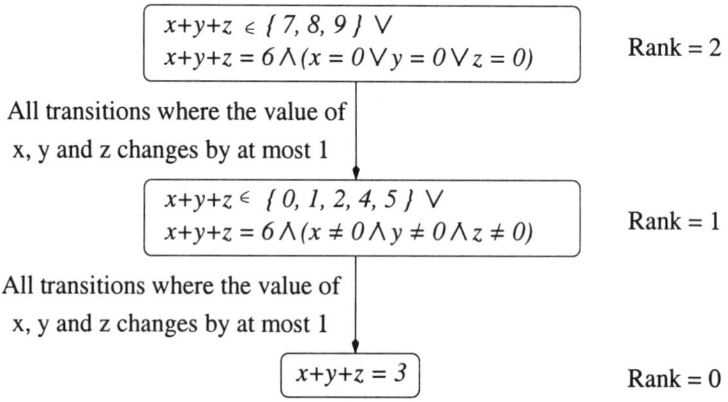

Fig. 5. Transitions of the Masking Fault-tolerant Program to Parking Lot Problem.

Remark. Note that all states in T_1 are not reached in the presence of $F2$. However, as argued in Section 3, one of the goals of our algorithms is to compute the largest possible invariant and largest possible fault-span. This is desirable if the program output by our synthesis procedure is to be used as an input to add fault-tolerance to another fault. Also, the parking lot program designed in this section is masking fault-tolerant to the fault that increments/decrements the value of x, y and z such that the value of these variables is at 3 or less.

7. Related Work

Numerous approaches exist for automatic generation of the design of a system most of which produce a design from a given specification (i.e., *specification-based* approaches). Specifically, Arora, Attie and Emerson[1] present a method for automatic synthesis of fault-tolerant programs from their temporal logic specifications. Their approach has its roots in other specification-based methods,[25–28] where a design is generated from a satisfiability proof of the specification. One of the major differences between specification-based methods and our algorithm is in our input. We begin with an existing design, whereas the specification-based methods[1,25–28] begin with a specification in some temporal logic. For this reason, we believe that our algorithms will be especially useful if a fault-intolerant design is already known or if other constraints (such as unavailability of a complete specification of the given fault-intolerant design) require that we reuse the fault-intolerant design.

In control theory, several approaches[3–6,29–31] exist for automatic synthesis of the design of a discrete-event controller from the specification of a controlled system. Our work differs from synthesizing discrete-event controllers in that (i) the computation model for synthesizing controllers is based on prioritized synchronization, whereas ours is based on interleaving, and (ii) the complexity of synthesizing a fault-tolerant design in the context of the formulation presented in this chapter is polynomial (in design state space), whereas the complexity of synthesizing controllers is NP-hard.[32]

In the game-theoretic approaches, many techniques for the synthesis of controllers[7,33,34] and reactive programs[2] are based on the model of two-player games where a program makes moves in response to the moves of its environment. The program and its environment interact through a set of interface variables, and hence, the environment can only update the interface variables, whereas, in our model, faults can perturb all program variables. Moreover, in a two-player game model, players take turns and the set of states from where the first player can make a move is disjoint from the set of states from where the second player can move,[7] whereas, in our work, fault-tolerance should be provided against the faults that can execute from any state.

8. Impact of Proposed Algorithms and Open Problems

In this section, we discuss the role of the algorithms presented in this chapter in adding fault-tolerance to the design of distributed programs and automatic addition of *multitolerance* to fault-intolerant designs, where a multitolerant program provides different levels of fault-tolerance corresponding to different types of faults. We also discuss complexity issues and open problems for future work.

Application in adding multitolerance. We have reused our algorithms in adding multitolerance to fault-intolerant designs.[24] For example, if a program is simultaneously subject to two classes of faults f_1 and f_2, and failsafe fault-tolerance is expected against f_1 and masking fault-tolerance is expected against f_2 then we use the $Add\_failsafe$ and the $Add\_masking$ algorithms to transform the input fault-intolerant program to a multitolerant program that is failsafe f_1-tolerant and masking f_2-tolerant; i.e., *failsafe-masking* multitolerance. Using the soundness and completeness of our algorithms, we have developed sound and complete algorithms,[24] where we add failsafe-masking and *nonmasking-masking* multitolerance to fault-intolerant programs. We have shown that the complexity of such addition is polynomial in program state space. However, we have shown that adding *failsafe-nonmasking* multitolerance is NP-hard! This is a surprising result in that in this chapter we showed that the simultaneous addition of failsafe *and* nonmasking fault-tolerance (i.e., masking fault-tolerance) for one fault-type can be done in polynomial time, whereas adding failsafe fault-tolerance for a fault-type f_1 and nonmasking fault-tolerance for a different fault-type f_2 is NP-hard.[24]

The effect of the safety specification model. Given the significance of the proposed algorithms for adding fault-tolerance, it is equally important to determine the complexity of such addition of fault-tolerance in a weaker (i.e., more general) model of specification. In particular, in this chapter, we showed that if one represents a safety specification as a set of bad transitions that must not occur in program computations (i.e., bad transitions (BT) model) then the time complexity of adding failsafe, nonmasking, and masking fault-tolerance is polynomial (in program state space). The BT model is a restricted version of Alpern-Schneider's[13] general model of safety specifications, where safety is represented as a set of finite *sequences* of transitions that must not occur in program computations. We have shown[14] that if one uses Alpern-Schneider's general model of safety specification then the complexity of adding masking fault-tolerance will be NP-hard. A direct outcome of this result concerns the complexity of multitolerance in Alpern-Schneider's general model, which is NP-hard, in general, for failsafe-masking and nonmasking-masking multitolerance but unknown for failsafe-nonmasking multitolerance (see Figure 6). Hence, we argue that, for efficient automation, the focus should be on restricted models of safety specifications such as the BT model. We note that even though the BT model is not as expressive as Alpern-Schneider's general safety model, it is still sufficiently expressive to capture numerous practical problems. We have modeled the safety specification of several industrial applications (e.g., an altitude switch controller and a cruise control system[15]) using the BT model. The table in Figure 6 summarizes the effect of the safety specification model on the complexity of adding fault-tolerance and multitolerance in the high atomicity model.

	F	N	M	F+M	N+M	F+N
BT Specification Model	P*	P*	P*	P [24]	P [24]	NPC [24]
Alpern-Schenider's General Model of Safety Specification	?	P*	NPH [14]	NPH [14]	NPH [14]	?

Legend:

NPH: NP-Hard, but not known to be NPC
NPC: NP-Complete
F: Failsafe
F+M: Failsafe-Masking Multitolerance
P: Polynomial
N: Nonmasking
N+M: Nonmasking-Masking Multitolerance
? : Open problem
M: Masking
F+N: Failsafe-Nonmasking Multitolerance
* : Results shown in this paper
NP: Known to be in NP, but not known to be in P or to be NPC

Fig. 6. The effect of the safety specification model on the complexity of adding fault-tolerance and multitolerance. (The reference numbers refer to the papers in which the results have been appeared.)

Adding fault-tolerance to distributed programs. In this chapter, we addressed the problem of adding fault-tolerance in a high atomicity model, where program processes can read/write all program variables in one atomic step. We have also investigated the addition of fault-tolerance to the design of distributed programs, where processes have read/write restrictions with respect to program variables. Specifically, we illustrate that adding masking[22] and failsafe[35] fault-tolerance to distributed programs is NP-complete (in program state space). (Please see the second row, first and third columns of the table in Figure 7). To deal with the exponential complexity of the addition problem for distributed programs, Kulkarni, Arora and Chippada[36] present a set of deterministic polynomial heuristics. These heuristic are applied to provide a deterministic method for deciding about removing/retaining transitions (respectively, states) during the addition of fault-tolerance. Kulkarni and Ebnenasir[23] also present heuristics for enhancing the level of the tolerance of nonmasking distributed programs to masking fault-tolerance. Using these heuristics, Ebnenasir and Kulkarni[15] have developed an extensible software framework, called Fault-Tolerance Synthesizer (FTSyn), where developers can add fault-tolerance to (distributed) programs. We have used FTSyn for automatic addition of fault-tolerance to the design of several programs including Byzantine agreement, token rings, diffusing computation, and a simplified version of an altitude switch.[15] FTSyn has also been used in Networked Embedded Software Technology (NEST).[37] (The source code of FTSyn is available at `http://www.cs.mtu.edu/~aebnenas/research/tools/ftsyn.htm`.) To our knowledge,

FTSyn is the first software tool for automatic addition of fault-tolerance to distributed programs.

Another way to reduce the complexity is to identify sufficient conditions for polynomial-time addition of fault-tolerance. Kulkarni and Ebnenasir[35] have identified a class of distributed programs and a class of specifications for which failsafe fault-tolerance can be added in polynomial time. They have also shown that programs and specifications for commonly encountered problems such as consensus, commit and agreement fall in this class. It follows that failsafe fault-tolerant programs for these problems can be designed in polynomial time. We have used these results[38] to identify heuristics that strengthen the given specification (respectively, add determinism to the given fault-intolerant program) in such a way that failsafe fault-tolerance can be added in polynomial time by using the modified specification (respectively, program). Yet another approach for dealing with the exponential complexity of adding fault-tolerance to distributed programs is to provide reuse during synthesis. Towards this end, we have presented a synthesis method[39] for adding pre-synthesized fault-tolerance components during the synthesis of different programs. We have used such components[39,40] for dealing with message loss, link/node failure, and process-restart faults.

	F	N	M	F+M	N+M	F+N
High Atomicity Model	P*	P*	P*	P [24]	P [24]	NPC [24]
Distributed Programs	NPC [35]	NP [22]	NPC [22]	NPC [24]	NPC [24]	NPC [24]

Fig. 7. The effect of program model on the complexity of adding fault-tolerance in the bad transition (BT) safety specification model.

Even though the algorithms presented in this chapter add fault-tolerance to high atomicity programs, they provide an upper bound for reasoning about the possibility of adding fault-tolerance to distributed programs. For example, we have used[23] the high atomicity algorithms of this chapter in reasoning about the feasibility of enhancing the level of fault-tolerance from nonmasking to masking for distributed programs. Specifically, we search the recovery paths provided by a nonmasking fault-tolerant program from each state s outside the invariant to find those paths of execution where safety specification is preserved; i.e., safe recovery paths. To find safe recovery paths in distributed programs, we have to ensure the safety of the actions of each individual process considering all possible combinations of the states of other processes, which is a computationally expensive task. Hence, we first use the high atomicity algorithms of this chapter to investigate whether the high atomicity version of the nonmasking program provides a safe recovery path originated at s. If the high atomicity nonmasking program does not provide any safe recovery originated at s then we infer that providing such a safe recovery for a distributed version of that programs would be impossible.

9. Conclusions and Future Work

In this chapter, we considered the problem of adding fault-tolerance to the design of a given fault-intolerant program represented as a finite state machine. The input to the problem was the design of a fault-intolerant program, its invariant, its safety specification and faults. The output of the problem was the design of a fault-tolerant program with a new invariant.

While solving the addition problem, we considered three commonly encountered fault-tolerance levels in a high atomicity program model, where a process could read and write all variables in an atomic step. The three levels –failsafe, nonmasking and masking– were based on the extent to which the original specification is satisfied when faults occur. We presented three polynomial-time (in the program state space) algorithms for adding fault-tolerance to a fault-intolerant program. We also illustrated that the invariant output by our algorithm is maximal and that the fault-tolerant program output by our algorithm provides maximal non-determinism inside the invariant. As argued in Section 3, this property is desirable when designing multitolerant programs where one adds fault-tolerance for multiple classes of faults in a stepwise fashion. Kulkarni and Ebnenasir[24] illustrate how they use the algorithms presented in this chapter to design sound and complete algorithms for stepwise addition of multitolerance. We also summarized the impact of the proposed algorithms on the addition of fault-tolerance to distributed programs.

In a broader perspective, we are interested in identifying the problems and formulations where the addition of fault-tolerance can be achieved efficiently (in polynomial time), and also the problems for which exponential complexity is inevitable (unless $P = NP$). By identifying such a boundary, we can determine the problems and formulations that can reap the benefits of automation and the problems for which heuristics need to be developed in order to benefit from automation. This chapter helps to make this boundary more precise in that we presented a high atomicity model of computation and a bad transition (called BT) model of safety specification for which adding three levels of fault-tolerance to existing programs can be done in polynomial time (in program state space). Furthermore, we discussed the effect of the safety specification model on the complexity of adding fault-tolerance.

We are currently investigating the application of different state space reduction techniques in the addition of fault-tolerance. Specifically, we plan to incorporate techniques used in model checking (e.g., partial ordering, state compression) in the implementation of the software framework Fault-Tolerance Synthesizer (FTSyn)[15] so that we extend the scope of synthesis to programs with large state space.

References

1. P. C. Attie, A. Arora, and E. A. Emerson. Synthesis of fault-tolerant concurrent programs. *ACM Transactions on Programming Languages and Systems (TOPLAS). (A preliminary version of this paper appeared in Proceedings of the 17th ACM Symposium on Principles of Distributed Computing (PODC), 1998.)*, 26(1):125 – 185, 2004.
2. A. Pnueli and R. Rosner. On the synthesis of a reactive module. In *ACM Symposium on Principles of Programming Languages*, pages 179–190, Austin, Texas, 1989.
3. P.J. Ramadge and W.M. Wonham. The control of discrete event systems. *Proceedings of the IEEE*, 77(1):81–98, 1989.
4. K.H. Cho and J.T. Lim. Synthesis of fault-tolerant supervisor for automated manufacturing systems: A case study on photolithography process. *IEEE Transactions on Robotics and Automation*, 14(2):348–351, April 1998.
5. Karen Rudie, Stephane Lafortune, and Feng Lin. Minimal communication in a distributed discrete-event systems. *IEEE Transactions On Automatic Control*, 48(6), June 2003.
6. Kurt Ryan Rohloff. *Computations on distributed discrete-event systems.* PhD thesis, University of Michigan, MI, USA, 2004.
7. N. Wallmeier, P. Hütten, and Wolfgang Thomas. Symbolic synthesis of finite-state controllers for request-response specifications. In *CIAA, LNCS, Vol. 2759*, pages 11–22, 2003.
8. A. Arora and Sandeep S. Kulkarni. Detectors and correctors: A theory of fault-tolerance components. In *International Conference on Distributed Computing Systems*, pages 436–443, May 1998.
9. A. Arora and Sandeep S. Kulkarni. Component based design of multitolerant systems. *IEEE Transactions on Software Engineering*, 24(1):63–78, January 1998.
10. S. S. Kulkarni. *Component-based design of fault-tolerance.* PhD thesis, Ohio State University, OH, USA, 1999.
11. Wilfried Steiner, John Rushby, Maria Sorea, and Holger Pfeifer. Model checking a fault-tolerant startup algorithm: From design exploration to exhaustive fault simulation. In *The International Conference on Dependable Systems and Networks*, pages 189–198, Florence, Italy, June 2004. IEEE Computer Society.

12. M. J. Fischer, N. .A. Lynch, and M. S. Peterson. Impossibility of distributed consensus with one faulty processor. *Journal of the ACM*, 32(2):373–382, 1985.
13. B. Alpern and F. B. Schneider. Defining liveness. *Information Processing Letters*, 21:181–185, 1985.
14. S. S. Kulkarni and A. Ebnenasir. The effect of the safety specification model on the complexity of adding masking fault-tolerance. *IEEE Transaction on Dependable and Secure Computing*, 2(4):348–355, 2005.
15. Ali Ebnenasir and Sandeep S. Kulkarni. FTSyn: A framework for automatic synthesis of fault-tolerance. `http://www.cs.mtu.edu/~aebnenas/research/tools/ftsyn.htm`.
16. A. Arora and M. G. Gouda. Closure and convergence: A foundation of fault-tolerant computing. *IEEE Transactions on Software Engineering*, 19(11):1015–1027, 1993.
17. E. W. Dijkstra. Self-stabilizing systems in spite of distributed control. *Communications of the ACM*, 17(11), 1974.
18. A. Arora and Sandeep S. Kulkarni. Designing masking fault-tolerance via nonmasking fault-tolerance. *IEEE Transactions on Software Engineering*, 24(6):435–450, 1998. A preliminary version appears in the Proceedings of the Fourteenth Symposium on Reliable Distributed Systems, Bad Neuenahr, 174–185, 1995.
19. G. Varghese. *Self-stabilization by local checking and correction.* PhD thesis, MIT/LCS/TR-583, 1993.
20. Sandeep S. Kulkarni and Anish Arora. Automating the addition of fault-tolerance. Technical Report MSU-CSE-00-13, Department of Computer Science, Michigan State University, East Lansing, Michigan, June 2000.
21. E. W. Dijkstra. *A Discipline of Programming.* Prentice Hall, 1976.
22. S. S. Kulkarni and A. Arora. Automating the addition of fault-tolerance. In *In Proceedings of the 6th International Symposium on Formal Techniques in Real-Time and Fault-Tolerant Systems*, pages 82–93, 2000.
23. Sandeep S. Kulkarni and A. Ebnenasir. Enhancing the fault-tolerance of nonmasking programs. In *Proceedings of the 23rd International Conference on Distributed Computing Systems*, pages 441–449, 2003.
24. Sandeep S. Kulkarni and Ali Ebnenasir. Automated synthesis of multitolerance. In *In Proceedings of International Conference on Dependable Systems and Networks (DSN), Palazzo dei Congressi, Florence, Italy*, pages 209–218, July 2004.
25. E. A. Emerson and E. M. Clarke. Using branching time temporal logic to synchronize synchronization skeletons. *Science of Computer Programming*, 2:241–266, 1982.
26. P. Attie and E. Emerson. Synthesis of concurrent systems with many similar processes. *ACM Transactions on Programming Languages and Systems*, 20(1):51–115, 1998.
27. Z. Manna and P. Wolper. Synthesis of communicating processes from temporal logic specifications. *ACM Transactions on Programming Languages and Systems*, 6:68–93, 1984.

28. P. Attie and A. Emerson. Synthesis of concurrent programs for an atomic read/write model of computation. *ACM TOPLAS (a preliminary version appeared in ACM Symposium on Principles of Distributed Computing, 1996)*, 23(2), March 2001.
29. Feng Lin and W. Murray Wonham. Decentralized control and coordination of discrete-event systems with partial observation. *IEEE Transactions On Automatic Control*, 35(12), December 1990.
30. S. Lafortune and F. Lin. On tolerable and desirable behaviors in supervisory control of discrete event systems. *Discrete Event Dynamic Systems: Theory and Applications*, 1(1):61–92, 1992.
31. Karen Rudie and W.M. Wonham. Think globally, act locally: Decentralized supervisory control. *IEEE Transactions On Automatic Control*, 37(11):1692–1708, 1992.
32. P. Gohari and W. M. Wonham. On the complexity of supervisory control design in the RW framework. *IEEE Transactions on Systems, Man and Cybernetics, Part B*, 30(2):643–652, October 2000.
33. Wolfgang Thomas. On the synthesis of strategies in infinite games. In *STACS*, pages 1–13, 1995.
34. Wolfgang Thomas. Infinite games and verification (extended abstract of a tutorial). In *14th International Conference CAV, Copenhagen, Denmark, July 27-31, LNCS, Vol. 2404*, pages 58–64, 2002.
35. S. S. Kulkarni and A. Ebnenasir. Complexity issues in automated synthesis of failsafe fault-tolerance. *IEEE Transaction on Dependable and Secure Computing*, 2(3):201–215, July-September 2005.
36. S. S. Kulkarni, A. Arora, and A. Chippada. Polynomial time synthesis of Byzantine agreement. In *Symposium on Reliable Distributed Systems*, pages 130 – 139, 2001.
37. A. Arora, M. Gouda, T. Herman, S. Kulkarni, and M. Nesternko. Self-stabilization in networked embedded software technology (NEST). Available at: http://www.dsic-web.net/meetings/urb3butp/index.html, July 2002.
38. Ali Ebnenasir and Sandeep S. Kulkarni. Efficient synthesis of failsafe fault-tolerant distributed programs. Technical Report MSU-CSE-05-13, Computer Science and Engineering, Michigan State University, East Lansing, Michigan, April 2005.
39. Sandeep S. Kulkarni and Ali Ebnenasir. Adding fault-tolerance using pre-synthesized components. In *Fifth European Dependable Computing Conference (EDCC-5), LNCS, Vol. 3463, p. 72*, 2005.
40. Ali Ebnenasir and Sandeep S. Kulkarni. Hierarchical presynthesized components for automatic addition of fault-tolerance: A case study. In *In the extended abstracts of the ACM workshop on the Specification and Verification of Component-Based Systems (SAVCBS), Newport Beach, California*, 2004.

REPLICATION IN SERVICE-ORIENTED SYSTEMS

JOHANNES OSRAEL*, LORENZ FROIHOFER, KARL M. GOESCHKA

Institute of Information Systems, Vienna University of Technology, Vienna, 1040, Austria

**E-mail: johannes.osrael@tuwien.ac.at*

www.tuwien.ac.at

Replication is a well-known technique to enhance dependability of distributed systems. A plethora of replication techniques for distributed object, file, and database systems has been proposed in the past decades. However, replication in service-oriented systems is still in its infancy. Thus, in this chapter we address replication on a conceptual level and contribute to the understanding of replication in service-oriented systems by (i) analyzing replication *protocols* regarding their suitability for service-oriented systems and by (ii) identifying commonalities in existing service replication middleware *architectures* and deriving a system architecture pattern for replication of services. Our main conclusion is that neither replication protocols nor replication middleware architectures need to be re-invented from scratch for service-oriented systems. Thus, we recommend software and service engineers to take a look at the well-established replication algorithms and architectures for distributed object, database, and file systems and apply these techniques in service-oriented systems. However, there are some subtle differences that have to be taken into consideration.

Keywords: service replication, stateful services, replication protocols, middleware for service replication, architectural replication pattern

1. Introduction

1.1. *Motivation*

Service-oriented architectures are more and more adopted by industry in almost all areas of computing. If the success shall continue and the service-oriented computing approach shall be applied in critical, vital systems — such as air traffic control systems, health care systems, nuclear power plants, chemical refineries, public transportation, etc. — *dependability* needs to be ensured.

Dependability is the "ability of a system to avoid service failures that are more frequent or more severe than is acceptable"[1]. Dependability can be achieved by the combined utilization of fault prevention, fault removal, fault forecasting, and fault tolerance techniques. Fault prevention aims at software and hardware development methodologies to prevent the occurrence or introduction of faults. Fault removal techniques (e.g. verification, diagnosis, correction) reduce the number and severity of faults both during system development and system use. Fault forecasting techniques (e.g. qualitative and quantitative evaluation) estimate the present number, future incidence, and the likely consequences of faults. Finally, fault tolerance, which we address in this chapter, ensures that a service failure can be avoided when faults are present in the system[1].

Redundancy is the key to fault tolerance. Fault tolerance cannot be achieved without redundancy. *Replication* of both hardware and software resources is one important means to introduce redundancy and thus to enable fault tolerance.

A plethora of replication methods have been proposed and thoroughly investigated since the 1970's for various domains such as databases, file systems, and distributed object systems. However, applying the well-known principles of replication in service-oriented systems is still not trivial, though urgently required to close the dependability gap[2] we currently face in large-scale, heterogenous (service-oriented) systems and to continue the success of the service-oriented paradigm in critical settings. As pointed out by Ken Birman[3], "only replication can ensure access to critical data in the event of a fault."

Thus, in this chapter[a] we address replication on a conceptual level and contribute by (i) analyzing replication *protocols* regarding their suitability for service-oriented systems and by (ii) identifying commonalities in existing service replication middleware *architectures* and deriving a system architecture pattern for replication of services.

Software and service engineers that need to build fault-tolerant service-oriented systems can benefit from these contributions, especially in the design phase of the software life cycle.

Chapter overview: After classifying services (Sec. 1.2) and presenting our model of a service-oriented system (Sec. 1.3), we discuss how traditional replication protocols can be applied in service-oriented systems for replication of stateful atomic services (Sec. 2.1). We show that replication

[a]This work has been partially funded by the European Community under the FP6 IST project DeDiSys (Dependable Distributed Systems, contract number 004152, http://www.dedisys.org)

protocols used in distributed object systems can be applied on the service level and database or file replication protocols can be used on the data level of a service-oriented system. Moreover, we discuss possible combinations of these replication techniques for composite services (Sec. 2.2).

Existing database or file replication solutions can be used if state synchronization is performed on the data level. However, new middleware solutions are required if state synchronization shall be performed on the service level. Thus, we analyze state-of-the-art service replication middleware architectures (Sec. 3.1 and Sec. 3.2), identify the common key components and derive a system architecture pattern (Sec. 3.3) for replication of services if state synchronization is performed on the service level.

1.2. *Types of services*

A service is a self-describing computational element that performs some function[4], e.g. a flight booking service. The capabilities of the service are defined by a service description language such as the Web Service Description Language (WSDL[5]). With respect to state, we distinguish between stateless and stateful services (Fig. 1). With respect to the functionality of the services, business services and infrastructure services need to be distinguished.

1.2.1. *Stateful vs. stateless services*

A stateless service does not maintain state; thus, the actions performed by a stateless service only depend on the content of the invocation message. In contrast, the actions performed by a stateful service depend on the content of the invocation message and the state maintained by the service. A stateful service keeps state either in memory (non-persisted, transient state) or persists it in a data store (persisted state) such as a file or database. The latter type of stateful services can be modeled as a stateless "access" service plus a stateful resource[b].

Examples for stateless services are file compression/decompression services, temperature conversion services (e.g. Fahrenheit to Centigrade), file comparison services, etc. Many stateful services allow only read access to data: e.g. services for retrieving stock quotes, the current weather conditions, zip codes for a city name, etc. Most e-commerce services are stateful and require both read and write access to data, for example booking ser-

[b]Thus, this category is also called "service that acts upon a stateful resource"[6].

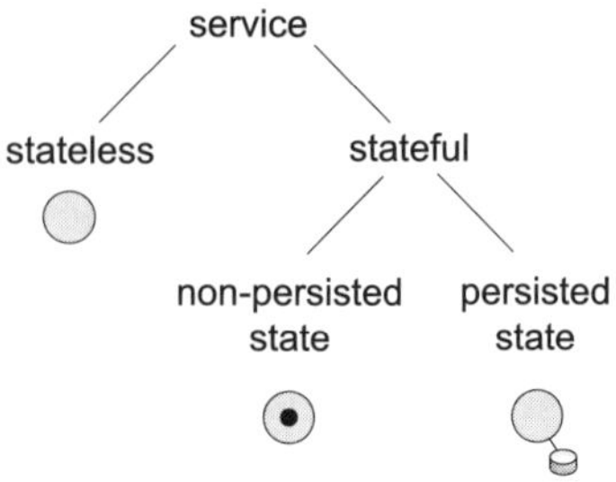

Fig. 1. Types of services

vices (flights, hotels, cars, etc.). Besides accessing persistent data, many stateful services need to maintain conversational state[6], which can be either transient (i.e. stored in memory) or persisted in a database or file.

1.2.2. *Business services vs. infrastructure services*

Service-oriented systems typically contain both pure business services (as illustrated above) and infrastructure services. Business services can be divided into atomic[c] services and composite services. While atomic services provide their functionality without interaction with other services, composite services are an aggregate of several services that — together — deliver a business function. A popular example for such a composite service is a booking engine of a travel agency, which combines several atomic services such as a flight booking service, a hotel booking service, and a car rental service. The service that coordinates these individual services in order to provide a composite service is typically called an orchestration or composition service.

Examples for infrastructure services in a service-oriented environment are directory services (e.g. UDDI registry[7]), messaging intermediaries (e.g. based on WS-Reliability[8]), and transaction coordinators. Business services often require such infrastructure services in order to provide their own functionality. For example, the above mentioned travel agency service may benefit from a transaction service.

---

[c]Note, that an atomic service is a service which does not require other services. This has not to be mixed up with atomic transactions between several services.

1.3. *Model of a service-oriented system*

Figure 2 presents a service-oriented system with both stateful and stateless atomic and composite business services. We have omitted infrastructure services in order to enhance the comprehensibility of the figure.

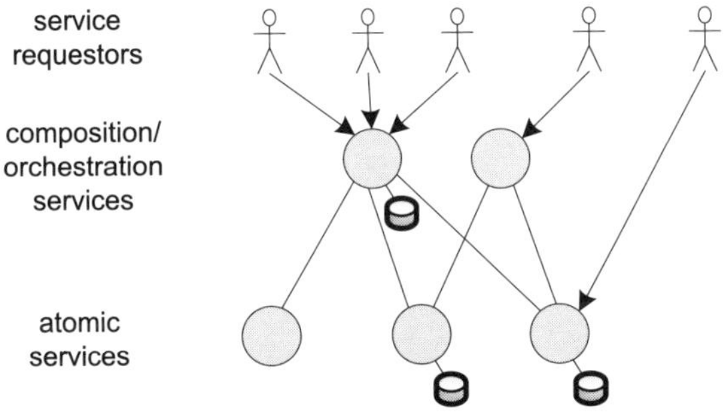

Fig. 2. Service-oriented system without replication

Figure 3 shows an extension of the system by introducing replication of both stateful and stateless services.

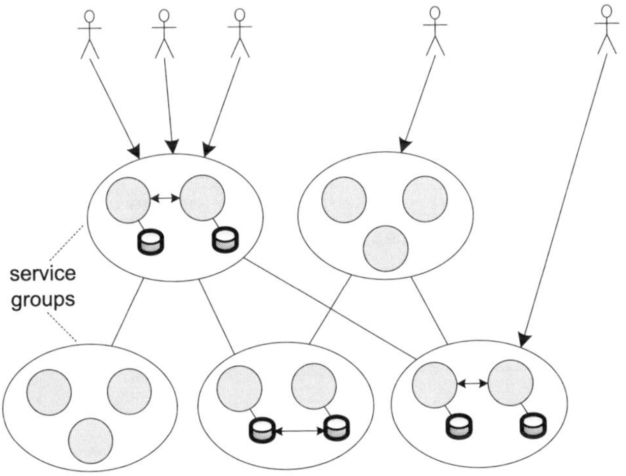

Fig. 3. Service-oriented system with replication on the service and data layer (see Sec. 2)

Replication techniques differ depending on the degree of consistency they can guarantee, ranging from strict consistency such as linearizability or sequential consistency[9], to weaker forms such as eventual consistency. Sequential consistency has similarities with one-copy serializability[10], a common correctness criterion for replicated databases in combination with transactions. Replication techniques that can guarantee strict consistency are feasible for a small number of service replicas. If the number of replicas needs to be large, consistency requirements have to be relaxed or only immutable data (e.g. mp3 music files in a peer-to-peer sharing network) is replicated.

2. Replication Options

In this section, we primarily discuss options for replication if a small number of replicas is sufficient, which is the case in many real-life applications.

Replication of stateless services: Stateless services are not considered, due to the fact that replicating them is comparatively easy (w.r.t. stateful services) since no state needs to be synchronized. Thus, in principle, merely several instances of a service need to be deployed on different hosts in the distributed system. Nevertheless, middleware (see Sec. 3) can be beneficial for replication of stateless services, since it typically provides — besides facilities for the deployment of replicas — the abstraction of a logical service group (comprising several replicas), which reduces complexity for the application programmer.

2.1. *Replication of stateful atomic services*

Stateful services that persist state in a data store can perform replication either on the service level or on the data level[d]. In the first case, the state is synchronized by the "access" service while the underlying stateful resource (data store) takes care of state synchronization in the latter case. This second option does not exist for stateful services that keep their state in memory.

2.1.1. *State synchronization via the data store*

Data is typically either persisted in a database or a file. Both commercial database management systems (DBMS) such as Oracle[11], IBM DB2 Universal Database[12], or Microsoft SQL Server[13] and open-source DBMS such as

---

[d]In order to avoid a single point of failure on the service level, both the stateless "access service" and the underlying data store (stateful resource) should be replicated.

PostgreSQL[14] and MySQL[15] provide replication mechanisms[16]. Distributed file management systems such as the Network File System (NFS)[17], Coda[18], or Microsoft's Distributed File System (DFS)[19] offer replication as well.

Thus, if the stateful service builds upon a data store capable of replication, state synchronization of replicated services can be achieved on the data level via the data store.

2.1.2. *State synchronization on the service level*

An alternative is to synchronize replicated state on the service level. In principle, two different options need to be distinguished: either the original client invocation is processed on all replicas or the invocation is only processed on one replica and the results are propagated to the other replicas which update the state accordingly.

The first approach works only if requests are processed by all replicas in a deterministic way, i.e. the same state needs to be reached by all replicas if the same sequence of invocations is applied. Sources for non-determinism are for example calls to non-deterministic functions (e.g. time() or random()), or the scheduling of concurrently executing conflicting transactions. Thus, non-deterministic sources need to be avoided (e.g. by using a deterministic scheduler and by removing all non-deterministic function calls) if this technique is to be applied.

The second approach does not impose the determinism requirement: the replica which processes the original client invocation determines the result. For instance, a client invocation could cause an update of a data item with a random value between 1 and 100. The random function would only be called at one replica, while the other replicas only get the result, but do not call the random function again.

2.1.3. *Fundamental replication methods for service-oriented systems*

A plethora of replication protocols has been proposed in the past decade. One way to categorize replication protocols is the level of replica consistency they guarantee (Fig. 4). Informally speaking, replica consistency denotes to what extend replicas can differ from each other. Two dimensions of consistency need to be distinguished: temporal and spatial. Temporal replica consistency refers to the update propagation policy. An eager (synchronous, blocking) update propagation policy ensures that the return message to the client (that initiates the update) is returned after all replicas (that need to be updated) are updated. Lazy (asynchronous, non-blocking) variants update only a subset of replicas immediately and defer update propagation to the other replicas. Thus, the eager variant ensures strict consistency of all replicas while the lazy variant yields better response time for the client at the cost of relaxed consistency. A special form of lazy update propagation techniques are probabilistic variants such as epidemic replication[20]. Consistency in the spatial sense can be categorized into full and partial replication: full replication means that the whole state is available at all replicas while partial replication means that each replica contains only a subset of the state[e]. Now we discuss the most important replication techniques and show how they can be applied in service-oriented systems. Most of them can be configured for different consistency guarantees.

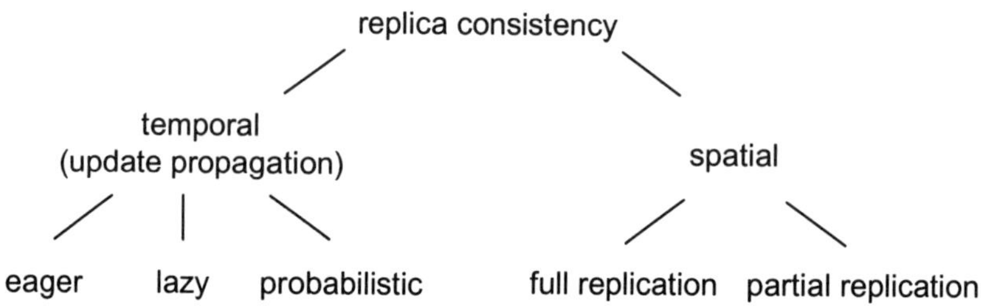

Fig. 4. Replica consistency

Primary-backup replication: In the *primary-backup* approach[22], only the primary service receives a client's request. The backups are either updated on the service level (Fig. 5a) or directly by the underlying data store (Fig. 5b). S1 denotes instance 1 of service S. S1' is a replica of this instance. In the original primary backup variant, only the primary replica processes the requests and forwards the results to the backups. Thus, primary-backup replication is also called *passive* replication. A slight variation is to forward the invocations instead of the results to the backups. Primary-backup replication can be performed in an eager or lazy fashion. An example of a primary-backup replication middleware for Web services is FT-SOAP[23] (see Sec. 3.1).

[e]For example, Sousa *et al.*[21] use the database state machine approach for partial replication.

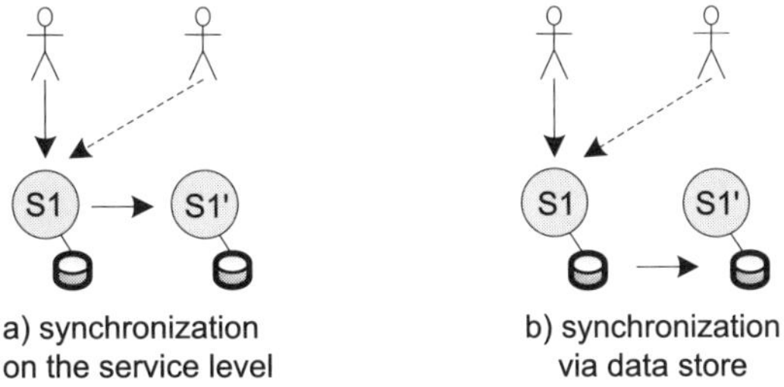

Fig. 5. Primary-backup replication

Coordinator-cohort: The *coordinator-cohort*[24] (Fig. 6) replication method is similar to the primary-backup approach in the sense that requests are sent to one replica (coordinator), which is responsible for distribution to the other replicas (cohort). However, each client invocation might be served by a different coordinator. Hence, some kind of distributed concurrency control such as distributed locking is required. If this replication concept is used on the database layer, it is usually called *update everywhere*[25] or *multi master*[16] replication. Coordinator-cohort (update-everywhere) replication can be performed in an eager or lazy fashion. To our knowledge, no implementation of a coordinator-cohort replication protocol for Web services currently exists.

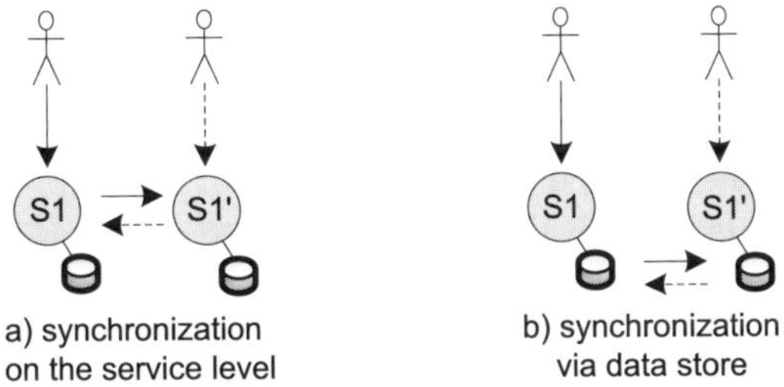

Fig. 6. Coordinator-cohort/Update-everywhere replication

Active replication: In *active replication*, which is also known as the *state machine approach*[26] (Fig. 7a), all replicas receive and process a client's request. In contrast to primary-backup or coordinator-cohort replication, the client contacts all replicas — either directly or via a communication module (proxy)[25]. All invocations need to be issued in the same order to all replicas (total order) and services need to be deterministic. Active replication can also be performed on the data layer (Fig. 7b). In that case, the stateless part ("access service") of a stateful service becomes the client for the replicated data store.

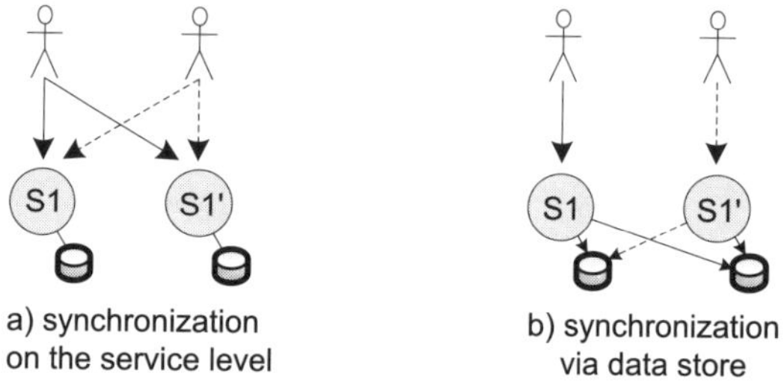

Fig. 7. Active replication

WS-Replication[27] is an example of an implementation of active replication for Web services (see Sec. 3.2).

Quorum consensus replication: In quorum consensus (QC) replication protocols, read/write operations have to be performed by a read/write quorum of replicas. The quorums must overlap in a way that read-write and write-write conflicts are avoided, i.e. any read set must overlap with any write set and two write sets must overlap respectively. Quorum consensus protocols have been proposed for file[28,29], database[30], and data-centric distributed object[31] systems. Though conceptually reasonable, quorum consensus (and also active replication) protocols are hardly used in database systems outside the research community: most of the state-of-the-art (commercially relevant) database management systems offer primary-backup and update everywhere replication. However, in principle, quorum consensus protocols can be used for replication on the data level of a service-oriented system.

Epidemic replication: Demers *et al.*[20] applied the principles of epidemics for propagation of updates. In the anti entropy model, a replica randomly selects another replica and exchanges updates with it in a push, pull, or push-pull fashion. Anti entropy guarantees that all replicas are updated eventually, i.e. they become fully consistent only if no new updates are started. Another model is rumor mongering (rumor spreading, gossiping), which (however) does not guarantee that all replicas eventually receive an update.

Epidemic algorithms scale well but separate algorithms are needed to cope with update conflicts. In practice, this is only feasible if the data semantics are relatively simple. The Bayou[32] system is the most prominent example where epidemic algorithms are used and support for conflict resolution is provided.

Epidemic replication protocols might be used in service-oriented systems where a large number of replicas is needed, update conflicts rarely happen, and consistency requirements are mild. Similar to Bayou, the state could be stored in a database in such a system, but state synchronization and conflict resolution should be provided on the service level. To our knowledge, currently no implementation of an epidemic replication protocol for (Web) services exists.

2.2. *Replication of composite services*

Section 2.1 introduced fundamental replication methods for replication of an atomic service. With the exception of epidemic protocols, the above mentioned protocols are targeted to systems with a small number of replicas, which is sufficient in many real life applications. Replication becomes more complex if the system is composed of several services that interact with each other as depicted in Fig. 2. In order to discuss various combinations of the most important (most widely used) replication methods (primary-backup, active, and coordinator-cohort/update-everywhere replication), without loss of generality, we consider a chain of two stateful services as depicted in Fig. 8a and thereby introduce the concept of layering with respect to replication. The client directs its request to the service on the upper layer which in turn needs to invoke the service on the lower layer in order to fulfill a task. It is also possible to perform replication on only one of the service layers or to use no replication at all.

2.2.1. *No replication at all*

Figure 8 shows three different alternatives as to how a system without replication can be built. Figure 8a is the most obvious case with only one service instance at each layer. U1 is instance 1 of service U at the upper layer. U2 is instance 2 of this service. The service instances of the service L on the lower layer follow the same scheme. Although two instances of the same service type exist on the upper layer in Fig. 8b, this approach is *not* replication with respect to state since the state of the services is not synchronized, i.e. the services are of the same type but independent instances. Figure 8c shows how this concept is applied on both layers. This structure is only useful for stateless services or as building block in composite services with replication on only one out of several layers.

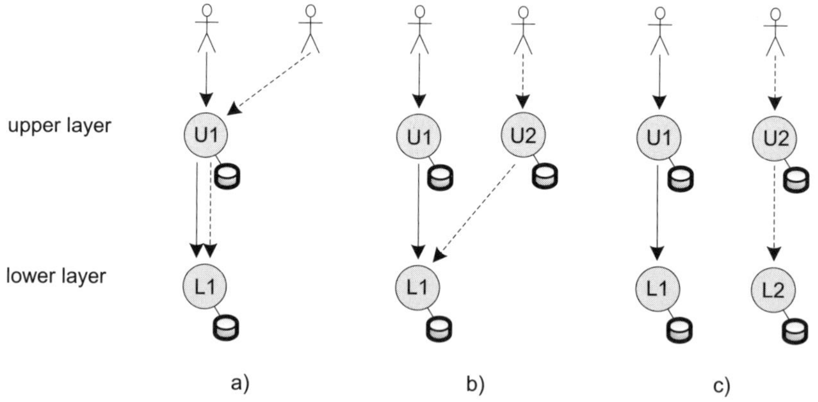

Fig. 8. No replication at all

2.2.2. *No replication on the lower layer*

Figure 9 shows combinations if replication is only applied on the upper layer but not on the lower layer. This situation can occur in service-oriented environments if services with different availability/reliability guarantees (typically of different service providers) are combined: e.g. if a replicated flight booking service on the upper layer accesses a non-replicated weather information service on the lower layer.

U1' denotes the replica of instance 1 of service U on the upper layer. Coordinator-cohort replication is used on the upper layer in these examples. Figure 9a shows that no special treatment is necessary on the lower layer if replication is performed by the data store on the upper layer and only one service instance exists on the lower layer. In contrast, if invocations are replicated via service invocation on the upper layer as depicted in Fig. 9b, messages to the lower layer are duplicated as well and hence need to be detected. This is called the *redundant nested invocation problem*[33].

Finally, Fig. 9c depicts what happens when each replicated service on the upper layer invokes a different, independent service on the lower layer: although these two service instances on the lower layer are not coordinated within their layer, consistency of the states can indirectly be established via coordination on the upper layer.

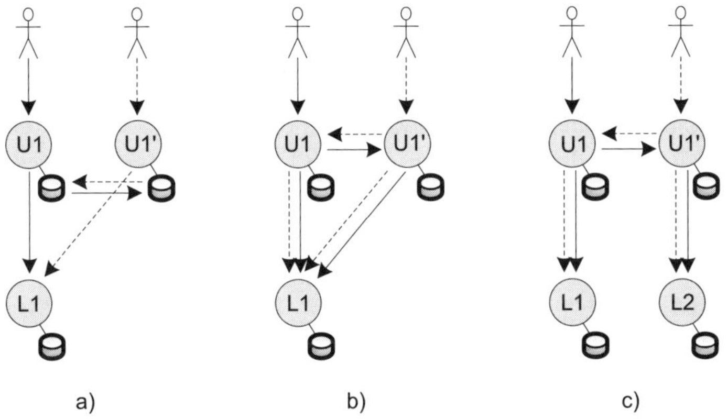

Fig. 9. No replication on the lower layer

2.2.3. *No replication on the upper layer*

Replication on the lower layer is not influenced, whether only one instance (Fig. 10a) or several independent, un-coordinated instances (Fig. 10b) of a service exist on the upper layer.

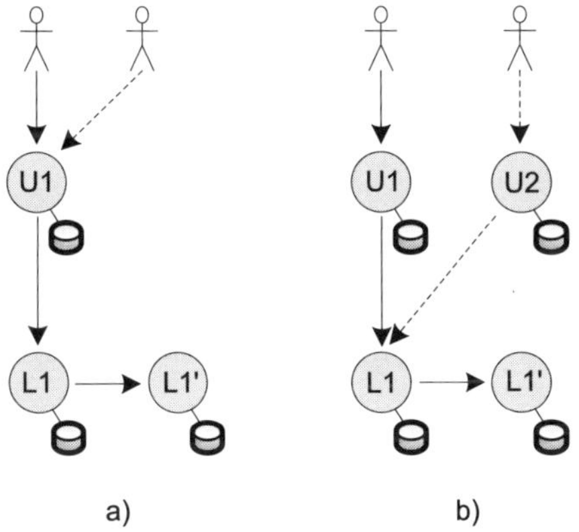

Fig. 10. No replication on the upper layer

As in the previous case with no replication on the lower layer, such configurations are quite natural in service-oriented systems, e.g. if services with different availability/reliability guarantees (typically offered by different service providers) are combined.

2.2.4. *Replication on both layers*

Figure 11 gives some examples how the fundamental replication techniques discussed in Sec. 2.1.3 can be combined: in Fig. 11a, the data stores on both layers perform primary-backup replication. In Fig. 11b, active replication is applied on the upper layer and primary-backup replication is applied by the data store on the lower layer. Replicated messages need to be detected if invocations are replicated on the upper layer. In Fig. 11c, update-everywhere replication is applied by the data store on the upper layer and active replication is used on the lower layer.

Other combinations and replication on additional layers follow the same principle. The most important subtlety that needs to be considered is redundant nested invocations if invocations are replicated.

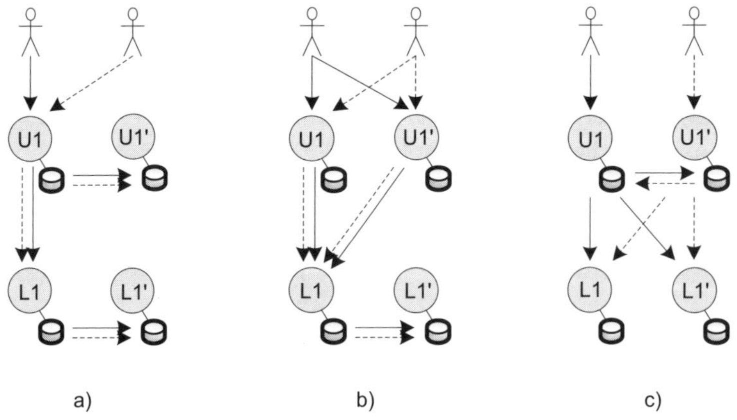

Fig. 11. Replication on both layers

Again, such combinations are quite natural in service-oriented systems if services (of typically different service providers) are combined: e.g. as depicted in Fig. 11c, a Web service based application of an online bookshop (upper layer) might use active replication while the (via a Web service accessible) clearing system (lower layer) of the credit card company uses replication on the database level.

Suppression of redundant nested invocations: A suppression mechanism for redundant nested invocations (RNI) needs to (i) automatically detect RNI, (ii) forward only one of the RNI and suppress the other RNI, and (iii) return the invocation reply to all replicated services. For single-threaded services (i.e. one nested invocation is served at a time), the RNI problem can be solved by simply assigning sequential number identifiers to invocations. For example, suppose an actively replicated service U which in turn invokes an actively replicated service L. Figure 12a depicts the situation without a suppression mechanism: the replicated instances of service L receive invocations twice. This leads to an incorrect state if the invocations are not idempotent, e.g. new state = old state + 4, assuming the state is represented by an integer value. Figure 12b depicts the solution: redundant invocations are detected by the RNI suppression mechanism by comparing the sequence numbers of the invocations. An invocation is suppressed if the sequence number has already been processed.

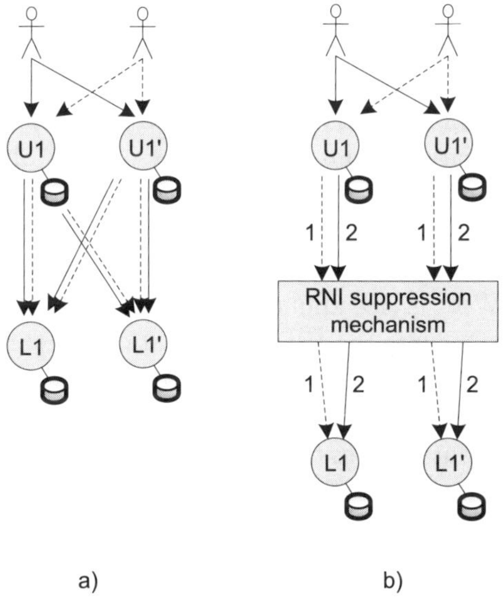

Fig. 12. RNI suppression for single threaded services

This solution also works for multi-threaded services (i.e. nested invocations are served in parallel) if a deterministic thread scheduler is used. If this is not the case, more sophisticated invocation identifiers (taking into account the thread contexts, etc.) need to be created in order to allow detection of identical invocations. Fang *et al.*[33] describe the redundant nested invocation problem in detail and provide a solution for multi-threaded actively replicated Web services.

3. Service Replication Middleware

The previous sections show that traditional replication algorithms can be applied in service-oriented systems. Naturally, the next questions from the perspective of a software engineer are: "How can these traditional replication protocols be implemented in a service-oriented environment? How does middleware need to be built in order to support these techniques?"

In this section, we tackle these questions and compare some of the proposed service replication middleware solutions. All of the currently existing service replication middleware solutions do not use the replication mechanism of the underlying data store. We identify six major infrastructure components and present an architectural pattern for service replication middleware.

We consider middleware that can cope with crash failures[34] and link failures but we do not focus on Byzantine fault-tolerant middleware[35]. Few middleware solutions have been proposed for service-oriented systems: the middleware systems presented by Ye and Shen[36] and Salas *et al.*[27] offer transparent active replication based on group communication[37]. Primary-backup replication of Web services is offered by the FT-SOAP (Fault-Tolerant SOAP) middleware[23]. Thema[35] is a byzantine fault-tolerant middleware for Web service applications. ADAPT[38] is a J2EE replication framework integrated into the JBOSS application server that allows to plug-in replication protocols. Besides replication of Enterprise JavaBeans, it supports replication of AXIS Web services as well. The Web services might contain session state, but services that invoke other EJBs or call a database are not supported. Among these few solutions, we concentrate on FT-SOAP[23] and the active replication middleware systems,[27,36] since primary-backup and active replication are the most commonly used replication techniques in real-life applications.

3.1. *Primary-backup replication middleware*

Figure 13 shows the architecture of the FT-SOAP replication middleware[23], which has many similarities with FT-CORBA[39] and is based on the Apache Axis SOAP engine[40]. As in the FT-CORBA architecture, the key components in FT-SOAP are the *Replication Manager*, the *Fault Management* unit and the *Logging & Recovery* unit. SOAP engine interceptors, which are associated with each service, are used to intercept client requests. WSDL files of replicated services are published in a UDDI registry.

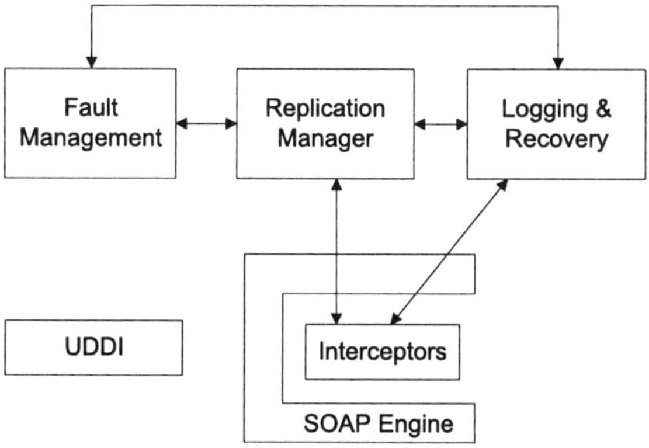

Fig. 13. FT-SOAP

The FT-SOAP replication manager basically provides interfaces for

- setting the desired replication properties like the replication style, initial number of replicas, etc. and
- creating and managing service groups.

FT-SOAP extends WSDL by introducing a ⟨WSG/⟩ element in order to describe Web service groups.

The fault management unit, used to monitor replicated services, consists of a fault detector and a fault notifier. The fault detector actively polls Web services (according to a configurable polling frequency) in order to detect crashes and reports faults to a notification component, which in turn propagates the information to interested components, e.g. the replication manager.

Invocations and periodical checkpoints of the primary's state are logged in a database management system by the logging/recovery unit. Moreover, checkpoints are periodically transferred to the backups and logged invocations are replayed during the recovery stage if necessary.

3.2. *Active replication middleware*

The middleware presented by Ye and Shen[36] offers transparent active replication based on group communication. The system implements the TOPBCAST[41] probabilistic multicast protocol using the JGroups toolkit[42]. Both synchronous and asynchronous interaction between the client and the Web service are supported.

WS-Replication[27] is a framework for wide area replication of Web services and offers transparent active replication. The major components in WS-Replication are a *Web service replication component* and a *reliable multicast component*. The former component enables active replication of Web services while the latter — called WS-Multicast — provides SOAP-based group communication. Moreover, WS-Multicast performs failure detection (which is required for group communication) by a SOAP-based ping mechanism. WS-Multicast can also be used independently from the overall WS-Replication framework for reliable multicast in a Web service environment. The SOAP group communication support has been built on the JGroups[42] toolkit.

3.3. *Replication system architecture pattern*

Based on existing architectures — some of them presented in the previous sections and in previous work[43] — six major architectural units for service replication middleware can be identified as shown in Fig. 14: a *Multicast Service*, a *Monitoring Service*, a *Replication Manager*, a *Replication Protocol* unit, an *Invocation Service* and an optional *Transaction Service*. Some of the units such as the replication protocol and the multicast service are naturally distributed since they realize distributed algorithms. The other components should also be implemented in a distributed fashion in order to avoid single points of failure and to provide an adequate level of fault-tolerance for the infrastructure itself. For instance, a replication manager instance resides on every node in the system that hosts business services. Even more so, the state of the replication manager is also subject to replication. Besides these six major components, replication middleware typically comprises further supportive components such as a naming service (e.g. for resolving human-readable names to identities) or some kind of persistence service (e.g. for object-relational mapping[44]).

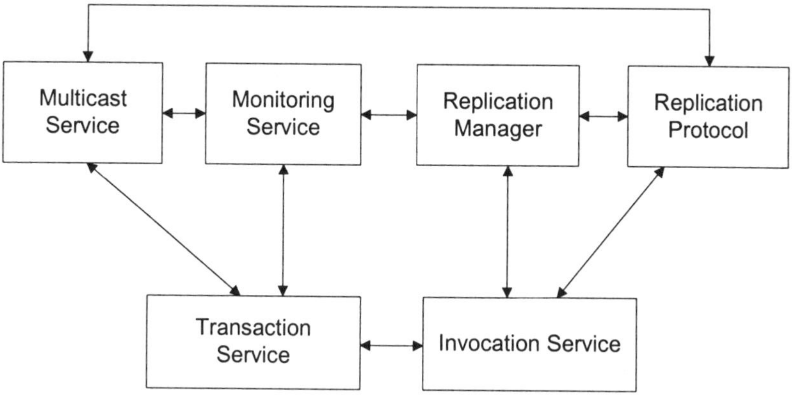

Fig. 14. Replication architecture pattern

3.3.1. *Multicast service*

Schiper[45] points out that group communication, a communication infrastructure that eases the implementation of replication techniques, is beneficial for both active and primary-backup replication. Active replication requires ordering of operations, which can already be provided by a group communication primitive. Group communication primitives hide most of the (implementation) complexity of primary-backup replication: for instance, group communication can cope with undesirable situations such as the crash of the primary during a multicast. Indeed, most of the presented middleware architectures rely on group communication. Examples for state-of-the-art group communication toolkits are JGroups[42], Spread[46], or the newly proposed SOAP-based WS-Multicast toolkit[27], which is specifically targeted to service-oriented systems. The only noteworthy difference compared to traditional group communication toolkits is that WS-Multicast exposes its operations via a WSDL (Web Services Description Language)[5] interface. However, this could also be realized for the other toolkits.

3.3.2. *Monitoring service*

Monitoring of replicated services is required, since replication middleware needs to take appropriate action in case of a fault. For instance, in case of primary-backup replication, it has to promote a backup to a new primary replica if the original primary crashes.

A monitoring service typically distinguishes three entities: *monitors* (failure detectors) collect information about failures of *monitorable entities* and disseminate this information to *notifiable entities.* In a push-model, monitorable entities periodically inform monitors about their status by using heartbeat messages. In a pull-model, monitors actively request liveness messages from monitorable entities.[47]

If a group communication toolkit is used as in WS-Replication[27], the group membership unit already provides the functionality of a monitoring service on the node level. Vogels and Re defined a monitoring and membership service called WS-Membership[48] which is specifically targeted to Web services environments.

3.3.3. *Replication manager*

A certain component is necessary to manage replicated services, including tasks such as storing the location and role (e.g. primary, backup) of replicas, maintaining service groups, general configuration of the replication middleware such as the replication style, etc. Typically, this component is called the replication manager (e.g. in FT-SOAP[23]). The *Web service replication component* of the WS-Replication framework[27] provides similar functionality.

For instance, the interface of a simple primary-backup replication manager might contain the following methods:

- `getPrimary()`: returns the location of the primary replica
- `getBackups()`: returns the locations of the backup replicas
- `getReplica(replicaID)`: returns the location of a replica with the given identifier
- `addReplica(location,role)`: adds a new replica with its location and role
- `changeRole(replicaID,role)`: changes the role of a replica
- `deleteReplica(replicaID)`: deletes a replica

3.3.4. *Replication protocol*

The actual replication logic (i.e. triggering of update propagation, recovery, etc.) is typically either a separate component or embedded in the replication management unit (e.g. WS-Replication middleware[27]). The advantage of a separate replication protocol component is that a change of the protocol (e.g. necessary due to system evolvement) is easier to achieve.

3.3.5. *Invocation service*

An invocation service provides the invocation logic used for invocation of operations and provides specific guarantees with respect to node or link failures. It further provides the possibility to intercept service invocations and transmits additional data with an invocation, e.g. the identifier of a transaction to associate a specific call with a transaction. The Web service replication component of the WS-Replication framework[27] comprises a proxy generator which generates a proxy for each Web service operation. The proxy intercepts invocations to the replicated Web service and triggers the further replication logic.

The SOAP engine Axis2[49,50] allows the definition of customizable message interceptors, so-called "handlers", which ease the implementation of an invocation service in a Java-based Web service environment. Microsoft's new SOAP-based communication platform Windows Communication Foundation (WCF[51]), which is part of the .NET Framework[52] 3.0, also allows the interception of message calls.

3.3.6. *Transaction service*

Transactions are a fault tolerance technique by themselves; specifically the atomicity and durability properties of traditional ACID[f] transactions are related to fault tolerance[45]. Atomicity denotes that either all or none of the transaction's operations are performed. Durability requires that the committed effect of transactions is permanent, such that the data is available after a failure or system restart. However, since durability has its limitations (e.g. some failures such as a disk crash are not recoverable), replication needs to be introduced in critical transactional systems. Thus, transactions need to be performed on replicated services. While distributed object replication middleware often supports transactions (e.g. DeDiSys middleware[53]), support for transactions in replication middleware for service-oriented systems is rather in its infancy. To our knowledge, only WS-Replication[27] has been combined with transactional support. WS-Replication has been successfully tested in combination with long running transactions as defined in the Web Services Composite Application Framework (WS-CAF)[54]. In contrast to short-running ACID transactions, long running transactions provide atomicity guarantees, despite relaxing the isolation property. Compensation actions are required to reverse the effects of

[f]Atomicity, Consistency, Isolation, Durability

long running transactions in case of conflicts. Although the combination of WS-Replication with transactions yielded promising results, there is clearly a need for further research in this area, especially with different replication protocols and other transaction models.

4. Related Work

As this chapter has survey character, we have already cited literature excessively. Here, we summarize references to other research on the application of fault tolerance techniques in service-oriented systems.

Moser *et al.*[55] discuss fault tolerance techniques for Web services including replication, checkpointing and message logging. However, they do not focus on replication of composite services. Nevertheless, their paper complements our work by discussing which infrastructure components need to be replicated in a service-oriented system to achieve dependability: e.g. the UDDI registry, the transaction coordinator, etc.

Birman[3] stresses the importance of replication in service-oriented mission-critical systems in order to achieve robustness and trustworthiness. The same author suggests[56] using the virtual synchrony process group computing model and the state machine model (e.g. exemplified by Lamport's Paxos[57] algorithm) to deploy replication in Web services based systems. Indeed, some of the replication methods for stateful services that we have discussed require multicast primitives[58] which could be provided by toolkits (targeted to service-oriented systems) that follow the virtual synchrony model, for example.

Dependability of composite Web services with online upgrades has been discussed by Gorbenko *et al.*[59], but replication is only indirectly addressed with respect to the parallel execution of several releases of a Web service. Other dependability mechanisms for composite services (but not replication) such as backward or forward error recovery are for example addressed by Tartanoglu *et al.*[60].

Besides conceptual considerations regarding replication in the above mentioned publications, some literature exists on the implementation of specific replication techniques in service-oriented systems as discussed in the previous section.

Replication of data stores such as databases or file systems has been extensively discussed in scientific literature. Oliveira *et al.* give an excellent overview about state-of-the-art in database replication[16]. Saito and Shapiro[61] provide a survey on optimistic replication techniques (weak consistency guarantees) including both file and database replication techniques.

Wiesmann *et al.*[25] compare replication in database systems with replication in distributed object or process systems. However, combinations of these approaches with replication on the service layer have not been investigated to our knowledge.

5. Conclusions and Future Work

This chapter discussed two major aspects of replication in service-oriented systems: replication protocols and replication middleware architectures.

Firstly, we discussed the two principle options for replication of a stateful service: state synchronization is either performed on the service level or via the underlying data store (database or file management system). In the first case, either the original client invocation is processed on all replicas or the invocation is only processed on one replica and the results are propagated to the other replicas, which update the state accordingly. Almost all database management systems and some distributed files systems offer replication mechanisms which can be used in a service-oriented system as well. Before introducing the concept of layering for composite services, we have shown how fundamental replication methods can be applied for atomic services. Without loss of generality, we assumed a chain of two services in order to show that replication techniques can be combined for composite services by following an approach of layered replication. Our key conclusion is that in principle, all combinations of the fundamental replication methods primary-backup, active, coordinator-cohort/update-everywhere and quorum consensus are feasible; however, redundant nested invocations need to be detected if invocations are replayed on several replicas. Besides this, these variants require deterministic service replicas on both layers and can indirectly yield to consistent states on the lower layer even if replication (with respect to state) is not used on the lower layer.

Secondly, we analyzed state-of-the-art service replication middleware systems, which provide primary-backup or active replication. The middleware solutions which we discussed do not use the replication mechanisms of the underlying data store (database or file system). Based on these middleware architectures, we identified six major infrastructure components and derived a replication architecture pattern for service-oriented systems.

Previously[43] we compared state-of-the-art service replication middleware solutions with distributed object middleware such as FT-CORBA[39]. Object and service replication middleware share many architectural commonalities and only subtle differences such as (i) the most suitable internal data structures of the replication middleware, which are caused by the different granularity of the replicated entities (services vs. objects), and (ii) different transaction models.

Thus, our message to software and service engineers is the following: the wheel need not be re-invented from scratch and new solution approaches should complement, but not replace, existing ones:

(1) Traditional, well-established replication protocols can be applied as long as particularities such as redundant nested invocations in the case of composite services, the granularity of services, and specific transaction models for service-oriented systems are considered.
(2) Well-established replication middleware architectures from distributed object systems such as FT-CORBA can be applied in a similar way in service-oriented systems in order to perform state synchronization on the service level. In addition, or as alternative, state-of-the-art database or file management system replication mechanisms can be used for state synchronization on the data level if the state of a service is persisted in a data store.

A future research challenge for replication in service-oriented systems is the combination of replication techniques with novel transaction models.

References

1. A. Avizienis, J.-C. Laprie, B. Randell and C. Landwehr, Basic concepts and taxonomy of dependable and secure computing, in *IEEE Transactions on Dependable and Secure Computing*, (1) (IEEE CS, 2004).
2. J.-C. Laprie, Resilience for the scalability of dependability, in *Proc. 4th Int. Symposium on Network Computing and Applications*, (IEEE CS, 2005).
3. K. Birman, The untrustworthy web services revolution, in *IEEE Computer*, (2) (IEEE CS, 2006).
4. M. Papazoglou, Service-oriented computing: Concepts, characteristics and directions, in *Proc. of the 4th Int. Conf. on Web Information Systems Engineering*, (IEEE CS, 2003).
5. W3C, Web services description language WSDL 1.1 (2001), http://www.w3.org/TR/wsdl.html.
6. I. Foster, J. Frey, S. Tuecke, K. Czajkowski, D. Ferguson, F. Leymann, M. Nally, I. Sedukhin, D. Snelling, T. Storey, W. Vambenepe and S. Weerawarana, Modeling stateful resources with web services (2004).
7. OASIS, UDDI version 3.0.2 (2004), http://www.oasis-open.org.
8. OASIS, WS-Reliability 1.1 (2004), http://www.oasis-open.org.
9. H. Attiya and J. Welch, Sequential consistency versus linearizability, in *ACM Transactions on Computer Systems*, (2) (ACM Press, 1994).
10. P. Bernstein and N. Goodman, The failure and recovery problem for repli-

cated databases, in *Proc. 2nd ACM Symp. on Principles of Distributed Computing*, (ACM Press, 1983).
11. Oracle, Oracle Database, http://www.oracle.com/database/.
12. IBM, IBM DB2 Universal Database, http://www.ibm.com/db2/.
13. Microsoft, Microsoft SQL Server, http://www.microsoft.com/sql/.
14. PostgreSQL Global Development Group, PostgreSQL, http://www.postgresql.org.
15. MySQL AB, MySQL, http://www.mysql.com.
16. Rui Oliveira (ed.), *D1.1 - State of the Art in Database Replication*, tech. rep., Gorda Consortium (http://gorda.di.uminho.pt/) (2005).
17. S. Shepler, B. Callaghan, D. Robinson, R. Thurlow, C. Beame, M. Eisler and D. Noveck, Network File System (NFS) version 4 protocol, in *RFC3530*, (RFC Editor, 2003).
18. M. Satyanarayanan, J. J. Kistler, P. Kumar, M. E. Okasaki, E. H. Siegel and D. C. Steere, Coda: A highly available file system for a distributed workstation environment, in *IEEE Transactions on Computers*, (4) (IEEE CS, 1990).
19. Microsoft, Distributed File System (DFS), http://www.microsoft.com/windowsserver2003/technologies/storage/dfs/.
20. A. Demers, D. Greene, C. Hauser, W. Irish, J. Larson, S. Shenker, H. Sturgis, D. Swinehart and D. Terry, Epidemic algorithms for replicated database maintenance, in *PODC '87: Proc. of the 6th ACM Symp. on Principles of Distributed Computing*, (ACM Press, 1987).
21. A. Sousa, F. Pedone, R. Oliveira and F. Moura, Partial replication in the database state machine, in *Proc. of the IEEE Int. Symp. on Network Computing and Applications (NCA'01)*, (IEEE CS, 2001).
22. N. Budhiraja, K. Marzullo, F. Schneider and S. Toueg, The primary-backup approach, in *Distributed systems*, ed. S. Mullender (ACM Press, Addison-Wesley, 1993) pp. 199–216, 2nd edn.
23. D. Liang, C.-L. Fang, C. Chen and F. Lin, Fault tolerant web service, in *Proc. of the 10th Asia-Pacific Software Engineering Conf.*, (IEEE CS, 2003).
24. K. Birman, T. Joseph, T. Raeuchle and A. E. Abbadi, Implementing fault-tolerant distributed objects, in *IEEE Transactions on Software Engineering*, (6) (IEEE CS, 1985).
25. M. Wiesmann, F. Pedone, A. Schiper, B. Kemme and G. Alonso, Understanding replication in databases and distributed systems, in *Proc. of the 20th Int. Conf. on Distributed Computing Systems*, (IEEE CS, 2000).
26. F. Schneider, Replication management using the state-machine approach, in *Distributed Systems*, ed. S. Mullender (ACM Press, Addison-Wesley, Wokingham, United Kingdom, 1993) pp. 17–26, 2nd edn.
27. J. Salas, F. Perez-Sorrosal, M. Patiño-Martínez and R. Jiménez-Peris, WS-Replication: a framework for highly available web services, in *Proc. 15th Int. Conf. on World Wide Web*, (ACM Press, 2006).
28. D. Gifford, Weighted voting for replicated data, in *SOSP '79: Proc. of the 7th ACM Symp. on Operating Systems Principles*, (ACM Press, 1979).
29. R. Thomas, A majority consensus approach to concurrency control for mul-

tiple copy databases, in *ACM Transactions on Database Systems*, (2) (ACM Press, 1979).
30. R. Jiménez-Peris, M. Patiño-Martínez, G. Alonso and B. Kemme, Are quorums an alternative for data replication?, in *ACM Transactions on Database Systems*, (3) (ACM Press, 2003).
31. J. Osrael, L. Froihofer, M. Gladt and K. Goeschka, Adaptive voting for balancing data integrity with availability, in *On the Move to Meaningful Internet Systems: OTM Confederated Int. Workshops Proc.*, LNCS 4278 (Springer, 2006).
32. D. Terry, M. Theimer, K. Petersen, A. Demers, M. Spreitzer and C. Hauser, Managing update conflicts in Bayou, a weakly connected replicated storage system, in *Proc. 15th ACM Symp. on Operating Systems Principles*, (ACM Press, 1995).
33. C.-L. Fang, D. Liang, C. Chen and P. Lin, A redundant nested invocation suppression mechanism for active replication fault-tolerant web service, in *Proc. of the Int. Conf. on e-Technology, e-Commerce and e-Service*, (IEEE CS, 2004).
34. F. Cristian, Understanding fault-tolerant distributed systems, in *Communications of the ACM*, (2) (ACM Press, 1991).
35. M. Merideth, A. Iyengar, T. Mikalsen, S. Tai, I. Rouvellou and P. Narasimhan, Thema: Byzantine-fault-tolerant middleware for web-service applications, in *Proc. 24th Symp. on Reliable Distributed Systems*, (IEEE CS, 2005).
36. X. Ye and Y. Shen, A middleware for replicated web services, in *Proc. of the 3rd Int. Conf. on Web Services*, (IEEE CS, 2005).
37. G. Chockler, I. Keidar and R. Vitenberg, Group communication specifications: a comprehensive study, in *ACM Computing Surveys*, (4) (ACM Press, 2001).
38. O. Babaoglu, A. Bartoli, V. Maverick, S. Patarin, J. Vuckovic and H. Wu, A framework for prototyping J2EE replication algorithms, in *On the Move to Meaningful Internet Systems 2004: CoopIS, DOA, and ODBASE*, LNCS (Springer, 2004).
39. Object Management Group, *Common Object Request Broker Architecture: Core Specification, v3.0.3* 2004.
40. Apache, Axis, http://ws.apache.org/axis/.
41. M. Hayden and K. Birman, *Probabilistic Broadcast*, tech. rep. (Ithaca, NY, USA, 1996).
42. JGroups: A toolkit for reliable multicast communication http://www.jgroups.org.
43. J. Osrael, L. Froihofer and K. Goeschka, What service replication middleware can learn from object replication middleware, in *Proc. of the 1st Workshop on Middleware for Service Oriented Computing in conjunction with the ACM/IFIP/USENIX Middleware Conf. 2006*, (ACM Press, 2006).
44. Jboss, Relational Persistence for Java and .NET, http://www.hibernate.org/.
45. A. Schiper, Group communication: From practice to theory, in *SOFSEM 2006: Theory and Practice of Computer Science*, LNCS 3831 (Springer,

2006).
46. J. S. Y. Amir, C. Danilov, A low latency, loss tolerant architecture and protocol for wide area group communication, in *Proc. of The Int. Conf. on Dependable Systems and Networks*, (IEEE CS, 2000).
47. P. Felber, X. Défago, R. Guerraoui and P. Oser, Failure detectors as first class objects., in *Proc. Int. Symp. on Distributed Objects and Applications*, (IEEE CS, 1999).
48. W. Vogels and C. Re, Ws-membership - failure management in a web-services world., in *Proc. 12th Int. World Wide Web Conf. (Alternate Paper Tracks)*, 2003. http://www2003.org/cdrom/papers/alternate/P712/p712-vogels.html.
49. Apache, Axis2, http://ws.apache.org/axis2/.
50. S. Perera, C. Herath, J. Ekanayake, E. Chinthaka, A. Ranabahu, D. Jayasinghe, S. Weerawarana and G. Daniels, Axis2, middleware for next generation web services, in *Proc. Int. Conf. on Web Services (ICWS'06)*, (IEEE CS, 2006).
51. Microsoft, Windows Communication Foundation (WCF), http://msdn2.microsoft.com/en-us/netframework/aa663324.aspx.
52. Microsoft, .NET Framework 3.0, http://msdn2.microsoft.com/en-us/netframework/.
53. J. Osrael, L. Froihofer, K. Goeschka, S. Beyer, P. Galdámez and F. Muñoz, A system architecture for enhanced availability of tightly coupled distributed systems, in *Proc. of 1st Int. Conf. on Availability, Reliability, and Security*, (IEEE CS, 2006).
54. Arjuna, Fujitsu, IONA, Oracle and Sun Microsystems, Web services composite application framework ws-caf ver 1.0 (2003), http://developers.sun.com/techtopics/ webservices/wscaf/primer.pdf.
55. L. Moser, P. Melliar-Smith and W. Zhao, Making Web services dependable, in *Proc. of the 1st Int. Conf. on Availability, Reliability, and Security*, (IEEE CS, 2006).
56. K. Birman, Can web services scale up?, in *IEEE Computer*, (10) (IEEE CS, 2005).
57. L. Lamport, The part-time parliament, in *ACM Transactions on Computer Systems*, (2) (ACM Press, 1998).
58. R. Guerraoui and A. Schiper, Software-based replication for fault tolerance, in *IEEE Computer*, (4) (IEEE CS, 1997).
59. A. Gorbenko, V. Kharchenko, P. Popov and A. Romanovsky, Dependable composite web services with components upgraded online, in *Architecting Dependable Systems III*, , LNCS Vol. 3549 (Springer, 2005).
60. F. Tartanoglu, V. Issarny, A. B. Romanovsky and N. Lévy, Dependability in the web services architecture, in *Architecting Dependable Systems*, LNCS 2677 (Springer, 2003).
61. Y. Saito and M. Shapiro, Optimistic replication, in *ACM Computing Surveys*, (1) (ACM Press, 2005).

PART B

Verification and Validation of Fault Tolerant Systems

EMBEDDED SOFTWARE VALIDATION USING ON-CHIP DEBUGGING MECHANISMS

JUAN PARDO, JOSÉ C. CAMPELO, JUAN C. RUIZ, PEDRO GIL
Fault-Tolerant Systems Group (GSTF). Polytechnic University of Valencia. Camino de Vera, s/n, E-6022 Valencia, Spain. Phone:+34963877577, Fax:+34963877579

Everyday thanks to technological advances software of embedded systems is more complex and its increasing utilization for critical applications, makes necessary the development and later validation of fault tolerant embedded systems. Moreover, the increasing utilization of commercial off-the-shelf (COTS) components to develop such systems increases the necessity of verifying the behavior properties exhibited by each system component in presence of faults. To face this challenge, verification and validation techniques becomes essential to evaluate the fault tolerant properties of such embedded systems. But in order to obtain representative results of fault tolerance, the verification and validation processes have to be non-intrusive, mainly when evaluating fault tolerant real-time systems. Using the on-chip debugging capabilities available in most modern embedded systems it is possible to perform fault injection experiments in a non-intrusive manner and observe the system behavior in front of such faults. This paper argues how to use such on-chip debugging (OCD) facilities for verification and validation of fault tolerant real-time embedded systems constructed from COTS components integration.

1. Introduction

In the field of embedded systems, semiconductors technology has had a vertiginous advance having increased the integration of peripherals and memories of different technologies and big capacities in microcontrollers. The example are the Systems-on-a-chip (SoCs) or chip-embedded computers. As everyday they become more complex, SoCs are able to assume further complex control tasks since they can run more sophisticated fault tolerant software. Transportation and telecommunications are some of the critical areas where SoC-based solutions are gaining importance.

That increasing complexity of the embedded software together with the need of reducing time-to-market costs lead manufacturers to consider the (re-) use of software components that collaborate to deliver the final system service. These components are typically designed and constructed separately. But the heterogeneity of such software components motivates the need of verifying their behavior in the system in absence, but also in presence, of faults. It is important to verify, if they are able to play their roles despite the occurrence of faults. For such validation software components have to be evaluated in front of external faults in its interfaces to see how they robust are. In case of using commercial off-the-self (COTS) components, the problem increases due to these ones have serious certification problems because their design and development process is usually unknown. Moreover, they are constructed for general purposes and systems, and they usually have poor dependability specifications. This is mainly why the research of solutions to verify and validate the fault tolerance properties of software components in real-time embedded systems is becoming a priority in the embedded domain [18].

Fault injection techniques are basic bricks for fault tolerance evaluation. Basically, these techniques establish processes to emulate faults in computer systems and monitor the resulting behavior [11]. Such techniques have approached the problem from either hardware or software perspectives. From a hardware perspective [3], faults of interest are typically those affecting memory cells, which are mainly emulated using the bit-flip fault model, where bits are randomly changed. From a software perspective [12], considered faults are those induced in a system component by its execution environment. These second type of faults are typically emulated by corrupting information targeted components receive through their interfaces.

These faults can be assimilated to software residual defects that have not been detected during previous testing phases [11]. It is well-known that increasing the presence of COTS components in embedded systems augments the likelihood of existence of these faults. Due to interactions among components, consequences of residual fault activations may propagate (in form of errors) to other system components. This is why robustness verification to external faults is so important in today's embedded components. However, the strong degree of encapsulation imposed by SoC packages makes emulation of any type of fault a real challenge. This is a known problem that some authors [15][4] have already tried to solve using On-Chip Debugging (OCD) mechanisms. This suggestion is interesting since currently, most SoCs embed such type of mechanisms.

Using OCD mechanisms it is feasible, as it is demonstrated in [17], to perform fault injection of hardware and software faults in SoC-based systems for validation and verification of their fault tolerance properties. It is possible to carry out non-intrusive fault injection experiments in order to see the system reaction in front of errors. Next, it is proposed a methodology for such evaluation having these main properties:

- Portability: Only standard OCD features are considered;
- Non-intrusiveness: Both fault emulation and monitoring processes do not require target system modifications. Temporal overhead is also minimized, which is essential to support the verification and validation of real-time components;
- The solution allows faults to be injected under real-life operational conditions, i.e. without using models to simulate neither the execution environment of the target system nor the physical process under control (if any). This is important for (i) SoCs running software devoted to the control of physical processes whose complexity prevents the definition of detailed and precise models, and (ii) embedded systems with safety-critical constraints where validation under real operational conditions is most of time mandatory for certification;
- The approach applies on any software component embedded in a SoC and this despite the unavailability of its source code.

But not only it is important the considered faults and fault injection process, also the monitoring constitutes a basic step in the definition of any valid fault injection technique. Formally speaking, monitoring can be defined as the process of extracting and gathering information regarding the behaviour of a particular system. In the absence of faults, system activity is typically monitored with the purpose of defining golden runs, i.e. traces of the system normal activity. During fault injection experiments, such activity is perturbed in order to observe how the target system reacts in presence of the injected faults. In this second case, traces obtained from the monitoring of the system activity can be exploited to detect potential deviations from golden runs (or fault-free executions). It must be noted that any interference between the real-time activity of embedded system components and the monitoring process may distort conclusions derived from the analysis of observations. This is why it is so important to minimize system temporal and spatial intrusion when characterizing the behaviour of an embedded system in the absence, but also in the presence, of faults.

This paper extends the work presented in [14][17] to target the problem of verifying and validating fault tolerant properties through robustness tests of SoC-embedded components from a software perspective. Basic questions addressed are how to emulate external residual faults, and how to study component robustness to such type of faults, and how to monitor (measure, collect and analyze) the effects of such faults on the normal activity deployed by system components on embedded systems.

2. Research Context

As stated in [2], the main problem in today's SoC dependability evaluation is that the most existing work only considers the third letter of the acronym; that is, they consider SoCs only from a chip viewpoint. However, the increasing complexity within SoCs motivates the need of solutions to study the problem from a software perspective. From an abstract viewpoint, SoC applications can be defined as an aggregation of components that interact among them through a set of well-established interfaces.

Each interface defines (i) the type of service offered by a component to the system, (ii) the type of input information required to carry out the service; and (iii) the type of output information finally returned. In practice, monitoring and manipulation of components execution is very hard due to strong encapsulation imposed by SoC packages. OCD mechanisms enable to overcome these problems by providing a vision of the system structure and execution defined in terms of (i) SoC internal memory locations and (ii) system control and data flows.

2.1. *Related Work*

Diverse efforts in the domain have already explored the idea of exploiting OCD mechanisms with fault injection purposes. Most of them have adopted a low (chip) level point of view, which consists in exploiting test facilities currently available in many integrated circuits, like those specified in standards like JTAG (IEEE 149.1 [7]), in order to trigger and carry out the fault injection process. These test facilities implements scan-chains that can be used in order to inspect the internal state of a SoC. First, the SoC is programmed through the debug scan-chain to halt its execution when a specific program memory address is reached. The fault is then injected by shifting out the scan-chain, changing one or several bits and shifting the modified chain back. Since the access to the scan-chains is made through a serial interface, the time required for fault injection may be non-negligible. In addition, target system must be halted. The main benefit of such approach is that it enables faults to be injected in internal registers that are not accessible via software. Interested readers can find in [10], a fascinating discussion about the pros and cons of using boundary scan for fault injection.

More related to our vision of the problem, we find fault injection techniques based on the BDM (Background Debug Mode) port. This port defines a proprietary on-chip debugging solution that can be found on microprocessors from Freescale. When the debug mode is enabled, and external host can access memory and I/O devices through a serial interface. BDM is evaluated for fault injection purposes in [16]. The paper concludes that although BDM-fault injection techniques are able to inject faults in both memory and internal (non-memory mapped) registers, introduces an important slow-down in the system. The main benefit of the approach is the portability of fault injection controller, which is a platform-independent software running on an external host. Despite this, the portability of the approach itself remains questionable, since it is based on a set of OCD proprietary mechanisms. Therefore, most of existing fault injection techniques mainly lacks of two things: portability and solutions for minimizing temporal overhead in the target system during fault injection and monitoring. To cope with the aforementioned limitations, another fault injection technique was proposed in [15].

The technique was based on the OCD IEEE-ISTO processor independent standard called Nexus [13]. It showed that (i) Nexus-based fault injection can be performed on-the-fly, i.e. without stopping the execution of the target SoC, (ii) the approach enables solutions to be portable, since applicable to any SoC supporting the Nexus standard, and (iii) no modification is required in the target system for carrying out fault injection. The type of injected faults was hardware faults and fault injection was carried out in SoC internal memory positions. The research report available at [4] also focused on how to inject hardware faults in SoC registers using OCD interfaces. The drawback of the approach relied on the fact that the target system needs to be stopped during experimentation. It must be noted that this requirement is admissible in evaluation contexts where SoCs are studied using model-based execution environments. However, it is not recommended when SoCs must be checked under real-life conditions. To the best of our knowledge, OCD mechanisms have never been exploited with the purpose of injecting software (residual) faults in SoC components. The main challenge in this work is to marry the low-level (hardware-oriented) vision that OCD mechanisms provide with the high-level (software-oriented) vision that the consideration of software components require.

2.2. *Nexus Interface*

The Nexus 5001™ Forum, a program of the IEEE-ISTO, is an industry group chartered to define and implement a global, open microcontroller development interface standard for all embedded controller applications [13]. Many of the Nexus 5001 Forum members are embedded processor manufacturers and tool vendors. The founding members include representatives from ETAS, Hewlett-Packard, Hitachi Semiconductor, Infineon, and Motorola.

One of the aims of the Nexus consortium is the specification of an open industry standard that provides a general-purpose interface. This interface enables the development of debugging tools that runs on any system providing a Nexus-compliant port. As a result, any tool or technique that follows the Nexus specification will benefit from this portability. But despite its original purposes for the software development and debugging of embedded processors, this paper defends that the Nexus interface is also of great interest for verifying and validating, through fault injection, the dependability of SoC applications.

As stated before, most software fault injection techniques introduce an overhead that may alter the temporal behaviour of the system under study. This overhead typically results from (i) the selection of the moment in which faults must be injected (fault injection trigger); and (ii) the corruption of the selected system memory locations (fault injection). This computation results in a certain overhead that may be non-negligible from the viewpoint of the system application, especially when this application needs to meet with some real-time execution constraints. In order to solve the above issues Nexus enables the definition of two types of application events interesting for our research: (i) the execution of a given code instruction, and (ii) the access to a predetermined data memory word.

Thus, in order to obtain this data and among the different characteristics of this standard, two important interface features for our purposes are the watchpoints, which can be used in order to signal application events without halting the execution. These watchpoints are part of the Nexus debug circuitry. And on the other hand, the on-the-fly run-time memory access capabilities, which make possible to observe/substitute memory contents on real-time without producing any interference with the system normal activity. This enables to inject faults in memory before its contents is used by the application. According to the Nexus standard, the use of these two main features must not induce any temporal overhead in the considered target system.

Moreover, the observation capabilities offered by Nexus interface make possible to build traces of the real-time execution of the target application. For instance, Branch Trace Messaging is useful in order to produce (at run-time) a graph of the application control flow. Thus, Nexus data tracing provides the possibility of monitoring read and write memory accesses to the application data. The combined use of the above tracing features with watchpoints enables to know when a (dormant) fault in memory becomes an error. The idea consists in using watchpoints in order to detect when the execution flow of the target application access a (code or data) memory word containing a fault. This event signals the activation of the fault (i.e. an error appears in the system). Other events that can be traced using this approach are the detection of an error through the activation of an exception and the end of the error recovery process.

Therefore, using the sole management capabilities offered by Nexus our fault injection approach does not depend on any particular feature supplied by the considered target system. On the other hand, its specification only relies on features defined in the core of the Nexus standard. Next, it is shown how to profit such Nexus capabilities in order to verify and validate software on embedded systems.

2.3. *Software Residual Faults and SoCs*

Software residual faults are defects in components that have not been detected during previous testing or evaluation phases. For the emulation of the occurrence of such faults in a particular SoC-embedded component, it is considered that each component has a public interface that centralizes the reception of all incoming invocations. This interface is thus the conduct through which fault manifestations (errors) may propagate from one component to another. This error propagation can be emulated by corrupting values of invocation parameters the component sends to others. But the problem is that in practice, it must be noted that parameter value corruption is synonym of SoC internal registers modification. In order to understand that point, we need to know that, due to performance considerations, most compilers use SoC registers in order to carry out parameter exchange during function invocations. This choice enables optimizations to be applied on binary code to speed-up the execution of the system. Unhopefully, it also makes very complex the definition of a non-intrusive process for parameter corruption. According to the state of the art, corruption of the contents of SoC registers is conventionally approached by stopping the execution of the target system. And this type of solution violates the requirement of non-temporal intrusiveness.

On the other hand, robustness to external faults can be defined as the capacity of a system to operate correctly in presence of exceptional inputs or stressful environmental conditions. When applied to a system component, robustness evaluation must be understood as a way to obtain indications on the component capacity to resist/react to the manifestation of faults [3]. It is worth mentioning that robustness evaluation claims for target components to be considered as black boxes. Accordingly, it is considered a component model in which, as stated before, each component has a public interface that centralizes the reception of all external information, and it is the conduct through which components interact with their environment. Component interfaces are populated with functions containing a set of input/output parameters. And as it was mentioned before, due to performance considerations, most compilers use internal registers to carry out parameter exchange during function invocations. Unfortunately, it also makes the definition of a non-intrusive process for monitoring the values of these parameters very complex. Instead of monitoring the value of functions parameters when they are stored in the system internal registers, it is proposed a solution based on accessing input parameter values before they are loaded into registers. Memory locations for input and output parameters can be determined following the next inspection procedure [17].

3. OCD-based Software Fault Emulation

In this section, it is explained how register corruption can be performed in a non-intrusive way and how the behavior of the targeted component can be monitored after such corruption. The proposed approach executes in five successive steps:

1. Determine where faults can be injected. This step establishes the mapping among the logical view of components and their memory footprint. This mapping requires four tasks to be accomplished:

a. Select one component for experimentation. Name that component the *target component*;
b. Locate the memory addresses where functions of the target component interface are allocated. Call such addresses *callee addresses*;
c. Determine where other system components invoke functions in the callee addresses. Call such invocation locations *caller addresses*.
d. Fix your attention in memory addresses preceding each caller address. These addresses are those coding storage of parameter values in registers, i.e. they implement parameter exchange among caller and callee components. So, values handled at these addresses are those susceptible of corruption. Let us name these memory locations as *potential target addresses*;

2. Choose a fault location and emulate the fault:
a. Among all potential target addresses, select one and call it the *target address* of your experiment;
b. Define a system workload, i.e. a stimuli for exercising the system during experimentation. This workload varies from one type of system to another.
c. Launch the execution of the system and define a trigger to launch the fault emulation process;
d. Determine which is the parameter value handled by the target address instruction. Then, modify it using the read/write on-the-fly mechanisms that many OCD interfaces provide today for calibration. These mechanisms enable memory locations content to be modified without disturbing systems execution. In such a way, registers content will be changed using modified values during parameters exchange;

3. Monitor the behavior of the callee component in presence of the emulated fault. Do this adopting a black-box viewpoint, i.e. observe only outputs of the callee component. Call the resulting observations *the trace of the system in presence of faults*;

4. Golden run execution: Re-execute steps 1, 2.2, 2.3, 2.4 and 3. Do not inject any fault in the system, only observe how system behaves. Name resulting observations the *fault-free trace*;

5. Compare the set of observations stored in the fault-free trace with those obtained in presence of faults. Differences between these traces signal misbehaviors resulting from the emulated fault. It is obvious, that this can only be true if we consider equivalent activation conditions in both executions. Next sections detail the work behind each one of the aforementioned steps.

3.1. *Step 1: Determine Where Faults Can Be Injected*

According to section 2, it is considered SoCs applications as aggregations of software components that interact at runtime through their interfaces. This abstract view contrast with the low-level (memory-oriented) vision of that one obtain when observing the activity of those components using the inspection mechanisms provided by SoC-embedded OCD interfaces. What is needed is a method to correlate the abstract view of a component with its memory mapping. This is an essential step to determine where faults can be injected during experimentation.

3.1.1. *Target Components*

The first thing to do is to select a target component and obtain from its specification the definition of its interface. Then, an interface function and a parameter of such function must be chosen. It must be noted that, according the constraints imposed to our approach, components source codes are unavailable. However, it is assumed that the object code file of each individual component exists. Object code files contain the code machine defining the behavior and state of each component. Once the set of components in the system has been selected, they are linked and allocated in the SoC internal memory. As a result a SoC memory map is generated. This map reflects at which memory location component functions are placed.

3.1.2. *Callee Address*

It is trivial to locate target component functions using information supplied by SoC memory maps. The only thing to do at this end is to locate the previously selected component interface function in the memory map of the SoC application under study. This can be done since memory locations in memory map files maintain high-level function names. Function locations are translated to physical memory ones when memory maps are transferred to SoCs. The start physical memory location of a component function constitutes what we name the callee address.

3.1.3. *Caller and Target Addresses*

Once the callee address has been determined, function calls from other components to that address can be located on the SoC memory. Positions containing instructions coding those calls are named caller addresses. In order to cope with the location of caller addresses, memory maps must be analyzed. The goal of this analysis is to find out function calls to the selected callee address. To do that, one must know the pattern his compiler follows to code a function call*. Due to the intrinsic formal nature of compilers, this is the kind of information that is well-established and documented for each compiler and it must be known. In general, the strategy followed by compilers to carry out parameter exchange can be characterized by:

- A set of machine code instructions in which parameter values are copied to SoC registers;
- The caller instruction that jumps to the callee address, i.e. the location of the function call;
- In case of returning values, instructions coding the retrieval of such values.

By identifying this pattern, one can automate the process of obtaining the set of addresses in which parameter values are manipulated. These are the addresses where one must act during fault injection.

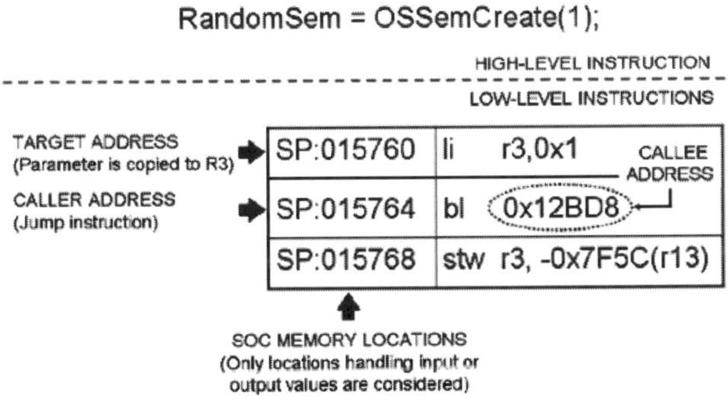

Figure 1. Caller, callee and target addresses

---

* Compilers can rely on global memory, stack or registers for function parameter exchange. Our interest goes to the last of these possibilities, since it is the one where parameters cannot be directly corrupted using OCD on-the-fly memory read/write mechanisms.

As shown in Figure 1, finding out instructions where parameters are loaded into (or stored from) registers when invoking component interface operations involves the analysis of the component object code. For the sake of understanding, both high-level and low-level instructions have been included.

In the example, we can see an application instruction invoking an operating system call. This instruction is coded at memory ranges [0x15760, 0x15768]. Memory position 0x15764 (the caller address) codifies the branch instruction to the operating system call (located at position 0x12BD8, the callee address.). According to the pattern described above, instructions coded in memory locations preceding caller addresses manipulate values of system call parameters and load them in SoC registers. They are our potential target addresses. By corrupting parameters in these instructions, it is possible to study robustness of system components with respect to external faults. In case of returning a value, this value is stored in the memory location following the branch instruction. Name the instruction in this location the *store instruction*. Consequently, monitoring inputs (and outputs) received (and produced) by system components requires the ability of monitoring information in load (and store) instructions preceding (and following) branch instructions in which component functions, a real-time operating system in this example, are invoked.

3.2. *Step 2: Fault Location Choice and Emulation*

Once all potential target addresses have been determined, it is time to choose one of them to inject the fault. This selection can be performed deterministically or following a random approach. For the time being, we only consider this second alternative. Let us name target address the potential target address finally selected for fault injection.

The contents of selected target address must be analyzed with the purpose of fault emulation. Basically, this memory address contains an instruction with three fields: a load instruction code, a register and a function parameter. The distribution, and the number of bytes associated to each one of these fields, depends on the type of SoC architecture considered. Consider that function parameters are coded in the lower bytes of the instruction. If the parameter is a constant, then the value stored in such bytes is the one to corrupt. If the parameter is a variable, then the value stored at the address pointed by such bytes is the one to corrupt. In both cases, parameter values are corrupted before being loaded in registers, in that way we can rely on the use of OCD on-the-fly memory read/write capabilities to perform parameter corruption. These capabilities run in parallel with the rest of the SoC internal circuitry and do not interfere with the nominal execution of the target system.

Parameter corruption is performed in three successive steps. First, target address instruction content is read. Then, value of the parameter handled in that instruction is corrupted. Finally, modified version of the instruction is written back. In order to determine the corruption value two different approaches can be followed. The first one consists in flipping one bit in the binary representation of the value. The second option relies on a selective substitution of the current value with a different (invalid, special or custom) new one. This new value must be selected according to the data type of the considered parameter. It must be noted that studies have demonstrated the equivalence of the errors provoked by these two techniques [9] in the context of general purpose systems. Further work is required to translate such affirmation to our embedded context.

Although interesting from an injection viewpoint, OCD mechanisms provide limited capabilities to synchronize the injection trigger with the target component execution. One can adopt a strategy based on triggering the injection based on execution of a particular memory instruction. However, it is difficult to ensure that such injection will be carried out before another instruction (like the target one) was executed. This issue, which is not relevant when the target system is halted for fault injection, becomes a great challenge when non-intrusion is a requirement. Hence, further research is necessary on that topic. For the time being, we use pure temporal triggers that are initialized with a count value randomly chosen within a specified time interval. Afterwards, the emulation controller (an external host machine) waits for a timeout to happen and then launches the fault emulation process.

3.3. *Step 3: Target Component Value Monitoring*

Monitoring the activity of SoC applications using OCD interfaces is not very difficult. The idea is to exploit the existing trace capabilities to observe what is happening inside the SoC. Observations of interest are target component interface output parameters and return values. The idea is select memory positions where such values are handled and program the OCD interface to follow their evolution. Each time a read or write access is performed on the selected positions; the internal OCD circuitry generates a trace message identifying the type of access and the value used.

Hardware exceptions are also a valuable monitoring source, since they denote conflictive situations derived from inability of components to exhibit a robust behavior in presence of the emulated faults. Since system detection capabilities are not infallible, certain of the emulated faults may propagate to the component execution environment and may lead the system to hang. To detect such situation, our advice is to involve the external experiment controller in the monitoring process. Thanks to its external view of the system, this controller should able to determine whether the SoC reacts to new inputs or not.

3.4. *Step 4: Golden Run Execution*

Every fault injection experiment must be followed by the execution of a golden run. Golden run experiments executes under the same operational conditions than fault injection experiments. The difference is that in golden runs, no faults are emulated. Traces obtained in that case are thus fault-free traces that define the reference for the analysis of the traces obtained in fault injection experiments.

3.5. *Step 5: Result Analysis*

In this step, golden run traces are compared to ones retrieved from fault injection experiments. As Nexus has been initially specified for debugging purposes, its specification proposes a number of observation capabilities that are very useful for observing the effects produced by fault injection in a target system. The idea is to build execution traces of the system that are rich enough in order to deduce both event- and time-oriented measures from their analysis.

The resulting execution traces represent the knowledge that can be obtained through Nexus from the internal activity of an embedded SoC application. Basically, they are the image that must be used in order to analyze the behaviour of the system after a fault injection experiment. It is worth noting that these execution traces should maintain an association between the occurrence of each event and its time. So, for this comparison be feasible and meaningful, it is important to note that equivalent activation conditions must be guaranteed for the target system in both fault-free and fault injection experiments. In addition, these conditions must also ensure a deterministic behavior of the target system. This means, that under equivalent execution conditions (system configuration, workload, state of controlled processes, etc.), the behavior of the system should be the same. Thus, experiments can be repeated. Under those conditions, golden run traces and fault injection ones can be compared.

From a pure event viewpoint, two traces are comparable if events they reflect are the same and have occurred in the same order and same time frame in each experiment. This aspect is important when considering components with real-time constraints. In that case, two different traces are equivalent if they reflect that same events have happened in the same order and these events, when compared one by one, refer to the same system state and reflect the same behavior with respect to deadlines, i.e. none (or both) events violate a deadline. In this way, the monitoring process becomes a crucial step and it is of prime interest to define how to observe the system functioning without producing any intrusion.

Most traditional monitoring solutions are breakpoint-oriented. This means that they stop the system execution at selected points in the source code. However, if the program execution is interrupted, the physical time is stopped and the system is not anymore consistent in the timing domain [5]. This is the main reason why breakpoint-oriented techniques are not the best choice for monitoring the activity of real-time systems. Moreover, they are not recommended when the system is checked under real-life experimental conditions, i.e. when the system behaviour must be certified in a real environment as stated in IEC 61508 standards [6]. But using the On-Chip Debugging (OCD) mechanisms, it is possible to overcome the limitations existing in conventional monitoring approaches [1][17][16]. These OCD interfaces enable developers to debug their applications without stopping the real-time execution, due to any interference produced by a monitoring activity in a real-time system is intolerable and must be consequently avoided [5]. It may invalidate conclusions derived from the analysis of gathered information. In this context the OCD Nexus interface emerge as an interesting standard for non-intrusive monitoring solutions [13]. Next it is explained how to use Nexus interface to validate the system under test in the content and timing domains.

4. A Nexus-based Approach for Monitoring and Time Measurement

In [5] Kopetz defines a real-time system as a computer system in which the correctness of the system behaviour does not only depends on the logical results of the computations, but also on the physical instant of time at which these results are produced. Therefore the retrieval of time measurements is significant for a complete characterization of the real-time capabilities of an embedded application. Thus, this section describes (i) how to monitor, under real-life conditions, the temporal behaviour of real-time systems using the tracing information provided by the Nexus circuitry, and (ii) the type of temporal measures that can be deduced from the measurements provided by such monitoring process. It is focused on the how to compute component error detection latencies and real-time tasks execution times.

4.1. *Nexus Traces*

The proposed technique exploits the observation capabilities of Nexus in order to build traces of the target component execution. Nexus data tracing [13] provides the possibility of monitoring read and write on-the-fly memory accesses, which combined with watchpoints enables to know when a defined event (like the activation of a fault) occurs. These watchpoints are part of the microcontrollers built-in Nexus debug circuitry and they are used in order to signal events without halting the system execution. Basically, Nexus enables the definition of two types of application events that can be used for our purposes: (i) the execution of a given code instruction, and (ii) the access to a predetermined data memory word. This information is essential to detect component function calls and inspect outputs provided by these calls in order to determine whether an error code has been returned. Data obtained from the Nexus trace includes a time footprint for the target component execution flow. The treatment and filtering of such information, makes possible to gather data in order to measure the delay between two different events. This capability is very useful to obtain for example operating system error detection latencies, or the time spent by a task during its execution in a multitasking system.

4.2. *Component Error Detection Latencies*

Component error detection latency times refer to the time passed between errors become activated and component detects such errors. Error detection latencies are computed by subtracting two temporal measures: *t1*, the instant when an injected fault becomes activated, i.e. when the memory address containing the fault is executed; and *t2*, the moment when the component notifies (return code) to its environment an error code. Thus, error detection latencies are equal to *t2-t1*. To obtain *t1* and *t2*, it is necessary to follow four successive steps:

1. Establish an on-chip watchpoint at the code memory address where the fault has been injected – As it has been explained in section 3, this memory address is chosen among those memory addresses preceding a branch instruction to a function call. These addresses contain instructions that load the parameter values into registers. This approach is followed to corrupt the parameter values before they are stored in the system internal registers, thus avoiding the need of stopping the target system.

2. Set this watchpoint as the temporal reference of the monitoring process – The activation of the watchpoint will define an event that will become the temporal reference for successive events. This temporal reference has been previously named t1.

3. Establish a second on-chip watchpoint in the memory address where the error detection routine of the component under study store error codes – This memory address can be obtained, as explained in a previous section 3, by inspecting the memory map file generated by the linker tool (source code is not necessary). Let t2 reflect the activation instant of this second watchpoint.

4. Filter the Nexus trace to take the temporal difference between the activation of previously established watchpoints – The Nexus program execution trace is filtered to obtain the difference between t1 and t2. Next figure illustrates how component error detection latency times are computed and the type of information provided by Nexus traces after filtering.

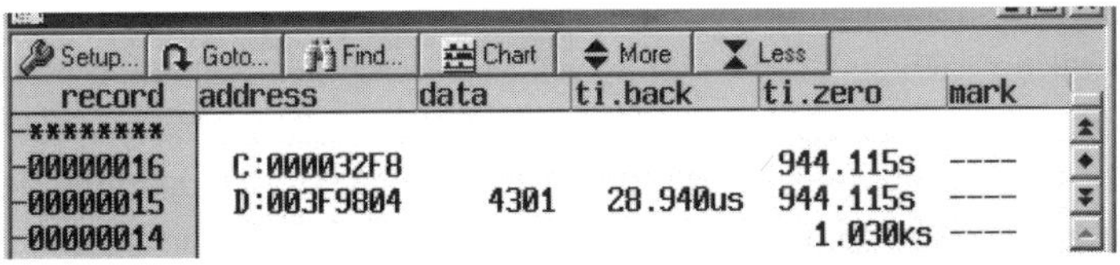

Figure 2. Example of a filtered Nexus trace

As the above figure 2 shows, *t1* is established in the code memory address C:0x32F8. This address stores the instruction where parameters are loaded into registers before performing the component call. By monitoring the execution of this address it is possible to observe whether or not the injected fault becomes activated, then the temporal reference *t1* is defined. Then, another watchpoint (defining *t2*) is placed at memory position D:0x3F9804. That address corresponds to the memory address in which the targeted component returns error codes for the invoked function call. In this case, the error code returned was the 4301 and the relative time between both *t2* and *t1* was of 28,940 μs.

4.3. *Real-Time Tasks Execution Times*

A similar approach could also be applied to obtain the execution times of the system real-time tasks. The idea is to profit the Nexus capabilities to observe the effect of the introduced errors in the system in its execution time, to study the real-time system response although the appearance of errors.

To carry out this analysis, you should follow next four steps:

1. *Put a watchpoint at the task entry point address*
2. *Establish the activation of this watchpoint as a temporal reference (t1)*
3. *Define a second watchpoint at the task output point address (t2)*
4. *Filter the Nexus trace to compute the difference between both watchpoints occurrences (t2-t1)*

But due to the limitation of Nexus implementations (only 2 or 4 on-chip watchpoints) [13], it is not possible to measure all tasks execution times in a single experiment. To be able to measure all tasks execution times, an alternative way can be used. Such way is to obtain the application execution trace to analyze the address memory ranges executed. So, groups of memory addresses could be established for each task to provide to the system the framework for each task to be monitored. Such temporal evaluation offers great possibilities to real-time application designers, who can measure all tasks response times (including those related to recovery tasks) in order to better analyze task scheduling under a considered set of fault-hypothesis.

5. Case Study

To show the feasibility of the methodology proposed, our approach has been used to study the behaviour exhibited by a real-time operating system (RTOS) component in presence of residual design faults in control components running on top of it. The main objective is to demonstrate the capacities of the technique to verify and validate embedded (fault or non-fault tolerant) software using OCD mechanisms.

A MPC565 microcontroller from Freescale is the core of the experimental setup. This 32-bit PowerPC RISC microcontroller works at 40MHz and it implements an OCD class-3 Nexus interface. A PC manages this interface using a commercial in-circuit Nexus debugger distributed by Lauterbach GmbH. The in-circuit Nexus debugger used provides 96 trace channels running at up to 200MHz with a 16MFrames trace depth. Each trace has a 32bit time stamp and a resolution of 20ns. The targeted system is composed by a real-time operating system and a set of application tasks devoted to the control of traffic lights. Next figure 3 shows the evaluation board and the Lauterbach Nexus in-circuit debugger.

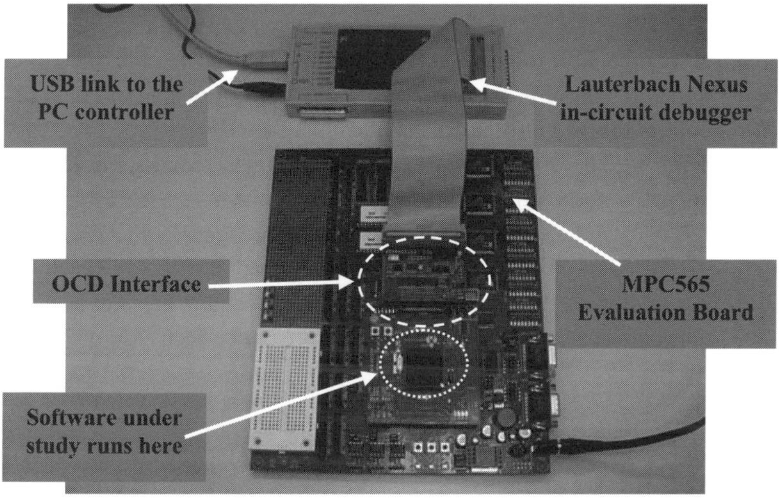

Figure 3. MPC565 evaluation board and Lauterbach debugger

The studied RTOS is an implementation of the OSEK/VDX specification called 'osCAN' [8]. OSEK/VDX is a joint project of the automotive industry. It aims at an industry standard for an open-ended architecture for distributed control units in vehicles. The specification of the OSEK operating system is to represent a uniform environment which supports efficient utilisation of resources for automotive control unit application software. The OSEK operating system is a single processor operating system meant for distributed embedded control units. Automotive applications are characterised by stringent real-time requirements. Therefore the OSEK operating system offers the necessary functionality to support event driven control systems.

The software running on top of the considered OSEK RTOS is a traffic lights control application that controls the traffic on an intersection of two streets. There are four traffic lights and one control unit for all them. Each traffic light has a sensor (4 sensor tasks) which monitors the incoming traffic and sends the information to a control task which manages the traffic lights [8]. Next, it is described in detail each task which have been implemented at the control application.

The system has the following real-time tasks:

1. *Traffic_In*: Simulation of the incoming traffic on each street.
2. *Sensors*: Each traffic light has a sensor which monitors the incoming and outgoing traffic on each street. If more than ‘n’ cars are waiting at a traffic light or at least one car is waiting longer than the time ‘T’ the control unit (Control task) shall be notified.
3. *Control*: The control unit services all streets round-robin. If for one street no notification from the sensor has been received it is skipped. Changes in the setting of the traffic lights are signalled to *Traffic_Out*.
4. *Traffic_Out*: Simulation of the outgoing traffic on each street. Depending on the traffic light setting departures are signalled to the appropriate sensor. Equidistant departures have been assumed

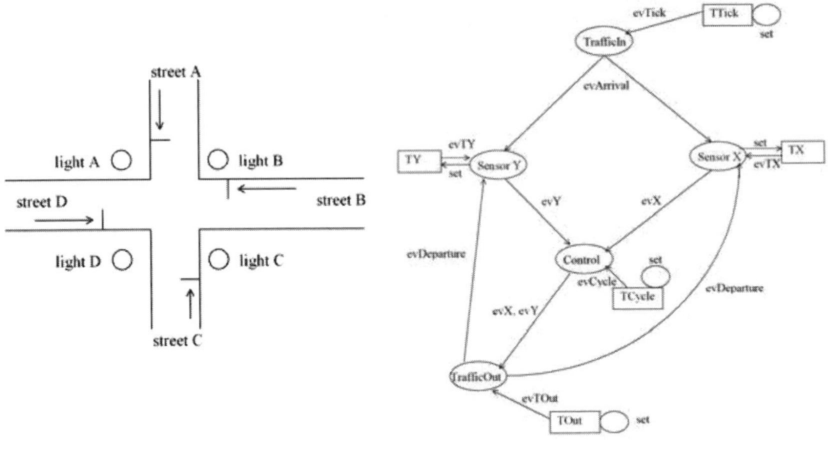

Figure 4. Control application topology and states diagram for sensors and streets

At left in figure 4 it is possible to see the topology of the control application implemented with the sensors and traffic-lights. And on the right side, it is show the diagram of states for the sensors and streets. Note that for the sake of clearness, the states diagram you can find in the above figure, only applies to two streets and therefore only considers input from two sensors. Four streets can be easily obtained by duplicating the sensors and their associated events and alarms.

5.1. *Experiments*

First, fault-free experiments (golden runs) were carried out in order to measure tasks response times and trace application outputs in absence of faults. Then, fault injection experiments were performed in order to study and characterise the system behaviour in the presence of faults in the content and timing domains. Injected faults were based on operating system call parameter corruption. And the fault injection process was performed under the following experimental conditions: (i) All OSEK RTOS system calls were selected as possible targets for the fault injection experiments. However, at each experiment only one parameter of one of these possible targets was selected for fault injection; (ii) the bit-flip technique described in [17] was used for parameter corruption. The bit of the parameter value that was modified in each experiment was randomly selected.

The purpose was to measure not only the ability of the operating system to detect the emulated errors but also to study to what extent the operating system is permeable to them. The capacity of the operating system to content error propagation is reflected on the impact of error on the real-time task running on top of it. This is why it is also collected information for measuring the impact of faults injected in the operating system onto execution times of application tasks.

5.2. *Experimental Results*

Parameter corruption at the operating system (OS) interface level has led us to observe the following different situations: i) the corrupted parameter does not affect the computation and the results are correct in content and timing domain; ii) the corrupted parameter lead the OS to generate an error code; iii) the corrupted parameter does not generate an OS error code, but it corrupts its internal state, leading the system to fail in either the content or the timing domain, iv) the corrupted parameter activates the underlying hardware error detection mechanisms and v) the system may hang without providing any answer.

From the 1792 fault injection experiments that were conducted, 443 errors were detected by the OS and reported with the appropriate error code, 477 errors generated content failures, 57 were detected by the hardware detection mechanisms of the considered microcontroller, 82 generated hang failures, and 733 experiments do not affect the system computation in the content domain. Next figure 5 shows the results obtained after the fault injection experiments.

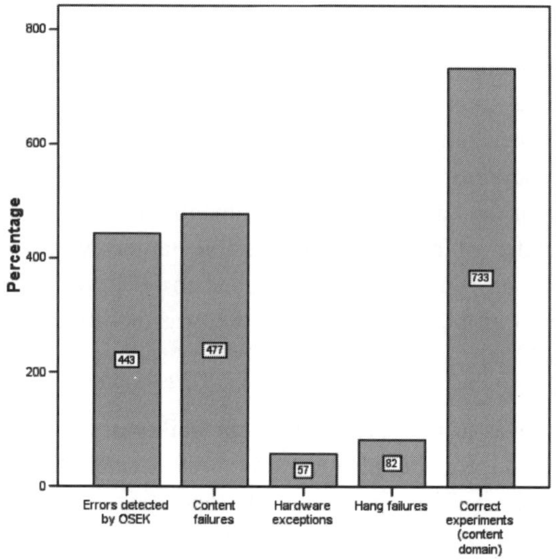

Figure 5. Control application topology and states diagram for sensors and streets

Next section focuses on OS error detection latency times related to the 443 experiments where an error code was returned by the OS. Later, the 733 experiments that do not affect the system computation in the content domain will be studied from a temporal perspective.

5.3. *OS Error Detection Latency Time*

The OSEK operating system provides system specific hook routines to allow user-defined actions within the OS internal processing. An error service is provided to handle temporarily and permanently occurring errors within the operating system. Its basic framework is predefined and shall be completed by the user. This gives the user a choice of efficient centralised or decentralised error handling. Two different kinds of errors are distinguished: (i) *Application errors* when the OS system could not execute the requested service correctly, but assumes the correctness of its internal data. In this case, centralised error treatment is called. Additionally the operating system returns the error by the status information for decentralised error treatment. It is up to the user to decide what to do depending on which error has occurred. (ii) *Fatal errors* when the OS can no longer assume correctness of its internal data. In this case the operating system calls the centralised system shutdown. All those error services are assigned with a parameter that specifies the error [8].

Next table 1 shows the generation frequency of the error codes obtained after the experiments and their meaning in relation to the OS services. As table 1 shows, the most typical error codes were related to the control events system services (nearly 60%). Around 44% of the produced error codes were related to alarms and synchronization events and only a 3,5% due to overflow problems.

Table 1. Description of the generated error codes

Error Code	Related to	Generation Frequency
0x4101	Control events	198 out of 443 (45 %)
0x4301	Control events	37 out of 443 (8,4 %)
0x5301	Alarms & synchroniz.	78 out of 443 (17,7 %)
0x5302	Alarms & synchroniz.	26 out of 443 (6 %)
0x5501	Alarms & synchroniz.	88 out of 443 (20 %)
0x6101	Overflow problem	16 out of 443 (3,5 %)

Table 2. OSEK RTOS error detection latencies

Error Code	Minimum	Maximum	Mean value	Standard deviation
0x4101	28,24us	28,26us	28,25us	0,01
0x4301	28,58us	40,66us	32,57us	5,6
0x5301	30,10us	30,10us	30,10us	0
0x5302	40,34us	63,94us	44,81us	9,1
0x5501	27,78us	27,82us	27,8us	0
0x6101	286us	310,393ms	82,859ms	100869,9

Table 2 shows the minimum, maximum and mean values about OS error detection latencies, i.e. the time required by OSEK to notify the error to the real-time tasks running on top of it. From the table 2, it is possible to see that error code detection and subsequent error notification had a temporal cost that vary, except in the case of overflow errors, from 27,82us (minimum latency) to 63,94us (maximum latency). About the overflow errors, these ones go from 286us to 310,4ms with a mean value around 83ms.

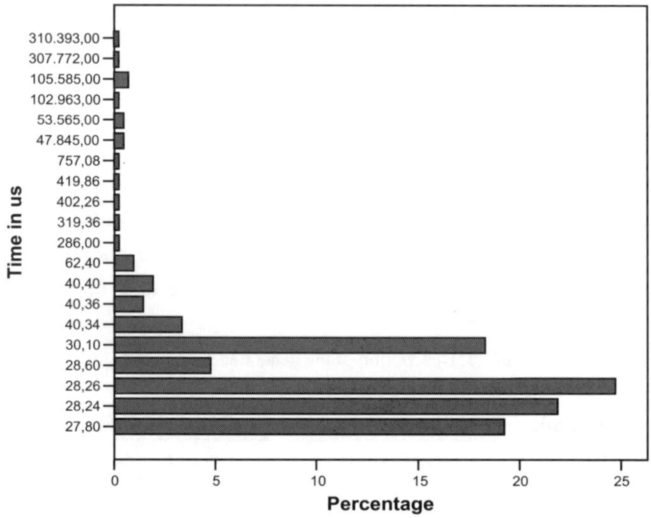

Figure 6. Percentage of detected errors with their detection latency

At the above figure 6, it is possible to see the distribution of the latencies. The figure shows that more than 85% of the errors were detected in less than 40us. On the other hand, around 3,5% of the errors were detected before 286us. These results can be very interesting for real-time systems designers since let them estimate the temporal delay exhibited by the error detection and notification mechanisms integrated in a particular RTOS. Thus, decisions can be taken in consequence regarding the pertinence of a particular RTOS for a given real-time application.

5.4. *Real-Time Tasks Execution Times*

Sometimes experiments leading to correct content values are labelled as correct results without taking into account the timing domain. In this section, it is explained how the system behaves in presence of errors affecting only its temporal behaviour, and more particularly for the case study, the execution time of the considered traffic light control tasks. As stated in a previous section, 733 from the 1792 experiments performed were content valid experiments. Now it is studied how many of them have lead to an early, on-time or late service and in which cases early and late service is synonym of timing failure.

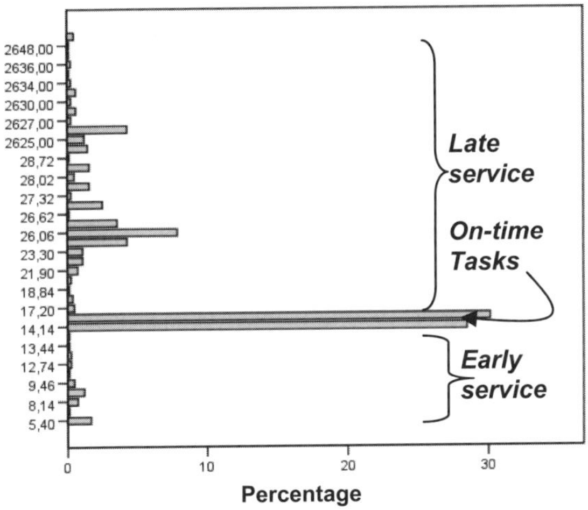

Figure 7. Percentage of *Control* task providing an early, on-time (14,14μs) and late service

Take the example of the *Control* task, which receives from the sensors at the traffic lights the incoming/outgoing traffic and sends the different notifications to the *Traffic_Out* task, in charge of changing corresponding traffic lights. Figure 7 shows the percentage of executions of such *Control* task that lead to an early, on-time and late service. It must be noted that in absence of faults the mean of the maximum execution times computed for this task was of 14,14us. As Figure 7 reflects only 30% of the experiments which are correct in the content domain, they are also correct in the timing domain. The rest of the experiments, although produced correct output values, manifested timing (early of late) variations.

Table 3. Mean of max. tasks execution time

Errors	**SensorA**	**SensorB**	**SensorC**	**SensorD**
Without	5,61us	5,61us	5,61 us	5,61 us
With	238,7 us	151,67 us	94,05 us	54,07 us
	Control	**Traffic_In**	**Traffic_Out**	
Without	14,14 us	2633,4 us	874,01 us	
With	341,06 us	2367,8 us	933,84 us	

Other interesting results can be obtained with the presented methodology. For example, worst case execution times, means of the maximum times or percentage of worst-case execution times can be easily obtained to better understand the behavior of a real-time application under faults with the purpose of verification and validation. Table 3, for example, shows means of the maximum execution times of each considered real-time task in absence but also in presence of errors. With these data a real-time designer can study their application and detect, as in this case, accumulative delays between tasks blocked waiting a signal. Other times, tasks can exhibit an early timing failure as for example in this case Traffic_In, which has been caused for an event signalled with a wrong identifier, which unlocks this task before expected.

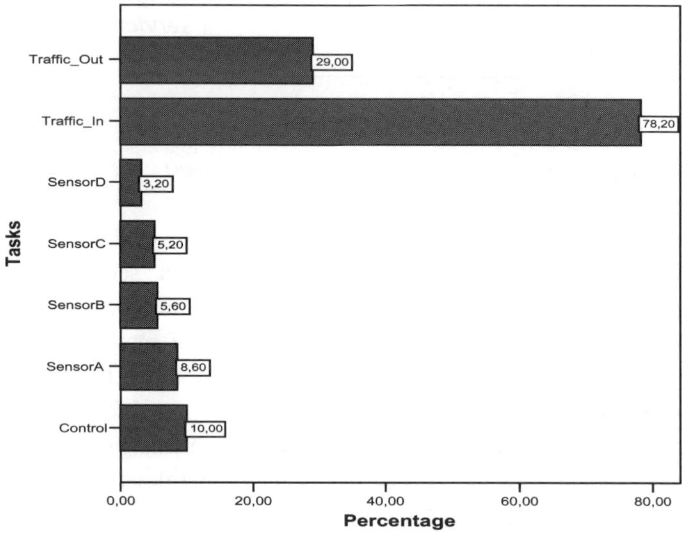

Figure 8. Percentage of worst-case execution time under errors

Figure 8 shows the percentage of times that each task arrives to its worst-case execution time. As it can be seen, the Traffic_In task a 78.20% of the times the task is in its worst-case execution time, this means that this task is the most prone to produce timing failures. The rest of the tasks are in their worst-case execution time in less than 30% of the cases.

6. Conclusions

This paper defines a step forward in the use of OCD features for fault injection. Until now, all the efforts on that topic were concentrated on the injection of hardware faults in SoC internal elements (memory and registers). However, the increasing complexity of the software integrated in such systems claims for new injection solutions enabling SoC validation to be studied from a software perspective. In this research, it is studied to what extend on-chip debugging (ODC) mechanisms are suitable to emulate residual software faults in SoC-embedded software components. A new emulation methodology for verification and validation of embedded systems, mainly for those systems where fault tolerant properties are mandatory, has been presented. To fulfill this objective, the approach has faced the challenge of marrying the low-level (hardware-oriented) vision that OCD mechanisms offer with the high-level (software-oriented) vision required by components and residual design faults. The result is an approach in which propagation of errors from one system component to another is performed by interface parameter corruption.

On the other hand, it is explained how to exploit, after the fault injection, the OCD capabilities provided by Nexus-based systems to analyze the temporal behavior of real-time embedded applications under faulty conditions in a non-intrusive manner. Data about error detection latencies and tasks execution times can be obtained by means of the Nexus on-the-fly memory read/write capabilities. This aspect seems crucial for a future exploitation of the approach in some certification context where real-time systems must be evaluated in real-life conditions, i.e. without stopping the system execution. Moreover, the temporal information provided by the presented methodology can enrich the vision that real-time system designers have on their systems. We claim that these temporal measures will be of great interest to schedule real-time applications taking into account the temporal delays induced by errors.

The solution is portable (since OCD requirements meet capabilities provided by nowadays OCD standards, like those defined by the Nexus consortium), non-intrusive (since the target system must neither be modified nor stopped during experimentation) and it does not require the source code of the (off-the-shelf) software component under study.

The feasibility of such methodology has been illustrated by evaluating a real-time operating system component in presence of residual faults in control components running on top. Preliminary results are promising and show the solution usefulness. They also lead us to note that, according to the current formulation of our technique, the degree of observation and control over targets is not as fine as the one attained by more conventional “stop-oriented” approaches. This is why we claim that ODC-based fault emulation must not be considered as replacement, but rather as a complement, to existing solutions supporting evaluation and testing of real-time embedded software.

References

1. Barbosa, R., et al. “*Assembly-Level Pre-Injection analysis for improving fault injection efficiency*”. LNCS 3463. Fifth European Dependable Computing Conference (EDCC-5). Hungary, April 2005.
2. B. Dervisoglu “*Design for Testability: It is Time to Deliver it for Time-To-Market*”, IEEE. Test Conference, pp. 1102-1111, USA, 1999.
3. “*DBench Dependability Benchmarks*”. Deliverables and final report of the DBench Project, IST 2000-25425.
4. D. Skarin, et al. "*Implementation and Usage of the GOOFI MPC565 Nexus Fault Injection Plug-in*," Tech. Report No. 04-08, Chalmers University. Sweden, 2004.
5. Idriz Smaili. “*Monitoring and Debugging of Real-Time Systems: A Survey*”. Research Report 17/2004, T.U. Wien.
6. International Electrotechnical Commission. “*Functional safety of electrical/electronic/programmable electronic safety-related systems*”. IEC standard 61508.
7. IEEE-1149.1-2001, IEEE Standard Test Access Port and Boundary Scan Architecture.
8. Janz W., Stehle J. “*OSEK real-time operating system. osCAN User manual*”. Vector Technische Informatik.
9. K. Kanoun et al. "*DBench: Dependability Benchmarking*", Chapter 4 of the DBench IST-2000-25425 final project report, available at http://www.laas.fr/dbench/Final.
10. L. Santos and M. Rela. “*Constraints on the Use of Boundary-Scan for Fault Injection*”, 1st Latin-American Symp. on Dependable Computing, pp. 33-55. Brasil, 2003.
11. Madeira, H. et al. “*Emulation of Software Faults: Representativeness and Usefulness*”.1st Latin-American Symp. on Dependable Computing, pp. 23-38. Brasil, 2003.
12. Madeira, H. et al. “*On the Emulation of Software Faults by Software Fault Injection*”. IEEE Int. Conf. on Dep. Systems and Networks, pp. 417-426. NY, USA, June 2000.

13. Nexus 5001 Forum™ Standard for a Global Embedded Processor Debug Interface. IEEE-ISTO 5001-1999.
14. Pardo, J, Campelo, JC., Ruiz, JC. Gil, P. "*Temporal Characterization of Embedded Systems Using Nexus*". Sixth European Dependable Computing Conference (EDCC-6), pp. 47-52. Portugal, 2006.
15. P. Yuste et al. "*Non-intrusive Software Implemented Fault Injection in Embedded Systems*", 1st Latin-American Symp. on Dependable Computing, pp. 23-38. Brasil, 2003.
16. Rebaudengo, M., Sonza, M. "*Evaluating the Fault Tolerance Capabilities of Embedded Systems via BDM*". 17th IEEE VLSI Test Symposium, 1999, pp. 452-457, Dana Point (USA), April 1999.
17. Ruiz JC., et al. "*On-chip Debugging-based Fault Emulation for Robustness Evaluation of Embedded Software Components*". 2005 Pacific Rim International Symposium on Dependable Computing. Changsha (China), December 2005.
18. Winter M., et al. "*Components for Embedded Software — The PECOS Approach*", In 16th European Conference on Object-Oriented Programming. Málaga, Spain, June 11, 2002.

ERROR DETECTION IN CONTROL FLOW OF EVENT-DRIVEN STATE BASED APPLICATIONS*

G. PINTÉR and I. MAJZIK

Budapest University of Technology and Economics
Department of Measurement and Information Systems
E-mail: {pinter, majzik}@mit.bme.hu

This chapter presents two *runtime error detection techniques* for UML 2.0 statechart implementations. The first technique aims at detecting errors caused by *model refinement faults* (introduced in early phases of the development) by proposing a temporal logic language to be used for defining and checking temporal correctness criteria on statecharts. The second solution is a watchdog structure aiming at detection of errors caused by *implementation faults*. The solutions can detect a subset of errors emerging from operational fault as well.

Keywords: Statecharts, error detection, temporal logic, watchdog.

1. Introduction

The two dominating trends in modern software industry are the increasing complexity and the ever higher dependence of the society on the correct operation of IT systems. Complexity is to be ruled by high-level visual modeling languages like UML, while achieving software dependability is aimed by model checking, code generation, runtime error detection techniques and fault tolerance solutions. This chapter presents two techniques for *runtime detection of errors* in the behavior of software specified by UML statecharts. Error detection is a prerequisite of error recovery, fault handling and continuation of service.

There have been multiple proposals published in the literature aiming at the detection of *faults in the implementation* of algorithms based on asserting pre- and postconditions in functions or using some sort of software di-

*This research was supported by the Hungarian National Research Fund (OTKA T-046527). A part of the work was carried out in the framework of the Embedded Information Technology Research Group of the Hungarian Academy of Sciences and Budapest University of Technology and Economics.

versification techniques. Assertions are a viable solution for sanity checking the input provided to functions or results of numeric computations but are not applicable for checking the complex state-based behavior specified by a statechart. Diversification techniques (N-version programming, recovery block, etc.) are based on parallel execution of multiple diverse implementations of the same algorithm and comparing/checking the results delivered by them; the obvious drawback of these solutions is the high resource consumption emerging from having to execute multiple implementations of the same algorithm. In this chapter we will propose a *watchdog architecture* derived from the formal operational semantics of UML statecharts for runtime detecting semantic errors in the implementation of the statechart (e.g., selecting an invalid set of transitions for firing on the reception of a trigger, errors in the maintenance of the configuration, incorrect initialization etc.).

Modeling faults introduced during early phases of the development are usually addressed by model checking, e.g., for detecting invalid refinement of a draft statechart to a more elaborated version violating this way some dependability requirements. Unfortunately, it is widely recognized that model checking is a complicated task and may be even infeasible in case of complex systems. This drawback results in a need for runtime detection of erroneous behavior. There is an inherent semantic contradiction in the detection of errors caused by faults in the abstract model: we can not check the behavior of the application against its fully elaborated statechart model (as in case of implementation faults) since we are aiming at handling faults in the model itself. In this chapter we present a technique for bridging this semantic gap by proposing a temporal logic language to be used for defining temporal correctness criteria in the context of statecharts prepared in early development phases (before the possibly faulty model refinement process) and a method for runtime detection of violating these requirements.

The discussion is structured as follows. Since both error detection approaches require a formal operational semantics for UML 2.0 statecharts, we present the semantics used by us in Sec. 2; we will focus on statecharts that honor some well-formedness and semantic consistency criteria called precise statecharts (PSC). Our propositional linear temporal logic for precise statecharts (PSC-PLTL) is presented in Sec. 3, the method for evaluating PSC-PLTL expressions on execution traces of statechart implementations (PSC-PLTL checker) is outlined in Sec. 4. Our watchdog architecture for precise statecharts (PSC-WD) is discussed in Sec. 5. The error detection capabilities of our solutions are experimentally evaluated in Sec. 6. Finally Sec. 7 concludes the discussion and outlines the directions of future research.

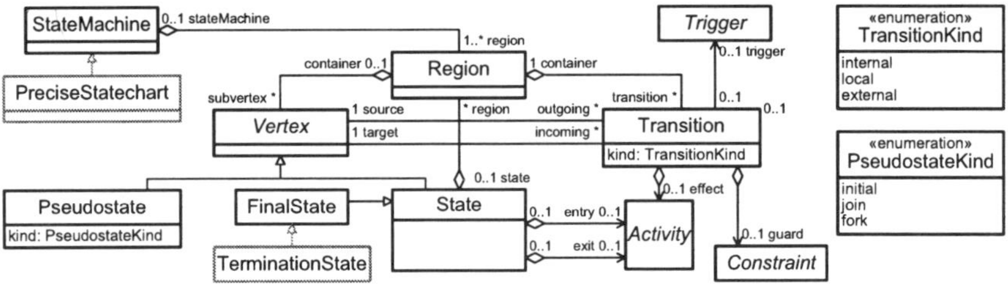

Fig. 1. Precise Statechart Metamodel

2. A Formal Semantics for UML 2.0 Statecharts

This section outlines a formal operational semantics for UML 2.0 statecharts that was introduced by us primarily for code generation and error detection purposes. As the entire discussion including the detailed formalism [1] would be too lengthy, below we will focus on those aspects that are inevitable for understanding our error detection techniques.

In order to rule the complexity we distinguished two sets of modeling facilities: *basic concepts* are the ones that represent some fundamental artifacts of finite state-transition systems while *advanced concepts* are shorthand notations that make the visual modeling more comfortable but do not increase the expressive power of the language. We considered junction and choice pseudostates, history vertices and facilities for embedding state machines as advanced constructs and defined a set of formal transformation rules for their substitution with basic concepts [1]. From this point on, we will focus on those statecharts that contain basic constructs only (or are transformed to this form using the transformations mentioned above) and we will call these statecharts as *precise statecharts* (PSC). The metamodel of precise statecharts is shown in Fig. 1. The remaining differences between the PSC and the original UML 2.0 statechart metamodel are as follows: (i) the ambiguously defined "do activity" and "deferred trigger" concepts were removed and (ii) termination of execution is represented by "termination states" (newly introduced metaclass `TerminationState` derived from the metaclass `State`) instead of terminate pseudostates (this modification was needed for fixing the semantic inconsistency in the standard i.e., representing a terminated *status* by a *transient vertex*.

It is easy to see that transitions can not be considered in isolation since, e.g., a transition connecting a fork and a join pseudostate is practically meaningless without the transitions targeting the join and originating in the fork vertex. Thus below we will identify six *transition conglomerate*

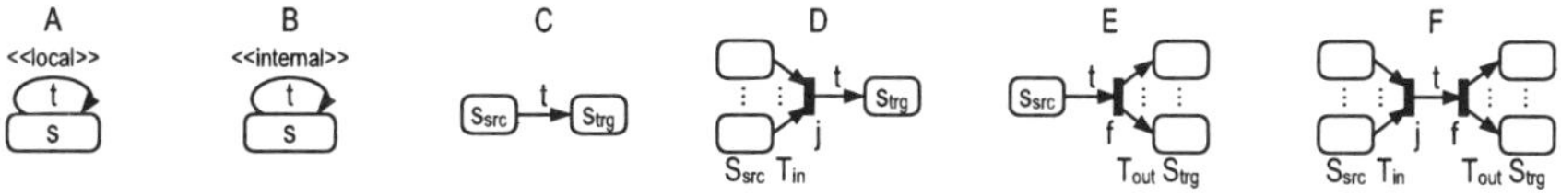

Fig. 2. Transition Conglomerate Classes

classes (class A, B, ... F) representing the possible application patterns of transitions (Fig. 2) and refer to these classes as sets $\mathbf{TC}_a$, $\mathbf{TC}_b$, ... $\mathbf{TC}_f$ respectively; we will use the $\mathbf{TC} = \mathbf{TC}_a \cup \mathbf{TC}_b \cup \mathbf{TC}_c \cup \mathbf{TC}_d \cup \mathbf{TC}_e \cup \mathbf{TC}_f$ set for referring to all transition conglomerates in the actual model.

Class A and *B* represent *local* and *internal transitions* respectively. The remaining classes correspond to *external transitions* (external transitions are the most common ones, while internal and local transitions can be seen as rare cases that are not even supported by many modeling tools). *Class C* corresponds to simple transitions originating in a state and targeting another state (maybe the same state) i.e., no pseudostate vertices are involved. *Class D* represents compound transition paths consisting of multiple $t_{in} \in T_{in}$ transitions originating in $s_{src} \in S_{src}$ concurrent source states targeting a join vertex j, the join pseudostate itself and the single transition t originating in j and targeting the state s_{trg}. *Classes E* and *F* can be defined similarly using the notation of Fig. 2.

It is easy to see that the usual concepts like source and target states, trigger, guard and least common ancestor (LCA) can be defined in the context of transition conglomerates derived from the corresponding properties of individual transitions building up the conglomerate. Based on these concepts the notion of *enabled* conglomerates can be introduced (i.e., ones whose source states are active, triggered by the currently processed trigger and guard evaluates to true) and priority relations can be specified according to the standard (for formal definitions see [1]). Below we will use the function $\mathbf{Enabled}(C, t)$ that selects *enabled transition conglomerates* i.e., ones that are triggered by t, set of source states is active in the configuration C (set of active states) and guard evaluates to true. The function $\mathbf{Frbl}(C, t)$ selects *fireable transition conglomerates* i.e., ones that are enabled and are not overpowered by another conglomerate of higher priority.

The effect of firing a conglomerate can be defined by a compound activity structure possibly consisting of multiple effects with various subsequence relations amongst them. In [1] we generalized the concept of compound activity structures to a flexible formalism based on PERT graphs. PERT graphs are used similarly to represent the activities to be performed on firing one or multiple transition conglomerates involving any number of exit and entry activities and transition effects. We will use the function **FireSingle** for calculating the states left and entered by a single conglomerate and the PERT graph of activities to be performed on firing. The higher level function **Fire** will be used for calculating the state sets and the PERT graph corresponding to firing multiple transition conglomerates in parallel. (Due to space restrictions the discussion below is restricted to the maintenance of configuration and selecting transitions to be fired, for a detailed discussion involving formalism for extended variables and PERT graphs see [1]). Having outlined the basic concepts we can define the operational semantics of PSCs by a Kripke transition system (KTS).

Definition 2.1. Let P be a precise statechart. The operational semantics of P is specified by a Kripke transition system $\mathbf{B}^{\mathrm{KTS}} = (S, \Rightarrow, \mathbf{L}^{\mathrm{S}})$ over the $\mathbf{A}_{\mathrm{S}}$ set of *state labels* and $\mathbf{A}_{\mathrm{T}}$ set of *transition labels*, where (i) S is the *set of states*, (ii) $\Rightarrow$ is the *labeled transition relation* and (iii) $\mathbf{L}^{\mathrm{S}}$ is a composite *state labeling function.*

The S *state set* of $\mathbf{B}^{\mathrm{KTS}}$ corresponds to *statuses* of the precise statechart P. The *status* concept is a compound representation of (i) the actual *configuration* of P and (ii) the actual *phase of the operation.* These concepts are mapped to *compound state labels*: $\mathbf{A}_{\mathrm{S}} \subseteq 2^{\mathsf{State}} \times \mathbf{Phs}$ (for $a_s = (C, p) \in \mathbf{A}_{\mathrm{S}}$: C is the actual configuration and p is the actual phase of the operation). The $I \subseteq S$ *set of initial states* contains a single state: $I = \{s_\alpha\}$.

The *labeling function* $\mathbf{L}^{\mathrm{S}} : S \to \mathbf{A}_{\mathrm{S}}$ is used for associating the state labels to elements of S. For simplicity reasons we will decompose $\mathbf{L}^{\mathrm{S}}$ into two individual labeling functions $\mathbf{L}^{\mathrm{S}}_{\mathrm{Cnf}}$ and $\mathbf{L}^{\mathrm{S}}_{\mathrm{Phs}}$: (i) $\mathbf{L}^{\mathrm{S}}_{\mathrm{Cnf}} : S \to 2^{\mathsf{State}}$ assigns the *actual configuration* of P or the empty set representing the "uninitialized configuration" to S; for the single initial state $s_\alpha : \mathbf{L}^{\mathrm{S}}_{\mathrm{Cnf}}(s_\alpha) = \emptyset$, for any other states $\forall s \in (S \setminus I) : \mathbf{L}^{\mathrm{S}}_{\mathrm{Cnf}}(s) \neq \emptyset$ and (ii) $\mathbf{L}^{\mathrm{S}}_{\mathrm{Phs}} : S \to \mathbf{Phs}$ assigns one of four labels to states in S indicating the *phase of operation*: $\mathbf{Phs}_\alpha$ if P is in the *uninitialized configuration*, $\mathbf{Phs}_{\mathrm{S}}$ if P is in a *stable configuration* (i.e., idle between RTC steps), $\mathbf{Phs}_{\mathrm{U}}$ if P is actually *performing an RTC step* (i.e., the configuration is considered to be *unstable*) and (iv) $\mathbf{Phs}_\omega$ if P is *terminated*; for the single initial state $s_\alpha : \mathbf{L}^{\mathrm{S}}_{\mathrm{Phs}}(s_\alpha) = \mathbf{Phs}_\alpha$. The entire $\mathbf{L}^{\mathrm{S}} : S \to \mathbf{A}_{\mathrm{S}}$ labeling function can be seen as being composed of these functions: $\mathbf{L}^{\mathrm{S}}(s|_{s \in S}) = (\mathbf{L}^{\mathrm{S}}_{\mathrm{Cnf}}(s), \mathbf{L}^{\mathrm{S}}_{\mathrm{Phs}}(s))$.

Transitions of $\mathbf{B}^{\mathrm{KTS}}$ indicate the possible *steps between statuses* of P (note that we are talking about the transitions of the KTS and not about ones in the statechart). Steps are initiated by one or zero *triggers* and result in *firing* zero or more transition conglomerates. These concepts are mapped to the set of *compound transition labels*: $\mathbf{A}_\mathrm{T} \subseteq (\mathsf{Trigger} \cup \{t_0\}) \times 2^{\mathbf{TC}}$ where for a $a_t = (t, \mathrm{TC_f}) \in \mathbf{A}_\mathrm{T}$, t is the trigger and $\mathrm{TC_f}$ is the set of transition conglomerates fired. We use the special symbol $t_\emptyset \notin \mathsf{Trigger}$ for indicating the "empty trigger" (i.e., not a valid trigger in the statechart just a symbol used for indicating that no trigger is processed in the step). The labeled transition relation $\Rightarrow$ indicates the possible steps between states of $\mathbf{B}^{\mathrm{KTS}}$: $\Rightarrow \subseteq (S \times \mathbf{A}_\mathrm{T} \times S) = (S \times ((\mathsf{Trigger} \cup \{t_\emptyset\}) \times 2^{\mathbf{TC}}) \times S)$. The members of the tuple represent the following concepts: (i) *source state* of the step, (ii) the *label of the transition* (including the *trigger* consumed in the step and the *set of transition conglomerates fired* in the step) and (iii) the *target state* of the step. For simplicity reasons we will decompose $\Rightarrow$ into six subsets: $\overset{init}{\Longrightarrow}, \overset{open}{\Longrightarrow}, \overset{inter}{\Longrightarrow}, \overset{close}{\Longrightarrow}, \overset{term}{\Longrightarrow}$ and $\overset{drop}{\Longrightarrow}$ representing initialization, opening run-to-completion (RTC) steps, internal steps, closing RTC steps, termination and dropping a trigger respectively.

In the *initialization step* the statechart enters the initial configuration while *opening an RTC step* means receiving a trigger and performing one or multiple transitions resulting in a new configuration. Initialization and opening an RTC step result in states of unstable phase indicating that the RTC step of the statechart has not yet been finished and transitions without triggers may still be fired. Firing these transitions is done in *internal steps*; internal steps also result in states of unstable phase since the number of subsequent internal steps is not restricted. The series of internal steps ends if there are no transition conglomerates without triggers that can be fired; this is represented by the *closing an RTC step* operation (obviously resulting in a state of stable phase). The operation *terminates* in a state of unstable phase if the configuration contains a termination state (termination steps end in states of terminated phase). Finally a trigger is *dropped* in a state of stable phase if none of the transitions triggered by it can be fired. Below we give the formal definition of opening RTC steps, internal and closing RTC steps; the remaining steps can be specified similarly:

$$\overset{open}{\Longrightarrow} = \{(s_s, (t, \mathrm{TC_f}), s_u) | (\mathbf{L}^{\mathrm{S}}_{\mathrm{Phs}}(s_s) = \mathbf{Phs_S}) \wedge (\mathrm{TC_f} = \mathbf{Frbl}(\mathbf{L}^{\mathrm{S}}_{\mathrm{Cnf}}(s_s), t)) \wedge (\mathrm{TC_f} \neq \emptyset) \wedge \exists S_l, S_e : ((S_l, S_e) = \mathbf{Fire}(\mathbf{L}^{\mathrm{S}}_{\mathrm{Cnf}}(s_s), \mathrm{TC_f})) \wedge (\mathbf{L}^{\mathrm{S}}(s_u) = ((\mathbf{L}^{\mathrm{S}}_{\mathrm{Cnf}}(s_s) \setminus S_l) \cup S_e), \mathbf{Phs_U})\}$$

$$\overset{inter}{\Longrightarrow} = \{(s_u, (t_\emptyset, \mathrm{TC_f}), s'_u) | (\mathbf{L}^{\mathrm{S}}_{\mathrm{Phs}}(s_u) = \mathbf{Phs_U}) \wedge ((\mathsf{TerminationState} \cap \mathbf{L}^{\mathrm{S}}_{\mathrm{Cnf}}(s_u)) = \emptyset) \wedge (\mathrm{TC_f} = \mathbf{Frbl}(\mathbf{L}^{\mathrm{S}}_{\mathrm{Cnf}}(s_u), t_\emptyset)) \wedge (\mathrm{TC_f} \neq \emptyset) \wedge \exists S_l, S_e : ((S_l, S_e) = \mathbf{Fire}(\mathbf{L}^{\mathrm{S}}_{\mathrm{Cnf}}(s_u), \mathrm{TC_f})) \wedge (\mathbf{L}^{\mathrm{S}}(s'_u) = ((\mathbf{L}^{\mathrm{S}}_{\mathrm{Cnf}}(s_u) \setminus S_l) \cup S_e, \mathbf{Phs_U}))\}$$

$$\overset{close}{\Longrightarrow} = \{(s_u, (t_\emptyset, \emptyset), s_s) | (\mathbf{L}^{\mathrm{S}}_{\mathrm{Phs}}(s_u) = \mathbf{Phs_U}) \wedge ((\mathsf{TerminationState} \cap \mathbf{L}^{\mathrm{S}}_{\mathrm{Cnf}}(s_u)) = \emptyset) \wedge (\emptyset = \mathbf{Frbl}(\mathbf{L}^{\mathrm{S}}_{\mathrm{Cnf}}(s_u), t_\emptyset)) \wedge (\mathbf{L}^{\mathrm{S}}(s_s) = (\mathbf{L}^{\mathrm{S}}_{\mathrm{Cnf}}(s_u), \mathbf{Phs_S}))\}$$

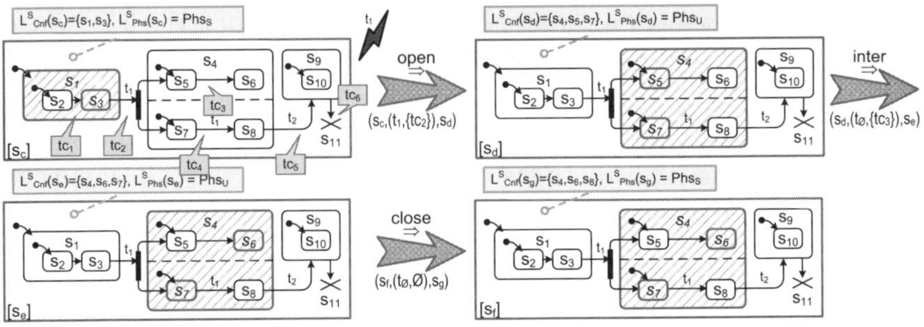

Fig. 3. Processing a Trigger

The meaning of sub-expressions in the definition of $\overset{open}{\Longrightarrow}$ are as follows: (i) s_s is a stable state, (ii) the set of fireable transition conglomerates (with respect to the actual configuration and trigger t) is $\mathrm{TC_f}$ (iii) $\mathrm{TC_f}$ is a non-empty set, (iv) firing the set $\mathrm{TC_f}$ results in leaving the set of states S_l and entering the set of states S_e and (v) the labeling of the target state s_u indicates that it represents the configuration obtained by removing S_l from the original configuration and adding S_e and s_u is unstable. The meaning of sub-expressions in the definition of $\overset{inter}{\Longrightarrow}$ is as follows: (i) s_u is an unstable state, (ii) there are no active termination states in the configuration, (iii) the set of transition conglomerates that have no triggers and can be fired (with respect to the actual configuration) is $\mathrm{TC_f}$, (iv) $\mathrm{TC_f}$ is a non-empty set, (v) firing the set $\mathrm{TC_f}$ results in leaving the set of states S_l and entering the set of states S_e and (vi) the labeling of the target state s'_u indicates that it represents the configuration obtained by removing S_l from the original configuration and adding S_e and s'_u is still unstable. The meaning of sub-expressions in the definition of $\overset{close}{\Longrightarrow}$ is as follows: (i) s_u is an unstable state, (ii) there are no active termination states in the configuration, (iii) there are no transition conglomerates that have no triggers and can be fired and (iv) the labeling of the target state s_s indicates that it represents the same configuration as s_u and s_s is stable.

Having defined $\mathbf{B}^{\mathrm{KTS}}$ we have outlined a formal semantics for UML 2.0 statecharts. The example shown in Fig. 3 presents the entire processing of a trigger t_1 received in the state s_c. States of the KTS are indicated by rectangles with the actual configuration of the statechart indicated in them (active states are filled with a dashed pattern). Transition conglomerates are indicated by small callouts attached to s_c, labels of KTS states are shown in callouts above the corresponding rectangles, labels of KTS transitions are written under the arrows. The reception of the trigger is indicated by a

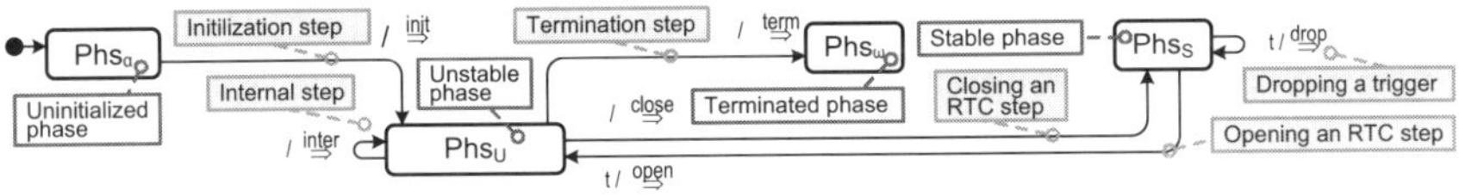

Fig. 4. High-Level View of the KTS Operation

small lightning. Since t_1 triggers tc_2 an RTC step is *opened*, taking $\mathbf{B}^{\mathrm{KTS}}$ to the state s_d. As indicated under the arrow, the step is initiated by the trigger t_1 and involves the firing of tc_2 and ends in the unstable state s_d. In s_d the tc_3 transition conglomerate without trigger is fireable, therefore in the next *internal step* tc_3 is fired resulting in the unstable state s_e. Since there are no more fireable transition conglomerates (and there are no active termination states) the RTC step is *closed* resulting in the stable state s_f.

The operation specified by the KTS is visualized by grouping states by their phase of operation and indicating $\stackrel{init}{\Longrightarrow}$, $\stackrel{open}{\Longrightarrow}$ etc. transition sets amongst them as transitions of an automaton in Fig. 4. This high-level view will be the basis for constructing the watchdog in Sec. 5.

3. A Temporal Logic Language for UML 2.0 Statecharts

This section presents the PSC-PLTL temporal logic language defined by us for reasoning about temporal correctness of PSC implementations. After an overview on temporal logic languages, we derive the finite state-transition model of PSC-PLTL from the KTS used for defining PSC semantics in Sec. 2 and finally we present the syntax and semantics of PSC-PLTL.

According to our knowledge there were relatively few proposals about mapping temporal logic (TL) languages to artifacts of statecharts. Sowmya and Ramesh proposed the FNLOG language [2] based on predicate calculus and TL for proving various dependability criteria on statecharts primarily aiming at model checking. Drusinsky proposed TLCharts [3], that are extensions of Harel statecharts allowing TL to be used in guard predicates.

Temporal logic languages were originally suggested by Pnueli [4] for reasoning about concurrent programs. Since then several researchers have used TL variants for checking and proving temporal correctness of software, communication protocols and HW devices. The core concept of checking temporal criteria is to define a *finite state-transition system* representing an abstraction of the system and check that specific propositions hold for *execution traces* of the system. This abstraction is usually presented by a *Kripke-structure* (KS). A KS consists of simple *states*, *transitions* and *labels* assigned to states.

Definition 3.1 (Kripke-Structure). Having a label set P a *Kripke-structure* is a three-tuple: $K = (S, T, L)$ where S is the *set of states*, $T \subseteq S \times S$ is the *state transition relation* and L is the *labeling function* that assigns labels to states: $L : S \to 2^P$.

Definition 3.2 (Finite Trace, Trace Suffix). A $\Pi = (s_0, s_1, \ldots, s_{n-1})$ *finite trace* of the KS is a sequence of states connected by the state transition relation: $s_0, s_1, \ldots, s_{n-1} \in S$, $n > 0$ and $\forall_{0<i<n}(s_{i-1}, s_i) \in T$. A $\Pi^j = (s_j, s_{j+1}, \ldots, s_{n-1})$ *trace suffix* is obtained from $\Pi = (s_0, s_1, \ldots, s_{n-1})$ by removing the first j steps ($j < n$). By definition: $\Pi^0 \equiv \Pi$.

Execution traces may be considered to be finite or infinite; as we would like to use our TL language for reasoning about programs that may be terminated, in the definition above we defined *finite traces* (infinite trace semantics is primarily used in model checking and requires different approaches for evaluating TL expressions). Temporal logic languages can be classified according to the following criteria: (i) with respect to the *operator set* a temporal logic may be *propositional* (temporal and Boolean operators may be used) or *first order* (first order operators may also be used); (ii) the *evaluation of temporal operators* may be focused to atomic *points of time* or to *time intervals*; (iii) with respect to the *granularity of time* there are *discrete time* and *continuous time* temporal logics; (iv) the notion of *subsequence* may be simply interpreted over a *linear timeline* or, in *branching time temporal logics*, the life of a system is considered as a tree of states where states may have multiple subsequent states and (v) the temporal operators may refer to the *future* of the system or the *past* or both.

As the goal of our approach is to define a language for runtime error detection in PSC implementations, the following decisions were drawn: (i) since we can observe only the actual (single) execution of the system, we need a *propositional* TL; (ii) as statecharts operate in RTC steps, temporal operators are to be evaluated at atomic *points of time* and (iii) the granularity of time is a *discrete*; (iv) as we observe a single execution we cannot reason about *all* execution traces hence will use of *linear timeline* semantics; (v) whether temporal operators refer to the past or the future is of secondary importance, we choose the future-time syntax because most of TL languages follows this approach. To put together: we need a *propositional linear temporal logic language* (PLTL) of discrete time semantics.

Below we present the syntax for a PLTL language and introduce the notion of a formula ϕ being true at a trace suffix Π^i denoted by $\Pi^i \models \phi$.

$$\Pi \models p \quad \text{iff } p \in L(s_0) \quad \text{(Atomic propositions)} \quad (1)$$

$$\Pi \models \neg e \quad \text{iff } \Pi \models e \text{ is not true} \quad \text{(Boolean not)} \quad (2)$$

$$\Pi \models e_1 \wedge e_2 \quad \text{iff } \Pi \models e_1 \text{ and } \Pi \models e_2 \quad \text{(Boolean and)} \quad (3)$$

$$\Pi \models \mathcal{X} e \quad \text{iff } n > 1 \wedge \Pi^1 \models e \quad \text{(Temporal next)} \quad (4)$$

$$\Pi \models e_1 \mathcal{U} e_2 \quad \text{iff } \exists_{0 \leq i < n} \Pi^i \models e_2 \text{ and } \forall_{0 \leq j < i} \Pi^j \models e_1 \quad \text{(Temporal until)} \quad (5)$$

Informally: An *atomic proposition* $p \in P$ is true if the p label is a member of the labeling set of the first step of the trace suffix; the meaning of Boolean operators is obvious, $\mathcal{X}$ refers to the *next suffix* of the trace, $e_1 \mathcal{U} e_2$ requires the condition e_1 to hold *until* e_2 becomes true. We will also use the usual *Boolean constants* ($\top$ and $\bot$), the *or* ($\vee$) and *implication* ($\rightarrow$) operators according to their usual semantics and the *finally* $\mathcal{F}$ and *globally* $\mathcal{G}$ temporal operators: $\phi = \mathcal{F} e$ is a shorthand notation for $\phi = \top \mathcal{U} e$ representing that there is a suffix for which e holds; and $\phi = \mathcal{G} e$ is a shorthand notation for $\phi = \neg \mathcal{F} \neg e$ representing that e holds for all suffixes of the trace.

The fact that we are presenting a *finite trace* semantics can be captured in the definition of the $\mathcal{X}$ next-time and $\mathcal{U}$ operators: (i) for $\mathcal{X} e$ being true at a trace suffix Π we require that the trace is longer than 1 i.e., that the trace actually has a next state (Eq. 4) and (ii) for $\mathcal{U} e$ being true we require that e should evaluate to true before the *end of the trace.*

The first step for specifying our PSC-PLTL language is defining the KS model of the language. Since the operational semantics of PSCs was defined by a KTS, we do not have to build the KS model from scratch, our only task is to transform the KTS into a KS. The transformation is nearly just a syntactic rewriting as follows. Let a KTS S^{KTS} be specified by the tuple $S^{\text{KTS}} = (S, \Rightarrow, I)$ over the AP set of state labels and Act set of transition labels where S is the set of states, $\Rightarrow \subseteq S \times \text{Act} \times S$ is the labeled transition relation and $I : S \rightarrow 2^{\text{AP}}$ is the state labeling function. As we would like to construct a KS that represents the same semantics as the KTS, we have to move the information on KTS transition labels into the KS state labels by using $\langle s, a_t \rangle$ pairs as states where s is an original state of the KS and a_t is the label of a transition targeting s. This way the KS is specified by the tuple $S^{\text{KS}} = (S \times \text{Act}, R, I')$ over $\text{AP} \cup \text{Act}$ state labels where the transition relation is $R = \{(\langle s, a \rangle, \langle s', a' \rangle) | (s, a', s') \in \Rightarrow\}$ and the state labeling function is $I'(\langle s, a \rangle) = I(s) \cup \{a\}$ (the similar rewriting of $\mathbf{B}^{\text{KTS}}$ to $\mathbf{B}^{\text{KS}}$ is shown in Tab. 1).

As we have moved the transition labeling information into the state labeling function $\hat{\mathbf{L}}$, state labels are now four-tuples. Similarly to the def-

Table 1. Rewriting Kripke Transition Systems to Kripke-Structures

Kripke transition system	Kripke structure
$\mathbf{B}^{\mathrm{KTS}} = (S, \Rightarrow, \mathbf{L}^{\mathrm{S}})$ over $\mathbf{A}_{\mathrm{S}}$, $\mathbf{A}_{\mathrm{T}}$	$\mathbf{B}^{\mathrm{KS}} = (\hat{S}, \hat{R}, \hat{L})$ over $\hat{\mathbf{A}}_{\mathrm{S}} \subseteq \mathbf{A}_{\mathrm{S}} \times \mathbf{A}_{\mathrm{T}}$
$\mathbf{L}^{\mathrm{S}} : S \to \mathbf{A}_{\mathrm{S}}$	$\hat{S} = S \times \mathbf{A}_{\mathrm{T}}$, $\hat{\mathbf{L}}(\langle s, a_t \rangle) = \mathbf{L}^{\mathrm{S}}(s) \cup \{a_t\}$
$\Rightarrow \subseteq S \times \mathbf{A}_{\mathrm{T}} \times S$	$\hat{R} = \{(\langle s, a_t \rangle, \langle s', a'_t \rangle) \mid (s, a'_t, s') \in \Rightarrow\}$

inition of the KTS we decompose the composite labeling function to four sub-functions below for obtaining the (i) configuration (Eq. 6) and (ii) phase of operation (Eq. 7) from the original state labeling and (iii) the trigger that initiated the step (Eq. 8) and (iv) the set of transition conglomerates fired in the step (Eq. 9) from the original transition labeling.

$$\hat{\mathbf{L}}^{\mathrm{S}}_{\mathrm{Cnf}} : \hat{S} \to 2^{\mathsf{State}} \qquad \hat{\mathbf{L}}^{\mathrm{S}}_{\mathrm{Cnf}}(\langle s, (t, \mathrm{TC_f}, p) \rangle) = \mathbf{L}^{\mathrm{S}}_{\mathrm{Cnf}}(s) \tag{6}$$

$$\hat{\mathbf{L}}^{\mathrm{S}}_{\mathrm{Phs}} : \hat{S} \to \mathbf{Phs} \qquad \hat{\mathbf{L}}^{\mathrm{S}}_{\mathrm{Phs}}(\langle s, (t, \mathrm{TC_f}, p) \rangle) = \mathbf{L}^{\mathrm{S}}_{\mathrm{Phs}}(s) \tag{7}$$

$$\hat{\mathbf{L}}^{\Rightarrow}_{\mathrm{Trigger}} : \hat{S} \to \mathsf{Trigger} \cup \{t_{\emptyset}\} \qquad \hat{\mathbf{L}}^{\Rightarrow}_{\mathrm{Trigger}}(\langle s, (t, \mathrm{TC_f}, p) \rangle) = t \tag{8}$$

$$\hat{\mathbf{L}}^{\Rightarrow}_{\mathrm{TC}} : \hat{S} \to 2^{\mathbf{TC}} \qquad \hat{\mathbf{L}}^{\Rightarrow}_{\mathrm{TC}}(\langle s, (t, \mathrm{TC_f}, p) \rangle) = \mathrm{TC_f} \tag{9}$$

Definition of the temporal logic language PSC-PLTL consists of the definition of the Boolean and temporal operators used and the atomic propositions. We use the Boolean *not* and *and* operators and the temporal *next-time* and *until* operators according to their usual syntax and semantics as discussed above (Eq. 2, 3, 4, and 5 respectively). Atomic propositions are derived from state labels of the KS: (i) the predicate $\hat{\mathbf{P}}_{\mathrm{Cnf}}(C)$ is true if all states in C are active in the actual *configuration* of the statechart (Eq. 10), (ii) $\hat{\mathbf{P}}_{\mathrm{Phs}}(p)$ is true if the actual *phase of operation* is p (Eq. 11), (iii) $\hat{\mathbf{P}}_{\mathrm{Trigger}}(t)$ is true if the step ending in the actual status was initiated by the *trigger* t (Eq. 12) and (iv) $\hat{\mathbf{P}}_{\mathrm{TC}}(\mathrm{TC_f})$ is true if during the step ending in the actual status, all *transition conglomerates* in $\mathrm{TC_f}$ were *fired* (Eq. 13).

$$\Pi \models \hat{\mathbf{P}}_{\mathrm{Cnf}}(C|_{C \subseteq \mathsf{State}}) \qquad \text{iff } \forall c \in C : c \in \hat{\mathbf{L}}^{\mathrm{S}}_{\mathrm{Cnf}}(s_0) \tag{10}$$

$$\Pi \models \hat{\mathbf{P}}_{\mathrm{Phs}}(p \in \mathbf{Phs})\}) \qquad \text{iff } p = \hat{\mathbf{L}}^{\mathrm{S}}_{\mathrm{Phs}}(s_0) \tag{11}$$

$$\Pi \models \hat{\mathbf{P}}_{\mathrm{Trigger}}(t \in \mathsf{Trigger}) \qquad \text{iff } t = \hat{\mathbf{L}}^{\Rightarrow}_{\mathrm{Trigger}}(s_0) \tag{12}$$

$$\Pi \models \hat{\mathbf{P}}_{\mathrm{TC}}(\mathrm{TC_f} \subseteq \mathbf{TC}) \qquad \text{iff } \mathrm{TC_f} \subseteq \hat{\mathbf{L}}^{\Rightarrow}_{\mathrm{TC}}(s_0) \tag{13}$$

Having specified the model of computation with the syntax and semantics of operators and atomic propositions the definition of PSC-PLTL is complete. For convenience we will also use the Boolean and temporal shorthand operators ($\vee$, $\rightarrow$, $\mathcal{F}$ and $\mathcal{G}$) defined above.

4. Efficient Evaluation of Temporal Logic Formulae

For the implementation of the PSC-PLTL checker we needed a method for evaluation of PSC-PLTL formulae over finite execution traces. As PSC-PLTL is bound to statecharts only in the interpretation of atomic predicates, any method for evaluating PLTL formulae is applicable for our purposes (correspondingly below we will discuss PLTL languages in general without restricting our approach for PSC-PLTL).

The most straightforward naive approach is based on iterative rewriting of formulae. We can establish a *tree of expression nodes* rooting in the original expression to be evaluated: leaves of the evaluation tree are atomic propositions to be evaluated on the label set of the corresponding step of trace while internal nodes are Boolean operators ($\neg$ or $\wedge$) and next-time subexpressions (i.e., ones in the $\mathcal{X}\,\phi$ form); until subexpressions are to be moved into the scope of an $\mathcal{X}$ operator according to the $(\Pi \models e_1 \,\mathcal{U}\, e_2) \leftrightarrow (\Pi \models e_2 \vee (e_1 \wedge \mathcal{X}(e_1 \,\mathcal{U}\, e_2)))$ rewriting:

$$
\begin{aligned}
&\pi \models e_1 \,\mathcal{U}\, e_2 \leftrightarrow \exists_{0 \le i < n} \pi^i \models e_2 \wedge \forall_{0 \le j < i} \pi^j \models e_1 \leftrightarrow \\
&\quad (\pi^0 \models e_2) \vee (\exists_{1 \le i < n} \pi^i \models e_2 \wedge \forall_{1 \le j < i} \pi^j \models e_1 \wedge \pi^0 \models e_1) \leftrightarrow \\
&\quad (\pi^0 \models e_2) \vee (\pi^0 \models e_1 \wedge \exists_{1 \le i < n} \pi^i \models e_2 \wedge \forall_{1 \le j < i} \pi^j \models e_1) \leftrightarrow \\
&\quad (\pi^0 \models e_2) \vee (\pi^0 \models e_1 \wedge \pi^0 \models \mathcal{X}(e_1 \,\mathcal{U}\, e_2)) \leftrightarrow \pi \models \neg(\neg e_2 \wedge \neg(e_1 \wedge \mathcal{X}(e_1 \,\mathcal{U}\, e_2)))
\end{aligned}
$$

The tree resulting from the naive iterative decomposition of $\mathcal{G}(r \rightarrow (p \,\mathcal{U}\, d))$ is shown in part a of Fig. 5. The root of the tree is the $\mathcal{G}(r \rightarrow (p \,\mathcal{U}\, d))$ expression (represented without shorthand operators as $\top \,\mathcal{U}(r \wedge \neg(p \,\mathcal{U}\, d))$; the expression is rewritten to $(\neg(r \wedge (\neg d \wedge \neg(p \wedge \mathcal{X}(p \,\mathcal{U}\, d)))) \wedge \neg(\top \wedge \mathcal{X}(\top \,\mathcal{U}(r \wedge \neg(p \,\mathcal{U}\, d)))))$ resulting in two next-time expressions $\mathcal{X}(p \,\mathcal{U}\, d)$ and $\mathcal{X}(\top \,\mathcal{U}(r \wedge \neg(p \,\mathcal{U}\, d)))$ (indicated by white rounded boxes) that yield expressions $p \,\mathcal{U}\, d$ and $\top \,\mathcal{U}(r \wedge \neg(p \,\mathcal{U}\, d))$ to be evaluated in the next trace suffix Π^1 (orange rounded boxes). It is easy to see that the naive iterative rewriting starts the evaluation of $p \,\mathcal{U}\, d$ for each suffixes resulting in ever growing number of expressions to be evaluated; let L^n_e be the number of leaves in the tree built for expression e for a trace of length n and N^n_e be the number of all nodes in the tree built for the same case. It is easy to see that $L^n_{p \mathcal{U} d} = 2n$ and $N^n_{p \mathcal{U} d} = 9n$ hence $L^n_{\mathcal{G}(r \rightarrow (p \mathcal{U} d))}$ and $N^n_{\mathcal{G}(r \rightarrow (p \mathcal{U} d))}$ are proportional to n^2:

$$
L^n_{\mathcal{G}(r \rightarrow p \mathcal{U} d)} = 4n + \sum_{i=1}^{n} L^{i-1}_{p \mathcal{U} d} = 4n + \sum_{i=1}^{n} 2(i-1) = 4n + 2\left(-n + \sum_{i=1}^{n} i\right) = n^2 + 3n
$$

$$
N^n_{\mathcal{G}(r \rightarrow p \mathcal{U} d)} = 17n + \sum_{i=1}^{n} N^{i-1}_{p \mathcal{U} d} = 17n + \sum_{i=1}^{n} 9(i-1) = \frac{9n^2 + 25n}{2}
$$

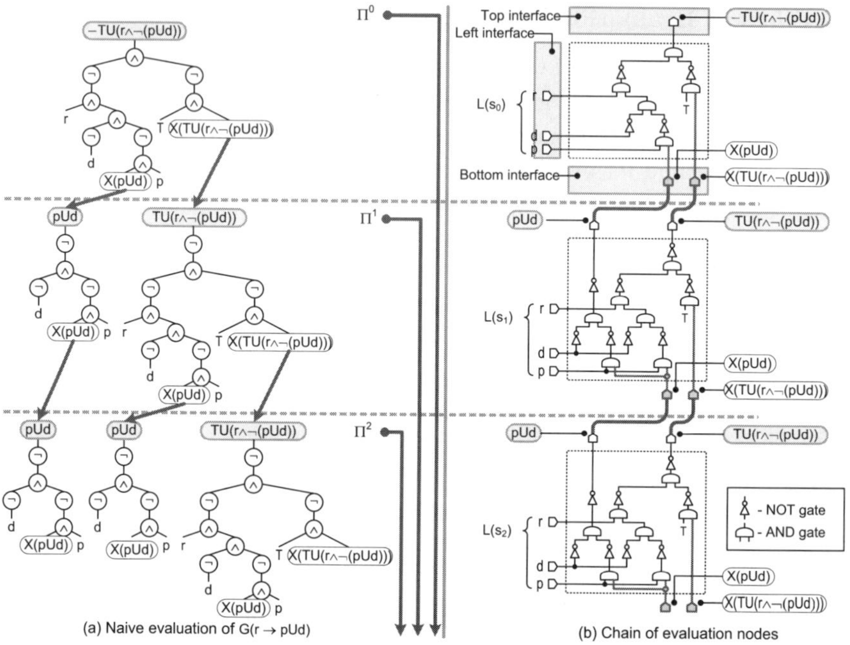

Fig. 5. Efficient Evaluation of Temporal Logic Formulae

The idea of our solution is shown in part *b* of Fig. 5. We introduced the concept of *evaluation nodes* as straightforward hardware analogy for (i) encapsulating a piece of evaluation logic and (ii) collecting the next-time subexpressions to be evaluated in the next suffix. The atomic predicates to be evaluated on the set of labels assigned to the actual step of trace appear on left interfaces of evaluation nodes while next-time subexpressions appear on bottom interfaces. This solution prevents the explosion of expression set to be evaluated as in case of the naive approach. We implemented a *code generator* that derives the interfaces and internal logic of evaluation nodes from a root expression and synthesizes source code implementing the evaluation nodes as C++ classes. The solution is discussed in-depth in [5]; we reported significant reduction of time needed for evaluating PLTL expressions on finite traces as compared to approaches published previously in the literature. This method was used for implementing our PSC-PLTL checker: as PSC-PLTL is bound to statechart artifacts only by its atomic propositions, the source code synthesized by our code generator was usable for evaluating PSC-PLTL formulae over execution traces of statechart implementations after a simple preprocessing phase.

5. A Watchdog Architecture for UML 2.0 Statecharts

This section presents PSC-WD, a watchdog architecture for detecting errors in the implementation of a precise statechart. Our solution was inspired by traditional watchdog approaches that observe the control flow of a software running on the main CPU and signal an error if it deviates from the correct control flow graph synthesized from the source code of the application. Our method elevates this scheme to the abstraction level of statecharts by observing the runtime behavior of a statechart implementation and checking whether it actually corresponds to the statechart with respect to the semantics defined in Sec. 2. After a short introduction to watchdogs proposed previously in the literature we will discuss the representation of runtime and reference information in PSC-WD and outline the implementation.

The structure of a program can be described by the *control flow graph* (CFG) whose *nodes* represent branch-free blocks of subsequent instructions and *directed edges* represent branch instructions, function calls etc.

Hardware elements or software applications that aim at detection of control flow errors are usually called *watchdogs* for historical reasons. *Watchdog circuits* attached to interfaces of devices were originally used for detecting such lethal conditions as loss of clock signal, power outage or lack of some life signals. The more advanced *watchdog processors* (WP) [6] are able to perform more sophisticated checks on the operation of the main processor: the WP observes the actual behavior of the program and checks it against the correct CFG. A WP can be characterized by the solutions chosen for (i) describing of the correct control flow (called the *reference information*), (ii) observing the actual behavior (called the *runtime information* and (iii) the actual *implementation* of the WP.

Runtime information is represented by compacted pieces of observed behavior called *signatures* (e.g., address of the actually fetched instruction without the actual operation code and arguments). The WP can *obtain the runtime signatures* in two ways: (i) observing the system buses (called *derived signatures*) or (ii) explicitly receiving messages from the program (called *assigned signatures*). Although the application of derived signatures promises totally non-intrusive observation, predictive prefetching, instruction caching, pipeline organization, out of order execution etc. applied in modern CPUs prevents the WP from unambiguously observing the execution by bus signals and renders assigned signatures the only viable solution.

There were three solutions proposed in the literature for the representation of the *reference information*: (i) storing the correct CFG in a *database* in the WP, (ii) executing a *watchdog program* on the WP that accepts correct runs of the main program or (iii) the reference information can be *embedded* in signatures themselves. The *stored database* approach uses an adjacency matrix or adjacency list for storing the directed control flow graph; unfortunately this approach may result in significant memory consumption (e.g., large, sparse adjacency matrix) or time-consuming lookup operations (e.g., searching for an edge in the adjacency list). The *watchdog program* approach considers the valid executions of the main program as sentences of a language where the words are signatures of execution; the watchdog program is a language parser that accepts valid sequences of signatures, i.e., valid executions of the main program; it is easy to see that having built the valid CFG of the main program, it is relatively easy to automatically synthesize such an automaton that accepts valid runs. The *embedded signatures* approach uses composite signatures whose first part identifies the actual point of execution and the second part identifies the set of signatures that may follow the actual one in a correct execution.

There were proposals for all combinations of representing runtime and reference information mentioned above. *Derived signatures* were used together (i) with *stored database* in the Asynchronous Signatured Instruction Stream approach by Eifert *et al.* [7], (ii) with *watchdog program* by Michel *et al.* [8] and (iii) with *embedded signatures* in Path Signature Analysis approaches of Namjoo [9] *Assigned signatures* were used together (i) with *stored database* in the Extended Structural Integrity Checking approach by Michel and Hohl [10], (ii) with *watchdog program* in Lu's Structural Integrity Checking method [11] and (iii) with *embedded signatures* in the Signature Encoded Instruction Stream (SEIS) approach by Majzik *et al.* [12].

The actual *implementation* of the WP can be (i) a real physical processor, but there were approaches proposed in the literature for (ii) utilizing the unused resources of the main processor for emulating the WP [13] and (iii) integrating watchdog processors into multiprocessor systems [14].

Having introduced the key concepts related to WPs, we can reason about choosing the most appropriate solutions for mapping CFG concepts to statecharts, the representation of runtime and reference information and the implementation of PSC-WD. To put together: we would like to construct a watchdog that observes the execution of an application and checks whether the actual behavior corresponds to the statechart specification, e.g., after the reception of a trigger a valid set of transition conglomerates is selected to be fired and the resulting configuration is reached correctly. The concepts of CFGs seamlessly map to the KTS specified in Sec. 2: *nodes* of the CFG are states of the KTS (i.e., statuses of the PSC representing the configuration, and phase of operation as defined in Def. 2.1) and *edges* of the CFG are labeled transitions of the KTS (e.g., $\stackrel{init}{\Longrightarrow}$, $\stackrel{open}{\Longrightarrow}$, etc.).

Using derived signatures as *runtime information* does not seem to be viable since the passive external observation of such a complex behavior is nearly impossible, therefore we will use assigned signatures to carry the relevant parts of $\stackrel{init}{\Longrightarrow}$, $\stackrel{open}{\Longrightarrow}$, etc. tuples, i.e., the source and target configuration, the trigger processed and the set of transition conglomerates fired.

It is important to highlight that tuples transmitted to PSC-WD are not necessarily members of the $\Rightarrow$ set; in contrary: we would like to detect those cases where the tuple $\Rightarrow_x$ describing the actual step violates a semantic rule, i.e., $\Rightarrow_x \notin \Rightarrow$. As an illustration: in traditional WP schemes the application sends a signature s to the WP to check whether the state represented by s is a valid successor of the previous state; in our approach the application sends a tuple $\Rightarrow_x$ to PSC-WD to check whether $\Rightarrow_x$ is valid, i.e., $\Rightarrow_x \in \Rightarrow$.

Storing the *reference information* in a database (e.g., adjacency matrix) is surely not viable since this requires flattening the statechart and precalculating all possible steps; due to orthogonal state decomposition the size of the flattened statechart may be an exponential function of the original. The application of embedded signatures is not an option again since embedding a "fragment of possible future behavior" seems to be semantically even more complicated than the definition of the entire statechart semantics itself. Thus we will present an approach similar to watchdog program approaches: we will synthesize an automaton from the KTS that accepts correct runs of the application with respect to the statechart specification. The watchdog automaton will run in synchrony with the observed application, and check the validity of its steps.

Since our watchdog has to perform quite complex checks, we will *implement* it purely in software; PSC-WD can run as a stand-alone application connected to the observed application by some IPC mechanisms or embedded in the observed application in a self-checking configuration. For simplicity reasons we will focus on checking a single object specified by the statechart but our approach can be extended to checking any number of objects specified by any number of statecharts as discussed in [15].

According to our knowledge there were no elaborated solutions proposed in the literature for runtime error detection in statechart implementations. A combination of the SEIS approach with a statechart-based high level specification was suggested in [16]. In their approach statecharts are flattened and the reference information is stored in an adjacency matrix; state exit and entry activities are considered to be implemented by functions and the execution of these functions is checked by the SEIS WD scheme. The solution uses statecharts for ensuring that functions are called in a valid order. Unfortunately due to the lack of a formal semantics for statecharts their approach can not exploit most of the description power of statecharts, the proposed solution is primarily an extension of the SEIS approach instead of a WP for statechart implementations.

In our approach we will construct a watchdog automaton $\mathbf{W}$ that *accepts the correct runs of a statechart implementation*. We will assume that the $\Rightarrow_x$ steps of the implementation can be observed (through a monitor interface or by instrumentation). The task of building $\mathbf{W}$ can be characterized as a computer linguistics problem: we would like to build an automaton that *accepts valid sentences of a language*: (i) the *grammar* of the language is specified by the actual statechart with respect to the semantics discussed in Sec. 2, (ii) *words* of the language are the $\Rightarrow_i$ steps, and (iii) *sentences* are the $S = (\Rightarrow_0, \Rightarrow_1, \ldots)$ step sequences. For a step sequence S_i we have to decide whether S_i is valid according to the statechart and the operation semantics i.e., S_i is a valid sentence of the language.

Let us imagine the implementation as an automaton shown in Fig. 4. In this aspect we can consider the implementation as another automaton that writes the $\Rightarrow_i \in \Rightarrow$ words to its output as indicated by the labels on arrows (e.g., writing $\Rightarrow_i \in \stackrel{\text{init}}{\Longrightarrow}$ in case of "Initialization" etc.).

Initially let us consider that $\mathbf{W}$ can only see the *type of the step* taken by the implementation (i.e., whether $\Rightarrow_i$ belongs to $\stackrel{\text{init}}{\Longrightarrow}$ or $\stackrel{\text{open}}{\Longrightarrow}$, etc.), but does not investigate the internal semantics of $\Rightarrow_i = (s, (t, \mathrm{TC_f}), s')$ tuples. Let us assign *observation states* in $\mathbf{W}$ for phases of operations in the implementation (e.g., $\mathbf{Obs}_\alpha$ for $\mathbf{Phs}_\alpha$, $\mathbf{Obs}_\mathrm{U}$ for $\mathbf{Phs}_\mathrm{U}$ etc.). Constructing an automaton that observes the actual phase of operation in the implementation is easy since a source phase-step type pair unambiguously determines the target phase. The observer automaton should be obviously started from the $\mathbf{Obs}_\alpha$ state corresponding to the initial phase $\mathbf{Phs}_\alpha$.

Until this point our watchdog automaton $\mathbf{W}$ can only indicate those abnormal situations when the implementation performs a step whose type is invalid in the actual phase (e.g., opening an RTC step in the uninitialized phase). The next step is adding more intelligence to $\mathbf{W}$ by enabling it to check the *internal semantics* of $\Rightarrow_i = (s, (t, \mathrm{TC_f}), s')$ tuples. The automaton extended this way is shown as a UML statechart in Fig. 6: $\mathbf{W}$ has two top states: *Observing* (the watchdog is currently observing the behavior of the implementation and has not detected any inconsistencies) and *Error* (an error was detected). The observer automaton is implemented as sub-

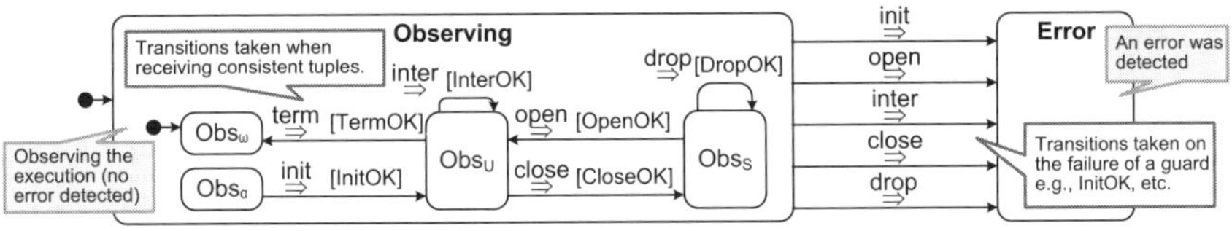

Fig. 6. The Watchdog Automaton

states and transitions in the Observing state. The predicates that check the internal consistency of $\Rightarrow_i = (s, (t, \mathrm{TC_f}), s')$ tuples are implemented as *guard predicates.* Note that according to priority relations, transitions between Observing and Error are only fireable if (i) a step of *invalid type* was performed (e.g., $\stackrel{\text{open}}{\Longrightarrow}$ in $\mathbf{Phs}_\alpha$) or (ii) a guard predicate evaluates to false indicating a *step consistency error.*

From this point our remaining work is only to specify the guard predicates that check whether a $\Rightarrow_i = (s, (t, \mathrm{TC_f}), s')$ tuple is a valid instance of the corresponding step type according to the semantics. The six guard predicates can be directly derived from the definitions of $\stackrel{\text{init}}{\Longrightarrow}$, $\stackrel{\text{open}}{\Longrightarrow}$, etc. Below we will present the formal definitions of guards **OpenOK**, **InterOK** and **CloseOK**, the remaining ones can be derived similarly.

The last observation to be considered before presenting the definitions is the following: the selection of fireable transition conglomerates involves the evaluation of guard predicates that possibly refer to variables of the application; since the WP does not know these values, all transition conglomerates whose source states are active and are triggered by the actual transition are considered to be *possibly fireable* i.e., if the application selects them for firing, then the watchdog will accept them. In the definitions we will use the symbol $\mathrm{TC_{pf}}$ representing possibly fireable transition conglomerates as discussed above and S_l^{ref} and S_e^{ref} as the reference sets of states left and entered: $(S_l^{\mathrm{ref}}, p^{\mathrm{ref}}, S_e^{\mathrm{ref}}) = \mathbf{Fire}(\mathbf{L}^{\mathrm{S}}_{\mathrm{Cnf}}(s), \mathrm{TC_f})$. The conflict of transition conglomerates tc_1 and tc_2 is indicated as $tc_1 \# tc_2$, the fact that tc_l is of higher priority that tc_h is indicated as $tc_l \prec tc_h$.

$$
\begin{aligned}
&\mathbf{OpenOK}((s,(t,\mathrm{TC_f}),s')) = (t \in \mathsf{Trigger}) \wedge (\mathrm{TC_f} \neq \emptyset) \wedge (\mathbf{L}^{\mathrm{S}}_{\mathrm{Cnf}}(s) \neq \emptyset) \wedge \\
&\quad (\mathbf{L}^{\mathrm{S}}_{\mathrm{Cnf}}(s) \cap \mathsf{TerminationState} = \emptyset) \wedge (\mathrm{TC_f} \subseteq \mathrm{TC_{pf}}) \wedge \\
&\quad (\forall tc \in \mathrm{TC_f} : \nexists tc^h \in \mathrm{TC_f} : tc \prec tc^h) \wedge (\nexists \{tc_1, tc_2\} \subseteq \mathrm{TC_f} : tc_1 \# tc_2) \wedge \\
&\quad (\mathbf{L}^{\mathrm{S}}_{\mathrm{Cnf}}(s') = (\mathbf{L}^{\mathrm{S}}_{\mathrm{Cnf}}(s) \setminus S_l^{\mathrm{ref}}) \cup S_e^{\mathrm{ref}}) \wedge (\mathbf{L}^{\mathrm{S}}_{\mathrm{Phs}}(s') = \mathbf{Phs}_{\mathrm{U}}) \\
&\mathbf{CloseOK}((s,(t,\mathrm{TC_f}),s')) = (t = t_\emptyset) \wedge (\mathrm{TC_f} = \emptyset) \wedge (\mathbf{L}^{\mathrm{S}}_{\mathrm{Cnf}}(s) \neq \emptyset) \wedge \\
&\quad (\mathbf{L}^{\mathrm{S}}_{\mathrm{Cnf}}(s) \cap \mathsf{TerminationState} = \emptyset) \wedge (\mathbf{L}^{\mathrm{S}}_{\mathrm{Cnf}}(s') = \mathbf{L}^{\mathrm{S}}_{\mathrm{Cnf}}(s)) \wedge (\mathbf{L}^{\mathrm{S}}_{\mathrm{Phs}}(s') = \mathbf{Phs}_{\mathrm{S}})
\end{aligned}
$$

$$\begin{aligned}&\mathbf{InterOK}((s,(t,\mathrm{TC_f}),s')) = (t = t_\emptyset) \wedge (\mathrm{TC_f} \neq \emptyset) \wedge (\mathbf{L}^{\mathrm{S}}_{\mathrm{Cnf}}(s) \neq \emptyset) \wedge \\ &\quad (\mathbf{L}^{\mathrm{S}}_{\mathrm{Cnf}}(s) \cap \mathsf{TerminationState} = \emptyset) \wedge (\mathrm{TC_f} \subseteq \mathrm{TC_{pf}}) \wedge \\ &\quad (\forall tc \in \mathrm{TC_f} : \nexists tc^h \in \mathrm{TC_f} : tc \prec tc^h) \wedge (\nexists \{tc_1, tc_2\} \subseteq \mathrm{TC_f} : tc_1 \# tc_2) \wedge \\ &\quad (\mathbf{L}^{\mathrm{S}}_{\mathrm{Cnf}}(s') = (\mathbf{L}^{\mathrm{S}}_{\mathrm{Cnf}}(s) \setminus S^{\mathrm{ref}}_l) \cup S^{\mathrm{ref}}_e) \wedge (\mathbf{L}^{\mathrm{S}}_{\mathrm{Phs}}(s') = \mathbf{Phs_U})\end{aligned}$$

The meaning of subexpressions in **OpenOK** is as follows: (i) the step consumed a trigger (i.e., not the empty trigger), (ii) there were one or more transition conglomerates fired, (iii) the source configuration was not empty, (iv) there were no termination states in the source configuration, (v) the transition conglomerates fired in the step were in the set of possibly fireable ones, (vi) none of the transition conglomerates fired in the step were disabled by priority relations, (vii) there were no conflicting transition conglomerate pairs fired, (viii) the resulting configuration is derived from the source configuration by removing S^{ref}_l and adding S^{ref}_e and (ix) the resulting phase is unstable. The meaning of subexpressions in **InterOK** is as follows: (i) the step did not consume any trigger, (ii) there were one or more transition conglomerates fired, (iii) the source configuration was not empty, (iv) there were no termination states in the source configuration, (v) the transition conglomerates fired in the step were in the set of possibly fireable ones, (vi) none of the transition conglomerates fired in the step were disabled by priority relations, (vii) there were no conflicting transition conglomerate pairs fired, (viii) the resulting configuration is derived from the source configuration by removing S^{ref}_l and adding S^{ref}_e and (ix) the resulting phase is unstable. The meaning of subexpressions in **CloseOK** is as follows: (i) the step did not consume any trigger, (ii) there were no transition conglomerates fired, (iii) the source configuration was not empty, (iv) there were no termination states in the source configuration, (v) the configuration was not modified and (vi) the resulting phase is stable.

The statechart in Fig. 6 coupled with formal definitions of guard predicates above defines the operation of PSC-WD. We implemented a prototype of PSC-WD as a stand-alone application that reads the statechart model of an application (using the XML metadata interchange format supported by most modeling environments), processes a trace of execution and signals an error on the violation of the behavioral specification.

6. Experimental Evaluation of Error Detection Capabilities

In order to demonstrate the error detection capabilities of our two solutions (PSC-PLTL checker and PSC-WD) we carried out a fault injection experiment campaign. This section outlines the goal of the analysis, the experiment setup and presents the results.

By definition, *fault injection* corresponds to artificial insertion of faults into a real target system [17]. A fault injection campaign is characterized by its goal, the system under investigation, and the input and output domains.

Fault injection experiments can aim at achieving the following *goals*: (i) understanding of the effects of faults in the system, (ii) assessing the efficiency of fault tolerance mechanisms and (iii) enhancement of fault tolerance mechanisms. The goal of our experiments is to experimentally assess the efficiency of our error detection techniques.

We used a desktop calculator application [18] as *system under investigation*. First we defined a draft statechart of the calculator (Fig. 7), specified some temporal correctness criteria in the context of the initial statechart, prepared the elaborated version of the calculator's statechart (Fig. 8) finally generated the source code of the application.

The *input domain* [19] corresponds to (i) the F set of injected faults, called the *faultload* and (ii) the W set of activities the system has to perform during the experiment, called the *workload*. In our experiments we used both model refinement faults (a transition was removed from model before code generation), implementation faults (two key functions were substituted by faulty implementations) and physical faults (a software-implemented fault injection (SWIFI) tool was used for enforcing bit flips in the memory) as *faultload*. The calculator had to perform calculations of various complexity as *workload*: (i) a "small" workload with three accumulated additions, (ii) a "medium" consisting of an addition, a percent calculation and a multiplication ($-0.123 + 4.56\% * -23.45 =$) and (iii) a "complex" containing multiple operations (note that since percent calculation takes the statechart to *ready* state, the medium workload does not contain accumulated operations).

The *output domain* corresponds to the R set of *readouts* that are collected to characterize the target system behavior in the presence of faults. The outcome of fault injection experiments is called the *measures* that are derived from the analysis and processing of the F, W and R sets. The direct *readouts* in our experiments were as follows: (i) everything written to the standard output (containing the result of computation), (ii) everything written to the standard error stream (possibly containing the error messages), (iii) the entire execution trace to be processed by PSC-WD and PSC-PLTL checker and (iv) errors detected by the operating system or the executer environment (e.g., occurrence of timeouts, signals delivered to the process etc.). Based on the raw readouts the following higher-level *measures* were derived: (i) failures delivered by the system (by comparing the con-

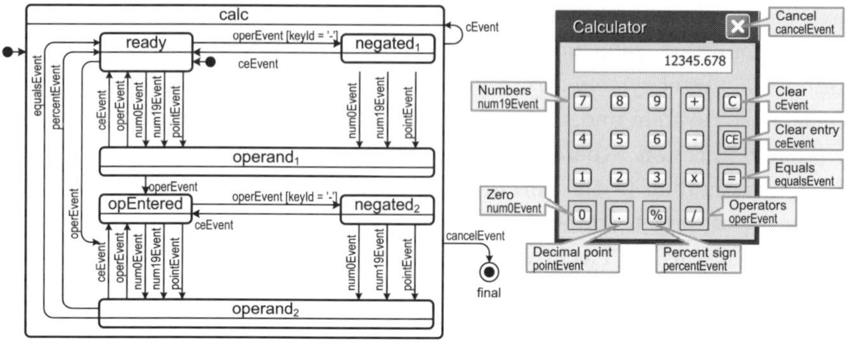

Fig. 7. Initial Statechart of the Desktop Calculator

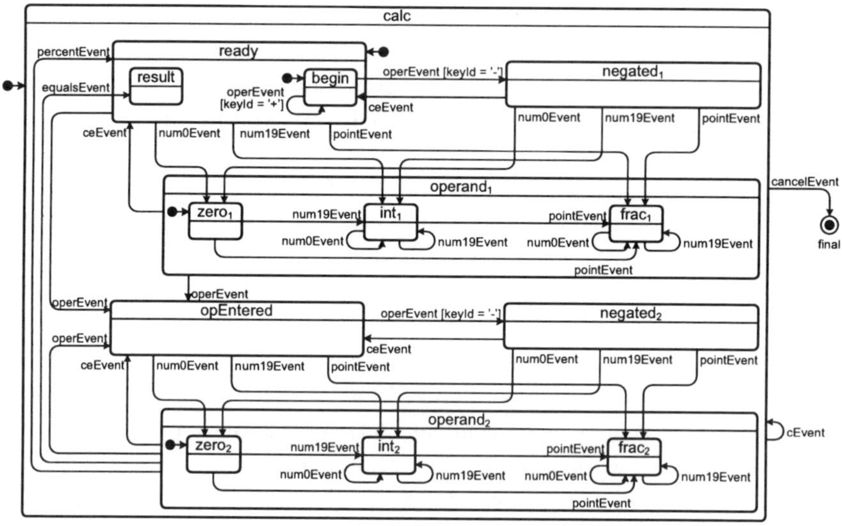

Fig. 8. Elaborated Statechart of the Desktop Calculator

tent of the standard output with the expected results of the computation), (ii) the errors detected by the PSC-PLTL checker and (iii) the PSC-WD (by processing the execution trace) and (iv) errors detected by the built-in mechanisms of the HW/OS mapped to UNIX signals (e.g., memory segmentation violations, etc.).

The initial statechart of the system (desktop calculator) is shown in Fig. 7. We defined the ϕ *temporal correctness criterion* in the context of the initial statechart: "the calculator should correctly handle operators

Table 2. Results of the Fault Injection Campaign

Faultload	**Workload**	**Observed phenomenon [%]**			
		Failure	PSC-PLTL	PSC-WD	Signal
Refinement	small	100.0	**100.0**	0.0	0.0
	medium	0.0	0.0	0.0	0.0
	complex	100.0	**100.0**	0.0	0.0
Implementation fault in **Enabled**	small	100.0	0.0	**100.0**	0.0
	medium	0.0	0.0	**100.0**	0.0
	complex	100.0	0.0	**100.0**	0.0
Implementation fault in **FireSingle**	small	0.0	0.0	**87.5**	0.0
	medium	100.0	0.0	**100.0**	100.0
	complex	12.5	0.0	**100.0**	12.50
Physical fault in **Enabled**	small	68.40	0.91	3.40	53.43
	medium	80.12	0.84	4.38	62.60
	complex	79.77	1.33	4.33	62.63
Physical fault in **FireSingle**	small	84.47	0.34	6.93	81.01
	medium	85.66	0.40	7.12	82.70
	complex	85.77	0.07	6.83	83.06

i.e., pushing an operator button in any of states $operand_1$ or $operand_2$ should take the calculator to *opEntered*": $\phi = \mathbf{G}(((\hat{\mathbf{P}}_{\mathrm{Cnf}}(\{\mathrm{operand}_1\}) \vee (\hat{\mathbf{P}}_{\mathrm{Cnf}}(\{\mathrm{operand}_2\}))) \wedge \mathbf{X}\,\hat{\mathbf{P}}_{\mathrm{Trigger}}(\mathrm{operEvent})) \to \mathbf{X}\,\hat{\mathbf{P}}_{\mathrm{Cnf}}(\{\mathrm{opEntered}\}))$.

The (correct) elaborated statechart of the calculator is shown in Fig. 8. We simulated *model refinement faults* by omitting the transition originating in $operand_2$, triggered by *operEvent* and targeting *opEntered* preventing this way the accumulation of operations in small and complex workloads.

Implementation faults were simulated by preparing faulty implementations of functions **Enabled** (collecting enabled transition conglomerates) and **FireSingle** (calculating the set of states left and entered when firing a transition conglomerate). The faulty version of **Enabled** was modified to return an invalid set of enabled transition conglomerates by first calculating the correct set than substituting an enabled transition conglomerate with a non enabled one. The faulty version of **FireSingle** was modified to return an invalid set of states left by adding a state to the correctly calculated set that should not be left. Both faulty implementations were prepared is such a way that the faulty behavior is exposed only once during the execution after a sufficiently long correct operation.

Physical faults were simulated by a custom SWIFI tool that was used for inverting bits in the code section targeting the binary implementation of **Enabled** and **FireSingle** functions.

The entire fault injection campaign consisted of over 180000 experiments (we used various slightly different options for code generation, building the binaries etc.) and resulted in a raw data set of over 10GB. The data set was processed and stored in a relational database. The results obtained by submitting queries to the database are shown in Tab. 2.

We were expecting *refinement faults* to be detected by the PSC-PLTL checker and remaining hidden from both PSC-WD and HW/OS mechanisms. The corresponding cells of Tab. 2 (highlighted by bold fonts) indicate that *all errors caused by refinement faults* that were forced to be activated by the workload were detected by the PSC-PLTL checker and there were no errors detected by PSC-WD or HW/OS mechanisms. It is important to highlight that the PSC-PLTL checker may detect errors only if (i) the PSC-PLTL predicate is violated (i.e., it is important to formally define all requirements that are to be checked) and (ii) the workload actually forces the application to expose faulty behavior (e.g., the omitted transition is not triggered by the medium workload therefore no error detection occurred).

We were expecting *implementation faults* to be detected by the PSC-WD and remaining hidden from the PSC-PLTL checker and HW/OS mechanisms. The corresponding cells of Tab. 2 (highlighted by bold fonts) indicate that a *very high percentage of errors caused by implementation faults* that were forced to be activated by the workload were detected by PSC-WD (87.5% of errors in case of the small workload and the **FireSingle** function and 100% of all other implementation errors and workloads). It was also indicated that some OS signals also occurred: taking a closer look on these signals we concluded that these were `SIGABORT` signals implementing standard ANSI-C assertions i.e., in these cases serious inconsistencies were detected by the application itself resulting in abortion of execution.

As our solutions were developed for detecting errors caused by refinement and implementation faults, in case of *physical faults* we were expecting low error detection potential from both the PSC-PLTL checker and PSC-WD and predicted better error detection potential for HW/OS mechanisms. Indeed: the corresponding cells of Tab. 2 indicate that the PSC-PLTL checker detected less than 2% of errors, the efficiency of PSC-WD fall into the [3.40% . . . 7.12%] interval while HW/OS mechanisms detected [53% . . . 83%] of faults in the code segment. The explanation for the high error detection ratio is as follows: bit inversions in the code section are likely to result in invalid operation codes or illegal memory addresses that are detected by the CPU or the memory management unit resulting in HW exceptions mapped to UNIX signals (e.g., segmentation violation, etc.).

It is interesting to outline the efforts needed for integrating our solutions into a software development process. In case of a UML-based development (where the delivered software is a result of subsequent iterative model refinement steps and finally the implementation), draft statecharts are constructed in early modeling phases while the implementation (manual programming or automatic code generation) is based on fully elaborated statecharts. This way the reference models of PSC-WD (elaborated statecharts) are already available without modifying the process, while the application of the PSC-PLTL checker still requires the definition of temporal correctness criteria in PSC-PLTL; the definition of requirements in temporal logic requires some practice in the mathematical formalism indeed, but on one hand this can be achieved with a minor effort, on the other hand the rigorous definition of temporal correctness and the corresponding communication with users is clearly beneficial for the entire process.

The prototype implementation of the LTL checker was used in the testing of a safety-critical railway application. Our industrial partner in this project was the Prolan Process Control Co. We are planning to port the PSC-PLTL checker and PSC-WD to the *mitmót* modular embedded platform [20] developed at the Embedded Information Technology Research Group of the Hungarian Academy of Sciences and Budapest University of Technology and Economics in order to prove the applicability of our solutions in resource constrained embedded platforms.

7. Conclusions and Future Work

This chapter has proposed two techniques for runtime detection of errors in the behavior of UML 2.0 statechart implementations. The main contributions are (i) outlining a *formal semantics* for statecharts that forms a solid foundation for reasoning about implementation, observation of behavior and runtime error detection; (ii) proposing the *PSC-PLTL language* for defining temporal correctness criteria in the context of statecharts and the corresponding evaluation method that enables the detection of errors caused by model refinement faults introduced during the development; (iii) presenting the *PSC-WD architecture* for detecting errors caused by faults in the implementation of statechart-based behavior and (iv) the *experimental evaluation* of our solutions that indicated the viability of our approaches. In our future work we would like to integrate these error detection techniques into a fault tolerance framework where errors detected by these techniques appear as high-level exceptions enabling the initiation of system-level recovery and fault tolerance measures.

References

1. G. Pintér and I. Majzik, *Formal Operational Semantics for UML 2.0 Statecharts*, tech. rep., Budapest University of Technology and Economics (DMIS/ESRG) (2005).
2. A. Sowmya and S. Ramesh, *IEEE Trans. on Software Eng.* **24**, 216 (1998).
3. D. Drusinsky and M.-t. Shing, TLCharts: Armor-plating Harel Statecharts with Temporal Logic Conditions, in *Proc. of the 15th IEEE Int. Workshop on Rapid System Prototyping*, (Switzerland, 2004).
4. A. Pnueli, The Temporal Logic of Programs, in *Proc. of the 18th Annual Symposium on Foundations of Computer Science,* (1977),
5. G. Pintér and I. Majzik, Automatic Generation of Executable Assertions for Runtime Checking Temporal Requirements, in *Proc. of the 9th IEEE Int. Symp. on High Assurance Systems Eng. (HASE 2005)*, eds. M. D. Cin, A. Bondavalli and N. Suri (Heidelberg, Germany, 2005).
6. A. Mahmood and E. J. McCluskey, *IEEE Trans. on Comp.* **37**, 160 (1988).
7. J. B. Eifert and J. P. Shen, Processor Monitoring Using Asynchronous Signatured Instruction Streams, in *Highlights from Twenty-Five Years: 25th Int. Symp. on Fault-Tolerant Computing,* (1995),
8. T. Michel, R. Leveugle and G. Saucier, A New Approach to Control Flow Checking Without Program Modification, in *Proc. of the 1991 Int. Symp. on Fault-Tolerant Computing (FTCS)*, (Canada, 1991).
9. M. Namjoo, Techniques for Concurrent Testing of VLSI Processor Operation, in *Proc. of the Int. Test Conf. 1982, ITC*, (IEEE Computer Society, Philadelphia, PA, USA, November 1982).
10. E. Michel and W. Hohl, Concurrent Error Detection Using Watchdog Processors, in *Proc. of the 5th Int. GI/ITG/GMA Conference*, eds. M. D. Cin and W. Hohl (Springer, Germany, September 1991).
11. D. J. Lu, *IEEE Trans. on Comp.* **C-31**, 681 (1982).
12. I. Majzik, W. Hohl, A. Pataricza and V. Sieh, *International Journal of Computer Systems – Science & Eng.* **11**, 125 (1996).
13. M. A. Schuette and J. P. Shen, *Trans. on Comp.* **43**, 129 (1994).
14. H. Madeira, *Microprocessors and Microsystems* **15**(April 1991).
15. C. Gacek, A. Romanovsky and R. de Lemos (eds.), *Architecting Dependable Systems* (Springer, 2005), ch. Run-time Verification of Statechart Implementations, pp. 148–172.
16. I. Majzik, J. Jávorszky, A. Pataricza and E. Selényi, Concurrent Error Detection of Program Execution Based on Statechart Specification, in *Proc. of the European Workshop on Dependable Computing,* (1999),
17. J. V. Carreira, D. Costa and J. G. Silva, *IEEE Spectrum* **36**, 50(August 1999).
18. M. Samek, *Practical Statecharts in C/C++* (CMP Books, 2002).
19. J. Arlat, M. Aguera, L. Amat, Y. Crouzet, J.-C. Fabre, J.-C. Laprie, E. Martins and D. Powell, *IEEE Trans. on Software Eng.* **16**, 166 (1990).
20. Cs. Tóth, Gy. Simon, T. Dabóczi, B. Scherer, L. Kádár, G. Samu, Z. Benesóczky and G. Péceli, A Modular Platform for Embedded Information Technology, in *Proceedings of the Design and Diagnostics of Electronic Circuits and Sytems, DDECS'05*, (Sopron, Hungary, 2005).

FAULT-TOLERANT COMMUNICATION FOR DISTRIBUTED EMBEDDED SYSTEMS*

C. KÜHNEL AND M. SPICHKOVA
Technische Universität München
Institut für Informatik
Bolzmannstr. 3
D-85748 Garching, Germany
E-mail: {kuehnelc,spichkov}@in.tum.de

Fault-tolerant communication is a crucial point in building distributed safety-critical real-time systems, as they are used today e.g. in the automotive and avionics domain. To argue about the timing properties of a distributed system and to show the fault-tolerance of its communication, a predictable timing of the system is needed. This can be solved using the time-triggered paradigm. In accordance with this paradigm, a time-triggered communication protocol, FlexRay, and an operating system OSEKtime with corresponding communication layer FTCom for the fault-tolerant communication were introduced by the FlexRay Consortium and OSEK/VDX respectively.

In this chapter we present the formal specifications of FlexRay and FTCom that allow us not only to argue about their properties in a precise, formal manner and to infer the dependences between their properties, but also to prove the correctness of the implementation formally.

1. Introduction

Embedded systems are one of the most challenging fields of systems engineering: Such a system must meet real-time requirements, is often safety critical and distributed.

Distributed embedded systems have been in an industrial environment for several years now, even for safety-critical applications, e.g. in avionics. Just like a modern aircraft, a premium car today consists of up to 70 electronic control units that communicate over several different networks. To reduce costs and increase functionality more and more features of a car are

*This work was partially funded by the german federal ministry of education and technology (bmbf) in the framework of the verisoft project under grant 01 is c38. the responsibility for this article lies with the authors.

controlled by software. In order to distribute even safety-critical functions over a network of control units, a fault-tolerant communication mechanism is required. Since the technical and economical constrains in automotive differ from those in avionics, a new communication stack fulfilling those automotive constraints has been developed.

The trend in the automotive industry to shift functionality from mechanics and electronics to software has been going on for several years now, but progress seems to have slowed down. Most of the manufacturers have presented drive-by-wire prototypes, but none of them has entered mass production. The experiences with increased software in the infotainment domain have shown severe quality issues. To overcome these, new technology for distributed fault-tolerant systems, is required. One major problem today is reliable, deterministic communication for distributed automotive systems. In avionics the time triggered paradigm was applied successfully to distributed systems. This idea is now being propagated to the automotive domain.

The system specified here is based on the time-triggered paradigm (both, the communication protocol and the operating system, are time-triggered). In a time-triggered system all actions are executed at predefined points in time. This provides a timing behaviour that is deterministic: Task execution times and their order, as well as message transmission times are deterministic. This property is important for distributed real-time systems, because for such types of systems it is possible to predict and even prove their timing properties with reasonable effort.

FlexRay and FTCom form, together with OSEKtime OS, the verification framework[4] that provides the methodology for the verification of application properties for time triggered systems. We abstract here from the detailed specification of the OS, as well as from the application components to concentrate on the representation of the fault-tolerant communication between application components via FlexRay and FTCom. The verification of an OSEKtime OS is being performed in the Verisoft project[25].

The architecture of the entire system is depicted in Figure 1. It consists of a micro controller and a FlexRay controller in each node and a network cable, connecting the FlexRay controllers of all nodes. Above that is the operating system consisting of OSEKtime OS and OSEK FTCom. On top of the operating system are the different applications that represent the desired behaviour of the system. The operating system and the hardware may be identical all over the network, the difference between the nodes are the configuration data of each node and the applications running on

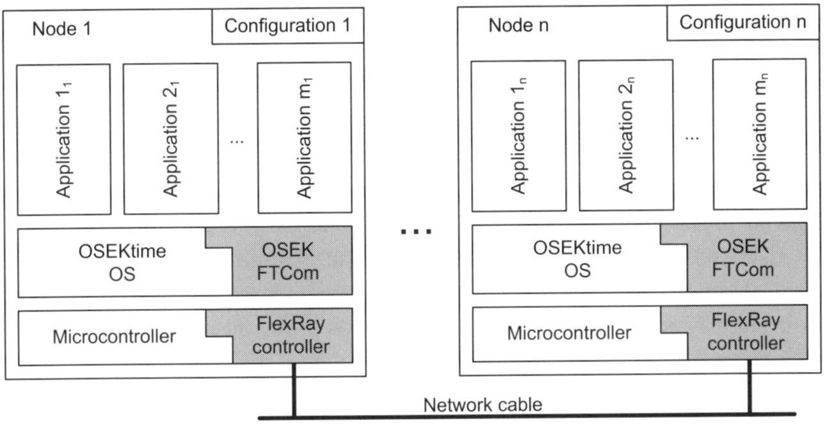

Figure 1. System architecture

the nodes. To make a formal analysis for FlexRay and FTCom possible, several aspects of the systems have been formalized[14]. This paper describes the major aspects of the formalization of the OSEK FTCom, the FlexRay controller and the network cable, as indicated by the gray colour in Figure 1.

For the development of embedded systems in most cases experts of different disciplines have to cooperate. For such cooperation a specification, i.e. a precise and detailed description of the behaviour and/or structure of the system under development is very important. One aim of formal methods is to prove or to evaluate automatically behavioural properties of a system in a systematic way, based on a clear mathematical theory. It is now widely recognized that only formal methods can provide the level of assurance required by the increasing complexity and the high safety and quality requirements of such systems. In order to design systems in a step-wise, modular style we use Focus[5], a framework for the formal specification and development of interactive systems. This framework provides a number of specification techniques and concepts of refinement for distributed systems. Focus is well suited for the formalization since it provides a synchronous notion of time and communication between components is message-based just as in FlexRay and OSEK FTCom.

Having the formal specification in Focus, it can be translated schematically into a specification in Isabelle/HOL[16](a specification and verification system implemented in the functional programming language ML) to prove the correctness of the implementation formally. The formal specifications of real-life systems can become very large and complex, and as a result hard to read and to understand. Therefore it is too complicated to start the specification process in HOL. To overcome this problem Focus is used as it supports a graphical specification style based on tables and diagrams, e.g. state transition diagrams.

FOCUS is preferred here over other specification frameworks since it has an integrated notion of time-synchrony and therefore matches the time-triggered paradigm of FlexRay and OSEKtime OS.[a] E.g., the B-method[1] is used in many publications on fault-tolerant systems, but it has neither graphical representations nor integrated notion of time, and the B-method also is slightly more low-level and more focused on the refinement to code rather than formal specification.

1.1. *FlexRay*

FlexRay is a time triggered communication protocol, developed by the FlexRay Consortium[8]. Its primary application domain is distributed real-time systems in vehicles. Today, most of these systems use a Controller Area Network (CAN)[21] as means of communication. The advantages of FlexRay over CAN are: higher bandwidth, integrated functionality for clock synchronisation, deterministic real-time message transmission and fault tolerance.

FlexRay will be used in the next generation automobiles, e.g. at BMW[6], for distributed control applications in chassis and power train[b]. FlexRay is especially suitable for these applications, since it provides synchronized clocks and deterministic message transmission times with a low jitter. Both criteria are a prerequisite for distributing control applications over an network. Furthermore its has enough bandwidth (up to 10 Mbit/s) to support applications with a high load of periodical messages, also typical for control applications.

1.2. *OSEKtime FTCom*

OSEKtime[19] OS is an OSEK/VDX[17] open operating system standard of the European automotive industry. OSEKtime OS is a time-triggered OS that supports static cyclic scheduling based on the computation of the WCETs (worst case execution times) of its tasks. WCETs are needed for

[a]Time-synchrony does not be restriction of FOCUS, in this framework an event-triggered system can also be modelled.
[b]Subsystem of a vehicle, usually consisting of engine, transmission, power steering and break controllers.

schedulability analysis and can be estimated from a compiled C program and the processor the program runs on[2].

FTCom[18] (Fault-Tolerant Communication) is a fault-tolerant communication layer for OSEKtime that provides a number of primitives for interprocess communication and makes task distribution transparent.

The rest of the chapter is organized as follows: Sect. 2 introduces the main concepts FOCUS. The formal specifications of FlexRay and FTCom as parts of a fault-tolerant embedded system are presented in Sect. 3, and the dependences between their properties are discussed in Sect. 4. The main ideas how the correctness of the implementation can be proven formally are introduced in Sect. 5. Sect. 6 gives an overview of related approaches and shows where the presented work goes beyond the existing techniques. Sect. 7 summarizes the chapter.

2. FOCUS

FOCUS [5] is a framework for formal specifications and development of distributed interactive systems. A distributed system in FOCUS is represented by its components that are connected by communication links called *channels*. Components are described in terms of their input/output behaviour which is total. The components can interact or work independently of each other.

The channels in this specification framework are *asynchronous communication links* without delays. They are *directed*, *reliable*, and *order preserving*. Via these channels components exchange information in terms of typed *messages*. Messages are passed along the channels one after the other and delivered in exactly the same order in which they were sent.

In FOCUS a specification characterizes the relation between the *communication histories* for the external *input* and *output channels*. The formal meaning of a specification is exactly this external *input/output relation*. The FOCUS specifications can be structured into a number of formulas each characterizing a different kind of property.

The central concept in FOCUS are *streams*. These represent communication histories of *directed channels*. Streams in FOCUS are functions mapping the indexes in their domains to their messages. For any set of messages M, M^{ω} denotes the set of all streams, M^{∞} and M^{*} denote the sets of all infinite and all finite streams respectively. $M^{\underline{\omega}}$ denotes the set of all timed streams, $M^{\underline{\infty}}$ and $M^{\underline{*}}$ denote the sets of all infinite and all finite timed streams respectively. A *timed stream* is represented by a sequence of messages and *time ticks* (represented by $\surd$), the messages are also listed in their order of transmission. The ticks model a discrete notion of time.

$$M^\omega \stackrel{\text{def}}{=} M^* \cup M^\infty \qquad M^{\underline{\omega}} = M^{\underline{*}} \cup M^{\underline{\infty}}$$

$$M^* \stackrel{\text{def}}{=} \cup_{n \in \mathbb{N}}([1..n] \to M) \qquad M^{\underline{*}} \stackrel{\text{def}}{=} \cup_{n \in \mathbb{N}}([1..n] \to M \cup \{\surd\})$$

$$M^\infty \stackrel{\text{def}}{=} \mathbb{N}_+ \to M \qquad M^{\underline{\infty}} \stackrel{\text{def}}{=} \mathbb{N}_+ \to M \cup \{\surd\})$$

An empty stream is represented in Focus by $\langle\rangle$, and $\langle x \rangle$ denotes an one-element stream. The following Focus operators will be used in the remainder of this chapter:

- $\#x$ denotes the length of the stream x;
- $x.j$ – the jth element of the stream x;
- $\mathsf{dom}.x$ – the domain of the stream x, $[1..\#x]$;
- $\mathsf{rng}.x$ – the range of the stream x, $\{x.j \mid j \in \mathsf{dom}.x\}$;
- the predicate $\mathsf{disjoint}(s_1, \ldots, s_n)$ is true, if all streams $s_1, \ldots, s_n$ are disjoint, i.e. in every time unit only one of these streams contains a message;
- to simplify the specification of the real-time systems we introduce the operator $\mathsf{ti}(s, n)$ that yields the list of messages that are in the timed stream s between the ticks n and $n+1$ (at the nth time unit)[c];
- we also define the operator $\mathsf{msg}_n(s)$, which holds for a timed stream s, if the stream contains at most n messages in every time unit.

In Focus we can have both *elementary* and *composite* specifications. Elementary specifications are the atomic blocks for system representation, and in this case we distinguish among three frames: the *untimed*, the *timed* and the *time-synchronous frame*, that correspond to the stream types in the specification.

Any *elementary* Focus specification has the following syntax:

Name (Parameter_Declarations)		Frame_Labels
in	*Input_Declarations*	
out	*Output_Declarations*	
Body		

[c]The reason to use this operator is also simplification and clarification the later translation into Isabelle/HOL to prove properties of the specified system and components.

Name is the name of the specification; *Frame_Labels* lists a number of frame labels, e.g. *untimed*, *timed* or *time-synchronous*, that correspond to the stream types in the specification; *Parameter_Declarations* lists a number of parameters (optional); *Input_Declarations* and *Output_Declarations* list the declarations of input and output channels respectively. *Body* characterizes the relation between the input and output streams, and can be a number of formulas, a table, or diagram or a combination thereof. The *Body* of an elementary FOCUS specification S is represented by a number of logic formulas – each formula represents some logic property – looks as follows:

P_1
P_2
$\ldots$
P_n

The line breaks denote a conjunction in FOCUS.

One special notion of body used in this specification is the *assumption/guarantee*[5] style, where the body consists of two parts: an assumption over the input declarations which must be met by the environment of the component (introduced by the asm keyword), and guarantee (introduced by the gar keyword) which holds over the output declarations of the component[d]. The semantics of such a specification in FOCUS is logical implication: the assumption part implies the guarantee part.

Having a timed specification we have always to deal with infinite timed streams by the definition of the *semantics of a timed frame.*

Definition 2.1. The semantics of any elementary timed specification S (written $[\![S]\!]$) is defined[5] to be the formula:

$$i_S \in I_S^{\underline{\infty}} \;\wedge\; o_S \in O_S^{\underline{\infty}} \;\wedge\; B_S \tag{1}$$

where i_S and o_S denote lists of input and output channel identifiers, I_S and O_S denote their corresponding types, and B_S is a formula in predicate logic that describes the body of the specification S. □

Composite specifications are built hierarchically from elementary ones using constructors for composition and network description.

Definition 2.2. For any composite specification S consisting of n subspecifications $S_1, \ldots, S_n$, we define its semantics, written $[\![S]\!]$, to be the

[d]Examples of such kind of specification are given in Sect. 3.3.2 by specifications *FlexRay* and *FlexRayArch*.

formula:

$$[\![S]\!] \stackrel{def}{=} \exists\, l_S \in L_S^{\infty} : \bigwedge_{j=1}^{n} [\![S_j]\!] \tag{2}$$

where l_S denotes a list of local channel identifiers and L_S denotes their corresponding types. □

System refinement provides a natural mechanism for structuring complex systems for increased readability. It is now widely recognized, that it is not advisable and in most cases even impossible to make a concrete implementation of a large system from its abstract requirements specification in a single step. In practice a stepwise development is used – the requirements specification is refined into a concrete implementation stepwise, via a number of intermediate specifications[5].

If a specification S_2 is a refinement of S_1, they must have the same syntactic interface. The refined specification S_2 may meet further requirements in addition to the requirements on the more abstract specification S_1. At the same time, the more concrete specification S_2 must meet all the requirements of the specification S_1. This kind of refinement is used to reduce the number of possible output histories for a given input history.

Definition 2.3. A specification S_2 is called a *behavioural refinement* ($S_1 \rightsquigarrow S_2$) of a specification S_1 if

- they have the same syntactic interface and
- every I/O history of S_2 is also an I/O history of S_1.

The relation $\rightsquigarrow$ of behavioural refinement is defined[5] by equivalence

$$(S_1 \rightsquigarrow S_2) \Longleftrightarrow ([\![S_2]\!] \Rightarrow [\![S_1]\!]) \tag{3}$$

□

The notion of the refinement relation is also essential for the verification of the system properties. If we summarise all properties of a system as an additional FOCUS specification (so called *requirements specification*), we can show that the system fulfils its requirements proving that the refinement relation between the system requirements specification and the (architecture) system specification holds. Thus, we can translate the formal FOCUS specifications schematically into the corresponding Isabelle/HOL (cf Sect. 5) specification and verify them. In this chapter we concentrate on the specification of the fault-tolerant communication for distributed embedded systems. The verification of the system's properties is presented exemplarily with the FlexRay specification – we have shown that the FlexRay architecture is a refinement of the specified FlexRay requirements.

3. Formal Specification

In this section we discuss the formal FOCUS specification of the fault-tolerant embedded system in general, and also the specification of the communication layer (FTCom and FlexRay) in detail.

3.1. *Fault-Tolerant Embedded System*

The architecture of the overall system is represented as a FOCUS specification *SystemArch*. The system consists of a number of nodes with an OSEKtime OS and a number of applications connected over a FlexRay network (cf. Figure 1). On each node there is a *FTComCNI* component that consists of two subcomponents: the *FTCom* itself and a *CNI_Buffer* (Communication Network Interface). In the *CNI_Buffer* all the messages that must be sent via FlexRay are stored, whereas the local communication on the node is done directly via *FTCom*.

To specify this system the following data types are used. The type *FT_CNI_Entity* represents the type of application messages. It consists of a message identifier of type *MessageId* and an application data type *DataType*. The data types *RCV_Type* and *Status_Type* represent the result types of the standard FTCom functions[18].The type *Slot* describes here one time slot during a FlexRay communication cycle and is equal to the type of natural numbers $\mathbb{N}$. The type *Frame* represents a FlexRay frame and consists of a slot identifier *slot* and the payload *Payload*, which is a (finite) list of type *FT_CNI_Entity*. The FlexRay bus configuration *Config* contains the bus scheduling table *schedule* of the node and the length of the communication cycle *cyclelength*.

$$
\begin{array}{lcl}
\textsf{type } FT\_CNI\_Entity & = & entity(mid \in MessageId,\ mdata \in DataType) \\
\textsf{type } Payload & = & FT\_CNI\_Entity^{*} \\
\textsf{type } Frame & = & frm(slot \in Slot,\ payload \in Payload) \\
\textsf{type } Config & = & conf(schedule \in Slot^{*},\ cycleLength \in \mathbb{N})
\end{array}
$$

The definition of the type *Payload* depends on the configuration of the FTCom (see Sect. 3.2 and Sect. 4).

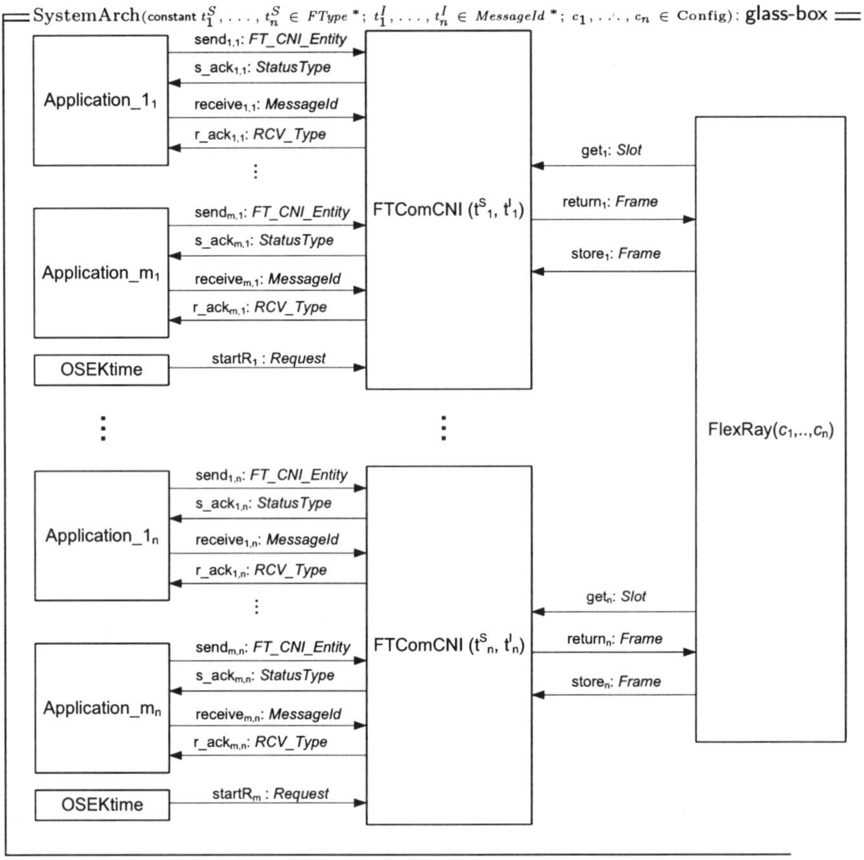
SystemArch(constant $t_1^S, \ldots, t_n^S \in FType^*$; $t_1^I, \ldots, t_n^I \in MessageId^*$; $c_1, \ldots, c_n \in$ Config): glass-box
Application_1$_1$
send$_{1,1}$: FT_CNI_Entity
s_ack$_{1,1}$: StatusType
receive$_{1,1}$: MessageId
r_ack$_{1,1}$: RCV_Type
Application_m$_1$
send$_{m,1}$: FT_CNI_Entity
s_ack$_{m,1}$: StatusType
receive$_{m,1}$: MessageId
r_ack$_{m,1}$: RCV_Type
OSEKtime
startR$_1$: Request
FTComCNI (t^S_1, t^I_1)
get$_1$: Slot
return$_1$: Frame
store$_1$: Frame
FlexRay(c_1,..,c_n)
Application_1$_n$
send$_{1,n}$: FT_CNI_Entity
s_ack$_{1,n}$: StatusType
receive$_{1,n}$: MessageId
r_ack$_{1,n}$: RCV_Type
Application_m$_n$
send$_{m,n}$: FT_CNI_Entity
s_ack$_{m,n}$: StatusType
receive$_{m,n}$: MessageId
r_ack$_{m,n}$: RCV_Type
OSEKtime
startR$_m$: Request
FTComCNI (t^S_n, t^I_n)
get$_n$: Slot
return$_n$: Frame
store$_n$: Frame

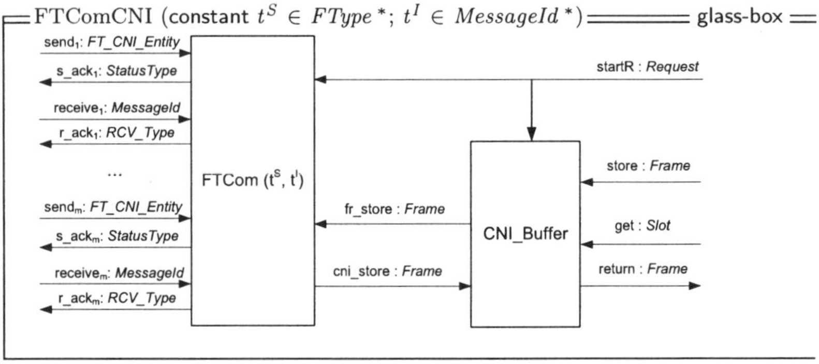
FTComCNI (constant $t^S \in FType^*$; $t^I \in MessageId^*$) glass-box
send$_1$: FT_CNI_Entity
s_ack$_1$: StatusType
receive$_1$: MessageId
r_ack$_1$: RCV_Type
...
send$_m$: FT_CNI_Entity
s_ack$_m$: StatusType
receive$_m$: MessageId
r_ack$_m$: RCV_Type
FTCom (t^S, t^I)
startR : Request
fr_store : Frame
cni_store : Frame
CNI_Buffer
store : Frame
get : Slot
return : Frame

Thus, to have fault-tolerant communication between n nodes of the system, we have a *FlexRay* component and n *FTComCNI* components (one for each node). According to the level of fault-tolerance (see Sect. 4.1) we either rely on the fault-tolerance of FlexRay transmission, or use the fault-tolerance components of FTCom (see Sect. 3.2).

3.2. *FTCom*

In the FOCUS specification the *FTCom* component consists of three subcomponents: *FTCom_Buffer*, *Replica* and *RDA* (Replica Determinate Agreement[18]). The *FTCom_Buffer* is used for the local communication – between applications that are deployed on the same node, so that local messages are not sent via FlexRay. The *Replica* and *RDA* components of *FTComArch* are needed for the fault-tolerant communication with other nodes of the system: every application message will be sent k times $(1 < k)$ according to the replication-tables. The receiver-node will compute the current value of the message from the arrived replicas of it.

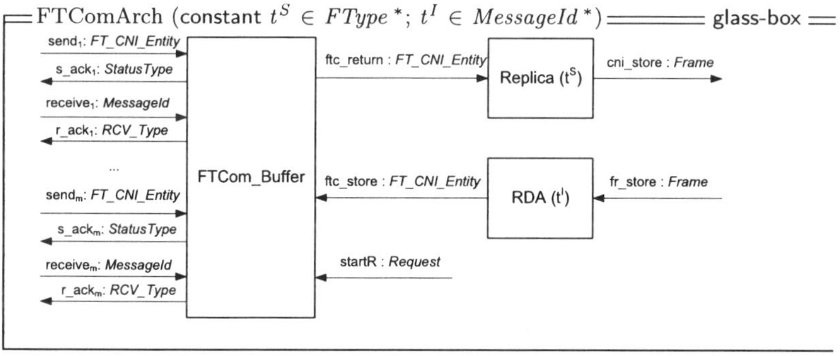

The *Replica* component performs the replication of messages: one application message is packed into several FlexRay frames using the replication-tables t^S – an application message will be transported during several FlexRay slots of each communication round. A replication-table is specified as list of type *FType*:

$$\text{type } FType = ft(slot \in Slot,\ msl \in MessageId^*)$$

Replica(constant $tableS \in FType^*$) — timed

in $ftc\_return : FT\_CNI\_Entity$

out $cni\_store : Frame$

asm

$CorrectTableS(tableS)$

gar

$$\forall t \in \mathbb{N} : \\ \mathsf{ti}(cni\_store, t) = \\ \quad \text{if } \mathsf{ti}(ftc\_return, t) = \langle\rangle \\ \quad \text{then } \langle\rangle \\ \quad \text{else } Replicate(tableS, \mathsf{ti}(ftc\_return, t)) \text{ fi}$$

The *CorrectTableS* predicate ensures that the replication-table is correct: the table must be nonempty, every slot identifier occurs in the table at most once, a new frame can be build only from the messages produced on this node, etc.

We define the *Replicate* function in FOCUS as follows:

Replicate

$$FType^* \times FT\_CNI\_Entity^* \rightarrow Frames^*$$

$$Replicate(\langle\rangle,\ b) = \langle\rangle$$

$$Replicate(ft(x_s, x_m) \,\&\, xs,\ b) = \\ \quad frm(x_s, ReplicateMessages(x_m, b)) \,\&\, Replicate(xs,\ t, send_1, \ldots, send_m)$$

where the function *ReplicateMessages* is defined as below:

ReplicateMessages

$$MessageId^* \times FT\_CNI\_Entity^* \rightarrow FT\_CNI\_Entity^*$$

$$ReplicateMessages(\langle\rangle,\ b) = \langle\rangle$$

$$ReplicateMessages(y \,\&\, ys,\ b) = \\ \quad \text{if } \exists\, a \in DataType :\ entity(y, a) \in \mathsf{rng}.b \\ \quad \text{then } entity(y, a) \,\&\, ReplicateMessages(ys,\ b) \\ \quad \text{else } ReplicateMessages(ys,\ b) \text{ fi}$$

The *RDA* component performs the elimination of the replicas: frames are unpacked using the RDA-tables t^I. A RDA-table is specified as list of type *MessageId*. From the replicated messages the current one is built using some RDA algorithm (it must be specified by the function *DoRDA*), e.g. average, majority vote, "pick any" (see also Sect. 4).

The *CorrectTableI* predicate ensures that the RDA-table is correct: the list of message identifiers must be nonempty, every message identifier occurs in the table at most once and does not belong to the identifiers of the messages produced on this node, etc.

The *Replica* and *RDA* components are called by the OSEKtime dispatcher every communication round. In the FOCUS specification this is represented by using request messages of type *Request* on the channel *startR*.

```
RDA(constant tableI ∈ MessageId*)                                timed
in     fr_store : Frame
out    ftc_store : FT_CNI_Entity
------------------------------------------------------------------
asm
   CorrectTableI(tableI)
- - - - - - - - - - - - - - - - - - - - - - - - - - - - - - - - -
gar
   ∀ t ∈ ℕ :
      ti(ftc_store, t) =
         if ti(fr_store, t) = ⟨⟩
         then ⟨⟩
         else DoRDA(tableI, Frame2Message(ti(fr_store, t))) fi
```

For the overall system the same correctness properties must also hold for the unions of all corresponding tables of the system, namely gS is the union of all t^S tables and gI of all t^I tables. Moreover, the gS and gI tables must be "inverse" in sense of the predicate *InverseSI*[14] (see below). In such a way we can formally show (using a theorem prover Isabelle/HOL[11,26]) for the concrete tables that they are correct according to these properties.

The property "gS and gI tables are correct and inverse" can also be seen as assumption part for the specification of the overall system.

InverseSI

$gS \in FType^*; \quad gI \in MessageId^*$

$\forall\, i \in \mathsf{rng}.gI : \ \exists\, s \in \mathsf{rng}.gS : \ i \in \mathsf{rng}.msl(s)$
$\forall\, ft(s,\ id\_list) \in \mathsf{rng}.gS : \ \forall\, i \in \mathsf{rng}.id\_list : \ i \in \mathsf{rng}.gI$
$\forall\, i,j \in \mathsf{dom}.gS : \ i \neq j \Rightarrow sl(gS.i) \neq sl(gS.j)$

We omit the discussion of the formal specifications of the *FTCom_Buffer* to concentrate on FlexRay.

3.3. *FlexRay*

FlexRay contains a set of complex algorithms to provide the communication services. From the view of the software layers above FlexRay only a few of these properties become visible. The most important ones are static cyclic communication schedules and system-wide synchronous clocks. These provide a suitable platform for distributed control algorithms as used e.g. in drive-by-wire applications. The formalization described here is based on the "Protocol Specification 2.0"[10].

3.3.1. *Abstractions*

To reduce the complexity of the system several aspects of FlexRay have been abstracted in this formalization:

(1) There is no clock synchronization or start-up phase since clocks are assumed to be synchronous[e]. This corresponds very well with the *time-synchronous* notion of FOCUS.[5]
(2) As they are optional, the model does not contain "bus guardians" that protect channels on the physical layer from interference caused by communication that is not aligned with FlexRay schedules.
(3) As the main interest of this chapter is time-triggered systems and since the transmission time of messages in the dynamic segment can, in general, not be guaranteed, only the static segment of the communication cycle has been specified here.

[e]A verification of the clock synchronization algorithm of FlexRay is in progress at LORIA, based on their framework[7].

(4) The time-basis for the system is one slot i.e. one FlexRay slot corresponds to one tick in the formalization. This is the abstraction level at which applications interact with FlexRay.

(5) The system contains only one FlexRay channel. Adding a second channel would mean simply doubling the FlexRay component (with a different configuration) and adding extra channels for the access to the *CNI_Buffer* component.

3.3.2. *FlexRay Requirements and Architecture*

The *FlexRay* component contains the assumptions and guarantees for the FlexRay network. In *IdenticCycleLength* it assumes that the length of the communication cycle is identical for all nodes, in *DisjointSchedules* and msg_1 that for each slot of a cycle there is at most one node sending at most one frame. These are the basic requirements of a static cyclic time division multiplexing network.

FlexRay (constant $c_1, ..., c_n \in$ Config) — timed

in $return_1, ..., return_n$: *Frame*

out $store_1, ..., store_n$: *Frame*; $get_1, ..., get_n$: *Slot*

---

asm $\forall\, i \in [1..n] : \mathsf{msg}_1(return_i)$

$DisjointSchedules(c_1, ..., c_n)$

$IdenticCycleLength(c_1, ..., c_n)$

gar $FrameTransmission(return_1, ..., return_n, store_1, ..., store_n, get_1, ..., get_n,$
$c_1 ..., c_n)$

$\forall\, i \in [1..n] : \mathsf{msg}_1(get_i) \wedge \mathsf{msg}_1(store_i)$

The guarantee $\mathsf{msg}_1(get_i) \wedge \mathsf{msg}_1(store_i)$ defines that over the channels get_i and $store_i$ at most one frame is transmitted in each tick. The former one is required by the *CNI_Buffer*, the latter by *Cable.*

The guarantee *FrameTransmission* describes how frames are transmitted over a FlexRay-network. This predicate specifies that if at time t the node k should be sending according to its schedule, it requests the frame which should be sent from the *CNI_Buffer* over the channels get_k and $return_k$. This frame is then sent to the other nodes of the system. These receive the frame and store it in their respective *CNI_Buffers* over the channel $store_j$.

FrameTransmission

$store_1, ..., store_n, return_1, ..., return_n \in Frame^{\underline{\omega}}$
$get_1, ..., get_n \in Slot^{\underline{\omega}}$
$c_1, ..., c_n \in Config$

$\forall\, t \in \mathbb{N}, k \in [1..n]$:

$\quad s \in schedule(c_k) : s = \mathsf{mod}(cycleLength(c_k), t) \rightarrow$

$\qquad \mathsf{ti}(get_k, t) = \langle s \rangle \wedge$

$\qquad \forall\, j \in [1..n], j \neq k : \mathsf{ti}(store_j, t) = \mathsf{ti}(return_k, t)$

The architecture of the FlexRay communication protocol is specified in *FlexRayArch*, which is a refinement of the component *FlexRay*. The assumption part of the specification *FlexRayArch* is equal to the assumption part of the specification *FlexRay*. The guarantee part is represented by the specification *FlexRayArchitecture* (see below).

FlexRayArch (constant $c_1, ..., c_n \in$ Config) — timed

in $\quad return_1, ..., return_n : Frame$

out $\quad store_1, ..., store_n : Frame;\ get_1, ..., get_n : \mathbb{N}$

---

asm $\quad \forall\, i \in [1..n] : \mathsf{msg}_1(return_i)$
$\quad DisjointSchedules(c_1, \ldots, c_n)$
$\quad IdenticCycleLength(c_1, \ldots, c_n)$

gar $\quad (store_1, \ldots, store_n, get_1, \ldots, get_n) :=$
$\qquad FlexRayArchitecture(c_1, \ldots, c_n)(return_1, \ldots, return_n)$

The *FlexRayArchitecture* component consists of several *FlexRayController* and a network *Cable*. The unconnected channels of each controller are to be connected to those of the *FTCom-CNI* components (cf. Sect. 3.2). Since FOCUS does not contain a concept for broadcast communication this is simulated in the *Cable* component: It forwards a received frame to all connected nodes unless it is lost due to a communication error (cf. Sect. 3.3.4).

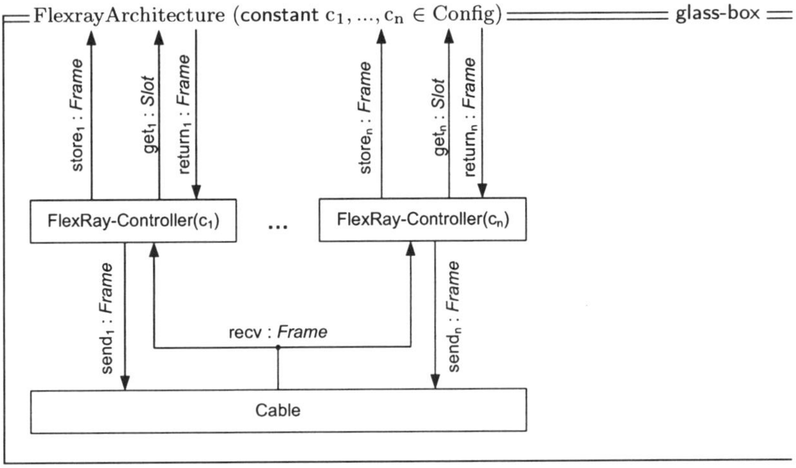

3.3.3. *FlexRay Controller*

A *FlexRayController* component consists of a *Scheduler* and a *BusInterface*. The *Scheduler* evaluates the schedule *schedule(c)*, whereas the *BusInterface* is responsible for the actual sending and receiving of the frames. The slot number in the schedule specifies the time slot when the frame should be sent and also the type of frame, since this mapping is static. Based on this information the *Scheduler* notifies the *BusInterface* in case a frame should be sent. The current slot s is the current time t modulo the length of a FlexRay cycle. If at time t, according to the schedule, the node is supposed to send a frame, the *Scheduler* sends the current slot number on the channel *activation*.

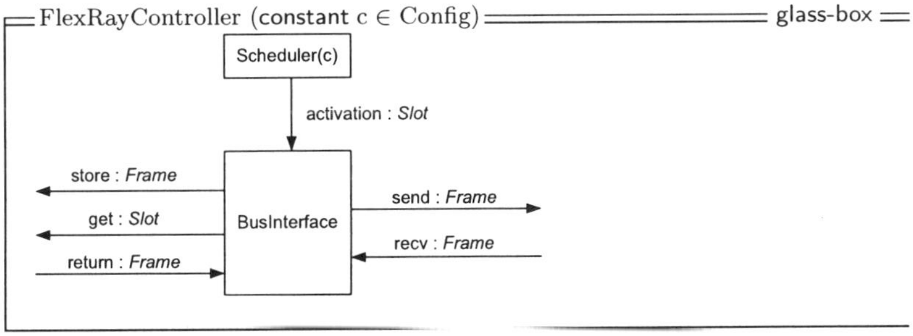

Scheduler(consttab c ∈ Config) — timed

out $activation : \mathbb{N}$

---

univ $s \in \mathbb{N}$

- - -

$\forall\, t \in \mathbb{N}:$

$\quad \mathsf{if}\ \mathsf{mod}(t, cycleLength(c)) \in schedule(c)$

$\quad\quad \mathsf{then}\ \mathsf{ti}(activation, t) = \langle \mathsf{mod}(t, cycleLength(c)) \rangle$

$\quad\quad \mathsf{else}\ \mathsf{ti}(activation, t) = \langle\rangle \quad \mathsf{fi}$

The *BusInterface* then fetches the corresponding frame from the *CNI_Buffer* and sends it on the channel *send*. If the node is not sending and a frame is received over the channel *recv*, this frame is forwarded to the *CNI_Buffer* over the channel *store*. This component is specified using the two predicates *Send* and *Receive* which define the FOCUS relations on the streams to represent respectively data send and data receive by the FlexRay controller. The details of the predicates *Send* and *Receive* are described in a technical report[14].

BusInterface — timed

in $activation : \mathbb{N};\ return, recv : Frame$

out $send, store : Frame;\ get : \mathbb{N}$

$\mathrm{Receive}(recv, store, activation)$

$\mathrm{Send}(return, send, get, activation)$

3.3.4. *Cable*

The FOCUS specification *Cable* describes the properties of FlexRay broadcast and is also an A/G specification. The *Cable* component simulates the broadcast properties of the physical network cable – every received FlexRay frame is resent to all connected nodes.

The assumption states, that all input streams of the *Cable* component are disjoint i.e. that at most one controller is sending during each slot. This holds by the properties of the *FlexRayController* components and the overall system assumption that the scheduling tables of all nodes are disjoint. The guarantee is specified by the predicate *Broadcast*.

Cable — timed

in $send_1, ..., send_n : Frame$

out $recv : Frame$

---

asm $\mathsf{disjoint}(send_1, ..., send_n)$

- - -

gar $Broadcast(send_1, ..., send_n, recv)$

Broadcast

$send_1, ..., send_n, recv \in Frame^{\underline{\omega}}$

$\forall\, t \in \mathbb{N}:$
  $\mathsf{if}\ \ \exists\, k \in [1...n] : \mathsf{ti}(send_k, t) \neq \langle\rangle$
    $\mathsf{then}\ \ \mathsf{ti}(recv, t) = \mathsf{ti}(send_k, t)$
    $\mathsf{else}\ \ \mathsf{ti}(recv, t) = \langle\rangle \quad \mathsf{fi}$

The *Cable* specification above represents the case, in which we fully rely the on the fault-tolerance of the FlexRay transmission – the FlexRay error correction is good enough for a certain system (see Sect. 4). Otherwise the following specification must be used:

Cable — timed

in $send_1, ..., send_n : Frame;\ loss : \mathbb{B}\mathrm{ool}$

out $recv : Frame$

---

asm $\mathsf{disjoint}(send_1, ..., send_n)\ \wedge\ \mathsf{ts}(loss)$

- - -

gar $Broadcast(send_1, ..., send_n, loss, recv)$

Broadcast

$send_1, ..., send_n, recv \in Frame^{\underline{\omega}};\ loss \in \mathbb{B}\mathrm{ool}^{\underline{\omega}}$

$\forall\, t \in \mathbb{N}:$
  $\mathsf{if}\ \ \exists\, k \in [1...n] : \mathsf{ti}(send_k, t) \neq \langle\rangle\ \wedge\ \mathsf{ti}(loss, t) \neq \langle \mathsf{true}\rangle$
    $\mathsf{then}\ \ \mathsf{ti}(recv, t) = \mathsf{ti}(send_k, t)$
    $\mathsf{else}\ \ \mathsf{ti}(recv, t) = \langle\rangle \quad \mathsf{fi}$

Please note, that in this specification we have an additional input channel *loss* (the corresponding stream is a time-synchronous one). It represents the connection status: the message true at slot t corresponds to the connection failure at this time unit, the message false at slot t means that at this time unit no data is losst on the *Cable*. In this case we also require the additional input channel *loss* in the specification of the components *FlexRay*, *FlexRayArch*, *FlexRayArchitecture* and *SystemArch*.

4. Collaboration between FlexRay and FTCom

The formal specifications of FlexRay and FTCom allow us to argue about their properties in a precise, formal manner[23] and also infer the dependencies between their properties. In this section we discuss the examples of the collaboration properties.

4.1. *Level of the Fault-Tolerance*

According to the FlexRay specification[10] a frame contains a 24 bit CRC (cyclic redundancy check) checksum to ensure the integrity of the frame's transmission. The probability of undetected network errors[20] is less than $6 \cdot 10^{-8}$, this means that at 10,000 messages per second and a bit error rate of 10^{-6}, this means approximately $2 \cdot 10^{-6}$ undetected erroneous frames per hour. This in turn means that only one percent of all vehicles will ever experience an undetected erroneous frame during an average lifespan of 6.000 hours of operation. Using FTCom's replication mechanisms we can reduce this probability even further and increase the fault-tolerance.

If the FlexRay error rate is good enough for a certain system, we can use simpler configurations of the *RDA* component of FTCom. Because of the high probability that a communication error is detected by FlexRay, we can assume that if such an error occurs, the wrong frame will be detected by the CRC and will not saved in the *CNI_Buffer*. Thus the RDA algorithm for this case a “pick first appropriate” can be chosen to make data processing faster. So the configuration of the replication table of the *Replica* component, depends on reliability of physical connection.

4.2. *FlexRay Frames*

The type of the *Payload* field in a FlexRay *Frame* (see Sect. 3.3) depends on the configuration of FTCom. In general, we represent the *Payload* as a list of application messages of type *FT_CNI_Entity*.

If the number of replicated messages in the system is smaller than the number of the FlexRay communication slots in a round, it is possible to use the model "One_message_per_frame", in which the types *Payload* and *FT_CNI_Entity* are equal. In the simple case, when the bus connection is reliable enough to send an application message without replication, i.e. once every FlexRay round, the message identifier can be used as slot number[f]: *Payload* = *DataType*.

4.3. *Schedule Dependences*

Combining a time-triggered OS with a time-triggered bus one can synchronize not only the communication, but also the computations in the systems. FlexRay provides OSEKtime OS with a globally synchronized clock. For this purpose, the length of the OSEKtime dispatcher round must be a multiple of the length of the FlexRay round (counted in FlexRay slots).

As mentioned in the Sect. 3.2, the Replica and RDA tasks must be called by the OSEKtime dispatcher every communication round to have current data both in the FTCom and CNI buffers. When generating the OSEKtime dispatcher tables, this property must be taken into account.

5. Verification of the Properties: FlexRay

To show that the specified system fulfills the requirements we need to show that the specification of the FlexRay architecture, *FlexRayArch*, is a refinement of the specification of the FlexRay requirements, *FlexRay*. It follows from the definition of behavioural refinement [5] that in order to verify that

$$FlexRay \rightsquigarrow FlexRayArch \tag{4}$$

it is enough to prove that

$$[\![FlexRayArch]\!] \Rightarrow [\![FlexRay]\!] \tag{5}$$

Thus, we translate these specification to syntax of the Isabelle/HOL schematically[23] and prove, using the verification framework Isabelle/HOL, that the refinement relation holds. Isabelle/HOL [16,26] is an interactive semi-automatic theorem prover[11]. To specify a system with Isabelle means

[f]This implies that the types *MessageId* and *Slot* ($\mathbb{N}$) are equal.

creating theories. Isabelle/HOL allows also to deal with induction without additional efforts. A theory is a named collection of types, functions (constants), and theorems (lemmas).

Therefore, we have to prove in Isabelle/HOL a lemma (let us call it *main_fr_refinement*), that says the Isabelle/HOL semantics of the specification *FlexRayArch* is a refinement of the Isabelle/HOL semantics of the specification *FlexRay*:

```
lemma main_fr_refinement:
"⋀ n nReturn nC nStore nGet.
  FlexRayArch n nReturn nC nStore nGet
  ⟹ FlexRay n nReturn nC nStore nGet"
```

The verification details are presented as technical report[23].

6. Related Work

An overview of the verification of TTA (Time Triggered Architecture)[13] was presented by J. Rushby[22]. The comparison of TTA (TTP/C) and FlexRay[12] comes to the conclusion that FlexRay and TTP/C were designed against the same set of automotive requirements, but that there is a difference in goals. Since the comparison has shown several differences, the results of the verification of TTA can not be transfered directly to FlexRay and FTCom. Nevertheless provide these TTA-publications some insights into the time triggered paradigm and its ongoing verification effort.

The time triggered standards for the fault-tolerant communication, FlexRay and FTCom, are relatively new, but auspicious. The formal verification of several aspects of these standards is required and is, therefore, an active research topic in different research groups. A verification of the clock synchronization algorithm of FlexRay is in progress at LORIA, based on their framework[7]. The verification of the startup behaviour[24] of the FlexRay protocol raised some noteworthy issues. The work on the verification of the lower layers[3] of the specified system is in progress in the Verisoft project[25].

This approach is similar to the behavioural refinement of Laibanis et al[15], but uses a different formalism as a different application domain is addressed (automotive instead of telecommunication). In contrast to the Omnibus approach[27], which is object oriented, a component-based formalism is used here as it is better suited for embedded applications.

7. Conclusion and Future Work

The paper presented the formal specifications of FlexRay and FTCom in FOCUS and also the correlation between their properties, which are inferred from the specifications. These FOCUS specifications allow us to argue about the properties of FlexRay and FTCom in a precise, formal manner. Using the presented specification of FlexRay we also have verified[23] that this FlexRay specification conforms the FlexRay requirements. On the basis of the verification of the FTCom and FlexRay, one might start the verification of applications, deployed on top of those two standards.

As future work, the extension of the formal specification with a second FlexRay-channel, Bus Guardians[9] and an explicit error model, would provide a more detailed insight on the fault-tolerance mechanisms of FlexRay.

Acknowledgments

We would like to thank Manfred Broy for his valuable feedback on the FOCUS specifications.

References

1. J.-R. Abrial. *The B-book: assigning programs to meanings.* Cambridge University Press, New York, NY, USA, 1996.
2. AbsInt Angewandte Informatik GmbH. Worst-Case Execution Time Analyzers. `http://www.absint.com/profile.htm`.
3. S. Beyer, P. Böhm, M. Gerke, M. Hillebrand, T. In der Rieden, S. Knapp, D. Leinenbach, and W.J. Paul. Towards the formal verification of lower system layers in automotive systems. In *23nd IEEE International Conference on Computer Design: VLSI in Computers and Processors (ICCD 2005), 2-5 October 2005, San Jose, CA, USA, Proceedings*, pages 317–324. IEEE, 2005.
4. J. Botaschanjan, L. Kof, C. Kühnel, and M. Spichkova. Towards Verified Automotive Software. In *ICSE, SEAS Workshop*, St. Louis, Missouri, USA, May 21 2005.
5. M. Broy and K. Stølen. *Specification and Development of Interactive Systems: Focus on Streams, Interfaces, and Refinement.* sv, 2001.
6. Peter Clarke. FlexRay drives to market in a BMW. *EE Times*, 2006.
7. D. Barsotti and L. Prensa Nieto and A. Tiu. Verification of Clock Synchronization Algorithms: Experiments on a Combination of Deductive Tools. In *Electr. Notes Theor. Comput. Sci. 145*, 2006.
8. FlexRay Consortium. `http://www.flexray.com`.
9. FlexRay Consortium. *FlexRay Communication System – Bus Guardian Specification - Version 2.0*, 2004.
10. FlexRay Consortium. *FlexRay Communication System – Protocol Specification – Version 2.0*, 2004.

11. Isabelle – Theorem proving environment. `http://isabelle.in.tum.de/`.
12. H. Kopetz. A Comparison of TTP/C and FlexRay. Technical report, Institut für Technische Informatik, Technische Universität Wien, 2001.
13. H. Kopetz and G. Bauer. The time-triggered architecture. In *Proceedings of the IEEE*. IEEE, 2003.
14. C. Kühnel and M. Spichkova. FlexRay und FTCom: Formale Spezifikation in FOCUS. Technical Report TUM-I0601, Technische Universität München, 2006.
15. Linas Laibinis, Elena Troubitsyna, Sari Leppanen, Johan Lilius, and Qaisar Malik. Formal service-oriented development of fault tolerant communicating systems. In *Proceesings of the Workshop on Rigorous Engineering of Fault Tolerant Systems*, 2005.
16. T. Nipkow, L. C. Paulson, and M. Wenzel. *Isabelle/HOL – A Proof Assistant for Higher-Order Logic*, volume 2283 of *LNCS*. Springer, 2002.
17. OSEK/VDX. `http://www.osek-vdx.org`.
18. OSEK/VDX. *Fault-Tolerant Communication – Specification 1.0*, 2001. `http://www.osek-vdx.org/mirror/ftcom10.pdf`.
19. OSEK/VDX. *Time-Triggered Operating System – Specification 1.0*, 2001. `http://www.osek-vdx.org/mirror/ttos10.pdf`.
20. M. Paulitsch et al. Coverage and the use of cyclic redundancy codes in ultra-dependable systems. In *2005 International Conference on Dependable Systems and Networks (DSN'05)*, pages 346–355, 2005.
21. Robert Bosch GmbH. *CAN Specification Version 2.0*, 1991.
22. J. Rushby. An overview of formal verification for the time-triggered architecture. In *Formal Techniques in Real-Time and Fault-Tolerant Systems*, volume 2469 of *Lecture Notes in Computer Science*. Springer-Verlag, 2002.
23. M. Spichkova. FlexRay: Verification of the FOCUS Specification in Isabelle/HOL. A Case Study. Technical Report TUM-I0602, Technische Universität München, 2006.
24. Wilfried Steiner and Hermann Kopetz. The startup problem in fault-tolerant time-triggered communication. *International Conference on Dependable Systems and Networks (DSN 2006)*, Jun. 2006.
25. Verisoft Project. `http://www.verisoft.de`.
26. M. Wenzel. *The Isabelle/Isar Reference Manual*. Technische Universität München, 2004.
27. Thomas Wilson, Savi Mahara, and Robert Clark. Omnibus: A clean language and supporting tool for integrating different assertion-based verification techniques. In *Proceesings of the Workshop on Rigorous Engineering of Fault Tolerant Systems*, 2005.

PART C

Languages and Tools for Engineering Fault Tolerant Systems

A MODEL DRIVEN EXCEPTION MANAGEMENT FRAMEWORK

SUSAN ENTWISLE AND ELIZABETH KENDALL

Faculty of Information Technology, Monash University, Melbourne, Australia

Programming languages provide exception handling mechanisms to structure fault tolerant activities within software systems. However, the use of exceptions at this low level of abstraction can be error-prone and complex, potentially leading to new programming errors. In this chapter, we present a model-driven framework to support the iterative development of reliable software systems. This framework is comprised of UML-based modeling notations and a transformation engine that supports the automated generation of exception management features for a software system. It leverages domain specific exception modeling languages, patterns, modeling tools and framework libraries. The feasibility of this approach is demonstrated through the development of a case study business application, known as Project Tracker.

1. Introduction

1.1. *Fault Tolerance and Exception Management*

There are many potential sources of faults in computer systems. These are the sources of deviations and errors, such as hardware, network, software, and human error [1, 2]. In order for fault tolerance to be addressed, each of these exceptions must be intercepted and managed. Exception management, also known as exception handling, is therefore a prerequisite for fault tolerance. Without exception handling, fault tolerance is impossible and reliability requirements can not be met. Fault tolerance is not guaranteed just because exception handling has been provided. But, improvements in exception handling should increase the fault tolerance of a system.

Modern programming languages, including Java [3] and C# [4], provide exception handling mechanisms [5]. However, the use of language-based exception handling is labor intensive, inflexible, and error prone [6-8]. Much of the research in exception handling to date has concentrated on addressing the objectives of exception handling as a language design issue [1], or providing the software developer with exception usage design patterns and software frameworks [7, 9, 10]. However, experience has shown that progress in understandability and reusability within most problem domains has failed to meet expectation [11, 12].

1.2. *Model Driven Development*

Progress in understandability and reusability has been disappointing across a large portion of software development. [11-16] argue that significant advances in reuse and the management of complexity can be potentially achieved through model driven development of system families, also known as product lines. The model driven development paradigm aims to facilitate the automatic construction of highly customized intermediate or end software products based on high-level problem domain models.

A model driven approach aims to promote productivity, maintainability, and expressiveness. It also manages complexity and reuse by supporting higher levels of abstraction that systematically reuse domain-specific assets. Assets include domain-specific languages, common architecture, components, documentation, etc.

This family based software development process is divided into two parts: domain engineering that focuses on engineering-for-reuse, and application engineering that focuses on engineering-with-reuse. The reusable problem domain knowledge, captured during domain engineering, is represented in domain specific models. The models can be interpreted by humans, promoting communication and understanding of the intent of the software system. They can also be processed by tools to facilitate the automated generation of the software system.

A domain specific language (DSL) is a specification language that aims to provide expressive power for a specific problem domain [17]. Domain specific languages specify the problem domain modeling paradigm, including key concepts, relationships, constraints, and the rules governing automated code generation. They can be represented either textually (e.g. SQL, declarative statements) or graphically (e.g. a modeling solution using domain concepts within a graphical environment) at varying levels of specialization.

[17] provides a list of references to a wide range of domain specific languages. Domain specific languages perform a pivotal role in model-driven development as they provide the basis to construct concrete instances of the system family.

Model transformation facilitates the automatic construction of customized applications from high-level problem domain models. There are two major categories of model transformation approaches: model to code transformation and model to model transformation [18]. The input into the transformation includes the source model, mapping rules and various markings that can be used to guide the transformation process. The result is the target model, which can be either source code or another model, and optionally a record of the transformation.

The two main approaches to model-to-code transformation are: visitor-based and template-based approaches. The visitor-based approach is a simple code generation technique that uses a visitor mechanism [19] to traverse the internal representation of the model in order to write source code to an output stream. The template-based approach consists of a text template that contains both literal text blocks and sections of meta-code. The model transformation engine uses the source model(s) to populate the meta-code sections in order to generate source code for the target programming language.

The advantages of the template-based approach compared to the visitor-based approach are [18]: the structure of the template closely resembles the code to be generated; templates can be based on boilerplate templates; and as they are independent from the target programming language, they can be used to simplify the generation of any textual artifact, including documentation. In addition to these aforementioned approaches, the OMG is currently ratifying a Query, View and Transformation (QVT) [20] specification. This specification aims to support querying models and defining model transformation.

1.3. *Horizontal and Vertical Domains*

[12] outlines that there are two different types of scope for the domain of software systems. They are:

•*Horizontal Scope:* addresses how many different systems are in the domain. The domain of exceptions has a large horizontal scope due to the number of different categories of exceptions (e.g. concurrent, sequential, web services, networking exceptions, etc).

•*Vertical Scope:* addresses what parts of the system are within the domain. The larger the parts of the system that are included in the domain, the deeper its vertical scope. For example, the domain of concurrent exceptions is deeper in vertical scope than the domain of web service exceptions. This is because web services exceptions capture a smaller slice of the range of exceptions that can occur within a system.

Software systems may belong to several domains. For example, a finance system includes workflow management, user interface, exception management, database management system, etc. Thus, a software system may not necessarily cover a whole domain and could potentially leverage several domains.

[21] distinguishes and outlines the relationships between the following types of domains on a per-system scope:

•Vertical and Horizontal Domains

•Encapsulated and Distributed Domains

Vertical domains are a complete system. Horizontal domains contain a part of a system within the domain scope. All horizontal domains are either encapsulated or distributed. Encapsulated domains are horizontal domains that contain well-localized system parts within domains, for example database systems. Distributed domains, also known as diffused domains [12], are horizontal domains but they consist of several different parts of the system in the domain scope. Exception management is an example of a distributed domain. [21] outlines strategies for determining the scope of a system.

1.4. *Model Driven Exception Management*

The limitations of language-based approaches to exception management and the potential benefits of model driven development have motivated our research into model driven development for exception management. [11, 22-25] also discuss the importance of providing model driven support for non functional requirements, such as security and exception handling.

To date model driven development of exception handling capabilities has been primarily restricted to high level discussions about the potential use of quality of service (QoS) aspect-oriented frameworks [22-25]. Preliminary research has focused on concurrent exceptions, and this is based on the Object Management Group (OMG) UML QoS and Fault Profile [26]. Our work rests on the same underpinnings as this research. However, we extend it. We investigate the model driven methods, generative programming techniques, frameworks and toolsets required to architect a generic, extensible exception management framework. This framework aims to automate the generation of exception management features for an application.

The remainder of this chapter is structured as follows: Section 2 provides a high level overview of the exception handling mechanisms in C# and the .NET framework. Section 3 describes the model-driven exception management framework. Section 4 illustrates the framework using a scenario from a Project Tracking application. Section 5 discusses related work in exception management and model-driven development, while Section 6 provides our conclusion and discusses future work.

2. Exceptions in C# and the .NET Framework

2.1. *Overview*

A software system should transition from one valid internal state to another during execution. However, under abnormal conditions, known as exceptions, a fault may cause it to transition into an erroneous internal state. Modern programming languages, including Java [2], and C# [3], provide exception handling mechanisms to systematically structure fault-tolerant activities to meet reliability requirements [1]. This approach provides fault tolerance in the form of structured units that define the area of error containment and recovery [2]. These mechanisms differ based on the design of the programming language but typically include language constructs, functions, runtime support and analysis tools that aid in the management of errors. This programming language based approach complements alternative fault tolerance mechanisms, such as hardware and software redundancy [1].

C# provides basic support to handle exceptional situations in an application [27]. Exceptions can be explicitly generated by the common language runtime (CLR), by software components, or by applications using the statement **throw** ***E***. The throw statement interrupts the normal control flow of the application and signals an error denoted by the expression *E*. E must have **`System.Exception`** (or a subclass thereof) as its effective base class. Exceptions can also be automatically raised by the .NET CLR when an operation cannot be completed because it misuses a virtual machine instruction (such as dereferencing null variable) or it exhausts some resource (such as memory).

In C#, the context of an exception is defined by a `try` block. A try block defines a region of the program where the same exception is always handled in the same manner, by the same exception handler. The catch blocks define the exception handlers.

The statement **try** { S } **catch** (E *e*) { H } catches exception of type *E* thrown in the statement block *S* and invokes the handler statement block *H*, when *E* denotes the exception thrown. A try block can have multiple catch clauses.

In .NET, the CLR searches for the nearest catch clause for the exception based on the runtime type of the exception that has been thrown. First it searches the current method for an enclosing try statement and the catch clauses are evaluated in order. This search continues up the application stack until either an appropriate catch clause is found or the search reaches the method that started the initial application thread. If no matching catch clause is located the execution of the thread is terminated.

Resource management in the event of an exception is handled by a `finally` statement. The statement **`try`** `{ S }` **`finally`** `{ R }` executes the statement *S* followed by the code to perform resource management "clean-up" functions (such as releasing file locks) in the finally statement block *R*. In the event of an exception, when a matching catch clause is found, the system executes any finally clauses that were associated with try statements more nested than the matching catch clause. This occurs prior to executing the catch clause handler.

`System.Exception` is the base type of all exceptions. This class contains common properties that all exceptions share: exception message and inner exception. The inner exception can be used to refer to the exception that caused the current exception. Below is a portion of the .NET exception hierarchy:

```
System.Exception
    System.SystemException
    System.ArgumentException
    System.ArithmeticException
    System.ContextMarshalException
    System.Data.DataException
    System.IO.IOException
     System.ApplicationException
```

The exception hierarchy can be further extended to create domain-specific exception types. Domain specific exception types are typically defined by extending from the `System.ApplicationException` type.

The Microsoft Exception Handling Application Block (MEHAB) [28] extends the exception hierarchy to provide basic exception management and notification services. MEHAB provides support for the inclusion of typical code that is found in catch statements in application components. Instead of repeating this code in identical catch blocks, the application block allows developers to encapsulate this logic as reusable exception handlers. These are .NET classes that encapsulate exception handling logic and implement the Exception Handling Application Block interface named IExceptionHandler.

2.2. *Concurrent Systems*

Concurrent software systems introduce new requirements on an exception handling mechanism in order to structure application-specific fault-tolerant activities into a software system. This is because, compared to sequential software systems, they should be structured to encapsulate complex behaviours.

Atomicity is a core concept in developing structured system designs for concurrent object-oriented systems [29]. Atomic units can be nested within other atomic units in order to manage system complexity in a scalable manner. Fault tolerance may be more easily provided in applications that are based on atomic units because these units can confine erroneous information and have error responses attached to them [29-33]. [32] argues that software systems based on atomic transactions are easier to design, verify, understand and provide fault tolerance for.

[34,35] classified concurrent systems into three types. They are: cooperative, competitive and disjoint systems. Each of these systems has different program structures and dynamic execution models. This leads to the need for different exception handling models and methodologies for each category. Competitive systems are structured based on atomic transactions. Cooperative systems are structured based on atomic actions. Complex systems that aggregate competitive and cooperative systems are based on coordinated atomic transactions.

Additional considerations for the design of fault tolerance in concurrent systems also include the need to: 1) recover multiple objects in a coordinated manner, 2) support the definition of error containment domains across several interconnected objects, and 3) structure complex behaviours as nested atomic actions comprised of groups of objects and method calls [29-33]. These requirements increase the complexity of both the software system and the exception handling mechanism.

C# provides guidance on the semantics of exception handling in concurrent programs. The C# exception handling mechanism is not integrated with the C# threading and synchronization model. Rather, a programming idiom based on releasing the acquired lock within a finally block is typically implemented. This idiom ensures that locks are released when a synchronized method signals an exception to the caller. [36] describes an extension to the C# language, referred to as Polyphonic C#, which provides new asynchronous concurrency constructs based on join calculus.

3. Model Driven Exception Management Framework

The primary focus of our model-driven exception management framework is to simplify the development of applications through a modeling framework that supports automated generation of exception management features. We have used a system-family engineering methodology for our model-driven exception management framework. This is depicted in Figure 1.

We have analysed the exception management domain to yield our domain specific language and models. We have also developed a model transformation engine that can be used to produce applications that incorporate exception handling code.

The framework provides the meta-level architecture, domain specific languages, model transformation engine and services upon which reusable domain specific exception management libraries (such as network exceptions, database exceptions, web services exceptions, and so on) can be added. This allows the software architect to model the exception management requirements for an application in architectural models using domain-specific modeling languages, rather than hand crafting the implementation. These models then provide the meta-data for the model transformation engine to facilitate the automated generation of source code to implement the exception management requirements.

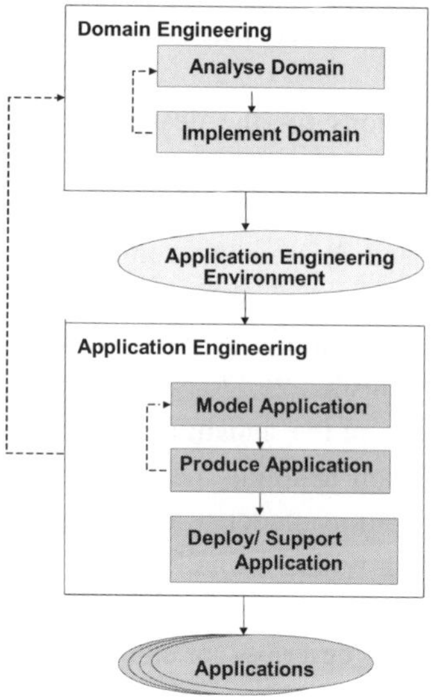

Figure 1. System Family Engineering Methodology

Figure 2 illustrates the layered architecture for the model-driven exception management framework. This architecture provides exception-agnostic modeling and management mechanisms to diagnose and resolve exceptions. This means that the mechanisms provided by the framework are not tied to one particular type of exception, or one particular way to represent exceptions.

The framework is made up of a number of components, including:

- *Platform:* This consists of the runtime environment and modeling tools required to support the reference implementation of the model-driven exception management framework.
- *Core Middleware:* This offers core services such as coordinated atomic actions, diagnostics, exceptions, monitoring, and so on.
- *User Level Middleware:* This includes the domain specific languages, domain-specific exception management libraries, and the model transformation coupled with custom application development tools that support the specification of an application's exception management requirements.
- *Model Driven Applications:* Model driven applications are developed by a software architect using domain specific languages and the model transformation engine.

The following sub-sections describe the model-driven exception management framework and illustrate the application of the system family engineering methodology.

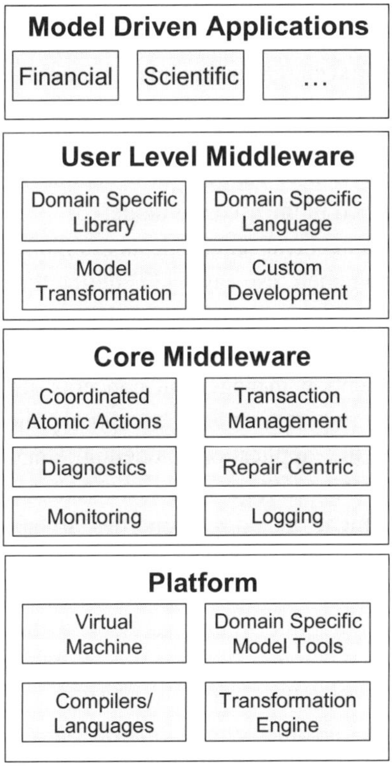

Figure 2. Layered Architecture of Framework

3.1. *Exception Management Modeling Language*

The model driven exception management framework is comprised of a set of domain-specific visual modeling languages that can be used together to architect applications. The models and languages are the following:

- Use Case: used to specify the requirements of an application.
- Application (Entities and Services): used to model the structure (entities) and behaviour (services) of an application. The entities represent the concepts in the problem domain and their composition. The services represent the integration points to support a service-oriented architecture.
- Publisher: used to specify the notification requirements for an application.
- Exception Policy: used to specify the strategies for handling an exception once it has occurred.

The purpose of the use case modeling language is to specify the functional and non-functional requirements for the application. Thus, the use case modeling language provides the notation to describe which actors are involved and what activities they perform. Traditionally, analysts do not include exception management requirements in use case models. However, we argue, as others have [37], that exception management requirements should be included as first class artifacts during the analysis phase to aid in verifying the reliability requirements throughout the software development lifecycle. Thus, if the system needs to perform an action to support an exception management requirement then it should be included in the use case model.

The exception management requirements are modeled as infrastructure use cases. Exception management use cases [37] define the sequence of events that need to occur when an exception occurs. The infrastructure use cases are modeled as extensions to application use cases. This approach supports the modularization of exception management concerns and the traceability of an exception management requirement to an exception policy.

Figure 3 shows the application modeling language that provides the notation to specify the entities and services for an application. The *ApplicationModel* element includes properties to specify global exception policies; the namespaces for the various tiers in the generated application; and the database connection. The *ModelType* elements *Entity* and *ServiceInterface* are used to specify the entities and services within the application. The *Operation* element enables the architect to specify an operation's method signature and exception policies. The *ModelType*, *Attribute* and *Operation* elements implement the abstract *ApplicationModelElement* element to support generic methods in the code generation process. The entity related model elements describe the entities, their attributes, operations, and relationships. The relationship types that are supported are the following: inheritance, aggregation, composition and bidirectional association.

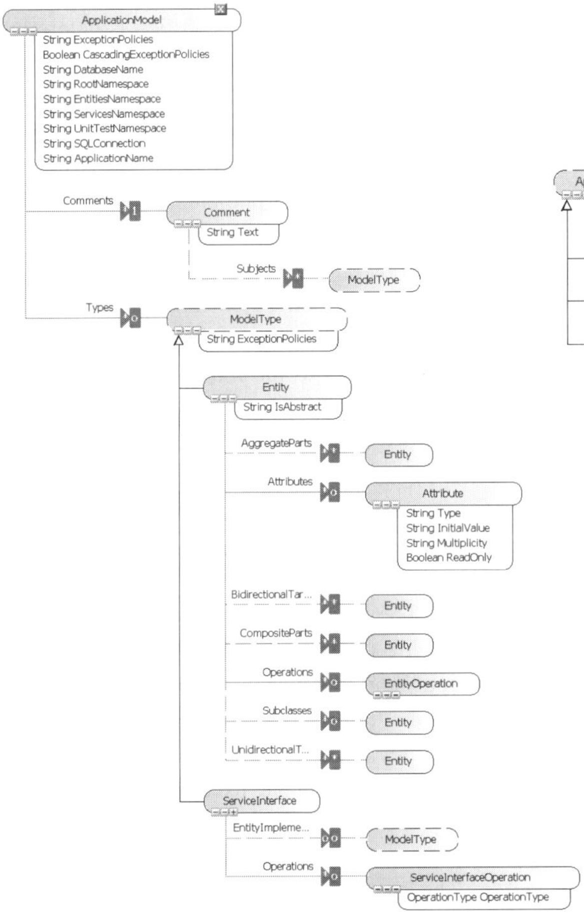

Figure 3. Application Modeling Language

The service model elements describe the service interfaces and operations. The services are the actions performed by the system on the entities in the model. The service model supports a limited set of operation types to support interacting with the entities.

Exception policies are linked to the application model, entities and services operations through the exception policies property. The sequence of events that occurs in the exception management use case guides the architect in identifying the exception policies. The use case also determines how the policies can be allocated to the model elements. Each model element can have zero to many associated exception policies. The order of policy execution is determined when the completed model is transformed to source code. The order is based on the set of policies associated with each element and the programming language's exception hierarchy.

The application model can be configured to support cascading exception policies, where multiple policies can be allocated to one element in an ordered sequence. With this approach, the architect can define exception policies at a global level, and these policies can then be enacted in multiple locations in the application. These policies are inherited by all model elements contained within the application model. This allows common exception management responses (such as logging and notification) to be bound to the model at a single point. This supports a separation of concern for selected exception policies at the model level. Model elements can also override inherited exception policies, if required.

The purpose of the publisher modeling language is to specify the notification actions for the application in the event of an exception. With the publisher notation, an architect can specify the notification sinks that should receive an exceptional event's details. The following notification sink elements are supported: Windows Event Log, File (Text or XML), Email and Custom. The custom element enables extensions, and it can be configured to specify any notification sink class that implements the framework's IPublisher interface.

Figure 4 shows the exception policy modeling language that is used to describe the continuation actions in the event of an exception. The notation allows a domain engineer to specify the resumption semantics for a domain specific exception type. Each *ExceptionPolicy* element has a defined exception type and a post handling action. The exception type defines the exceptional event that invokes the execution of the exception policy. Post handling occurs after the exception policy execution has completed. The following post handling actions are supported: none, rethrow and notify user. The rethrow is used to indicate that the exception could not be resolved and needs to be rethrown. The notify user post handling action is used to communicate across tiers that an exception occurred and has been resolved.

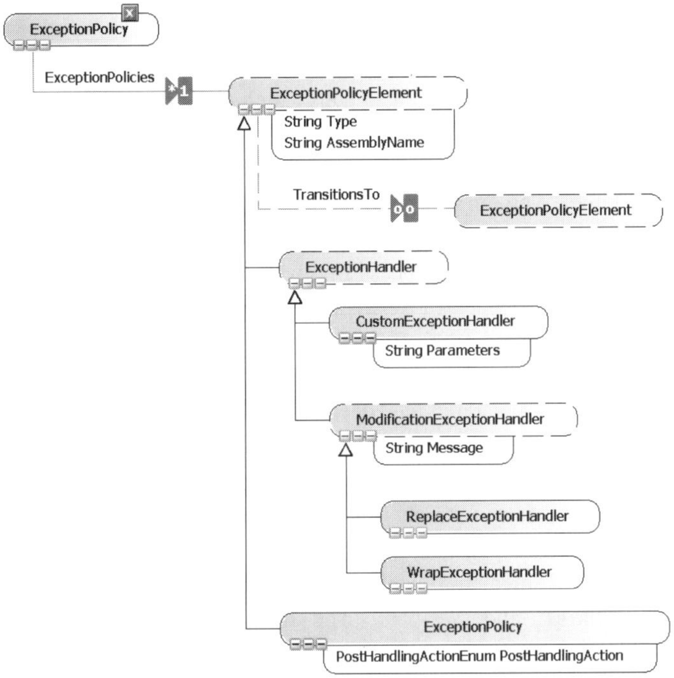

Figure 4. Exception Policy Modeling Language

Each exception policy has one or more corresponding exception handlers that perform actions to manage the exception. The supported exception handlers are:

- *WrapExceptionHandler:* used to wrap the exception type with another specified exception type.
- *ReplaceExceptionHandler:* used to replace the exception with another specified exception type.
- *CustomExceptionHandler:* used to perform custom actions to manage an exception. The *CustomExceptionHandler* element is configured with an exception handler type that extends the *ExceptionHandler* abstract class.

Our modeling approach aims to facilitate improvements in exception management and hence fault tolerance. The primary benefits of our modeling approach are: 1) supports a consistent strategy for managing exceptions across the tiers of an application, 2) allows exception policies to be defined and reused at the domain level, and 3) decouples exception policies from a particular application so they can be reused in other applications.

3.2. *Model Transformation*

The model transformation engine generates the implementation assets for the application based on its models. This includes the database and C# implementation of the entities, services, and unit tests. The generated entity and service classes use the exception management framework components and services, if required. The binding between the models and the implementation is achieved using template-based code generation.

The model transformation process involves two key activities: 1) metadata extraction from the models and 2) execution of the templates. The metadata for the application is extracted to XML files that are used as input into the model transformation engine. The benefits of this approach are: 1) simplified templates because the model's metadata has been extracted and transformed into the required format, 2) decoupling of the application's metadata from the underlying technology, and 3) reuse of metadata extracts in other transformation processes. The metadata extracts include: application model, data model, exception model, and the publisher model.

The application metadata schema defines the application's *Database*, *Namespace*, *Entities*, and *Services*. The *Application*, *Entity, Service* and *Operation* elements have an associated *ExceptionPolicy* element to store the modeled exception policies. If the exception policy is applied at the *Application*, *Entity* or *Service* level and exception cascading is applied, this will be inherited by the *Operation* element.

The exception policy metadata schema defines the domain-specific *ExceptionPolicies*. The *ExceptionPolicy* element represents a single exception policy that is associated to a specific *ExceptionType* within an *Assembly*.

The ExceptionHandlerChain element defines the set of ExceptionHandler classes that are invoked to manage the exception. The ExceptionHandler classes are of type: WrapHandler, ReplaceHandler, and CustomHandler. A GUID is used to link the ExceptionHandler element to its specific WrapHandler, ReplaceHandler, and CustomHandler elements. The SourceException element is application specific. This element is populated when the ExceptionPolicies are bound to a specific application during template execution. This binding is required to create an application-specific exception policy configuration file that is used by the exception management framework.

The templates codify the architectural design and implementation patterns for the entities, data access and services layers of a business transaction system. The application architecture that is generated is based on: C# [27, 36], Microsoft SQL Server [38], and Wilson's Object Relational Mapper (ORM) [39]. It also employs a customized version of Microsoft's Exception Handling Application Block [28] to encapsulate exception management behavior.

The entity and service classes leverage the customized version of the exception management application block. An exception management configuration file is also generated. This configuration file binds the exception source metadata within the application model with the applied exception policies. This therefore creates an application specific exception policy file that is used by the framework.

```
private string GetTryHandler (IList exceptionpolicieslist){
  if (exceptionpolicieslist != null){
  return "try{"; }
return String.Empty;
}
private string GetCatchHandler(IList exceptionpolicieslist){
  StringBuilder catchhandler =  new StringBuilder();
  XmlElement exceptionroot =
          ExceptionModelDocument.DocumentElement;
  if (exceptionpolicieslist != null){
  exceptionpolicieslist =  OrderExceptionPoliciesList(
                exceptionpolicieslist);
 foreach (String exceptionpolicy in exceptionpolicieslist){
   // 1. Search exception policy in exception policy metadata
   // 2. If exists write out associated catch handler
  }
  return catchhandler.ToString();
<%
  if (operationtype.Equals("Create")){
%>
  <%= GetAccessibility(operation) %>
  <%= Entity %> Create(){
  <%= GetTryHandler(exceptionpolicieslist) %>
  return DataManager.ObjectSpace.GetObject(
  typeof(<%= Entity %>)) as <%= Entity %>;
  <%= GetCatchHandler(exceptionpolicieslist) %>
<% } %>
```

Figure 5. Exception Handling Transformation

Figure 5 shows the transformation technique used to generate the exception handling code for the entity and service operations. As shown, if the operation has an associated exception policy the template outputs a *try {..} catch (..) {..} finally {..}* statement. Because a derived exception can be caught by handlers of its base class, the order of the catch statements is significant. Thus, if an operation has more than one exception policy the order of the catch handlers must be determined. The ordering algorithm uses a tree-based representation to map the inheritance hierarchy structure of the set of the associated exception types from the C# *System.Exception* base class. This order is then used to output the catch handlers from the most specific exception type to the most general.

3.3. *Exception Management Library*

The exception management library provides the necessary components and services to manage exceptional events. The management of exceptions includes: diagnosis, response and notification. The detection of the exceptions is performed by the application. The exception management library is based on Microsoft's Exception Handling Application Block [28]. This library has been extended to support the exception policies, coordinated atomic actions [30], and additional custom notification sinks (such as windows event log, email, etc).

The key classes in the exception management library are: `BaseDomainException`, `ExceptionManager`, `ExceptionHandler`, `ExceptionHandlerFactory`, and the `ExceptionPolicyConfigurationManager`. Domain-specific exception types extend the `BaseDomainException`. This class provides the common information about the source of the exception. This information may be required when attempting to resolve or communicate an exceptional event. This information includes the: application name, application domain, date, machine name, thread, and windows identity. The `BaseDomainException` class is serializable enabling it to be transmitted across processes.

Figure 6 shows the UML class diagram for the key classes responsible for exception resolution. The `ExceptionManager HandleException` method is called to resolve an exceptional event. This method accepts as input an exception and an exception source object. The exception source object includes information about the assembly, class and method name raising the exception. Model transformation generates the source code to invoke the `ExceptionManager`. The `ExceptionManager` queries the `ExceptionPolicyConfigurationManager` to find the appropriate exception policy by calling the `FindExceptionPolicy` method. If required, it loads the exception policy configuration file for the application. This file is generated during model transformation.

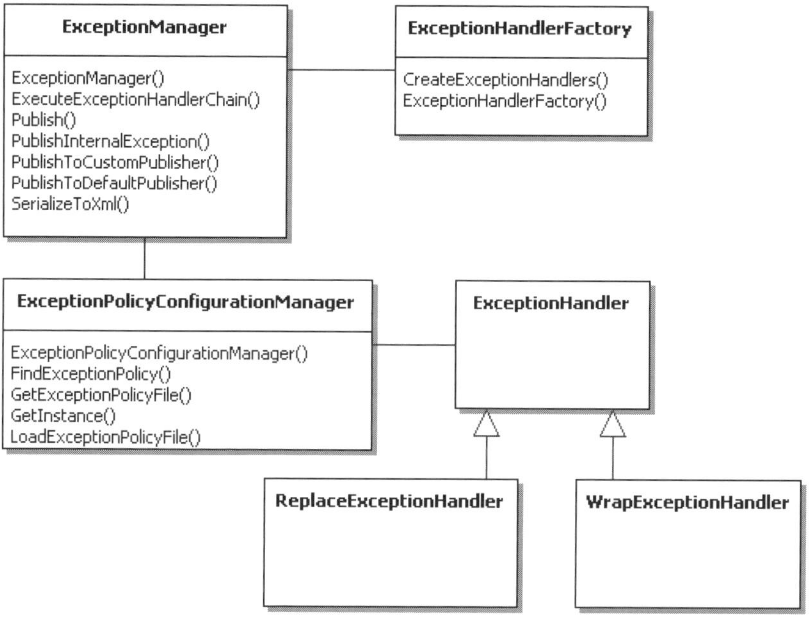

Figure 6. Exception Resolution Class Diagram

A query is then executed to find the appropriate exception policy based on the exception and exception source object. If no match is found the `ExceptionManager` returns the original exception to the client. If a match is found the `ExceptionManager` uses the `ExceptionHandlerFactory` [19] to construct a chain of `ExceptionHandler` objects based on the exception policy. The `ExceptionManager` then invokes the `HandleException` method for each of the `ExceptionHandlers`. This chain of responsibility [19] will continue to execute the `HandleException` methods until either the `ExceptionHandler` instance successfully resolves the exception or the chain is terminated. The successful resolution of an exception is indicated by the `HandleMethod` returning a null value. `ExceptionHandler` objects can also modify the exception being managed by the chain as each returns the exception object to be processed by the next `ExceptionHandler` object.

Once the `ExceptionHandler` chain has been traversed the notification framework is invoked. The notification framework is only invoked if the application has been configured to publish exceptions to notification sinks. This configuration file is generated during model transformation. The `ExceptionManager` calls the `Publish` method that iterates through all of the configured notification sinks invoking them to publish the exceptional event details. Finally, the `ExceptionManager` returns the `PostHandlingAction` to the client. The `PostHandlingAction` indicates if the exception needs to be rethrown, or if the client needs to take post handling actions that are application specific.

3.4. *Domain Specific Modeling Tools*

The model-driven exception management framework components described in the previous sections have been integrated together for evaluation purposes within Microsoft Visual Studio 2005 [40]. Microsoft Visual Studio 2005 includes the Domain Specific Language toolkit that supports the creation of custom graphical designers based on the exception management frameworks modeling languages.

The result aims to be a domain specific model-driven development tool focused on the development of reliable applications. The purpose of the tool is to support the software development team members during the analysis, design, and implementation phases of the software development lifecycle.

Figure 7 shows the high level iterative code generation process [41] supported within the tool:

- *Design Architecture:* design the application architecture using the exception management modeling languages.
- *Collect Metadata:* export the application's metadata from the models to an XML file. The application model has been marked up with the exception management and notification requirements. The metadata is used as input into the code generation templates tailoring the generated source code to the specific application.
- *Execute Code Generation Templates:* transform the models into source code that implements the exception management requirements. The transformation uses the metadata to fill in text templates that use the exception management framework components and services.
- *Customize Generated Code:* modify generated source code as required. Regeneration of the application is supported while preserving customized code through the use of merge management tools.
- *Test:* verify the functional and non-functional requirements of the application using standard testing tools.

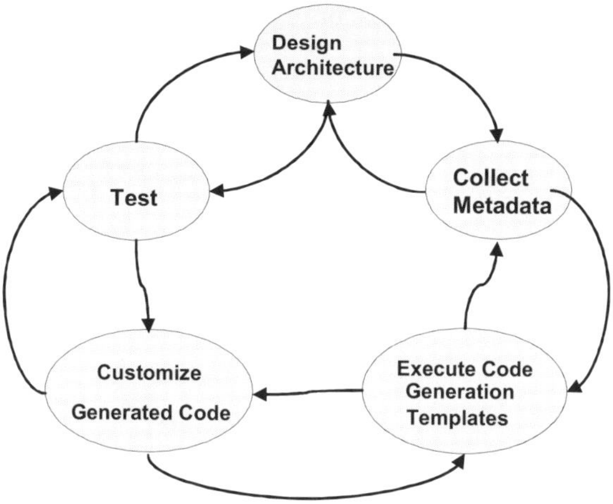

Figure 7. Domain Specific Modeling Tool Code Generation Process

4. Project Tracker Case Study

Our case study is based on the Project Tracker application. This application provides features for a manager to track projects and their associated resources. Figure 8 shows the use case for creating a new project. This use case includes the following infrastructure use cases:

- *Handle Database Server Unavailable:* if the database server is unavailable a system check should be executed to verify if the service is running. The exception details should be published to the windows event log. If the service is not running an attempt to restart the service should be executed. If this is successful, the end user should be notified that they must retry the failed transaction. If unsuccessful then rethrow the exception.
- *Handle Unexpected Failure:* an unexpected failure has occurred. The exception details should be published to the window event log. The end user should be notified to contact the system administrator of the failure.

For illustration purposes we focus our discussion on the Handle Database Server Unavailable use case.

The application model for the Project Tracker application consists of two services: `ProjectService` and `EmployeeService`. These services allow a manager to perform the standard online business transactions. The entity model consists of a project that has zero to many associated resources.

The design of the Create New Project use case is supported by the `ProjectService` `Save` method. The Save method has two exception policies associated to support the infrastructure use cases. The application has been configured with a notification sink for publishing exceptions to the windows event log.

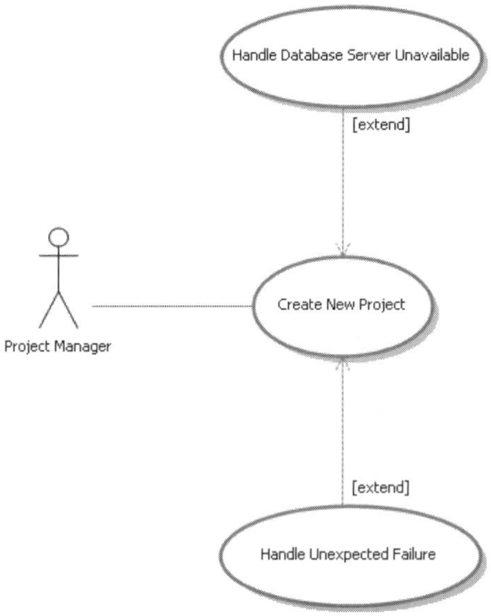

Figure 8 Create New Project Use Case

Figure 9 shows the exception policies. The database policy and the associated library support are based on a domain-specific extension to the framework we engineered for database errors. This extension includes support for the following exceptional events: database unavailable, constraint violations, row not in table, invalid constraint exception, and invalid attempts to access and modify nulls and read only fields.

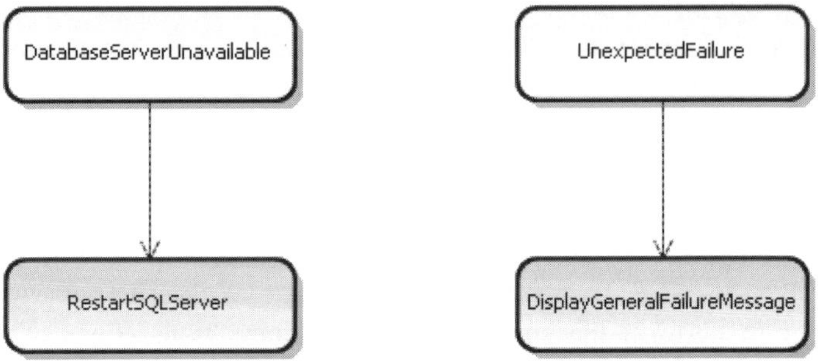

Figure 9. Exception Policies for Create New Project Infrastructure

The `DatabaseServerUnavailable` exception policy is associated with `System.Data.SqlClient.SqlException`. This exception indicates a failure has occurred when the client attempts to interact with the

Microsoft SQL Server [38] database. The policy's post handling action notifies the user that the exception has occurred, and that it has been handled. This enables the `ProjectService` to notify the end user that they should reattempt their failed transaction if the database is successfully restarted. The `RestartSQLServer` exception handler is responsible for attempting to restart the failed SQL Server using the `DatabaseStoppedExceptionHandler` in the exception management database library.

Figure 10 is an extract of the application specific exception policy configuration file generated during model transformation. As shown, the `CustomHandlerDatabaseStoppedExceptionHandler` is invoked if a `System.Data.SqlClient.SqlException` occurs in the ProjectService Save method.

```
<ExceptionPolicy>
<Name>DatabaseServerUnavailable</Name>
<ExceptionType> System.Data.SqlClient.SqlException
</ExceptionType>
<SourceExceptions>  <SourceException>
   <Assembly>ProjectTracker.Services</Assembly>
   <Class>ProjectService</Class>
   <Operation>Save</Operation>
  </SourceException> </SourceExceptions>
<ExceptionHandlerChain>  <ExceptionHandler>
    <Type>CustomExceptionHandler</Type>
    <GUID> 97960c6e-ae21-4c38-bae1-1c197ff2c065 </GUID>
  </ExceptionHandler> </ExceptionHandlerChain>
<WrapHandlers/>
<ReplaceHandlers/>
<CustomHandlers>  <CustomHandler>
   <GUID> 97960c6e-ae21-4c38-bae1-1c197ff2c065  </GUID>
   <Type> EMF.Database.DatabaseStoppedExceptionHandler </Type>
   <Assembly>EMF. Database</Assembly>
   <Parameters/>
   </CustomHandler>  </CustomHandlers>
<PostHandlingAction>NotifyUser</PostHandlingAction>
</ExceptionPolicy>
```

Figure 10. Exception Policies for DatabaseServiceUnavailable

Figure 11 shows the `ProjectService Save` method generated during model transformation. The method has catch handlers based on the modeled exception policies.

```
public void Save(Project project, bool
                 includeChildren){
  try
  {
    project.Save(includeChildren);
  }
  catch (System.Data.SqlClient.SqlException
         sqlexception)
  {
    PostHandlingActionEnum postHandlingAction =
      ExceptionManager.HandleException(
        new ExceptionSource(), sqlexception);
    if (postHandlingAction ==
      PostHandlingActionEnum.NotifyUser)
    {
      throw new ExceptionDisplayMessage("A
        database failure occurred. Please
        retry your database transaction.");
    }
    else if (postHandlingAction ==
      PostHandlingActionEnum.Rethrow)
    {
      throw;
    }
  }
  catch (System.Exception exception)
  {
    // . . generated source code for
    // . . unexpected failure exception policy
  }
}
```

Figure 11. Project Service Save Method

This service has been tested to verify that it could recover from a database server being offline. To perform these tests the database was manually stopped while the ProjectTracker application was running. A Save operation was then invoked while attempting to create a new project using the application's user interface. This resulted in the `DatabaseStoppedExceptionHandler` being invoked by exception management framework services. This handler successfully restarted the database service and returned a post handling action to notify the user of the exception. The notify post handling action is required in this exception policy as the user must retry their failed transaction. The message returned to the user is application specific. Thus, during model transformation a comment is generated in the source code informing the application developer to update the source code. In our sample this has been updated with an application specific message.

5. Related Work

The most closely related work to our research is the Correct Project and the research that preceded it [29-33]. The Correct Project aims to investigate the iterative development of complex fault tolerant systems from architectural descriptions. Our research has a number of similarities with this project. For example, the coordinated atomic actions protocol [30] is used to manage concurrent exceptions in multiple processes. However, our approach has a more broad scope as it investigates how to architect a generic framework for modeling various domain specific exception types. It also includes both sequential and concurrent exceptions.

The UML 2.0 [42] specification includes support for modeling exceptions in activity diagrams. However, no support for model transformation or library support has been proposed for exception management. We plan to evaluate this approach to modeling exceptions in activity diagrams as a notation to allow architects to model concurrent exceptions in our framework. Thus, we plan to build on the UML 2.0 specification.

The UML Profile for Fault Tolerance and QoS [26] provides modeling notation to define fault tolerance based on object replication strategies. The focus of our framework is on application faults that can be managed. Potentially, coupling our approach with an object replication strategy could provide failover support for exceptions that could not be managed. For example, this may involve attempting to access a remote service where the network connection has failed.

[44,45] have investigated using policies as a mechanism to manage exceptions in agent and workflow systems. Our approach to modeling exceptions is also based on the use of policies. To support this we defined a modeling notation and framework support for exception policies.

[46] explored the use of the aspect-oriented paradigm (AOP) to model and implement exceptions as a separate concern. The case-study based assessment concluded that this approach significantly reduced the number of lines of code, and provided greater support for extensibility and design evolution. [22,24] found that the benefits of AOP can be found in the area of domain-specific modeling for horizontal, distributed domains (such as exception management, security, etc). [47] discusses model-driven development of QoS-enabled distributed applications using AOP. [22] presents an extensible AOP meta-weaver framework to integrate cross-cutting constraints into a software system. However, [48] argues that failures and concurrency are particularly difficult to

separate from a distributed system. Furthermore, [11] argues that AOP breaks encapsulation and increases complexity in software systems.

There are a large number of domain engineering analysis and design methods being used in the development of software-product lines. To date, three surveys on domain engineering analysis and design have been published. [49] and [50] focus on domain analysis methods while [12] builds on these surveys by providing more recent developments in domain engineering methods. The major domain engineering methods are Feature-Oriented Domain Analysis (FODA) [51] and Organizational Domain Modeling (ODM) [17]. FODA is a domain analysis method that is based on identifying the features of a family of systems. The FODA process consists of three phases: context analysis, domain modeling and architecture modeling. ODM is a domain engineering method that leverages ideas from many different domain engineering methods and other non-software disciplines, such as organizational management, re-engineering, etc. [12]. ODM [20] integrates both the organizational and strategic aspects of domain planning, domain modeling, architecture engineering and asset base engineering. FODA and ODM are insufficient alone to capture domain knowledge for non-functional areas, such as fault tolerance, real-time support, etc, as they require specialized modeling techniques to be integrated into a generic domain engineering method [12].

[18] provides a detailed discussion on the approaches for each of the major portions of model transformation. Model-to-code transformations can be viewed as a type of model-to-model transformations where the target model is a meta-model of the target programming language. However, for pragmatic reasons that aim to reuse existing compiler technology model-to-code, transformation is often performed by generating text that is then input into a compiler [18].

6. Conclusion and Future Work

In this chapter, we have reasoned that a system families approach for exception management could be adopted to address exception handling for reliability requirements. We have presented an approach for modeling exception management requirements based on a set of modeling languages that a software architect can use to specify the key entities, services and exception management requirements for an application. Domain engineers can also extend the framework to support domain-specific exception types. Thus, both domain engineering and application engineering are supported by our approach. This has been demonstrated in our case study, where we developed a reusable domain-specific extension to the framework for database errors. This was used to architect the application and exception policies for the ProjectTracker infrastructure use cases. The exception management framework components and services were then leveraged by the generated application to support its exception requirements.

The framework provides a solution for architects to specify the architecture of an application independent of the underlying platform specific concerns. The focus is on service behaviour, domain entities and exception policies, which are described using high level abstractions that promote communication amongst various stakeholders. These user models reflect the functional and behavioural properties of the application. Furthermore, the model transformation engine and core exception management libraries provide a sound architectural foundation for code generation. The model transformation engine and core libraries could be extended to support multiple languages and platforms.

The adoption and use of the model driven framework for exception management does present challenges in terms of flexibility, modification and change management. The domain-specific visual modeling languages for exception management only permit a limited amount of customization at specified variation points. The architect may discover they need a richer set of modeling concepts, relationships and constraints to effectively model the exception management requirements for an application. This iterative development of the exception management framework is to be expected. To address this domain engineering must be performed to extend and refine the modeling language and other domain assets as new and updated requirements for the exception management domain are developed.

Another consideration is that the framework requires familiarity with exception management concepts and the framework itself. Thus, the initial adoption may lead to temporary decreases in productivity. The application development team must also follow change management processes and be proficient in the use of version control and merge tools to support managing changes in the model and in the previously generated assets when regenerating a model.

In the future, we plan to investigate the use of aspect-oriented programming as an implementation approach for integrating the application with the exception management framework. We are also planning to investigate the feasibility of modeling concurrent exceptions in UML collaboration diagrams.

References

1. A. F. Garcia, C. M. F.Rubira, A. Romanovsky, and J. Xu, "A Comparative Study of Exception Handling Mechanisms for Building Dependable Object-Oriented Software," *The Journal of Systems and Software*, vol. 59, pp. 197--222, 2001.
2. D. A. Patterson, A. Brown, P. Broadwell, G. Candea, M. Chen, J. Cutler, P. Enriquez, A. Fox, E. Kiciman, M. Merzbacher, D. Oppenheimer, N. Sastry, W. Tetzlaff, J. Traupman, and N. Treuhaft, "Recovery-Oriented Computing (ROC): Motivation, Definition, Techniques, and Case Studies," UC Berkeley Computer Science Technical Report UCB//CSD-02-1175 15th March 2002.
3. K. Arnold, J. Gosling, and D. Homes, *The Java Programming Language*, Third Edition ed: Addison-Wesley Pub Co, 2000.
4. M. Williams, *Microsoft Visual C# .NET*. Redmond: MS Press, 2002.
5. D. E. Perry, A. Romanovsky, and A. Tripathi, "Current trends in exception handling," *Software Engineering, IEEE Transactions on*, vol. 26, pp. 921-922, 2000.
6. M. Klein and C. Dellarocas, "Domain-Independent Exception Handling Services That Increase Robustness in Open Multi-Agent Systems," *M. Klein and C. Dellarocas, Domain-Independent Exception Handling Services That Increase Robustness in Open Multi-Agent Systems, Massachusetts Institute of Technology, Cambridge MA USA, Center for Coordination Science Working Paper CCS-WP-211, http://ccs.mit.edu/papers/pdf/wp211.pdf.*, 2000.
7. D. Reimer and H. Srinivasan, "Analyzing Exception Usage in Large Java Applications," *Exception Handling in Object-Oriented Systems Workshop at ECOOP 2003*, 2003.
8. C. Howell and G. Vecellio, "Experiences with Error Handling in Critical Systems," vol. Advances in Exception Handling Techniques in Object-Oriented Systems Workshop at ECOOP 2000, 2000.
9. T. Anderson, M. Feng, S. Riddle, and A. Romanovsky, "Error Recovery for a Boiler System with OTS PID Controller," *Exception Handling in Object-Oriented Systems Workshop at ECOOP 2003*, 2003.
10. A. F. Garcia and C. M. F. Rubira, "An Exception Handling Software Architecture for Developing Robust Software," *2nd Exception Handling in Object-Oriented Systems Workshop at ECOOP'2000*, 2000.
11. J. Greenfield, K. Short, S. Cook, S. Kent, and J. Crupi, *Software Factories: Assembling Applications with Patterns, Models, Frameworks, and Tools*: Wiley, 2004.

12. J. Eisenecker and K. Czarnecki, *Generative Programming: Methods, Tools, and Applications*, 1st ed: Addison-Wesley Professional, 2000.
13. S. J. Mellor, K. Scott, A. Uhl, and D. Weise, *MDA Distilled*: Addison-Wesley Professional, 2004.
14. J. O. Coplien, *Multi-Paradigm Design for C++*, 1st ed: Addision-Wesley, 1998.
15. P. Clements and L. Northrop, *Software Product Lines Pràctices and Patterns*, 1st ed: Addison-Wesley Professional, 2001.
16. D. M. Weiss and C. T. R. Lai, *Software Product-Line Engineering: A Family Based Software Development Process*: Addison-Wesley Professional, 1999.
17. A. Van Deursen, P. Klint, and J. M. W. Visser, Domain-Specific Languages. 2000, National Research Institute for Mathematics and Computer Science: Amsterdam, The Netherlands. p. 15.
18. K. Czarnecki, and S. Helsen, Classification of Model Transformation Approaches. in OOPSLA'03 Workshop on Generative Techniques in the Context of MDA. 2003. Anaheim, CA, USA: Online Proceedings.
19. E. Gamma, R. Helm, R. Johnson, and J. Vlissides, *Design Patterns Elements of Reusable Object-Oriented Software*, 1st Edition ed: Addison-Wesley Professional, 1995.
20. Query/View/Transformation RFP v2.1, http://www.omg.org/mof/, 2005
21. M. Simos, D. Creps, C. Klinger, L. Levine, and D. Allenmang, Organizational Domain Modeling (ODM) Guidebook, Verison 2.0, in Informal Technical Report for STARS. 1996
22. .J. Gray, T. Bapty, S. Neema, and J. Tuck, "Handling crosscutting constraints in domain-specific modeling," *Commun. ACM*, vol. 44, pp. 87--93, 2001.
23. R. E. Filman, S. Barrett, D. Lee, and T. Linden, "Inserting Ilities by Controlling Communications," *Communications of the ACM*, vol. 45, pp. 116-122, 2002.
24. J. G. Gray, "Aspect-Oriented Domain-Specific Modeling: A Generative Approach using a Metaweaver Framework," in *Computer Science*. Nashville, Tennessee: Vanderbilt University, 2002, pp. 225.
25. R. R. N. Guelfi, A. Romanovsky, S. Vandenbergh, "DRIP Catalyst: An MDE/MDA Method for Fault-tolerant Distributed Software Families Development," presented at 19th Annual ACM Conference on Object-Oriented Programming, Systems, Languages, and Applications, Vancouver, Canada, 2004.
26. O. M. Group, "UML Profile for QoS and Fault Tolerance", http://www.omg.org/cgi-bin/doc?ptc/2005-05-02, 2005.
27. Anders Hejlsberg, Scott Wiltamuth, and P. Golde, The C# Programming Language. 2003: Addison-Wesley Professional. 432.

28. Microsoft, "Microsoft Patterns and Practices: Exception Handling Application Block", http://msdn.microsoft.com/library/default.asp?url=/library/en-us/dnpag2/html/ehab.asp, 20th March 2005.
29. A. Romanovsky, and J. Kienzle, Action-Oriented Exception Handling in Cooperative and Competitive Concurrent Object-Oriented Systems. in Advances in Exception Handling Techniques. 2003. Darmstadt, Germany: Springer-Verlag Heidelberg.
30. A. Romanovsky, "Coordinated atomic actions: how to remain ACID in the modern world," *SIGSOFT Softw. Eng. Notes*, vol. 26, pp. 66--68, 2001.
31. Alexander Romanovsky, Action-Oriented Exception Handling in Cooperative and Competitive Concurrent Object-Oriented Systems. in Advances in Exception Handling Techniques. 2003. Darmstadt, Germany: Springer-Verlag Heidelberg.
32. J. Xu, A. Romanovsky, and B. Randell, Coordinated exception handling in distributed object systems: from model to system implementation. in Distributed Computing Systems, 1998. Proceedings. 18th International Conference on. 1998.
33. J. Xu, A. Romanovsky, and B. Randell, Concurrent exception handling and resolution in distributed object systems. Parallel and Distributed Systems, IEEE Transactions on, 2000. 11(10): p. 1019-1032.
34. C. A. R. Hoare, ed. Parallel programming: an axiomatic approach. 1973, Stanford University.
35. J. J. Horning, and B. Randell, Process Structuring. ACM Comput. Survey., 1973. 5(1): p. 5-30.
36. N. Benton, L. C. Cardelli, and D. Fournet, *Modern concurrency abstractions for C\#.* ACM Trans. Program. Lang. Syst., 2004. **26**(5): p. 769--804.
37. P.-W. N. Ivar Jacobson, *Aspect-Oriented Software Development with Use Cases*: Addison-Wesley Professional, 2004.
38. P. B. Ray Rankins, Chris Gallelli, Alex T. Silverstein, *Microsoft SQL Server 2005 Unleashed*: Sams, 2006.
39. P. Wilson, "Wilson ORM Mapper for .NET", http://www.ormapper.net/, 21st January 2006.
40. R. Hundhausen, *Working with Microsoft Visual Studio 2005 Team System*: Microsoft Press, 2005.
41. K. Dollard, *Code Generation in Microsoft .NET*: Apress, 2004.
42. O. M. Group, "Unified Modeling Language (UML): Superstructures version 2.0", http://www.omg.org/cgi-bin/doc?formal/05-07-04, 2004.
43. A. F. Zorzo and R. J. Stroud, "A distributed object-oriented framework for dependable multiparty interactions," in *OOPSLA '99: Proceedings of the 14th ACM SIGPLAN conference on Object-oriented programming, systems, languages, and applications*: ACM Press, 1999, pp. 435--446.

44. J. Li, Y. Mai, and G. Butler, "Implementing exception handling policies for workflow management system," presented at Software Engineering Conference, 2003. Tenth Asia-Pacific, 2003.
45. H.-X. Huang, Z. Qin, and J.-W. Guo, "Abstract exception handling policies in agent communication," presented at Machine Learning and Cybernetics, 2003 International Conference on, 2003.
46. M. Lippert and C. V. Lopes, "A Study on Exception Detection and Handling using Aspect-Oriented Programming," in *Proceedings of the 22nd international conference on Software engineering*: ACM Press, 2000, pp. 418--427.
47. T. Weis, "Model Driven Development of QoS-Enabled Distributed Applications," in *Intelligent Networks and Management of Distributed Systems*. Berlin: Berlin University of Technology, 2004, pp. 231.
48. J. Kienzle and R. Guerraoui, "AOP: Does It Make Sense? The Case of Concurrency and Failures," presented at ECOOP 2002 - Object-Oriented Programming: 16th European Conference, Malaga, Spain, 2002.
49. G. Arango, Domain analysis: from art form to engineering discipline, in IWSSD '89: Proceedings of the 5th international workshop on Software specification and design. 1989, ACM Press. p. 152--159.
50. S. P. Wartik, and R. Prieto-Díaz, Criteria for Comparing Reuse-Oriented Domain Analysis Approaches. International Journal of Software Engineering and Knowledge Engineering, 1992. 2(3): p. 403-431.
51. K. Kang, S. Cohen, J. Hess, W. Novak, and A. Peterson, *Feature-Oriented Domain Analysis (FODA) Feasibility Study*. 1990, Software Engineering Institute.

RUNTIME FAILURE DETECTION AND ADAPTIVE REPAIR FOR FAULT-TOLERANT COMPONENT-BASED APPLICATIONS*

RONG SU, MICHEL R.V. CHAUDRON and JOHAN J. LUKKIEN

System Architecture and Networking Group (SAN)
Department of Mathematics and Computer Science, Eindhoven University of Technology
PO Box 513, 5600 MB Eindhoven, The Netherlands
E-mails: r.su@tue.nl, m.r.v.chaudron@tue.nl, j.j.lukkien@tue.nl

In software engineering appropriately developed reusable components may significantly reduce the design cost, shorten the time to the market and reduce the maintenance effort. For those reasons more and more attention has been paid to the component-based framework recently. In this chapter, to improve availability of each individual service instance in a component-based system, we propose a runtime configurable fault management mechanism (FMM) which utilizes model-based failure detection and rule-based repair. When more than one repair action is possible, FMM picks one that incurs the best tradeoff between the success rate, the cost of repair and the post-repair reliability measure. Furthermore, in order to gradually improve the quality of fault tolerance, FMM is designed to be able to accumulate knowledge and adapts its capability accordingly.

Keywords: Component-Based Software; Model-Based Failure Detection; Adaptive Rule-Based Repair; Fault Tolerance

1. Introduction

It is well known in the software community that it is highly difficult, if at all possible, to guarantee fault-free software. Here, we adopt from[3,4] the term *fault* to describe an implementation that violates design specifications, and the term *failure* for abnormal symptoms during execution caused by some fault(s). A fault may be triggered in different ways, causing different *errors*, which then lead to different failures. Owing to our belief that appropriately developed reusable components may significantly reduce the design cost, shorten the time to the market and reduce the maintenance effort, we use a component-based framework,[1] where each application is formed by assembling several *service instances* (i.e. runtime instantiations of individual services), which may fail during an execution. Even

*This work is supported by the ITEA grant number 04003 (and the Dutch national grant number 18044021) for the EU-ITEA Trust4All Project.

when individual services are fault-free, their interaction in an application may lead to failures. Thus, to achieve high *reliability* of an application, it is necessary to achieve reliability of each relevant service instance. To achieve this goal, a fault management mechanism is proposed, which runtime instantiates a *configurable* wrapper in the sense that its data and logic controls can be dynamically changed, to encapsulate each service instance in use. By intercepting operation calls to and from the encapsulated service instance, the wrapper can detect deviations from the specification, and if repair is necessary, the wrapper is able to take a repair action, which is optimal in terms of a specific criterion. There is a large volume of publications on failure monitoring, diagnosis and repair of softwares, e.g.[7–9,11] Many are about component-based application, e.g.,[19–22] where failure detection and repair are discussed in terms of exception testing and handling. Compared with those, our proposed approach contains two novel contributions: (1) an "intelligent" screening procedure that picks the best repair action according to a pre-specified optimal criterion; (2) an adaptive procedure that can improve the screening procedure (in terms of the parameter updating) and also generate appropriate failure prevention rules which can prevent some failures to happen after their first time exposures. Considering that it is rather difficult to obtain all knowledge about a target software application once for all, we believe an appropriate self-learning capability within a fault management mechanism holds one of the keys for the success of a large component-based application.

This chapter is organized as follows. In Section 2 the system setup is introduced. Then we describe model-based failure detection in Section 3, and rule-based failure repair in Section 4. An example is presented in Section 5 and conclusions are drawn in Section 6.

2. The System Setup

In this section we first introduce basic constituents of a software component. Then we use an example to illustrate them. A *component* c is a collection of *services* S_c, where each service $s \in S_c$ consists of a family of interfaces I_s. An interface $i \in I_s$ is a *required interface* of s if it is required by s but implemented in another service s'; otherwise i is a *provided interface* of s. A service s_1 *binds* a service s_2 on an interface i if i is a required interface in s_1 and a provided interface in s_2. An interface i in our framework consists of a list of *operations* O_i, where each operation $o \in O_i$ consists of (1) a set $o.P$ of *input parameters*, where for each parameter $p \in o.P$, its domain is denoted by $p.D$ (thus implicitly the input type is also defined) and $\partial o.P$ for the boundary of $p.D$ when applicable; (2) a set $o.R$ of *returns*, where each return argument $r \in o.R$ has a domain $r.D$; (3) a resource usage (RU) tuple $[CU, MU] \in \mathbb{R}^+ \times \mathbb{N}$, where CU and MU denote the maximum CPU usage and memory usage of executing codes within o (here we can also use CU to describe some simple timing constraints such as the maximum time that o can wait for its input arguments to be supplied); (4) a *behavior model* describing in which order the operation o calls operations provided by other interfaces (not necessarily in the same service). The behavior model can be a finite-state machine (FSM), a sequence diagram or a process algebra.

As an illustration, let us consider a simplified Video-Audio Decoder (VAD) application, which consists of the following services: a Data-Retrieval, a Video Signal Processor (VSP), an Audio Signal Processor (ASP), a Video-Audio Synchronizer (VAS), and four buffers: BV1 between DR and VSP, BA1 between DR and ASP, BV2 between VSP and VAS, and BA2 between ASP and VAS. Figure 1 depicts the topological structure of VAD. DR takes data from some external

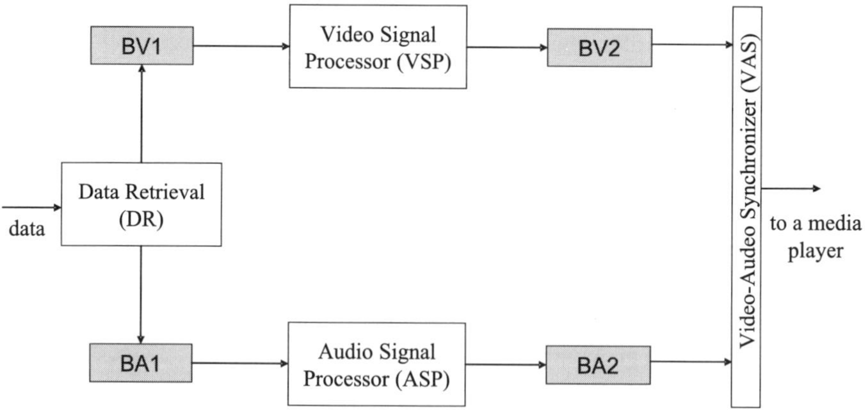

Fig. 1. The Simplified Video-Audio Decoder

source, then separates the video and audio signals from data, pushes the video signals to BV1 and audio signals to BA1. VSP takes video signals from BV1, processes them and pushes them to BV2. ASP takes audio signals from BA1, processes them and push them to BA2. Finally, VAS takes signals from BV2 and BA2, then synchronizes the video and audio signals that have the same time stamps. The output of VAS is fed to a media player such as a TV set or a DVD player.

Each buffer has one provided interface, e.g. IBV1 for BV1, IBA1 for BA1, IBV2 for BV2 and IBA2 for BA2. Each interface contains three operations:

PushIn, PopOut, BufferStatus. As an illustration, the service specification of BV1 may look as follows:

Service : BV1

provided IBV1
 operation PushIn
  input argument: { Item }
   domain of Item: $\{(v,t)|v \in \{1,\cdots,10\} \wedge t \in \mathbb{N}\}$
   /* v: the value of the item; t: the time stamp of the item */
  return argument: void
  CU = no restriction, MU = no restriction
  behavior model: no internal calls
 operation PopOut
  input argument: void
  return argument: Item
   domain of Item: $\{(v,t)|v \in \{1,\cdots,10\} \wedge t \in \mathbb{N}\}$
  CU = no restriction, MU = no restriction
  behavior model: no internal calls
 operation BufferStatus
  input argument: void
  return argument: Status
   domain of Status: { full, empty, neither full nor empty }
  CU = no restriction, MU = no restriction
  behavior model: no internal calls

The service specification for Data-Retrieval (DR) is as follows:

Service : DR

required IBV1
required IBA1
provided IDR
 operation ObtainData
  input argument: Item
   domain of Item: $\{(v,t)|v \in \{1,\cdots,10\} \wedge t \in \mathbb{N}\}$
  return argument: void
  CU = no restriction, MU = no restriction
  behavior model:
   IBV1.PushIn
   IBA1.PushIn

The service specification for Video Signal Processor (VSP) is as follows:

Service : VSP

1. **required** IBV1
2. **required** IBV2
3. **provided** IVSP
4. **operation** VideoProcessing
5. input argument: void
7. return argument: void
8. CU = 2 seconds, MU = no restriction
/* maximum waiting time for IBV1.PopOut is 2 seconds */
9. behavior model:
10. IBV1.PopOut
11. IBV2.PushIn

The service specification for Audio Signal Processor (ASP) is as follows:

Service : ASP

1. **required** IBA1
2. **required** IBA2
3. **provided** IASP
4. **operation** AudioProcessing
5. input argument: void
7. return argument: void
8. CU = 2 seconds, MU = no restriction
/* maximum waiting time for IBA1.PopOut is 2 seconds */
9. behavior model:
10. IBA1.PopOut
11. IBA2.PushIn

The service specification for Video-Audio Synchronizer (VAS) is as follows:

Service : VAS

1. **required** IBV2
2. **required** IBA2
3. **provided** IVAS
4. **operation** VideoAudioSynchronization
5. input argument: void

7. return argument: Item
8. domain of Item: $\{(v,t)|v \in \{1,\cdots,10\} \wedge t \in \mathbb{N}\}$
9. CU = 2 seconds, MU = no restriction
/*maximum waiting time for IBV2.PopOut & IBA2.PopOut is 2 seconds*/
10. behavior model:
11. IBV2.PopOut
12. IBA2.PopOut

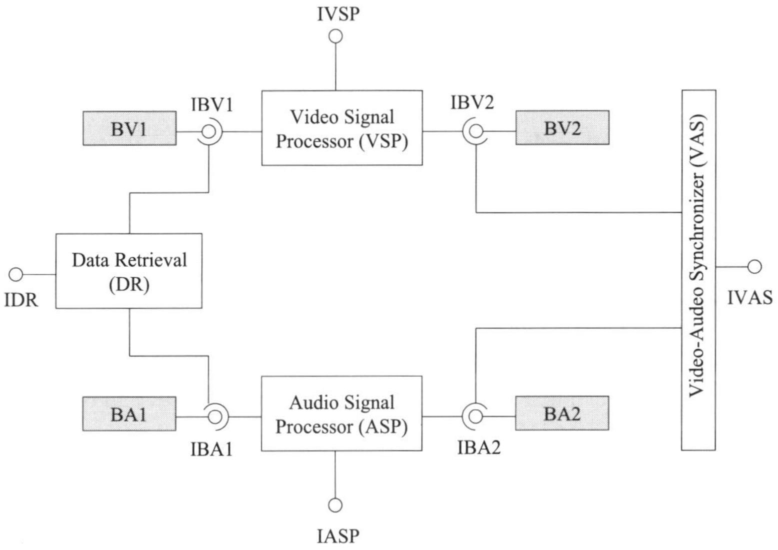

Fig. 2. Connections of Interfaces in VAD

Figure 2 depicts the connections among those interfaces. If IDR.ObtainData, IVSP.VideoProcessing, IASP.AudioProceesing and IVAS.VideoAudioSynchronization are called constantly and appropriately by an external user program or a control module, then there is a data flow from DR to VAS, namely a video-audio decoder is formed.

More generally, to form a specific *application* such as the above Video-Audio decoder, which is modeled as a finite set of *tasks*, where each task is a sequence of operation calls, each service instantiates some service instances, which are then bound to other service instances through interfaces connected by appropriate glue code. Each interface in a service instance is assigned a GUID (Global Unique

Identifier) number. A service instance may *fail* in the sense that it deviates from its specification, owing to reasons such as:[18] (1) input/output problems such as parameter incomplete or missing, type or value mismatches; (2) logic problems such as extreme value mishandled, missing condition test or iterating loop incorrectly; (3) memory problems such as insufficient memory allocation, data referenced out of bound or incorrect memory cleanup; (4) timing problems such as execution too slow/too fast; (5) computation problems such as equation insufficiency or incorrect sign conversion. The **fault management for service instances** is aimed to (1) detect any deviation as quickly and accurately as possible; and (2) if possible, remove a detected deviation from future executions. The first objective is about the *failure detection* and the second one about the *failure repair*.

3. Model-based Failure Detection

To perform failure detection, we use the wrapper pattern.[2] During runtime execution, a software entity called *Wrapper Generator* (WG) creates a wrapper for each service instance, which entirely encapsulates that service instance and intercepts every interface call to or from another service instance and every system call to or from the operating system. This can be done by manipulating GUID numbers. As an illustration, let us consider how to create a wrapper for the service instance DR in the VAD. Recall that DR has one provided interface IDR and two required interfaces IBV1 and IBA1. Figure 3 depicts the structure of DR with its dedicated wrapper M(DR).

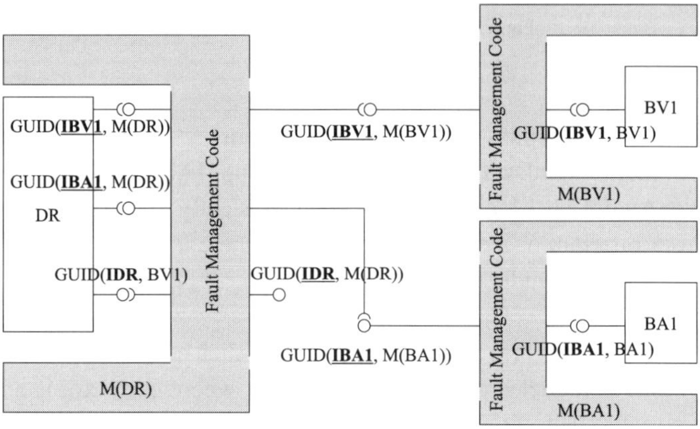

Fig. 3. The Wrapper for DR

The *runtime wrapper generation* procedure is described as follows:

Step (1): At runtime a service factory (SF) generates a service instance s, and each provided interface of s is assigned a unique GUID number.
Step (2): The wrapper generator takes information from SF, and generates a wrapper $M(s)$ for the service instance s with the following structure. For simplicity we use RU to denote resource usage and RA for return arguments.

/* wrapper code starts here */
outgoing interface calls from s:
  requires i_1: /* GUID(i_1,$M(s)$)) is to be filled in Step (5) */
  $\cdots$
  requires i_n: /* GUID(i_n,$M(s)$) is to be filled in Step (5) */
incoming interface calls to s:
  requires h_1: GUID(h_1,$M(s)$):=GUID(h_1,s)
  $\cdots$
  requires h_m: GUID(h_m,s):=GUID(h_m,s)
list of provided interfaces associated with outgoing calls:
  /* for each required interface i_k of s, create a provided interface $\underline{i_k}$ */
  provides $\underline{i_k}$ {
    /* for each o of the required interface i_k of s, create $\underline{i_k}.o$ in $M(s)$ */
    operation o
      /* check validity of inputs and RU of o; repair if necessary */
      operation call: GUID$(i_k, M(s)).o$
      /* check validity of RA of GUID$(i_k, M(s)).o$; repair if necessary */}
list of provided interfaces associated with incoming calls:
  /* for each h_k of s, creates a provided interface $\underline{h_k}$ in $M(s)$ */
  provides $\underline{h_k}$ {
    /* for each o of the provided interface h_k of s, create $\underline{h_k}.o$ */
    operation o
      /* check validity of inputs and RU of o; repair if necessary */
      operation call: GUID$(h_k, M(s)).o$
      /* check validity of RA of GUID$(h_k, M(s)).o$; repair if necessary */}
/* wrapper code ends here */

Step (3): Assign GUID numbers to provided interfaces in $M(s)$.
Step (4): For each required interface i_k $(k = 1, 2, \cdots, n)$ of s, which is the provided interface of s', assign GUID$(i_k, M(s))$:= GUID$(\underline{i_k}, M(s'))$.
Step (5): MG informs SF to bind every required interface of a service instance s

to the corresponding provided interface in $M(s)$, namely, for each required interface i_k $(k = 1, \cdots, n)$ in s, GUID(i_k, s) := GUID$(\underline{i_k}, M(s))$, where $\underline{i_k}$ is the corresponding provided interface in $M(s)$. □

Recall that the specification of a service instance s contains: (a) a list of required interfaces; (b) a list of provided interfaces; (c) for each operation in a provided interface a list of operations (input/output values and resource usages) and their ordering. Such information forms the *normal benchmark model* (NBM) of s and is stored in the wrapper $M(s)$. In some cases such an NBM can be obtained heuristically.[29] Although a fault without proper attention may eventually cause an execution to crash or simply idle, which then betrays the fault, service specifications may help to detect abnormality long before the fault leads to severe damages. There are many ways to store and use service specifications, e.g. $M(s)$ may initiate a new provided interface called ISispec, which serves as a database equipped with methods that can be used by other operations to retrieve data. ISispec may have the following structure:

provided interface ISispec: GUID(ISispec) {
  operation INIT() /* initialization */
    create list LI of provided interfaces of s:
      for each interface $i \in LI$ and each operation $o \in O_i$
        store the list of input arguments $o.P$ /* list of parameters */
          for each input argument $p \in o.P$
            store its domain $p.D$
        store the list of return arguments $o.R$ /* list of returns */
          for each return argument $r \in o.R$
            store its domain $r.D$
        store o's resource usage $Res(o)$=[CU, MU]
      encode the behavior model of o as a FSM $(X_o, \Sigma_o, CS_o, T_o)$ where
        X_o: the state set
        Σ_o: the alphabet where each element is an operation call made by o
        CS_o: the current state
        $T_o : X_o \times \Sigma_o \rightarrow X_o$: the transition map
  operation InputParameterCheck(operation-name o)
    search LI and return $(o.P, \{p.D|p \in o.P\})$
  operation ReturnCheck(operation-name o)
    search LI and return $(o.R, \{r.D|r \in o.R\})$
  operation ResourceCheck(operation-name o)
    search LI and return $Res(o)$

operation CurrentStatus(operation-name o)

  search LI and return CS_o and AO_o /* AO_o: legal operations at CS_o */

operation StatusUpdate(o, o') /* o' is an operation that is called by o */

  search LI and set $CS_o := T_o(CS_o, o')$ }

The wrapper $M(s)$ intercepts an incoming operation call (i.e. a call through a provided interface) and compares it with the specification stored in ISispec. Any observable deviation from the specification is called a *failure*. Such a failure detection approach is essentially a *model-based* approach, whose underlying idea can be found in many areas within or outside software engineering, e.g.[5–7,10,26–28] As for outgoing calls (i.e. calls through required interfaces), $M(s)$ does not have its normal benchmark model, thus, simply lets it pass without check. The call will be checked by the wrapper of the target service instance. As an illustration, in the fault management code part of each operation $h_k.o$ of $M(s)$, we can implement the failure detection approach by adding, e.g. the following code:

Upon intercepting an operation call $h_k.o$ to s, retrieve the NBM

  [P, L]=InputParameterCheck($h_k.o$)

  [CPU-usage, Memory-usage]=ResourceCheck($h_k.o$)

  [CS_o, AO_o]=CurrentStatus($h_k.o$)

if there is any deviation between $h_k.o$ and its normal benchmark model

  block the call $h_k.o$ to s and invoke methods of repair

otherwise, pass the operation call GUID$(h_k, M(s)).o$ to its destination in s

if o has internal calls, use CurrentStatus and StatusUpdate to check validity

if the return of o is different from its NBM ReturnCheck($h_k.o$)

  invoke methods of failure repair

In general, a service instance specification allows us to identify the following failures: (1) value mismatches such as illegal input parameter values and illegal return values of an operation call; (2) unspecified operation calls within an individual provides operation such as non-existing promised service functionality and unexpected service functionality; (3) unexpected resource usage for an individual operation such as insufficient memory allocation and timing problems.

4. Rule-Based Failure Repair and Adaptation

4.1. *Reliability Measure*

For a service s, ideally the service provider should supply a *reliability growth model*,[12] which tells users how the reliability of the service improves over a period of time, owing to changes in the service design such as bug fixings or extra fault tolerance mechanisms. In our case we are interested in how the reliability grows after each detected failure is removed. In case the provider does not fulfil his/her obligation on this matter, users may need to come up with their own models. Although there are a large volume of different growth models available in the literature,[15] we feel that, by constructing one with sufficient details, it may be helpful to illustrate how a reliability growth model can assist us in adaptive fault management. Then in practical applications a user may adopt the same fault management strategy described in the remaining of the chapter, but with his/her own reliability growth model.

Let $N(t)$ denote the expected number of defects (i.e. faults) present in the system at time t. The number of defects exposed during the time interval Δt is $N(t) - N(t + \Delta t)$. Let $k_s(t)$ be the expected fraction of existing defects exposed during a single execution, whose duration is T_s. We have the following equation[12]

$$N(t) - N(t + \Delta t) = k_s(t)N(t)\frac{\Delta t}{T_s} + O(\Delta t)$$

where $O(\Delta t)$ stands for a value that is a higher order of Δt. The term $k_s(t)$ is called the *fault exposure ratio*, whose value at each time instant t should be interpreted as an average over a large number of trials at t. Assumptions about defects such as whether they are independent of each other or correlated with each other are captured by $k_s(t)$ as well. Take Δt to be infinitesimal, then we have

$$\frac{dN(t)}{dt} = -\frac{k_s(t)}{T_s}N(t) \tag{1}$$

Thus,

$$N(t) = N(t_0)e^{-\int_{t_0}^{t} \frac{k_s(\tau)}{T_s} d\tau} \tag{2}$$

The term T_s can be approximately represented as follows:

$$T_s = \frac{I_s Q_x}{r}$$

where I_s stands for the number of source statements, Q_x the number of object instructions per source statement, and r the average object instruction execution rate of the computer being used. Notice that the reliability growth model predicts that, starting at t_0, by the time instant t there will be $N(t_0) - N(t)$ defects exposed to a user. If any exposed defect results in a failure, then the *time to the first failure* $\hat{t}$ (i.e. $N(t_0) - N(\hat{t}) = 1$) can be considered as a reliability measure of the current service instance. To make sure that $\lim_{t \to \infty} N(t) = 0$, meaning all defects will be exposed eventually, it is necessary that $\lim_{t \to +\infty} \int_{t_0}^{t} k_s(\tau)d\tau = +\infty$. The choice of $k_s(t)$ is quite subjective, e.g. it can be a constant, or $k_s(s) = \frac{a_1}{1+a_2 t}$ with $a_1, a_2 > 0$ as used in Musa-Okumoto model,[14] or $k_s(t) = \frac{a_1}{\sqrt{1+a_2 t}}$ as used in Littlewood-Verrall inverse linear model[16] etc. These parameters can be estimated based on real data collected in the runtime environment. If faults are correlated then the triggering of one fault may affect the chance of another fault being triggered, namely the fault exposure rate $k_s(t)$ is not only a function of time, but also a function of specific faults. In[23] the authors provide a model of $k_s(t)$ that takes some fault correlation into consideration. But validating such a treatment is rather difficult. We now discuss how to estimate those parameters in Equation (1).

There are three parameters in Equation (1): T_s, $N(t_0)$ and $k_s(t)$. We have discussed how to get an approximation of T_s, which should be provided by the service designer because knowledge of internal code is required. Of course, a few number of test trials can also reveal this value. The difficulty lies in obtaining good approximations of $N(t_0)$ and $k_s(t)$. In[25] we adopt a case-based reasoning approach described in.[24] The whole idea is to "guess" those two parameters by using knowledge of previously used *similar* service instances. Given a collection of service instances $S = \{s_1, \cdots, s_n\}$, suppose they share a set of software metrics (or independent variables), say MT, e.g. MT may contain the total number of lines of a service instance, the total number of distinct procedure calls to others, the number of entry/exit nodes, the number of control statements etc. For notation brevity, we use $\mathrm{MT}(s)$ to denote the values of those metrics for a specific service instance s. Imagine $\mathrm{MT}(s)$ as a vector. Define a *similarity function*

$$d : \{\mathrm{MT}(s) | s \in S\} \times \{\mathrm{MT}(s) | s \in S\} \rightarrow [0, 1] \subset \mathbb{R}$$

The function d is essentially a normalized distance map. Suppose $\mathrm{MT}(s) = (x_{1,s}, \cdots, x_{r,s})^T$ and $\mathrm{MT}(s') = (x_{1,s'}, \cdots, x_{r,s'})^T$. Depending on specific applications, the similarity function can be the *city block distance*,[24]

$$d(\mathrm{MT}(s), \mathrm{MT}(s')) := \sum_{j=1}^{r} w_j |x_{j,s} - x_{j,s'}|$$

or the Euclidean distance,

$$d(\mathrm{MT}(s), \mathrm{MT}(s')) := \sqrt{\sum_{j=1}^{r} [w_j (x_{j,s} - x_{j,s'})]^2}$$

or the Mahalanobis distance,

$$d(\mathrm{MT}(s), \mathrm{MT}(s')) := \sqrt{(\mathrm{MT}(s) - \mathrm{MT}(s'))^T W^{-1} (\mathrm{MT}(s) - \mathrm{MT}(s'))}$$

where W is the covariance matrix of metrics over all elements of S, and W^{-1} is the inverse of W. Clearly, W is positive definite. The degree of similarity between s and s' is simply the value of $d(\mathrm{MT}(s), \mathrm{MT}(s'))$.

Suppose we want to estimate $N(t_0)$ for a service instance s. We know that s is *very similar* to element in S in the sense that each value $d(\mathrm{MT}(s), \mathrm{MT}(s'))$ ($s' \in S$) surpasses a predefined threshold. Each element in S has been used for a long period, thus, we assume that we know the entire history of its fault exposure, namely we know the total number of faults $N_{s'}(t_0)$ at its first time usage. The predicted value of $N_s(t_0)$ can be described either as the unweighted average of $\{N_{s'}(t_0) | s' \in S\}$, namely

$$N_s(t_0) := \frac{1}{n} \sum_{s' \in S} N_{s'}(t_0)$$

or a weighted average

$$\delta(s, s') := \frac{1/d(\mathrm{MT}(s), \mathrm{MT}(s'))}{\sum_{s'' \in S} d(\mathrm{MT}(s), \mathrm{MT}(s''))}$$

$$N_s(t_0) := \sum_{s' \in S} \delta(s, s') N_{s'}(t_0)$$

As for estimating the fault exposure rate $k_s(t)$ of s, recall that we have a complete history for each element $s' \in S$, thus, we know $k_{s'}(t)$ in terms of either a finite set of values at discrete time instants or a continuous function interpolated from those discrete values. Suppose we have the latter. Then we simply take a weighted average as follows:

$$k_s(t) := \sum_{s' \in S} \delta(s, s') k_{s'}(t)$$

If we do not possess knowledge about those $s' \in S$, e.g. during the early stage of the system's usage, then we may try Bayesian reliability growth models[16,17] as long as we have an appropriate prior distribution of the failure rate. If we have no such prior knowledge, then we recommend not to include the factor of reliability in the fault management.

Suppose at time instant t some faults are revealed through failures. The fault management will take an appropriate repair, which is aimed to remove those failures and prevent them from appearing again in the future. If the repair succeeds in the sense that the previously presented failures disappear, then we *consider* that those corresponding faults have been exposed. Thus, we can update the reliability growth model, namely we update $k_s(t)$ and $N(t_0)$. More explicitly, the new initial time instant is set to t, and $N(t) := N(t_0) - a$, where a is the number of faults that we think have been exposed. $k_s(t)$ will be adjusted accordingly, as described above. Consequently, the reliability measure $\hat{t}$ is also updated. In the next subsection we will discuss how to take reliability into consideration when performing failure repair.

4.2. *Optimal Repair and Adaptation*

For a service instance s let $O_s = \{o_1, o_2, \cdots, o_n\}$ denote operations of provided interfaces in s. Notice that the wrapper $M(s)$ only does failure detection on operations provided by s, and allows operation calls required by s to pass without being checked. Of course, these calls will be checked later by relevant wrappers that encapsulate target service instances. For each $o \in O_s$, let o.MU and o.CU denote variables about memory and CPU usages of o respectively, and o.EP for the execution priority of o, whose domain is the list of available priorities. Let $F_s = \{\mu_1, \cdots, \mu_m\}$ denote known faults, e.g. *insufficient-stack* (IS) and *extreme-mishandling* (EM), and $W_s = \{\nu_1, \cdots, \nu_k\}$ denotes failures caused by faults in F_s, e.g. *stack-overflow* and *crash*. We usually couple O_s and F_s together and call each element $(o, \sigma) \in O_s \times F_s$ a *single fault* and $\omega \subseteq O_s \times F_s$ a *compound fault*. To repair a failure we first need to identify the failure. For that purpose we use a rule-based approach. There are *symptom rules* about causal relationship between faults and failures. Each symptom rule is expressed by a mapping SYM : $2^{O_s \times F_s} \to 2^{W_s}$, associating a set of *compound faults* to a collection of failures. When $\omega \subseteq O_s \times F_s$ is a singleton, say $\omega = \{(o, \sigma)\}$, then we also write SYM(o, σ) to denote SYM$(\{(o, \sigma)\})$. For example, a symptom rule may look as follows,

$$\begin{aligned}&\mathrm{SYM}(\{(o_1, \mathrm{IS}), (o_2, \mathrm{EM})\})\\ &= \{\textit{stack-overflow}, \textit{crash}, (\exists o \in O_s)(\exists p \in o.P)\ \mathrm{VALUE}(p) \in \partial p.D\}\end{aligned}$$

which says that if in operation o_1 the stack is insufficiently allocated and in o_2 the boundary value of some input argument are not correctly handled, then we expect to observe stack-overflow, execution crash and some input argument of an operation taking a boundary value.

For each single fault $(o, \sigma) \in O_s \times F_s$, let

$$\mathrm{IV}(o, \sigma) \subseteq o.P \cup \{o.\mathrm{MU}, o.\mathrm{CU}, o.\mathrm{EP}\}$$

denote the set of *influential variable* whose values can affect states associated with σ. Owing to inability to modify internal code of the service instance, we can only adjust values of input parameters of o, memory allocation, CPU allocation and execution priority to handle each potential fault (o, σ). If there exist some other means, the set $\mathrm{IV}(o, \sigma)$ may need to be extended accordingly. Suppose the domains of o.MU, o.CU and o.EP are $o.\mathrm{MU}.D$, $o.\mathrm{CU}.D$ and $o.\mathrm{EP}.D$ respectively. The *domain* of $\mathrm{IV}(o, \sigma)$ is a set of tuples:

$$\mathrm{IV}(o, \sigma).D := \prod_{x \in \mathrm{IV}(o,\sigma)} x.D$$

A *clock* associated with o and σ is a map: $T_{o,\sigma} : \mathbb{R}^+ \to \mathrm{IV}(o, \sigma).D$, where $\mathbb{R}^+$ denotes the set of all nonnegative reals. In our setup we are interested in some special time instant t^*, e.g. the initial time when the service instance s is in use, or when the latest non-failure operation execution in s starts. The goal of repair is to change state values at t^* so that the triggering of a specific failure can be avoided. To that end, we have *repair rules* describing how to perform repair, where each rule has the following format:

$$\mathrm{REPAIR}(o, \sigma, t^*) := f_{o,\sigma}(T_{o,\sigma}(t^*))$$

where the function $f_{o,\sigma} : \mathrm{IV}(o, \sigma).D \to \mathrm{IV}(o, \sigma).D$ tells how to update values of variables. For example, operation o may need a specific amount of memory to fulfil a computational task. The exact amount is unknown at the beginning. If there is not enough memory, namely the fault σ is *insufficient-memory*, the execution will crash. Here, $\mathrm{IV}(o, \sigma) = \{o.\mathrm{MU}\}$, meaning that we will repair the failure by adjusting the memory usage. We choose t^* as the beginning of the execution of o. Thus, $T_{o,\sigma}(t^*) = \mathrm{VALUE}(o.\mathrm{MU}, t^*)$, where $\mathrm{VALUE}(o.\mathrm{MU}, t^*)$ stands for the value of o.MU at t^*. The repair rule can be defined as

$$\mathrm{REPAIR}(o, \sigma, t^*) := \min\{3T_{o,\sigma}(t^*), C\}$$

where C is a pre-specified constant. The rule says that, to repair the failure we either increase the initial memory allocation by three folds or set it as C, whichever is smaller, and retry o.

A collection of faults $\omega \subseteq O_s \times F_s$ may be *correlated*[23] with each other in the sense that (1) the subsequent failures of a collection of faults may not be simply the union of failures caused by each individual fault; (2) failures of one fault may be masked by failures of others; and (3) the repair of one fault is indispensable of some other's repair. To avoid unnecessary complicity, in this chapter we only consider *independent faults* defined as follows.

Definition 4.1. A collection of faults $Y \subseteq O_s \times F_s$ are *independent* if

(1) For each $Z \subseteq Y$,

$$\mathrm{SYM}(Z) = \bigcup_{(o,\sigma)\in Z} \mathrm{SYM}(o,\sigma)$$

(2) For each $(o,\sigma) \in Y$ and $Z \subset Y$

$$(o,\sigma) \notin Z \Rightarrow \mathrm{SYM}(o,\sigma) \nsubseteq \bigcup_{(o',\sigma')\in Z} \mathrm{SYM}(o',\sigma')$$

(3) For any $(o_i,\sigma_i), (o_j,\sigma_j) \in Y$,

$$(o_i,\sigma_i) \neq (o_j,\sigma_j) \Rightarrow \mathrm{IV}(o_i,\sigma_i) \cap \mathrm{IV}(o_j,\sigma_j) = \varnothing$$

□

Def. 4.1 essentially says that the symptom of any collection of independent faults is simply the union of symptoms of each individual fault; the failures of one fault cannot be masked by the failures of others; and the repair of each individual fault will not affect others.

When a symptom $X \subseteq W_s$ is collected, we compute

$$\mathrm{SYM}^{-1}(X) := \{(o,\sigma) \in O_s \times F_s | \mathrm{SYM}(o,\sigma) \subseteq X\}$$

which consists of every single fault that may result in failures contained in the symptom X. For example, an operation o may crash owing to insufficient memory, or some logic error such as extreme-value-mishandled. Thus, given the symptom $X = \{crash\}$, we get that

$$\mathrm{SYM}^{-1}(X) := \{(o, \textit{insufficient-memory}),\ (o, \textit{extreme-value-mishandled})\}$$

We say $\mathrm{SYM}^{-1}(X)$ is *plausible* if

$$(\exists Z \subseteq \mathrm{SYM}^{-1}(X)) \bigcup_{(o,\sigma)\in Z} \mathrm{SYM}(o,\sigma) = X$$

Such a compound fault Z is called a *fault candidate*. In the above example, $\{(o,$ *insufficient-memory*$)\}$ is a fault candidate for $X = \{crash\}$, so are $\{(o,$ *extreme-value-mishandled*$)\}$ and the set $\{(o,$ *insufficient-memory*$)$, $(o,$ *extreme-value-mishandled*$)\}$. Let $\Phi(X)$ be the collection of every fault candidate, whose constituent faults are independent of each other. Suppose $\Phi(X)$ is not empty. A fault candidate $Z \in \Phi(X)$ is associated with a set of repair actions

$$\Omega(Z) := \{\mathrm{REPAIR}(o,\sigma,t^*_{o,\sigma}) | (o,\sigma) \in Z\}$$

where the time instant $t^*_{o,\sigma}$ is case-dependent because here we are considering compound faults. We call $\Omega(Z)$ a *repair* of X. Since all faults are independent (by the assumption), if the symptom X is resulted from the fault candidate Z, then performing repair actions in $\Omega(Z)$ will eliminate X. Considering that there may be more than one fault candidate in $\Phi(X)$, to decide which set of repair actions should be taken first, we assign priority numbers to repairs associated with different fault candidates.

Let $\text{RA}(X) := \{\Omega(Z)|Z \in \Phi(X)\} \cup \{\text{RETRY}, \text{REPLACE}\}$ be the collection of all possible repairs of the symptom X, and $\psi_X : \text{RA}(X) \to \mathbb{R}^+$ be a priority function. A repair with higher priority is chosen to execute first. We now describe how to choose a priority function.

Each repair $\Omega(Z)$ is associated with a 3-tuple

$$[\text{NS}(\Omega(Z))/\text{NT}(\Omega(Z)), \text{RC}(\Omega(Z)), \hat{t}(\Omega(Z))]$$

where $\text{NS}(\Omega(Z))/\text{NT}(\Omega(Z))$ denotes the *success rate* of $\Omega(Z)$, which is the ratio of the number of previous successful tries and the number of overall previous tries with the same symptom X. $\text{RC}(\Omega(Z))$ stands for the *repair cost* of $\Omega(Z)$ and $\hat{t}(\Omega(Z))$ is the reliability measure after the successful repair $\Omega(Z)$, which is derived from a reliability growth model as described in Section 4.1. To make $\Omega(Z)$ succeed is to require each repair action in $\Omega(Z)$ to succeed. Thus, we can define $\text{NS}(\Omega(Z))/\text{NT}(\Omega(Z))$ as follows:

$$\frac{\text{NS}(\Omega(Z))}{\text{NT}(\Omega(Z))} := \prod_{z \in \Omega(Z)} \frac{\text{NS}(z)}{\text{NT}(z)}$$

where $\text{NS}(z)/\text{NT}(z)$ denote success rate of repair action z and $\text{NT}(z) \neq 0$. If z has never been implemented before, we set $\text{NS}(z)/\text{NT}(z) = 50\%$. The total cost $\text{RC}(\Omega(Z))$ can be defined as:

$$\text{RC}(\Omega(Z)) := \sum_{z \in \Omega(Z)} \text{RC}(z)$$

where $\text{RC}(z)$ denotes the repair cost of z. Let $a_1 > 0$, $a_2 < 0$ be the weights. How to choose them properly is still a challenge. The priority $\psi_X(\Omega(Z))$ is,

$$\psi_X(\Omega(Z)) := a_1 \frac{\text{NS}(\Omega(Z))}{\text{NT}(\Omega(Z))} \hat{t}(\Omega(Z)) + a_2 \text{RC}(\Omega(Z))$$

Such a priority function suggests that, whenever a repair is necessary, we choose one with a low cost, but a high success rate and a high post-repair reliability value.

After $\Omega(Z)$ is taken we perform the following update (or *adaptation*) according to the result of the repair.

(1) Update Parameters:

For each repair action $z \in \Omega(Z)$, $M(s)$ updates $\mathrm{NS}(z)$ and $\mathrm{NT}(z)$ as follows. If the previous failures disappear after $\Omega(Z)$, then $\mathrm{NS}(z) := \mathrm{NS}(z) + 1$ and $\mathrm{NT}(z) := \mathrm{NT}(z)+1$, where the symbol ':=' denotes value assignment; otherwise, $\mathrm{NT}(z) := \mathrm{NT}(z) + 1$. If instances from the same service is constantly used, then by updating $\mathrm{NS}(z)$ and $\mathrm{NT}(z)$, the correct repair actions will gradually move to the top of the priority list. The duration of this process depends on the coefficient a_1, which is also called the *learning factor*.

(2) Update reliability growth model of s if previous failures disappear after $\Omega(Z)$.

(3) Generate a failure prevention rule if previous failures disappear after $\Omega(Z)$. For each repair action $z = \mathrm{REPAIR}(o, \sigma, t^*_{o,\sigma}) \in \Omega(Z)$, perform the following operations. Suppose the influential variable set is $\mathrm{IV}(o, \sigma) = \{p_1, \cdots, p_n\}$. Let

$$T_{o,\sigma}(t^*_{o,\sigma}) = \{\mathrm{VALUE}(p_1) = a_1, \cdots, \mathrm{VALUE}(p_n) = a_n\}$$

and the repair action is

$$f_{o,\sigma}(T_{o,\sigma}(t^*_{o,\sigma})) = \{\mathrm{VALUE}(p_1) = b_1, \cdots, \mathrm{VALUE}(p_n) = b_n\}$$

Then $M(s)$ adds a *failure prevention rule* (FPR) as follows:

$$[\mathrm{VALUE}(p_1) = a_1 \wedge \cdots \wedge \mathrm{VALUE}(p_n) = a_n] \Rightarrow [p_1 := b_1 \wedge \cdots \wedge p_n := b_n]$$

where VALUE is a valuation function which provides the current value of the corresponding variable. This new rule will be stored in the wrapper, which says that whenever the value of the tuple $\mathrm{IV}(o, \sigma)$ reaches $T_{o,\sigma}(t^*_{o,\sigma})$, $M(s)$ will forcefully change this value to $f_{o,\sigma}(T_{o,\sigma}(t^*_{o,\sigma}))$ before further execution. Such a value change is implemented by requiring new resource allocation through negotiating with the resource manager outside the wrapper and/or changing input parameter values of incoming calls to the service instance s. Thus, the potential failures caused by the fault σ within the operation o may be avoided (or at least their occurrence likelihood is reduced). This rule will also be stored in MG for future use.

Figure 4 depicts the architecture of a wrapper, which has three interfaces: IAdaptor, ISispec and IRepair. In IRepair the Decider is used to pick a repair with the highest priority value among untried ones. Each arrow-headed line points

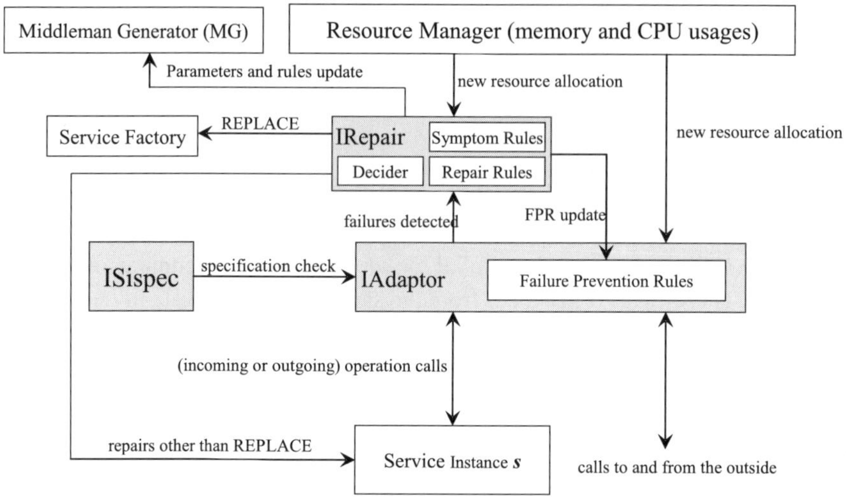

Fig. 4. Architecture of a Wrapper

to the entity which receives information.

In the next section we will describe how the proposed fault management approach affects the system performance in the audio/video decoder application.

5. Example

A fully functional runtime configurable adaptive fault management mechanism for component-based applications complying with the Robocop framework is still under development, which is expected to be demonstrated at the end of the Trust4All project in year 2007. A prototype (in C#) is currently operational and has been used to perform experiments on which the data in this section is based. In experiments we observe the effect of fault management on the system's performance by turning wrappers on and off.

For simple illustration purpose, in the Video-Audio Decoder application we consider three types of faults: (1) input/output problems within operation calls in DR, VSP and ASP; (2) buffer overflow; (3) timing mismatch among DR, VSP and ASP. We use mutation to inject faults (more accurately, errors) in the code. Each set of correct input/output values of an operation is associated with a set of wrong values that are out of relevant variable domains; in VSP and ASP a piece of mutated code simulate the value-mishandled fault, and the operation IDR.ObtainData in DR stops pushing data in BV1 and BA1, causing both missing their timing constraints. The buffer overflow problem exists in the system even without code mutation.

To simulate the random triggering of faults, each block of mutated code is executed as follows. A pseudo random number from a pre-specified range, say from 0 to 1, is first generated, which is then compared with a pre-specified threshold, say 0.9. If the random number is above the threshold, then the corresponding mutated code is executed; otherwise the correct code is executed. The distribution of the pseudo random numbers in C# within a small range is close to the uniform distribution. Thus, by using the above approach we can control the probability of execution of mutated code. Whenever mutated code is executed, it results in an exception, which halts the program.

Based on those faults we have the following symptom rules. For each service instance $s \in \{\text{DR, VSP, ASP, VAS, BV1, BA1, BV2, BA2}\}$, let O_s be the collection of all operations within provided interfaces. Recall that for each $o \in O_s$, $o.P$ stands for the input variables and $o.R$ the output variables. For each $p \in o.P \cup o.R$, $p.D$ stands for the domain of p, and VALUE(p) the current value of p.

- for an operation call o to s,
  - SYM(o, illegal-inputs) = $\{(\exists p \in o.P)\ \text{VALUE}(p) \notin p.D\}$
  - SYM(o, illegal-returns) = $\{(\exists p \in o.R)\ \text{VALUE}(p) \notin p.D\}$
- if s is VSP or ASP then
  - SYM(o, value-mishandled) = {a normal value incurs execution crash}
  - SYM(o, logic-error) = {execution crashes}
- if s is DR then
  - SYM(o, execution-too-slow) = {VSP, ASP miss timing constraints}
- if s is a buffer then
  - SYM(o, overflow) = { execution crashes}

For a service instance s, the wrapper $M(s)$ has the following repair rules:

- for an operation o from s'
  - Repair(o, illegal-inputs) = block the call, return the special code *ILLEGAL INPUTS* to $M(s')$.
  - Repair(o, illegal-returns) = retry o twice; if no success, replace s with a new instance.

- if s is VSP or ASP then
  - Repair(o, value-mishandled) = reduce the current item value x from BV1 by 5% per each repair and retry (maximum twice).
  - Failure Prevention: upon successful repair with, e.g. 5% reduction on the current value VALUE(x) =5, generate an FPR as: VALUE(x) $= 5 \Rightarrow$ VALUE(x) $= 4.75$
  - Repair(o, logic-error) = replace s with a compatible instance
- if s is DR then
  - Repair(o, execution-too-slow) = replace DR with a highly reliable compatible instance
- if s is a buffer then
  - Repair(o, overflow) = drop all items in the buffer and retry it.

Based on those symptom rules, the symptom $X = \{\text{execution crashes}\}$ in VSP is associated with three fault candidates:

$$Z_1 = \{(\text{VideoProcessing, value-mishandled})\};$$
$$Z_2 = \{\text{VideoProcessing, logic-error}\};\ Z_3 = Z_1 \cup Z_2$$

Based on repair rules, each fault candidate is associated with one of the following:

$$\Omega(Z_1) = \text{Repair(VideoProcessing, value-mishandled)}$$
$$\Omega(Z_2) = \text{Repair(VideoProcessing,logic-error)}$$
$$\Omega(Z_3) = \Omega(Z_1) \cup \Omega(Z_2) \text{ (because repairs for } Z_1 \text{ and } Z_2 \text{ are independent)}$$

It is interesting to notice that $\Omega(Z_3)$ is different from $\Omega(Z_2)$ because if a compatible instance is put in first then applying $\Omega(Z_1)$ on it may reduce its performance a little bit. We now associate parameters to each repair and construct a priority function ψ_X.

Suppose all repairs have not been taken before. Thus, their respective success rate (NS/NT) is chosen to be 50%. Suppose the cost for $\Omega(Z_1)$ is 20 dollars and for $\Omega(Z_2)$ is 50 dollars because a new compatible service is required, which is more expensive than simply adjusting the value of Stack and retrying in $\Omega(Z_1)$. The cost of $\Omega(Z_3)$ is 70. Suppose the reliability growth models for the current VSP and the compatible version are the same type but with different parameters:

$$\frac{dN_s(t)}{dt} = -\frac{k_s(t)}{T_s} N_s(t)$$

where s=VSP or s=VSP-compatible, $N_s(0) = 10$, $T_s = 1$ and $k_s(t)$ is a constant (for simplicity purpose), e.g. say $k_{VSP}(t) = 1.0536 \times 10^{-5}$ and

$k_{VSP-compatible}(t) = 7.024 \times 10^{-6}$. From equation (2) the reliability measure is

$$\hat{t} = -\frac{\ln(1 - \frac{1}{N_s(0)})}{k_s}$$

Thus, for VSP the post-repair reliability measure associated with $\Omega(Z_1)$ is $\hat{t}(\Omega(Z_1)) = 10^4$ and for the compatible VSP the associated reliability measure is $\hat{t}(\Omega(Z_2)) = 1.5 \times 10^4$. We assume that the associated reliability measure for the compatible VSP after $\Omega(Z_3)$ is the same as that after $\Omega(Z_2)$. Finally, we construct a priority function as follows:

$$\psi_X(\Omega(Z)) := 2 \times 10^{-3} \frac{\mathrm{NS}(\Omega(Z))}{\mathrm{NT}(\Omega(Z))} \hat{t}(\Omega(Z)) - 0.2\mathrm{RC}(\Omega(Z))$$

Then we have $\psi_X(\Omega(Z_1)) = 2 \times 10^{-3} \times 0.5 \times 10^4 - 0.2 \times 20 + 1 = 6$. Similarly we get $\psi_X(\Omega(Z_2)) = 5$ and $\psi_X(\Omega(Z_3)) = 1$. Thus,

$$\psi_X(\Omega(Z_1)) > \psi_X(\Omega(Z_2)) > \psi_X(\Omega(Z_3))$$

Therefore, when X is collected, Repair(VideoProcessing, value-mishandled) will be taken first. If the post-repair reliability measure of $\Omega(Z_2)$ is larger, say 5×10^4 (which means $k_{VSP-compatible} = 2.1072 \times 10^{-6}$), then

$$\psi_X(\Omega(Z_2)) = 40 > \psi_X(\Omega(Z_1))$$

In this case, when X is received, VSP will be replaced directly because the improvement on the post-repair reliability measure overtakes the repair cost.

The wrapper $M(s)$ for s has the following fault management procedure.

```
1.  wait for a call o to or from the service instance s
2.  if o is an outgoing call to s', then pass it to M(s') without any check
3.  if o is an incoming call to s
4.       check whether any above symptom rule is triggered
5.            if yes, then take the associated repair rule and goto Step 1
6.  loop until the return is intercepted or the execution crashes
7.  if X = {crashes} and s is VSP or ASP
8.       compute the optimal repair based on ψ_X, and execute it.
9.       based on the repair result, perform parameter update and generate a FPR
10. if X = {crashes} and s is a buffer
11.      take the Repair(o, overflow)
12. if the return is an error code ILLEGAL INPUTS
13.      ignore unless it has appeared 5 times, then replace s and goto Step 1
14. if SYM(o, illegal-returns) is collected
```

15.   take Repair(o, illegal-returns)
16.   else, pass o's return values to its final destination and goto Step 1.

We use C# to program the above VAD application and the fault management mechanism. First, we test whether the proposed fault management will significantly increase the overhead of each operation call in DR, VSP, ASP and VAS. To that end, we run the application 10 times. Among those runs half of them are with the wrappers being turned on and the remaining half with the wrappers off. In each run we measure the average duration of each operation call in every relevant required interface. In this experiment a Pentium M 2.0 GHz processor is used.

Table 1

No	1	2	3	4	5	average
DR BV1.PushIn	110.366 /118.628 /7.486%	132.748 /137.238 /3.382%	123.582 /130.422 /5.535%	117.668 /123.838 /5.243%	109.972 /117.226 /6.596%	118.867 /125.470 /5.555%
DR BA1.PushIn	101.242 /102.071 /0.819%	103.757 /104.242 /0.467%	100.871 /101.642 /0.764%	101.585 /103.614 /1.940%	102.871 /103.557 /0.667%	102.065 /103.025 /0.941%
VSP BV1.PopOut	103.164 /103.988 /0.799%	105.544 /106.161 /0.585%	103.100 /104.458 /1.317%	102.455 /104.367 /1.866%	104.782 /105.135 /0.337%	103.809 /104.821 /0.975%
VSP BV2.PushIn	99.224 /104.600 /5.418%	101.289 /107.467 /6.099%	107.667 /110.433 /2.569%	104.368 /109.853 /5.255%	112.428 /119.422 /6.221%	104.995 /110.355 /5.105%
ASP BA1.PopOut	117.933 /122.410 /3.796%	116.046 /119.6 /3.063%	113.180 /130.442 /15.252%	112.516 /132.1 /17.406%	119.117 /132.026 /10.837%	115.758 /127.315 /9.984%
ASP BA2.PushIn	107.369 /109.743 /2.211%	100.723 /104.528 /3.778%	116.159 /123.733 /6.520%	125.937 /129.746 /3.025%	108.482 /115.3 /6.258%	111.734 /116.61 /4.364%
VAS BV2.PopOut	98.193 /99.510 /1.341%	104.600 /108.806 /4.021%	101.466 /109.187 /7.609%	99.966 /105.879 /5.915%	100.580 /107.793 /7.171%	100.961 /106.235 /5.224%
VAS BA2.PopOut	157.222 /181.333 /15.336%	153.510 /156.148 /1.718%	157.629 /172.840 /9.650%	166.148 /179.652 /8.128%	151.666 /173.272 /14.246%	157.301 /172.649 /9.757%

Table 1 summarizes our test results, where each entry $a/b/c$ stands for the execution time a of an interface call without wrappers vs the execution time b of the interface call with wrappers and the percentage c of extra time caused by the involvement of wrappers. The time unit is millisecond. From Table 1 we can see that in average the overhead needed for fault management is less than 10% of the duration of each individual interface call in this example. Our ongoing software development for the Trust4All project will provide a better view on the overhead effect of fault management on a large component-based system.

Next, we inject faults by code mutation. As described before, by using random numbers and pre-specified thresholds, we can control the probability of occurrence of mutated code. We run the application 20 times with wrappers off and 20 times with wrappers on when all faults present. We measure the duration of each execution, which is also the time to the first failure when the execution fails. The time unit is second. Each mutation has a specific probability of occurrence, e.g. 5%, 10% or 15% in the following table. If the probability is 5%, then it means that each fault in an instance has 5% chance to be triggered and results in a failure.

Table 2

Probability of Each Single Mutation in an Instance	Execution Time	
	Without Fault Management	With Fault Management
5%	26.5 (all executions failed)	39.0 (all succeeded)
10%	15.9 (all executions failed)	42.0 (all succeeded)
15%	13.0 (all executions failed)	46.7 (all succeeded)

From Table 2 we can see that, when the probability of an instance failure increases, without fault management the overall system becomes less reliable, as manifested in the time to the first failure which gets shorter. If we add fault management, the overall system's reliability is significantly improved. Nevertheless, we need to pay a small price, as shown in the duration of each run, which becomes longer because runtime repairs may be needed to keep the system available when failures present. In this example, the main contribution to the increase of the execution time is the repair that replaces DR with another more reliable compatible instance when the timing mismatch between DR and VSP, ASP is detected.

6. Conclusions

In this chapter we have proposed an adaptive fault management mechanism, which is aimed to protect normal execution of each service instance by using model-based failure detection and rule-based failure repair. The proposed mechanism contains two novel features: (1) an "intelligent" screening procedure that picks the best repair action according to a pre-specified optimal criterion; (2) an adaptive procedure that can improve the screening procedure (in terms of the parameter updating) and also generate appropriate failure prevention rules which can prevent some failures to happen after their first time exposures. There are two immediate challenges facing us: (1) how to deal with correlated faults effectively? (2) how to systematically generate those symptom and repair rules and validate the effectiveness of the priority function? Our ongoing research is to solve those problems.

References

1. Szyperski, C.: 'Component Software: Beyond Object-Oriented Programming' (Addison Wesley Professional, 2nd edn, 2003)
2. Gamma, E., Helm, R., Johnson, R., and Vlissides, J.M.: 'Design Patterns: Elements of Reusable Object-Oriented Software' (Addison Wesley Professional, 1st edn, 1994)
3. Lyu, M.R.: 'Handbook of software reliability engineering' (McGraw-Hill Companies Inc., New York, 1996)
4. Avižienis, A., Laprie, J.C., Randell, B., and Landwehr, C.: 'Basic concepts and taxonomy of dependable and secure computing', IEEE Tran. on Dependable and Secure Computing, January-March 2004, 1, (1), pp. 11-33
5. Reiter, R.: 'A theory of diagnosis from first principles', Artificial Intelligence, 1987, 32, pp. 57–95
6. Sampath, M., Sengupta, R., Lafortune, S., Sinnamohideen, K., and Teneketzis, D.: 'Failure diagnosis using discrete-event models', IEEE Trans. Control Systems Technology, 1996, 4, (2), pp. 105–124
7. Stumptner, M., and Wotawa, F.: 'A model-based approach to software debugging'. Proc. 7th International Workshop on Principles of Diagnosis (DX-96), Val Morin, Canada, 1996
8. Hangal, S., and Lam, M.S.: 'Tracking down software bugs Using Automatic Anomaly Detection'. Proc. ICSE 2002
9. Podgurski, A., Leon, D., Francis, P., Masri, W., Minch, M., Sun, J., and Wang, B.: 'Automated Support for Classifying Software Failure Reports'. Proc. ICSE 2003
10. Popov, P., Strigini, L., Riddle, S., and Romanovsky, A.: 'Protective Wrapping of OTS Components'. Proc. 4th ICSE Workshop on Component-Based Software Engineering: Component Certification and System Prediction (part of the 23rd IEEE International Conference on Software Engineering (ICSE 2001)), Toronto, Canada, May 2006
11. Gao, J., Zhu, E.Y., and Shim, S.: 'Monitoring software components and component-based software'. Proc. 24th Annual International Computer Software & Applications Conference (COMPSAC00), Taipei, Taiwan, October 2000
12. Musa, J.D., Iannino, A., and Okumoto, K.: 'Software Reliability - Measurement, Prediction, Applications' (McGraw-Hill, 1987)
13. Kececioglu, D.: 'Reliability Engineering Handbook' (Prentice Hall, Inc., New Jersey, Vol. 1, 1991)
14. Musa, J.D., and Okumoto, K.: 'A logarithmic Poisson execution time model for software reliability measurement'. Proc. 7th International Conference on Software Engineering, Orlando, Florida, 1984, pp. 230-238
15. Kharchenko, V.S., Tarasyuk, O.M., Sklyar, V.V., and Dubnitsky, V.Yu.: 'The method of software reliability growth models choice using assumptions matrix'. Proceedings of 26th Annual International Computer Software and Applications Conference, Oxford, England, August 26-29, 2002, pp. 541-546

16. Littlewood, B., and Verrall, J.: 'A Bayesian reliability growth model for computer software', Applied Statistics, 1973, serials C 22, (3), pp. 332–346
17. Robinson, D., and Dietrich, D.: 'A nonparametric Bayes reliability Growth Model', IEEE Transactions on Reliability, December 1989, 38, (5), pp. 591–598
18. *IEEE Guide to Classification for Software Anomalies.* IEEE Std 1044.1-1995
19. Issarny, V., and Banatre, J.P.: 'Architecture-based Exception Handling'. Proc. 34th Annual Hawaii International Conference on System Sciences (HICSS'34), Hawaii, HA, USA, January 2001
20. Rubira, C.M.F., de Lemos, R., Ferreira, G.R.M., and Filho, F.C.: 'Exception handling in the development of dependable component-based systems', Software: Practice and Experience, 2005, 35, (3), pp. 195–236
21. Feng, Y., Huang, G., Zhu, Y., and Mei, H.: 'Exception handling in component composition with the support of middleware'. Proc. 5th international workshop on Software engineering and middleware, Lisbon, Portugal, 2005, pp. 90-97
22. da S. Brito, P.H., Rocha, C.R., Filho, F.C., Martins, E., and Rubira, C.M.F.: 'A Method for Modeling and Testing Exceptions in Component-Based Software Development'. Lecture Notes in Computer Science, 2005, 3747, pp. 61–79
23. Wu, K., and Malaiya, Y.K.: 'A Correlated Faults Model for Software Reliability'. Proc. IEEE Int. Symp. on Software Reliability Engineering, Nov. 1993, pp. 80-89
24. Khoshgoftaar, T.M., Seliya, N., and Sundaresh, N.: 'An empirical study of predicting software faults with case-based reasoning', Software Quality Journal, 2006, 14, pp. 85–111
25. Su, R., Chaudron, M.R.V., and Lukkien, J.J.: 'Adaptive runtime fault management for service instances in component-based software applications'. Proc. 10th IASTED International Conference on Software Engineering and Applications (SEA 2006), Dallas, Texas, USA, November 2006, pp. 216 – 221
26. Sen, K., Rosu, G., and Agha, G.: 'Runtime safety analysis of multithreaded programs'. Proc. 9th European Software Engineering Conference and 11th ACM SIGSOFT International Symposium on the Foundations of Software Engineering (ESEC/FSE'03), Helsinki, Finland, September 2003, pp. 337 – 346
27. Havelund, K., and Rosu, G.: 'Monitoring programs using rewriting'. Proc. 16th IEEE International Conference on Automated Software Engineering, Coronado Island, USA, November 2001, pp. 135 – 143
28. Kim, M., Viswanathan, M., Kannan, S., Lee, I., and Sokolsky, O.: 'Java-MaC: a runtime assurance approach for Java programs', Formal Methods in System Design, 2004, 24, (2), pp. 129 – 155
29. Fetzer, C., and Xiao, Z.: 'An automated approach to increasing the robustness of C libraries'. Proc. International Conference on Dependable Systems and Networks (DSN'02), Bethesda, Maryland, USA, June 2002, pp. 155 – 164

EXTENDING THE APPLICABILITY OF THE NEKO FRAMEWORK FOR THE VALIDATION AND VERIFICATION OF DISTRIBUTED ALGORITHMS

LORENZO FALAI and ANDREA BONDAVALLI

Dipartimento di Sistemi e Informatica, University of Florence
Viale Morgagni 65
I-50134, Firenze, Italy
E-mail: lorenzo.falai@unifi.it, bondavalli@unifi.it
Website: http://rcl.dsi.unifi.it

In this paper we present our recent work extending the applicability of a toolset for the fast prototyping, verification and quantitative validation of dependable distributed systems and algorithms.

Neko is a framework and a communication platform that allows rapid prototyping of distributed algorithms; the same implementation of an algorithm can be exercised both on top of real and simulated networks, allowing simulative and experimental qualitative and, using the NekoStat extension, quantitative analyses. The core of the Neko framework is written in Java (J2SE), being thus highly portable; however it requires the translation into Java of existing algorithms, written in other languages, that one wants to analyze. The Neko package contains also utilities that help users to configure campaigns of experiments; these supports are really useful, but they are made as Perl scripts and Unix C code and are thus directly usable only on Unix systems.

Our work aimed at extending the applicability of the tool was made towards two directions. On one side we included in the framework the utilities to allow a direct integration of existing C/C++ algorithms in Neko applications, avoiding the translation into Java that may be error prone and that may also fail in correctly represent some low level details of the algorithms. Since most of the running distributed algorithms are written in C/C++, allowing a direct analysis of C/C++ existing legacy distributed algorithms, we widely extend the applicability of Neko and improve the faithfulness of analyses performed. The paper describes the extensions made and illustrates the use of the tool on an algorithm whose Java translation does not have the original behavior. On the other side, we made a pure Java code (J2SE, Java 2 Standard Edition) porting of all utilities helping Neko users in the definition of simulative/experimental campaigns, obtaining thus a complete J2SE version of Neko.

Keywords: Verification, Validation, Tools, Distributed Algorithms, Legacy Systems

1. Introduction

The always increasing diffusion of distributed systems and the increasing dependency on their proper functioning led to the awareness of the need to assess their behavior both in qualitative and quantitative terms.[1] Thus methods for evaluations of functional properties and quantitative characteristics of such systems have been defined. To support these analyses the Neko framework, a rapid prototyping tool, was developed.[2] The core part of the Neko framework is made in Java, and it is thus portable. In Neko the same implementation of an algorithm can be *simulated* or *executed* on top of a real network, and from the log files automatically created by the Neko execution, on/off functional properties can be verified. To enhance the tool capabilities we have developed an extension of Neko, called NekoStat.[3] Using this extension, Neko users can perform *quantitative evaluations* of Neko distributed applications. The evaluations can be both *simulative* and *experimental*.

Our recent work on Neko, described in the paper, is aimed at extending the applicability of the tool for Verification and Validation (here after V&V) of distributed algorithms/systems. Neko is written in Java; an algorithm written in a different language must be translated in this language before proceeding to its analysis. Such translation to Java is not automatic, and it can be error-prone. Moreover, in many languages some low level constructs exist that do not have a corresponding form in Java. In these cases the translation can thus be partial and the behavior of the original algorithm and of its Java translation may differ. Despite Java is getting more and more popular and its diffusion is increasing, nevertheless most of the available distributed algorithms are written in different languages; in particular the most used in the distributed system community are the C language, and its evolution C++, especially for the implementation of real-time and critical systems (SourceForge[4] reports that currently 33890 open-source projects exist using C/C++ against 16906 using Java). For these systems Java is not (yet?) really used, especially for the current unpredictability of the timing behavior of actual JVM implementations (i.e. caused by the garbage collection and other dynamic mechanisms). It is thus clear that being able to analyze directly distributed algorithms written in C/C++ into the Neko framework is very important. Thus, motivated by the willingness to obtain more accurate and more reliable results in the evaluation of already existing C/C++ algorithms with Neko, we provided a methodology here presented.

On the side of portability, as we observed, despite the kernel part of Neko is coded in Java (J2SE, Java 2 Standard Edition), there are some utilities available only for Unix systems (made and tested in Linux). To make Neko usable on the largest possible class of systems, we thus decided to translate the Unix system specific code to J2SE: in this way, we can use the complete framework on top of the whole set of system for which a JVM conforming to J2SE is available.

Summarizing, the work on the tool was directed in extending the capability of analysis of the tool also for language different from Java, and in allowing the usage of the entire tool and its automated utilities to a larger class of systems.

The rest of the paper is organized as follow. In Section 2 we present the background of this work: the Neko framework, the methodologies that allow the integration of C/C++ code in a Java project, and the problem of the portability of code between different platforms. Section 3 contains a description of the architecture and of the components used to integrate C/C++ code in Neko; at the end of this Section we describe a case study of a quantitative and qualitative evaluation of a distributed algorithm whose original version, written in C code, has a different behavior respect to its Java translation. Section 4 illustrates the porting to J2SE of the utilities made available in the standard Neko only as Unix specific code. Finally, Section 5 contains our conclusions and future plans.

2. Background

2.1. *The Neko framework*

Neko[2] is a simple but powerful framework that allows the definition and the analysis of distributed algorithms. It shows the attracting feature that the same Neko-based implementation of an algorithm can be used for both simulations and experiments on a real network. This way, the development and testing phases are shorter than with the traditionally used approach, in which two implementations are made at different times and using different languages (for example, SIMULA for simulations and C++ for prototype implementation). The first version of the Neko framework was built at the Distributed Systems Lab of the EPFL in Lausanne. After the first version, the development was continued mainly by Peter Urban and by other research groups around the world. The core part of the framework is written in Java (J2SE) to assure high portability and has been deliberately kept simple, extensible and easy to use. The architecture of the current version of the Neko framework can be divided in three main components (see Figure 1): *applications*, *NekoProcesses* and *networks*.

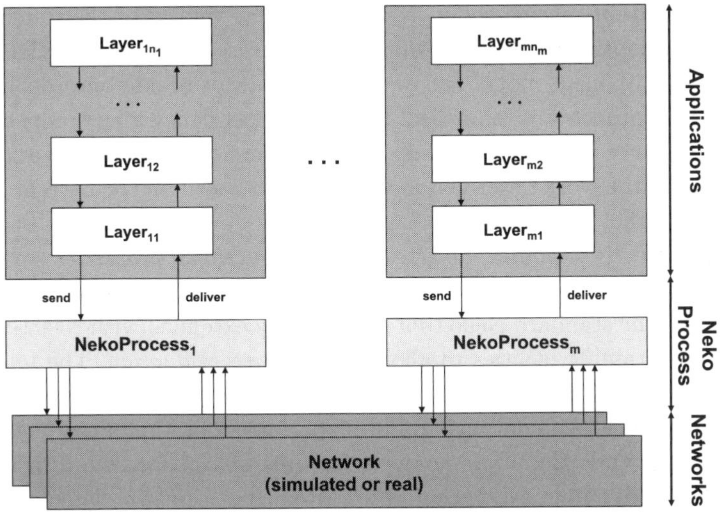

Fig. 1. Typical architecture of a Neko-based distributed application

Applications are built following a hierarchical structure based on multiple levels (called *layers*). Layers communicate using two predefined primitives for message passing: send and deliver. There are two kinds of layers in Neko: active (called *ActiveLayer*) and passive (called *Layers*). An ActiveLayer has its own thread: when a message arrives from another layer, it is stored and will be handled later on by the thread associated to the layer. A passive layer does not have its own thread, so messages are handled within the thread that delivered the message to the layer.

A typical Neko-based distributed application is composed of a set of m processes, numbered $1, ..., m$, communicating through a message passing interface: a *sender process* inserts, through the asynchronous primitive send, a new message in the communication infrastructure, that delivers the message to the *receiver process* through the deliver primitive. NekoNetworks are the communication supports used by the distributed algorithms. A variety of networks is supported. The network interface hides the details of the environment from the algorithm, and it allows to indifferently use real networks (like TCP/IP and UDP/IP communications channels) or simulated ones (for examples, networks characterized by a delay distribution function and by a loss probability). The framework is distributed with a library of fault tolerance algorithms already implemented and usable in combination with application specific codes. Note that a new version of the framework, Neko 1.0, adopting a different component model is now under development. The new component model is based on the concept of microprotocols; several microprotocols are composed, using the dependency injection pattern,[5] in a NekoProcess. At present only an alpha version of the new framework is available; the work described in this paper is based on the current stable release of Neko, Neko 0.9.

Neko directly supports the assessment of *functional properties* (so-called "on/off" properties) of distributed systems, following a dynamic verification approach. The standard Neko tool was recently extended with NekoStat,[3] a package containing utilities to allow *quantitative evaluation.* The interface of NekoStat was made in a way that it is usable, without differences for the user, both for simulations and for experiments on top of real networks. NekoStat extends the V&V analysis features of Neko in the direction of a statistical dynamic evaluation of a system, both on simulated and real execution. Neko with NekoStat is a powerful tool to perform V&V of distributed algorithms, both simulative and experimental, based both on testing of functional properties and on evaluation of quantitative metrics. One of its limitation is related to the *kind of systems* on which is can be directed used: Neko is restricted to prototype, test and evaluate Java implementations of distributed algorithms. The other main limitation addressed in this paper is related to portability: a quite large portion of the utilities, distributed with Neko, are tools made for Unix (especially Linux) systems. In the rest of the paper we describe how we extended the applicability of the tool, towards languages different from Java and towards platform different from Unix/Linux.

2.1.1. *Approaches for the Integration of C/C++ Code in a Java Framework*

To cope with the increasing size and complexity of software systems demands, among other features, the development of systems based on reusable components, known as *COTS (Commercial-Off-The-Shelf)*,[6] is increasing. The main advantages in using the COTS are reduced costs and faster development time. At the same time there are some drawbacks, problems and risks that one has to face when integrating COTS; in particular the conflicts between different components, and between a component and the Rest Of the System (ROS), and the possible incompatibility between the service provided by a component and what the ROS is expecting from it.

The integration of C/C++ code in a Java framework can be seen as an instance of the more general problem of the integration of COTS (in this case, the C/C++ code) into an existing system, the ROS (in this case, the Neko/NekoStat framework). In the following we thus describe the approaches used for integration of a general COTS.

The problems that arise in the integration of COTS can be addressed mainly resorting to three different techniques: *wrapping*, *glue code* and *component adaptation*. Wrapping is a technique that allows the integration of a COTS in a system, using a special component, called *wrapper*, which monitors and filters the control and data flow from/to the wrapped component.[6,7] Wrapping is particularly indicated for integration of *black-box* components; it supplies a standard interface to a set of components, increasing/decreasing the functionalities of existing components, and finally it gives a unique point of access to the component. *Glue code*[7] is additional code written with the purpose of connecting together the different components of the system; the main tasks of such code is flow control, that is the capability to invoke in the right way the functionalities provided by the components: glue code is used to resolve the incompatibility between component interfaces (e.g.: using data conversion), and also for exception handling. Finally, *component adaptation* is a method in which the functionalities of an existing component are increased, in general by adapting it to be usable in a different context.[8]

As we will describe in Section 3 with full details, we used both the idea of *glue code* and of *component adaptation* to allow integration of existing C/C++ code into the Neko/NekoStat, Java-based, framework.

2.1.2. *Approaches to make a tool usable in a larger class of systems*

Modern distributed computing system are very heterogenous and composed using several components and devices. Different kinds of hardware and operating systems are used. The usage of software components in a large distributed system thus generally requires particular *adaptation* or *modifications* of these components for the usage of these different execution environment (hardware/software). A characteristic of uttermost importance for the implementation of applications to be used in large distributed systems is the *portability*, or, also better, the direct *usability*, of the software components. In a sense the portability is a particular case of re-usability of software.

The portability of a software component essentially depends on the *programming language* used for its implementation.[9] We can thus identify four typical examples of language characterized by different portability:

- Assembler: An assembly language program is written for a specific CPU and will only run on that CPU.
- C/C++: we need a compiler, specific for the platform, able to transform the C/C++ program to executable code; essentially many C/C++ programs could be ported to different architectures, with a relative ease, also if not always this is true. In fact, some OS specific code is generally used in C/C++ programs, diminishing the portability of the programs; however some specific software engineering mechanisms can be used to increase the portability in these cases, e.g. handling system specific code by isolating the differences into separate modules. At compile time, the correct system specific module can be imported.
- Perl: an interpreted language; from this point of view, it can be consider as a "portable language", but the reality is different. Different Perl implementations have different syntax and semantics, and moreover Perl scripts usually call system specific commands.
- Java: it is a completely interpreted language with very good portability. In fact, Java is based on the idea of a complete independency from the platform used. A program written in Java generally works in all systems for which there is available a JVM conforming to the particular JAVA edition (e.g.: J2SE - Java 2 Standard edition, or J2ME - Java 2 Micro Edition).

Neko is composed by a core framework, described in the beginning of this Section, that allows fast prototyping of distributed algorithms. Beyond the basic framework, some important parts of the tool, related to instantiation of the algorithm on the nodes composing the distributed system and related to the process of system validation, are written as C code as well as Perl and shell script. These parts were written with specific platforms in mind: Linux, and more generally Unix-derived, platforms. For other operating system, as Microsoft Windows, no interpreter is available for these languages, or it has a different semantics which makes the direct usage of such supports impossible. An important part of these utilities are those allowing automatic instantiation of new processes and the ones allowing definition and execution of simulative/experimental campaigns, at the variation of one or more system/algorithm parameters. These last tools are the ones allowing the execution of multiple studies, necessary for a complete sensitive analysis.

In the list of languages reported in this Subsection we saw how Java is the typical example of completely interpreted language, an "almost perfectly portable" language. A large portion of the Neko framework and the whole NekoStat extension was already written in Java J2SE. To make Neko usable on the largest possible class of systems, we thus decided to translate the Unix system specific code (Perl and C code) to standard Java J2SE: in this way, we can use the complete framework on top of the whole set of system for which a JVM conforming to J2SE is available.

In Section 4 we describe in details the utilities available only for Unix platforms and how we translated them into pure Java J2SE code. This porting now allows to use the tool on every platform for which a J2SE JVM is available taking advantage of all the facilities and add-ons that were available only for Unix platforms.

3. How to directly include C/C++ code as components of a Neko application

In order to allow the integration of existing C/C++ code in a Neko application, we consider the legacy distributed algorithm, written in C/C++, as a *COTS*, and we use *glue code* and *component adaptation* methodologies to integrate it within the Java framework (the *ROS*). In particular, we build *glue code* to allow communication between Neko objects (written in Java) and the C/C++ legacy existing code; we instead *adapt* the C/C++ component to allow the communication between such code and the components of the Neko framework.

An existing C/C++ object (library, function, procedure, class) can be included in Java through the use of a API, developed by Sun for this purpose, called JNI (Java Native Interface).[10,11] JNI is an interface especially developed to allow in general the integration of *external, non-Java, code* into Java projects. It is part of the standard JDK implementations, and Java applications realized using it are thus highly portable. Using the Invocation API it is also possible to include a JVM in a non-Java application, making possible a *bidirectional communication* between Java and external code.

However many problems arise using JNI to include pieces of C/C++ code in Java, mainly:

i) the loss of type information between the two languages;
ii) the absence of error checking,
iii) the need of manual handling of the JINNEE, that is the structure

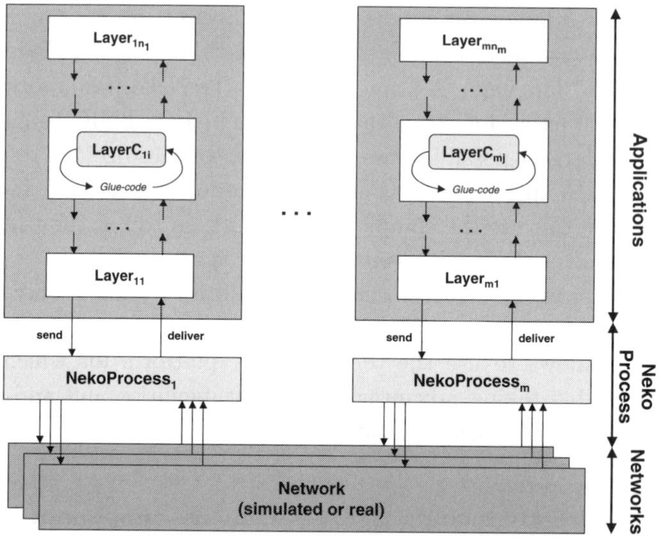

Fig. 2. Architecture that allows a direct integration of C/C++ code

containing information to connect C/C++ and Java.

To attack and solve these problems we used *Jack*[12] , an open-source toolkit developed to simplify programming with JNI. Jace supports the automatic generation of C++ *peer classes* and *proxy classes* from Java classes: the proxy classes allow the developer to instantiate and to manipulate Java objects from C/C++ code, whereas the peer classes facilitate the implementation of the methods declared native in the Java classes.

The resulting architecture of the typical Neko application in which we integrated some C/C++ code is depicted in Figure 2. The glue code is special Java code, integrated in a Neko Layer placed between the C/C++ code and the ROS (the rest of the Neko application). LayerC is a part of algorithm, written in C/C++, that we want to verify/evaluate. The instantiation of a Neko application is made as follow: the application begins with the initialization of all the layers, included the layers containing the glue code, whose task is to activate and establish a communication with the LayerC. The communication between the layers, typical of Neko, based on **send** and **deliver** primitives, is not influenced by the usage of these mechanisms: the communication infrastructure used (called NekoNetwork in the tool), both simulated and real, and the other Neko layers, communicate with LayerC using the glue code. LayerC is also adapted to use the glue code for sending/receiving messages from the other layers or the Neko network(s).

In the next two subsections we describe the task and the structure of the glue code, and the adaptation of the C/C++ source code of the distributed algorithm that we want to analyze.

3.1. *Glue Code*

The glue code can be an ActiveLayer or a Layer:[2] the choice depends on the kind of component of the system. In case of a component with *active* behavior we need an ActiveLayer as glue code, whereas for a component that only *reacts* to external actions (mainly messages from lower or upper layers) we can use a Layer. It is directly instantiated (and started, in case of ActiveLayer) during the application initialization phase.

The main task of this layer is the definition of the methods `native`, those methods that compose the distributed algorithm to integrate (e.g. the functions to be executed when a new message is received from the network, or the function of initialization of the component). This declaration allows to integrate external C/C++ functions and to execute them from within the JVM. The native methods call is made possible by the Jace toolkit, that allows to instantiate the C++ peer classes.

3.2. *Component Adaptation*

The inclusion of a LayerC in a Neko application requires some modifications to the original code. The C/C++ code must be modified to create the connection with the glue code, mainly for using the glue code to communicate with the other components of the protocol stack: in this way the C/C++ code can use the send/deliver primitives of Neko. It is thus necessary:

i) to find all the points in the code where the application makes calls to interact with the network or with other components;
ii) to substitute these calls with the proper calls of the glue code.

Note that the choice of the level of details of a single LayerC is free, and it depends on the level of the control that we want to establish on the behavior of the distributed algorithm. In particular, we can consider the whole C/C++ algorithm as a unique LayerC, or we can subdivide it into several LayerC, using send and deliver primitives of the glue code to allow the communication between these layers.

The modifications to be generally done to the code can be summarized as follows:

Includes: we have to include, using the #include directive, the header files of the glue code and of the Jace types that the glue code receives as input from the C/C++ methods; note that these headers can be automatically generated using `PeerGenerator` tool, available in the Jace distribution. To clarify this part, we make an example. Let suppose we want to integrate in Neko an original C algorithm that contains the procedure *P(...int num...)*. The header files to be included are thus: the header of the glue code and the file `jace/proxy/types/JInt.h`; this last one allows to use JInt class of Jace, that is a wrapper of the int Java type.

Deliver: the call to methods/functions/procedures used to receive, in the original C/C++ code, messages from the network (or from lower levels), must be substituted with a call to a method, declared as native in the glue code, that receives the messages from the Java glue code.

Send: the call to methods/functions/procedures to send messages to the network (or to lower levels) needs to be substituted with the call to the *send* method of the glue code. How to make a call to the *send* method of the glue code from the C/C++ code is described in the next Subsection.

3.3. *Communication between C/C++ code and Java*

So far we described how the glue code, built using the Jace tool, allows the information flowing from the Neko components to LayerC. The opposite flow, the communication between C/C++ code and the Neko framework (thus Java code), can be made directly using JNI technology. The usage of JNI can be made in two ways:

i) *Direct usage from C/C++ code:* we can directly insert as C/C++ code the calls to Java methods using specific JNI functionalities;
ii) *Indirect usage through a library:* we can insert in the C/C++ code specific calls to a user-defined library (from here after it is called LIBLayerC).

The second approach is preferable: the usage of an external library allows to make the minimum modifications to the original C/C++ code, limiting thus the introduction of errors. Many functions of this library are partially independent from the application: the skeleton of the library used for the case study in Section 3.5 could be successfully used also in other different contexts.

An example of call for which we need a communication from C/C++ code to Java method is for the *sending* of messages to lower layers of the structure. The sending of message can be made through the LIBLayerC in this way:

i) we define in the LIBLayerC a C/C++ function, called `c_send(...)` (with appropriate parameters), in which we call the real `send(...)` method of the glue code;
ii) we define in the glue code the `send()` method that prepare an object of type `NekoMessage` and uses the Neko supports for sending the message;
iii) we modify the calls to methods/functions/procedures to send messages to the network (or to lower levels) to calls to `c_send(...)` (with appropriate values).

3.4. *Quantitative Evaluation of C/C++ code with NekoStat*

Layers containing LayerC can also be perfectly integrated with the NekoStat extension to Neko:[3] the features and mechanisms made available in NekoStat are, in fact, compatible with these objects, and we can still use the glue code to connect LayerC to NekoStat utilities.

As described in details in the paper,[3] a quantitative evaluation made with NekoStat (both simulative and experimental) requires to *modify* the source code of the layers by introducing calls to a method, called log(), of the predefined (singleton for every JVM) object of the class StatLogger. The calls to log() must be put in the points in which the events of interest happen. The events of interest depend on the kind of evaluation that we want to do (especially, they depends on the metrics of interest). Such calls, as any call to Java methods from the C/C++ code, can be made through calls to a function of the glue code that in its turn calls the StatLogger.log() method.

The component adaptation, the modifications to the source code needed to use NekoStat for performing a quantitative evaluation of a C/C++ distributed algorithm inserted as a LayerC in a Neko application, are limited and simple and can be summarized along the following steps (we assume to use the external library LIBLayerC):

- to define in the LIBLayerC library a function logC(...), that calls logC_Java(...) of the glue code;

- to define in the glue code a method logC_Java(...), with proper parameters, whose purpose is to call the real log(Event) of the StatLogger;
- for each event of interest, to find the points of the C/C++ code in which the event has to be signaled and insert in these points the calls to logC(...) method.

3.5. *Analysis of C code using Neko: the ASFDA Case Study*

In the following pages we describe a case study in which we used the methodology presented for the evaluation, made by simulations, of an already existing C algorithm, ASFDA (Available and Safe Freshness Detection Algorithm.[13] ASFDA is one of the layers of a safe communication protocol stack currently in use in the Italian high speed railways communication infrastructure.

ASFDA is a mechanism for the *timing failure detection*, used in the communication between two entities (Sender and Receiver), that allows the detection of the *level of freshness* of received messages. The minimum level of freshness required can be specified assigning a value to the *maxDelay* parameter: the receiver closes the connection (and it informs the application level) when no information fresher than maxDelay is available. The algorithm reaches this goal by performing a conservative estimation δ of the delay of each received message: the δ estimation is by construction always greater than or equal to the actual delay of a message, under some assumption on the behavior of the system.

Using the modifications to Neko described in this Section, we have been able to directly analyze the C version of ASFDA, without a translation phase of the algorithm in Java code. In the remainder of this Section we show the usefulness of our framework by describing the results of the evaluation of the real C implementation and of the Java translation of ASFDA, and we make some comparison of the quantitative and qualitative results that have been obtained.

3.5.1. *Quantitative Analysis of ASFDA*

To make a quantitative evaluation of the C version algorithm these steps have been performed:

- integration of the original C algorithm as a LayerC, defining the

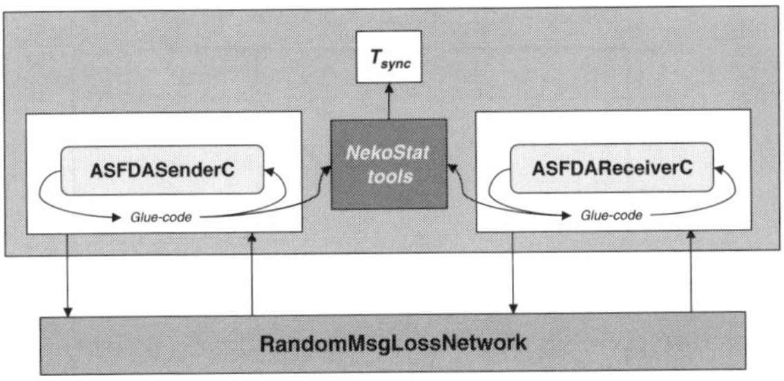

Fig. 3. Neko/NekoStat architecture used in the simulations

glue code as described in Section 3.1;

- definition of the connection between the LayerC and the NekoStat package, through a specific defined `LIB_ASFDA`;
- usage of NekoStat to evaluate T_{sync}, the time necessary to establish a new connection.

The architecture used for these simulations is depicted in Figure 3, where the ASFDASender and ASFDAReceiver are Java glue code that include the real C code (the LayerC ASFDASenderC and ASFDAReceiverC). We used a simulated communication infrastructure available in the package, called **RandomMsgLossNetwork**: a NekoNetwork characterized by exponential delays with mean value $meanDelay$ and a minimum value $minDelay$.

The parameter used in the simulation are those reported in Figure 4. Note that $minDelay$ and $meanDelay$ are parameters of the simulated network, whereas $maxDelay$ is a parameter of the algorithm. T_{sync}, the time necessary to establish a new connection, has been evaluated both on the Java and the C version of ASFDA. The comparison of results is reported in Figure 5: the results of the two simulations are clearly similar (the difference is almost zero - and below the precision of the simulation), demonstrating that the integration in Neko of the algorithm written in C does not modify the quantitative results obtained with NekoStat.

$$meanDelay \in \{150, 200, 250, 300\}\ msec$$
$$minDelay = 10\ msec$$
$$maxDelay = 1800\ msec$$

Fig. 4. Parameters used for the evaluation of the T_{sync} metric

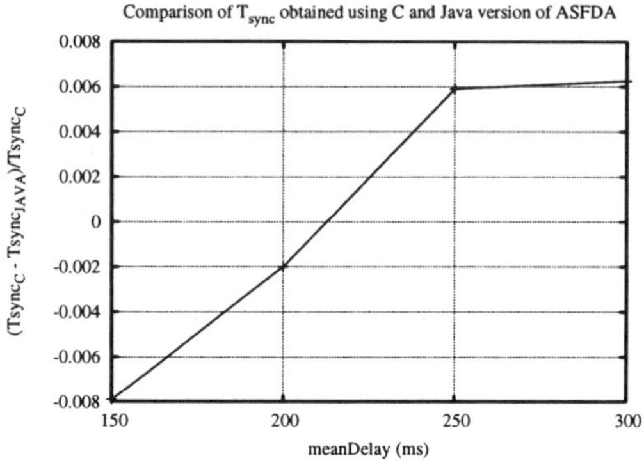

Fig. 5. Comparison of the results obtained with Java and C version of ASFDA: $\frac{Tsync_C - Tsync_{JAVA}}{Tsync_C}$

3.5.2. *Qualitative analysis of ASFDA*

ASFDA establishes its safety property on the ability to performing a *conservative estimation* (it means an upper estimation) of the delay of each received message. As described in detail in the paper,[13] the ability to correctly approximate floating point variables is necessary in order to obtain this safety properties. The approximation of a real value in the finite precision arithmetics of a computing system can be done in one of four ways:[14]

- TONEAREST - approximation to the nearest representable number;
- DOWNWARD - approximation to the greatest representable number lower than the real value;
- UPWARD - approximation to the lowest representable number greater than the real value;
- TOWARDZERO - approximation towards zero.

ASFDA requires different kinds of approximations for the computation of different floating point variables.[13] It is thus necessary, for a correct implementation of the algorithm, to use a language that allows to choose the approximation methods to use. Languages as C, C++ and Assembler allow to control the approximation methods to use for a floating point computation, whereas Java does not allow to choose the approximation method to use, that is set in many JVM implementations to the default TONEAREST method.

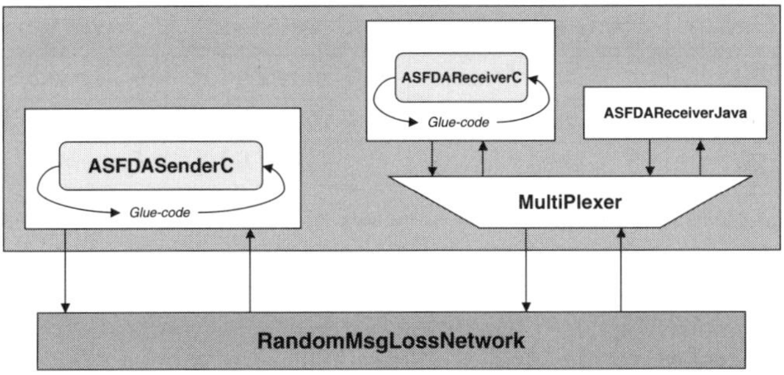

Fig. 6. Neko architecture used for the qualitative comparison

The comparison of the behavior of original C version of the algorithm and its Java translation was made through simulations, using the architecture depicted in Figure 6. On one side we put the ASFDASender layer, on the other a stack of two levels: a MultiPlexer as the bottom one, to forward the received messages to the upper level layers. The upper level is constituted by two separate layers: the Java version of the algorithm and the C one, defined through the methodology presented earlier. ASFDA is a cyclic algorithm; the Multiplexer checks in every cycle if the behavior of the upper layers is the same (in particular, it checks if the messages that the upper layers want to transmit are the same): when the behavior differs, the Multiplexer stops the Neko application and it exports information about the actual state of the two versions of ASFDA. Note that the sender is not duplicated with a Java and a C version: in fact in the ASFDA algorithm is the receiver that makes most of the work, evaluating the freshness of messages received from the sender. This architecture allows a *direct and non-intrusive* mechanism of control of differences of behavior of the two implementation of the ASFDA mechanism.

We made some simulations using the same **RandomMsgLossNetwork** used for the quantitative analysis of T_{sync}. For these simulations we vary the value of the *maxDelay* parameter. For some of these values the Java version, using always the TO_NEAREST approximation, *makes errors in the evaluation of the freshness of received messages.* The Figures 7 and 8 report the cases in which the C version and the Java one act differently. Two different error scenarios can be distinguished: in the first the Java version judges messages that are fresh as old (false positive detection); in the second, **more serious**, the Java version considers messages that are old as fresh (false negative detection).

$maxDelay$	**Real situation**	**C version**	**Java version**
1240	$\delta \leq maxDelay$	$\delta \leq maxDelay$	$\delta > maxDelay$
1590	$\delta \leq maxDelay$	$\delta \leq maxDelay$	$\delta > maxDelay$
2290	$\delta \leq maxDelay$	$\delta \leq maxDelay$	$\delta > maxDelay$

Fig. 7. Comparison between C and Java version of ASFDA: availability penalization of the Java one

Figure 7 refers to the first scenario: the Java version considers as old messages that are instead fresh enough. In this case a mistake made by the Java translation, caused by the impossibility to choose the approximation method to use, made the system *less available* than the original one.

The results reported in Figure 8 (corresponding to a $maxDelay$ of $889,9999999999864$) are related to the second scenario. Here the Java translation of ASFDA considers messages that are old as fresh, affecting the **safety** of the algorithm. In this scenario the C version correctly closes the connection because the delay experienced was greater than the maximum allowed, whereas the Java translation leaves the connection up: the application uses as good (and rely on) information that is instead too old. Such missed detection is very dangerous for safety-critical systems (as those for which ASFDA was designed).

This example shows what may happen analyzing and evaluating a Java translation of existing C/C++ code. The translation in Java of existing C/C++ code, also when performed with attention at maintain the behavior of the original system, as in this case study, can be error-prone: some constructs of the C language, which allow to interact at lower level with the hardware, may have no direct translation in Java. We have to take particular attention to these aspects when evaluating critical systems: a direct evaluation of the original code, made possible using the mechanisms described in this paper, allows to increase the confidence on the results obtained by our tool.

Last, we want to emphasize that these discrepancies among the two versions of the algorithm are rare enough not to affect the quantitative

$maxDelay$	**Real situation**	**C version**	**Java version**
889,9999999999864	$\delta > maxDelay$	$\delta > maxDelay$	$\delta \leq maxDelay$

Fig. 8. Comparison between C and Java version of ASFDA: safety violation of the Java one

evaluations reported earlier of metrics like the T_{sync}: mean values are not modified by such rare events.

The case study described in this Subsection is available for download on the webpage;[15] in the distribution the C/C++/Java sources of the case study, the sources of `LIB_ASFDA` (useful as skeleton of a general library LIBLayerC), and an usage guide have been included. This package can be installed on top of an existing standard Neko 0.9 installation.

4. Porting of Neko to pure Java code

The purpose of the work described in this Section is to make the entire Neko independent from the used platform. A large part of the utilities provided in standard Neko 0.9 distribution are compatible only with Linux/Unix systems; these tools are mainly of two classes:

i) the utilities to instantiate new Neko processes during the experimental setup;
ii) the utilities to define and to execute multiple simulations/experiments in sequence by varying the parameters of the algorithms; these are thus the supports that Neko users can use for definition and automatic execution of simulative/experimental campaigns.

4.1. *ServerFactory*

Neko uses an asymmetric approach for the bootstrap of experiments. For a distributed execution, one has to launch one JVM per process. The main process is the master process, that reads the configuration file and interprets the slave entry, which lists the addresses of all the other processes (called slaves). Then it builds a control network, including all the processes (by opening TCP connections to each slave), and distributes the configuration information. It is tedious to launch all the JVMs by hand for each execution of an application. For this reason, Neko provides the **slave factory** to automatically launch new slaves. Slave factories run as daemons on their hosts (one slave factory for each host). When bootstrapping begins, the master contacts each slave factory and it sends a request of a new JVM, which will act as a slave. Unfortunately standard Neko version do not give supports for automatic slave generation for every operating system: in fact, new slaves are generated through calls to an external program, called `start_server`, a C program that uses Unix specific system calls. Note that this asymmetric bootstrap is needed only for real executions; in case of simulations, Neko locally creates the simulation engine inside a single JVM, in which the whole distributed system is simulated.

The left part of Figure 9 depicts how standard Neko manages the generation of new slaves through the server factory. The ovals represent the involved Java classes, the rectangles the configuration file and `start_server`, the C code. We make a porting in pure Java code of `start_server`, maintaining all its functionalities, to allow the automatic generation of new slaves in a larger class of platforms. We substitute in the framework code the calls to `start_server` with instantiation and execution of a new object (of a new class *StartServerMain*) that directly creates the new slave.

The right part of Figure 9 depicts the new architecture for the instantiation of new slaves, and the behavior of this new Object StartServerMain. StartServerMain instantiates the object StartServer that creates two different threads: one thread ($SST1$ in Figure) is responsible of instantiating a new Slave, whereas the other thread ($SST2$ in Figure) remains listening to

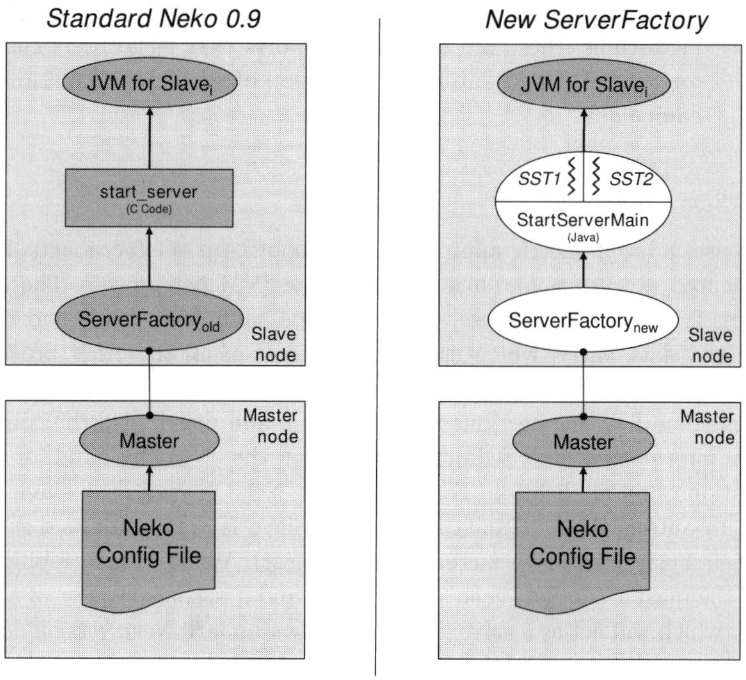

Fig. 9. ServerFactory: original version based on C program and complete J2SE version

the StartServerMain (for new Slaves execution, for killing existing Slaves and for the handling of the I/O of existing Slaves). The new Java code is depicted in white in the Figure. We realized a complete porting of the old functionalities from C to J2SE Java; in this way, we made these Neko functionalities usable on every platform for which a J2SE JVM is available.

4.1.1. *Utilities for campaign definition and execution*

An important and useful functionality offered by Neko is the capability of execute campaigns, both on top of real network or in simulations, defining the parameters to vary. This is particulary important to allow powerful sensitivity analysis, both on algorithm parameters and on parameters of the system in which the algorithm operates; e.g. a campaign of experiments allow to analyze how the Quality of Service of a middleware service varies to the varying of characteristics of the used network or to the varying of the workload. The utilities available in Neko for campaign execution allows to shorten the time necessary for experimentation: the collection of the results and the passage from an experiment to another are in fact completely automatic.

Unfortunately, also this functionality is available in standard Neko only for UNIX systems. In fact, the code for campaign execution is written as Perl and Shell scripts, working only for Linux and some other Unix systems.

The execution campaign in standard Neko is based on the definition of a template of the configuration file of the applications, in which some parameters are not instantiated as values, and in the definition of a Perl script able to generate the configuration file of every single experiment/simulation. The Perl scripts (called `run_test` and `run_all_tests`) execute the script file defined by the user to instantiate the single experiments and to execute them.

We decided to port the functionalities offered by these scripts into Java to allow the execution of multiple experiments in a larger class of platform. During this porting, we also decided to simplify the original method of definition of the parameters to vary, trying to improve the functionalities, simplifying the definition and execution of campaign of experiments.

The result of work made in this direction is NekoTestsGenerator, a Java program. The program takes as input the name of a configuration file and an integer number `numtest`. In the configuration file the user can declare the parameter to vary and how they vary. The integer number `numtest` can be used to perform multiple experiments using the same values: this can be really useful in order to increase the confidence on the results, using approaches as *batch-means* for the analysis of experimental or simulative quantitative results.[16]

The config file is composed by two parts:

i) The first part is closed within a block with the "%" symbol at the begin and at the end of the section; it includes the definition of the parameters to vary and how they vary. Every line of this section must follow the following syntax:
`$VarName` $= \{val_1 \ldots val_n\}$
`$VarName` $= val_{min} : val_{inc} : val_{max}$
In the first case, the variable `VarName` will take the values in the set $\{val_1, \ldots, val_n\}$; in the second one, the variable `VarName` will take the values in the set $\{val_{min}, val_{min} + val_{inc}, val_{min} + 2 * val_{inc}, \ldots, val_{max}\}$.

ii) The second part is closed within a block with the "@" symbol at the begin and at the end of the section. We can define in this section the value for the parameters of the experiments/simulations; we can use both constant values or we can instantiate values using $*, /, +, -$ operations and ? operator (an operator that choose the value on the base of the result of the evaluation of a boolean expression). In the section we can also use variables `VarName`, defined in the first part of the configuration file.

Here we do not enter in more details about operations available using NekoTestsGenerator; just to clarify its usage, Figure 10 depicts one configuration file, and the parameters used for first three tests defined and executed through NekoTestsGenerator using this configuration file. With the parameters inserted in the config file of the Figure, a total of $2 * 4 * 2 = 16$ tests will be executed: in fact we have 2 possible values for variable a (values 10 and 100), 4 possible values for variable b (values 2, 3, 4 and 5) and finally two possible values for *bool* (values *true* and *false*).

NekoTestsGenerator now allows to define and execute simulations/experiments campaigns on every system in which the core part of Neko already works.

4.2. *Compatibility of the new Java utilities*

We successfully tested the utilities described in this Section (new ServerFactory and NekoTestsGenerator) in the following systems:

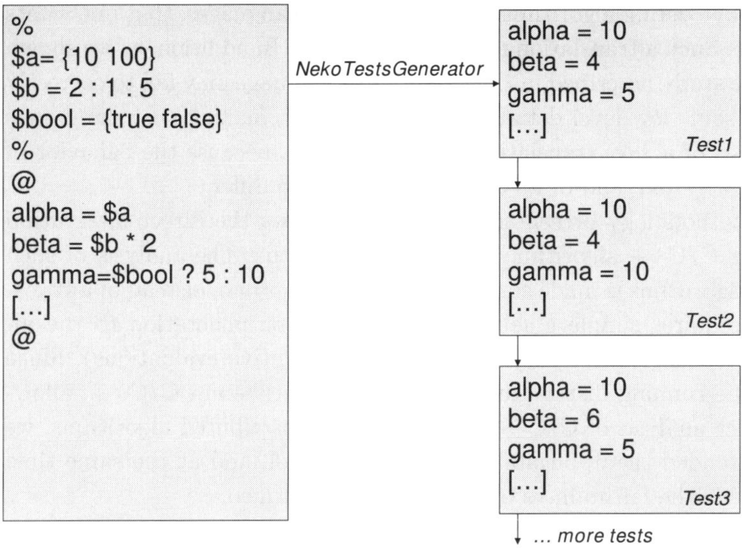

Fig. 10. Example of a configuration file of an campaign and the relative parameters generated through NekoTestsGenerator

i) JVM J2SE 1.5.0 on top of a Linux Fedora Core 4 distribution.
ii) JVM J2SE 1.5.0 on top of a Linux Fedora Core 3 distribution.
iii) JVM J2SE 1.5.0 on top of Mac Os X (Tiger).
iv) JVM J2SE 1.5.0 on top of Windows XP.
v) JVM J2SE 1.5.0 on top of Windows 2000.

The Java sources of the new utilities are available for download on the webpage.[15]

5. Concluding Remarks and Future Works

This paper presented our recent work on the Neko/NekoStat framework, aimed at extending the applicability of the tool in the simulative and experimental, qualitative and quantitative, V&V of distributed algorithms. We described two direction of this work: extending the applicability of the tool towards languages different from Java, and towards operating systems different from Unix.

In the paper we presented how it is possible to use concepts taken from software engineering, in particular component adaptation and glue code ideas, to allow a simple and direct integration of existing C/C++ code in Neko. The Neko framework is written in Java and requires the translation into Java of existing algorithms, written in other languages, that one wants to analyze. Such a translation may be error prone. In addition, as we shown in the case study described in the paper, Java language may fail to correctly represent some low level details of the algorithms, making very dangerous the analysis of a Java translation of an algorithm, because the behavior of the original system and of its Java translation can differ.

The methodology presented in Section 3 allows the direct integration of existing C/C++ algorithms in Neko applications. The analysis of such C/C++ algorithms is made simpler and less error-prone: instead of a translation it requires simple glue code and slight instrumentation to the algorithm (especially necessary to perform quantitative evaluations). Since most of the running distributed algorithms are written in C/C++, allowing a direct analysis of C/C++ existing legacy distributed algorithms, we widely extended the applicability of the Neko tool, and at the same time we improved the faithfulness of the analysis performed.

In Section 4 we described the work aimed at making the entire Neko independent from the platform used. We described the utilities originally available for Neko only when used on a Unix platform: these are useful utilities for automatic instantiation of new processes and for automatic execution of experimental campaigns. To be able to use the entire functionalities of Neko on a larger set of platform (e.g. Windows systems) we made the porting of these Unix specific code to J2SE code. The paper describes the work made and the results obtained.

With the new utilities, Neko is now a framework usable on a large class of systems (in particular, it can be completely used on top of every system for which a J2SE JVM is available). Neko can be used for rapid prototyping and for functional verification and validation of a large class of distributed algorithms: algorithms written in Java, and now also in C and C++ languages. NekoStat can be used for quantitative evaluation of distributed algorithms; despite NekoStat is usable, as already stated, for evaluation of algorithm written in Java and now also in C/C++, we have to pay attention to its usage for quantitative evaluation of distributed algorithms written in languages different from Java; in fact the execution of the typical mechanisms of current JVM implementations (e.g. garbage collection) can considerably modify, from a performance point of view, the behavior of the distributed system, altering the quantitative results obtained through our tool.

We are now working on a special, reduced, version of Neko framework able to be executed also on devices characterized by scarcity of available

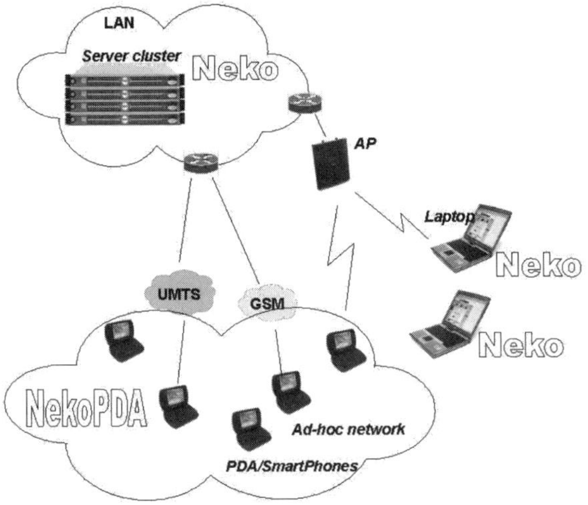

Fig. 11. Possible experimental architecture for the evaluation of distributed algorithms for futuristic applications, based on wired and wireless connections and on hybrid devices (PDAs, smartphone, laptop, servers, ...)

resources (in terms mainly of available memory and of CPU power). Nowadays, in fact, embedded systems and the idea of a "pervasive" and "ubiquitous" computing are always increasing their diffusion; objects of everyday life, like mobile phones, PDAs (Personal Digital Assistants), household appliances, cars, ... are based on computers. It is of uttermost importance to be able to perform fast prototyping and V&V of applications made for these new kind of devices. This reduced version of the framework, called NekoPDA, will be compatible with the standard Neko; it will be thus possible to use our framework for experimental validation and verification of distributed algorithms on top of the devices really used, as in the example of Figure 11. The Figure depicts a possible prototype of futuristic system, taken from the case studies of the HIDENETS project.[17,18]

Besides the direction of the current and future work aimed at extending the applicability of the tool, we are also working in the direction of increasing the *accuracy* of results obtained in the evaluation of distributed systems. Specifically our next objective is to be able to evaluate and improve the **trustfulness** that we can place on the results (especially quantitative but also qualitative) obtained using the framework.

Acknowledges

We would like to thank Giuseppina Bastone for her work, made during her master thesis, on the integration of C/C++ code in Neko/NekoStat, and Martina Albini and Vania Guarnieri, for their work on the porting of Neko utilities made for Linux/Unix to standard J2SE.

This work has been partially supported by the European Community through the IST Project HIDENETS (Contract n. 26979).

References

1. A. Avizienis, J. Laprie, B. Randell and C. Landwehr, Basic concepts and taxonomy of dependable and secure computing *IEEE Transactions on Dependable and Secure Computing* **(1-1)**2004.
2. P. Urbán, X. Défago and A. Schiper, Neko: A single environment to simulate and prototype distributed algorithms *Journal of Information Science and Engineering* **(6-18)**2002.
3. L. Falai, A. Bondavalli and F. D. Giandomenico, Quantitative evaluation of distributed algorithms using the neko framework: The nekostat extension, in *Dependable Computing: Second Latin-American Symposium, LADC 2005*, 2005.
4. SourceForge Repository. http://sourceforge.net/.
5. Dependency injection pattern. http://www.martinfowler.com/articles/injection.html.
6. B. W. Boehm and C. Abts, COTS integration: Plug and pray? *IEEE Computer* **(1-32)**1999.
7. I. Sommerville, *Software Engineering*, 7th edn. (Addison-Wesley, Harlow, UK, 2005).
8. A. W. Brown and K. C. Wallnau, Enginnering of component-based systems, in *Component-Based Software Engineering*, ed. A. W. Brown (IEEE Press, 1997) pp. 7–15.
9. J. C. Mitchell, *Concepts in Programming Languages* (Cambridge University Press, 2003).
10. *Java Native Interface*, (1997). Javasoft's Native Interface for Java (http://java.sun.com/products/jdk/1.2/docs/guide/jni/index.html).
11. S. Liang, *The Java(TM) Native Interface Programmer's Guide and Specification* (Addison-Wesley, 2002). Also available from http://java.sun.com/docs/books/jni.
12. Jace Tool. http://sourceforge.net/projects/jace/.
13. A. Bondavalli, E. D. Giudici, S. Porcarelli, S. Sabina and F. Zanini, A freshness detection mechanism for railway applications, in *Proc. of the 10th International Symposium Pacific Rim Dependable Computing. Papeete, Tahiti, French Polynesia*, March 2004.
14. S. Loosemore, R. M. Stallman, R. McGrath, A. Oram and U. Drepper, *The GNU C Library Reference Manual*, 0.10 edn.

15. Java Sources of the new utilities for Neko described in the paper (webpage). http://bonda.dsi.unifi.it/tools/.
16. A. M. Law and W. D. Kelton, *Simulation, Modeling and Analysis* (McGraw-Hill, 2000).
17. HIDENETS (Highly dependable IP-based networks and services) Web Page. http://www.hidenets.aau.dk/.
18. H. P. Schwefel, A. Pataricza, M. Radimirsch, M. Reitenspiess, M. Kaaniche, I. E. Svinnset, P. Verissimo, S. H. de Groot and A. Bondavalli, Hidenets highly dependable ip-based networks and services, in *Proc. of the 6th European Dependable Computing Conference, Coimbra, Portugal*, Oct 2006.